THIRTEEN LESSONS ON REVELATION

VOL. II (Revelation 12 - 22)

i

THIRTEEN LESSONS ON REVELATION

VOL. II (Revelation 12 - 22)

A Student Book
For Thirteen Weeks
Of Study

by

Paul T. Butler

College Press Publishing Company, Joplin, Missouri

Library of Congress Catalog Card Number: 82-71688
International Standard Book Number: 0-89900-176-9

Scripture used from Revised Standard Version (R.S.V.) of the Bible, copyright
1972 by Thomas Nelson, Inc. and used by permission.

iv

Contents

Lesson One
(12:1-17)

THE LAMB AND THE SPIRITUAL CONFRONTATION

With chapter 12 we begin the second main division of the Revelation. The first primary division, chapters 1 through 11, reveal the Lamb, Sovereign in historical predicaments. This second part reveals the Lamb, Sovereign in heavenly providences.

The second division of Revelation explains (in dramatic symbolism) that the earthly struggle of the church against its enemies is inseparably united to the unseen confrontation of God and the rebels of heaven for sovereignty over creation. As Paul put it, "For we are not contending against flesh and blood, but against the principalities, against the powers, against the cosmic-mighties of this present darkness, against the spiritual host of wickedness in the heavenly places" (Eph. 6:12). An angel of God revealed the same thing to Daniel (Dan. 10:1-21). History's *direct tie* to heaven's battle for the supremacy and sovereignty of God is taught in Zechariah, chapters 1-6 (especially in Zech. 3:1-10). In Revelation, chapter 12, the idea is sum-marized or condensed. There, graphically, the struggle is between God and Satan (the dragon). From chapter 13 through 19 the picture moves to the struggle between agents (beast, false prophet, harlot) in whom the forces of Satan are organized and the saints on earth. But the essential concept presented is the heavenly, spiritual involvement of history.

1

THIRTEEN LESSONS ON REVELATION

This section of the Revelation is, if you please, a window opened to heaven for the mental and spiritual eye. It gives reality to the promise, "If God is for us, who can be against us" (Rom. 8:31). It is as real as the vision of horses and chariots of fire given the prophet's servant (II Kings 6:15-19). "Fear not, for those who are with us are more than those who are with them." Revelation chapters 12—20:6 are not for some time future to 1982. It was a message for the seven churches of Asia Minor. *Their* struggle was tied to heaven's plans. *They* were wrestling with cosmic powers who were using Rome as their agent. *These* Christians needed to know the Lamb would win the struggle and had invited all who would to prepare for his "marriage supper." Of course, the message is as relevant for the church today as it was then—just as Romans 8, Ephesians 6, I Corinthians 15, and I Thessalonians 4-5 are.

The Babe (12:1-17)

12 And a great portent appeared in heaven, a woman clothed with the sun, with the moon under her feet, and on her head a crown of twelve stars; ²she was with child and she cried out in her pangs of birth, in anguish for delivery. ³And another portent appeared in heaven; behold, a great red dragon, with seven heads and ten horns, and seven diadems upon his heads. ⁴His tail swept down a third of the stars of heaven, and cast them to the earth. And the dragon stood before the woman who was about to bear a child, that he might devour her child when she brought it forth; ⁵she brought forth a male child, one who is to rule all the nations with a rod of iron, but her child was caught up to God and to his throne, ⁶and the woman fled into the wilderness, where she has a place prepared by God, in which to be nourished for one thousand two hundred and sixty days.

7 Now war arose in heaven, Michael and his angels fighting against the dragon; and the dragon and his angels fought, ⁸but they were defeated and there was no longer any place for them in heaven. ⁹And the great dragon was thrown down, that ancient serpent, who is called the Devil and Satan, the deceiver of the whole world—he was thrown down to the earth, and his angels were thrown down with him. ¹⁰And I heard a loud voice in heaven, saying, "Now the salvation and the power and the kingdom of our God and the authority of his Christ have come, for the accuser of our brethren has been thrown down, who accuses them day and night before our god. ¹¹And they have conquered him by the blood of the Lamb and by the word of their testimony, for they loved not their lives even unto death. ¹²Rejoice then, O heaven and you that dwell therein! But woe to you, O earth and sea, for the devil has come down to you in great wrath, because he knows that his time is short!"

13 And when the dragon saw that he had been thrown down to the earth, he pursued the woman who had borne the male child. [14]But the woman was given the two wings of the great eagle that she might fly from the serpent into the wilderness, to the place where she is to be nourished for a time, and times, and half a time. [15]The serpent poured water like a river out of his mouth after the woman, to sweep her away with the flood. [16]But the earth came to the help of the woman, and the earth opened its mouth and swallowed the river which the dragon had poured from his mouth. [17]Then the dragon was angry with the woman, and went off to make war on the rest of her offspring, on those who keep the commandments of God and bear testimony to Jesus. And he stood on the sand of the sea.

vv. 1-2   A great portent . . . a woman clothed with the sun . . . — The woman symbolizes God's wife, the church in both Old Testament and New Testament (cf. Isa. 54:1ff.; 62:4-5; Jer. 3:14-20; Hosea ch. 1-3; Eph. 5:21-33; Rev. 19:6-10; 21:2-4). As John sees God's wife she has been and is continuing to be *clothed* (Gr. perfect verb *peribeblemen*) with the glory of the sun and the *moon* (Gr. *selene,* Selena) underneath her feet. The investiture of God's people with glory and light, symbolized by the sun and moon, is prophetic imagery from the Old Testament (cf. Isa. 24:21-23; 30:26; 60:1-22; Dan. 12:3; Isa. 9:1ff.; 31:35-36; 42:6; 49:5; Zech. 14:6; Mal. 4:2). On the "woman's" head was a crown of twelve stars. Twelve stars may represent the 12 patriarchs of the Old Testament or the twelve tribes of Israel or simply completeness. The twelve stars symbolize the fact that all the glory of humanity and the universe was meant by God to *adorn, protect,* and *equip* his Bride. This Bride, clothed in all her glory is a great *portent* (Gr. *semeion,* sign). Her glory portends her invincibility. She was glorified and exalted to join with God in redeeming the world (cf. Eph. 1:3; 2:6; Rev. 20:4). All the world was made available (I Cor. 3:21-23) to her. That is the *signal* John was to get from this vision to relay to the seven churches. God's Bride (the redemptive people) was exalted and glorified so she might give birth to the "man-child." God protected her to this end and *will* continue to protect and exalt her. She will be victorious—not her enemy.

The Bride was "with child . . . and cried out in her pangs of birth." This picture of the "wife" of God crying in anguish for the birth of the "child" is also imagery from the Old Testament prophets (cf. Isa. 26:17ff.; 66:7-11; Micah 4:10). The cry of travail for the birth of this child fills all the Old Testament (cf. Isa. 7:14; 9:6-7; Micah 5:2, etc.). Abraham looked for it (Jn. 8:56); Isaiah looked for it (Jn. 12:41). The distress and trouble the Old Testament woman would have before the birth is predicted by Daniel as 490 years of trouble (Dan. 9:24-27). The covenant people travailed in anticipation from the time of their formation with the family of Abraham until the Child (Messiah) was born.

3

vv. 3-4   And another portent . . . a great red dragon — The word *dragon* is translated from a Greek word *drakon* which denoted, in classical Greek, a mythical monster with great powers of cleverness. The words *drakon* and *ophis* (serpent) were often used synonymously. The Hebrew word in the Old Testament often translated *dragon* is *tan* and could also be translated *monster* (cf. Isa. 27:1; 51:9; Jer. 51:34; Ezek. 29:3), or *sea monster. Leviathan* is the transliteration of a Hebrew word meaning *crocodile* (Job 40:25). That is why Egypt is symbolized as *Leviathan.* The *red dragon* is the unmistakable symbol of the devil (Rev. 12:9; 20:2). Satan is the *serpent* (Gen. 3:1ff.) seducing man in Eden. Satan's dragonlikeness here and in the Old Testament symbolizes his beastliness (carnality) and seductiveness.

This vision of the dragon saw him with seven heads and ten horns and seven diadems upon his heads. These heads, horns and crowns probably symbolize the emperors of Rome pictured in chapter 17:1-18 on the "scarlet beast" upon which the "harlot" rode. We learn in chapter 13:1-4 that the dragon invests the beast "rising out of the sea" with his power and authority. The dragon's power and authority is only pretended, of course, for the *point* of the book of Revelation is that God is all-powerful and has given all authority to the Lamb. Whatever authority the dragon exercises or gives to the "beast" he does so only because the Sovereign Lamb permits it.

The "dragon's" tail *drew* (Gr. *suro,* draw as with a net) a third part of the "stars" and cast (Gr. *ebalen,* aorist of *ballo,* throw) them to the earth. Some of the angels of heaven allowed themselves to be caught in the net of Satan's rebellion and were cast out of heaven (cf. Jude 6; II Pet. 2:4). These rebelled of their own choice and "did not keep their own position but left their proper dwelling" and God consigned them to the "nether darkness." There is a similar reference to the Lord punishing the "host of heaven" at some point in time in Isaiah 24:21-23, (see comments there in *Isaiah, Vol. II,* by Butler, pub. College Press). Satan's first rebellion must have preceded the Garden of Eden for it was there he seduced Eve and Adam to join it. His confrontation here with the woman and the man-child, his defeat and subsequent war "in heaven" and that defeat must be all one and the same. We do know from the moment of the promise of the "seed of woman" in Eden the devil tried over and over again to cause a miscarriage or still-birth by tempting Israel. A remnant, by faith in God, perpetuated the messianic seed until "in the fulness of time, God sent forth his Son, born of woman . . ." (Gal. 4:4). As the time neared for the Son to be born, the devil was positioning himself to devour the Son. Satan found willing accomplices in the Jewish rulers and in the Roman procurator of Judea.

vv. 5-6   she brought forth a male child . . . — The faithful remnant of Israel, through a God-fearing virgin of Nazareth, brought forth the "male-child" Messiah. It is clear this child is the Son of God and the Anointed Savior for He was to rule with a rod of iron which is specifically a messianic

4

term (cf. Psa. 2:9; Rev. 2:27; 19:15). The "rod of iron" symbolizes *absolute* sovereignty (cf. Isa. 9:6-7; 11:1-9; 16:5; Zech. 9:9-10, etc.). The Son's dominion is universal and everlasting (cf. Dan. 7:13-14). Ultimately every knee will bow and every tongue will confess his absolute sovereignty (Phil. 2:9-11). While the devil seduces some into believing the Son does not have a "rod of iron" by the power of the fear of death (Heb. 2:14-15), God has destroyed the devil's power by raising Jesus Christ from the dead. Christ's resurrection proves he has absolute power. Christ, the Lamb, exercises absolute sovereignty over the worst and most final thing Satan claims to control—death. The "man-child" has the keys to death, Hades and Life. The Son, therefore, has sovereignty over all the world. No one takes his life from him—he lays it down and he takes it up again (Jn. 10:17-18). He has promised and demonstrated the sovereignty to do the same for all who trust him (Jn. 10:27-29). When the "man-child" suffered the ultimate pretensions of the devil and proved the devil really had no power, then the Father caught him back up to heaven and exalted him to co-rulership over all that exists (cf. Phil. 2:5-11). There the "male-child" as the Lamb, slain from the foundation of the world, sits enthroned as sovereign of history (cf. Rev. 5:1ff.).

When the man-child was caught up to heaven, the woman (the church) fled because the devil turned upon her to take out his malicious hatred. After the ascension of Christ, the church began to move out of Jerusalem and Judea in an ever-broadening infiltration of the world. The "wilderness" is symbolic of the world into which the church went after the exaltation of Christ. There the church temporarily received protection from the devil and she was nourished. This dispersion of Christians away from Judea was deliberately *prepared* (Gr. *etoimasmenon,* perfect participle meaning, having been prepared in the past and continuing in a prepared state) for the church by God. God had prepared the world for the growth (nourishment) of the church by dispersing the Jews, by Pax Romana, by *koine Greek* dialect, and by a hundred other providential details. Furthermore, this preparation was *in order* (Gr. *hina*) that the woman might be nourished. It was no accident that the gospel began to be nourished among the Gentiles when it was evident that the majority of the Jews rejected it. Daniel predicted the Jews would have 490 years (from 457 B.C. to 34 A.D.) and their time would be up (see our notes, *Daniel,* College Press, chapter 9:24-27). After the stoning of Stephen, the church fled into the "wilderness" and was nourished (Acts 8:1ff.).

The woman (the church) is to be nourished for 1260 days. These are evidently the same 1260 days of Rev. 11:3 where the two witnesses are preserved but clothed in sackcloth. The nourishing (Gr. *trephosin,* fed, reared) was in the form of spiritual exercise in the "wilderness" producing growth.

vv. 7-8 Now war arose in heaven . . . — The *time* sequence of this war must fit this context. Contextually it has to do with the devil being thwarted in his attempt to devour the man-child and the fleeing of the church into the wilderness. The *place* of this war cannot be Paradise where the Father and the Son dwell. It cannot be the throne-room of God for no wickedness dwells in his presence. The battleground of this war cannot be the where God reigns as absolute sovereign for there His will is done perfectly. It must, therefore, be in some *heavenly* place. The church is a heavenly place (Eph. 1:3; 2:6; Heb. 12:22). Unsuccessful in devouring the man-child the devil tries to conquer the heavenly place, the church, and take it over.

This is not a reference to Satan's original status—it is apocalyptic imagery to pictorialize vividly his intense hatred for anything heavenly. It apparently is a reference to the attempt of the Jews (cf. Phil. 3:2-3) to subvert the gospel of grace and the church of Christ back to Judaism by persecution. Hebrews 6:1-8 warns that Christians who return to Judaism commit apostasy and crucify the Son of God afresh. Hebrews 10:26-39 repeats it. After the Son of God atoned once for all for sin and established the New Covenant community (the church), Satan attacked the church through Judaizers (cf. Galatians, Romans, Hebrews). The book of Revelation refers to those who say they are *Jews* but are of the *synagogue of Satan* (Rev. 2:9; 3:9)! This "war of the dragon" probably parallels the predictions of Jesus in Matthew 24:1-28 concerning the early Jewish persecutions of Christians, false prophets and false messiahs. Satan made a great effort to destroy the church through the war of Judaism against the early church. There was even a skirmish between two of the great apostles over this matter (cf. Gal. 2:11ff.). It took a council at Jerusalem to get some matters of Jewish prejudice straightened out (cf. Acts 15:1-35). Judaizers constantly plagued the life of Paul and opposed his preaching. Jesus predicted a war-like struggle from Jewish persecutors against His new kingdom (cf. Mat. 10:16-33; 24:4-14).

But the devil could not take over the heavenly-place (the church) through Judaizers. There was no longer any place for the devil and his angels in the church. Jewish attempts to bring Christians back to Judaism and apostasy, and Jewish persecutions became minor. They were no longer threats to the church.

vv. 9-12 **And the great dragon was thrown down . . .** — The dragon is unmistakably identified. He is the archaic (Gr. *archaios,* old) serpent (seducer) from Eden; he is called the devil (accuser); he is called Satan (adversary). He is the one who leads the whole world astray. The word *deceiver* in Greek is *planon* and is often translated, *go astray* or *err* (Heb. 3:10). It is the same word from which we get the English word *planet.* It means to *wander off.* When the devil deceives or lies or leads people astray he does so because it is his nature; he is a liar and the father of lies—there is *no truth at all* in the devil (Jn. 8:44).

This deceiver, accuser and adversary of man was thrown down from the heavenly place. He was thrown out of the church. There was no room for

6

him there because that is a community committed to the truth even at the cost of life itself. Satan is cast "down" into the "world"—he must now carry on his hate campaign toward God through "the world." He is not totally restrained, he is simply given boundaries. His angels are cast out of the heavenly-place with him.

The Greek word *arti,* translated *now,* signifies *coincidence* or "just now." A loud voice in heaven said, "Coincidentally, the salvation and the power and the kingdom of our God and the authority of his Christ have come, for the accuser of our brethren has been thrown down. . . ." Once Judaism was conquered in the church, it became evident that the church was indeed the "kingdom" predicted in the Old Testament and it became evident that Jesus Christ's authority was equal with God's. It was through the incomplete system of Judaism that Satan could accuse the brethren (cf. Zech. 3:1-10) but when the Servant of God (the "branch") came the accuser would be cast out. Once the war to subvert the church of Christ to Judaism was won, the accuser could no longer find any of God's brethren to accuse for they were free of the guilt of the law.

The brethren *conquered* (Gr. *enikesan,* aorist, at some point past) *on account of* (Gr. *dia to*) the blood of the Lamb and on account of the word which they testified. It is significant that it is the *blood of the Lamb* and the *word* of the New Testament (the church's testimony) that gave the brethren their victory in the war of Jewish subversion. Those are exactly the weapons used by the apostle Paul in his many struggles against the Judaizers (cf. Gal. 3:1-29; Heb. 10:1-25; Rom. 3:19-33; etc.). Rejoice then, O church of God and all that *dwell* (Gr. *skenountes,* tabernacle, tent) therein. This is another indication that *heaven* in this context is referring to the *church.* It is plain that the New Testament occasionally connects the church on earth to the church in heaven immediately and presently without any break in time or reality (cf. Eph. 1:3; 2:6; Heb. 10:19ff.; 12:1; 12:22-24).

The heavenly kingdom, the church, may rejoice because it is protected from the devil's wrath—but the world of Rome is not. Woe to that Roman world (the wilderness) into which the church fled, for the devil is going to seduce that world, exploit it and use it as an instrument to fight against God. The devil is not really the ally of the world—he only uses it and would eventually lead that Roman world to *destroy itself* (Rev. 17:1—18:24). Once the devil had been defeated in his attempt to destroy the church through Judaism, he knew his time to destroy the church by the use of "the world" (Rome) was also short. He therefore set himself to infect that world with every despicable and depraved evil possible to the human nature. The devil knew that with the fall of Rome he would be bound to a great extent (cf. comments Rev. 20:1-6). The "short time" allotted to the devil (12:12) does not have to refer to sometime near the end of all time. It is certain that *no one* knows how to anticipate the end of all time—whether by a short or long period (cf. Mt. 24:36). The Son of man is going to bring an end to all time when it is *unexpected!* Those who will not be expecting it will certainly include the devil. Christians live in expectation of Christ's return at every moment—but they do so by faith. The devil doesn't live in that expectancy for he does not believe. What the devil could know in terms of time, however, was that Rome would fall, and it would be the last great universal opposition to God's kingdom. How could he know that? The same way you can know it—from the prophecies of Daniel (cf. Dan. 2:1-45; 7:1-27)! The devil does know scripture (cf. Mt. 4:6). Knowing he would only have a short time with Rome (two or three centuries) to try to kill the church, the devil came upon the world of that time with great wrath. It was beastly (Rev. 13:1ff.), foul (Rev. 16:13-14), blasphemous (Rev. 17:3) and abominable (17:5). It has already been described in general terms in the Seals and the Trumpets. It will be symbolized in great detail and with awesome drama in the remaining chapters of Revelation.

vv. 13-17 . . . he pursued the woman who had borne the male child. — When the devil realized he had been thrown out of the heavenly place (the church) and that he could not destroy the church from within (by Judaizing), he knew his last, short, hope was "the world." He therefore set himself to *pursue* the "woman" (the church) by using the world. The Greek word *edioxe* means "to put to flight, drive away, persecute." It is translated *persecute* in the KJV.

The church was given wings of an eagle (symbolizing power and swiftness) that she might fly from the serpent into the *wilderness* (Gr. *eremon,* "uninhabited places"). This scene is not intended to portray the church protected from all persecution and trial. It pictures the church so swiftly and widely flown into the far reaches of the Roman world it cannot be stamped out. It is no longer provincially Jewish. The faith once for all delivered to the saints has now reached the very household of Caesar and his praetorian guard (cf. Phil. 1:12). It will go with Roman soldiers, merchants and other citizens all over the world, to the British Isles, to Africa, and to India. About 200 A.D. the Christian writer Tertullian said: "Men proclaim that the state is beset with us. Every age, condition, and rank is coming over to us. We are only of yesterday, but already we fill the world." As noted earlier, nourishing does not preclude the possibility of pain. With all forms of growth there is struggle and trial and pain. So it was with the church. The "time, times, and half a time" is the same period of time referred to in 12:6 and 11:3 and predicted in Daniel 7:25. Three and one half "times" are half of seven. The Roman attempt to stamp out the church, looked at from only a human perspective, by those living through it, would appear to have no end in sight. A man really knows only that history he lives through. He certainly cannot see the future. A man living in second century Rome would have thought Rome would last forever and Christianity

8

would soon be crushed out of existence. But in God's perspective here Rome will never complete the crushing. The persecution of the woman by the serpent, using the world, will not be perfected (not reach the number seven) but will be over in a "short" time.

When the devil gained his hold on Rome as the instrument of his war against God (beginning with Domitian) a flood of persecution almost swept the church away. The imagery of persecution and tribulation on God's saints as a "flood" is Old Testament imagery (cf. Psa. 18:4; 32:6; 42:7; Isa. 43:2). This *flood* cast out of the mouth of the devil is probably both persecution and false religion and pagan degeneracy. Many thousands of Christians lost lives and property in this flood of pagan hostility toward the church.

But the earth (world) came to the help of the woman and the earth opened its mouth and swallowed the flood. Some have interpreted this to mean that God used nature or providence to protect his church. Even the natural order of God's creation is against the devil. This can certainly be established as a practice of God in Biblical history. Both the Old Testament and the New Testament are replete with instances of God's use of nature and creation to sustain his saints. The world's swallowing of the flood may, on the other hand, refer to the period of toleration of Christianity and relaxation of persecution by some Roman emperors. For 130 years from the time of Domitian to Septimius Servus (81-211 A.D.) the church endured a flood of heathen hostility all over the empire. But with the coming of the emperor Caracalla (211 A.D.) there began a period of toleration for Christianity which lasted some 30 years through the reign of the emperor Phillip (244-249 A.D.). One emperor during this period (Alexander Severus, 222-235 A.D.) was very favorably inclined toward Christianity. He quoted the "Golden Rule" frequently and had it engraved on the walls of the palace and many other public buildings. He recommended the morals of the Jews and the Christians to the Roman people. His mother favored the Christians, protected Origen, and summoned him to the palace to explain to her his theology. After the emperor Phillip, the church had to endure another 50 years of persecution. This last raging flood of hatred found its culmination in Diocletian (284-305 A.D.). But then Constantine became emperor (306-337), issued the imperial edict of toleration, became a Christian himself, and once again the earth swallowed up the flood from the devil's mouth.

This thwarting of the devil's attempt to stamp out the church made him exceedingly angry. The Greek text uses the word *orgisthe* (English, *orgasm*) to describe the devil's anger—it was an orgasm of anger. The devil, frustrated in his attempt to inundate the church and sweep it away with a flood of evil, did not give up but went off to make war on the *offspring* (Gr. *spermatos,* seed) of the woman wherever they might be found susceptible and vulnerable to his deception. Now the devil has to search out his victims individually—his collective war against the church has failed. The church was

9

scattered over the face of all the earth and could no longer be vulnerable to the Roman empire. The power of the devil would be severely limited with the fall of the Roman empire and the universal spread of Christianity.

Although the Roman emperors who were tolerant of Christianity were of some help in preserving the church, it was really the faith of these early Christians which kept the church alive. John describes them as those continually *keeping* (Gr. present participle, *terounton*) the commandments of God and those continuing to *hold on to* (Gr. pres. part. *echonton*) the testimony of Jesus.

Chapter 12 is the introductory chapter to the second main division of Revelation. It summarizes the issue to be amplified and detailed in the remainder of the book. That issue is: the flood of persecution about to come upon the church has its roots in the great cosmic hatred of the devil for God. Rome is merely the tool of the devil. Chapter 12 pictures for us God sending his Son as the "Child" of the Old Testament redemptive program; the devil attempts to devour that Son; God defeats the devil and catches his Son up to glory; Satan attacks the heavenly kingdom of the Son, the church; again, God defeats the devil, while the church flees into the Roman world; the devil pursues the church into the world; God protects the church and her offspring there, even using the world to swallow up the devil's flood of hate. Chapters 13-22 is a highly-figurative, apocalyptically-symbolized, detailed dramatization of the issue of chapter 12.

APPREHENSION AND APPLICATION:

1. What is the second main division of Revelation? Do you think of the struggle of the Christian life as a warfare involving the issue of the control of creation? Does there seem to you a great struggle for supremacy of right and wrong?

2. What does the woman's domination of the sun and moon symbolize? How does the glory of the church become a sign to the world? Do you see the church giving the world a portent of God's ultimate victory by her glorious testimony today? How?

3. Why symbolize the devil as a dragon? How do you think of him? What do the heads and horns symbolize? Does he have that much power now? When did the devil sweep some of the angels ("stars") from heaven? Did they have a choice?

4. Who is the "male-child"? Why does he have a "rod of iron"? How does he prove his sovereignty? How was the woman "nourished" in the wilderness? For what period of time? How did God prepare the "wilderness" for this?

5. Where would God permit the devil, in heaven, to wage war? Do you think of the church as a place (piece) of heaven? If Christians were more

like Christ, would the church be more like heaven? Should it? How could the devil get away with a subversion of the early church by Judaism while he cannot today?

6. When was the devil thrown down to "the world"? What is "the world"? How did the devil know his "time was short"? What did that motivate the devil to do to the world?

7. How did the woman's fleeing into the wilderness give her nourishment? Does nourishment preclude the possibility of trial and pain? What about the nourishment of the church today? Is the time (3-1/2) the same as 12:6 and 11:3?

8. What is the "flood" from the mouth of the devil? Will such a "flood" ever occur again? How did the "world" come to the aid of the church? Does the world aid the church in much the same way today?

9. While the devil was defeated in his attempt to swallow up the church by the "flood" from his mouth, he did not give up his hatred on the "seed" of the church—how does he manifest that hatred now?

10. Are you ready now to look at chapters 13-22 as detailed dramatizations of the issue of chapter 12?

Lesson Two
(13:1-18)

THE LAMB AND THE SPIRITUAL CONFRONTATION

John is now given a vision which connects the Roman empire's hostility against the church to the cosmic spiritual war of the devil against God. Rome is implicated as a tool of the devil in the blasphemous rebellion against the sovereignty of God and His Christ. Rome's attempt to kill the church is not merely human goodness in error—it is complicity with all that is evil.

The clear teaching of the Old Testament prophets is that no human form of government is adequate to produce the fellowship of man with his Creator. In fact, human government at its worst or best stands, by its very nature, opposed to man's allegiance to the absolute sovereignty of God. Therefore, the message of the prophets is that all human government is doomed while the government of God through the messianic kingdom (the church) will be established forever.

Revelation, chapter 13, while continuing that theme, applies specifically to the seven churches of Asia Minor in their struggle with the Roman empire. It has only general fulfillment beyond those centuries of early Rome. The beast of Revelation 13 is tied directly to the fourth beast of Daniel 7:1ff., as will be shown in later comments.

12

It is not unusual for men or governments to be called "beasts" in the Bible. Isaiah called Egypt, "leviathan" (monster) (Isa. 27:1; 51:9); Nahum called Assyria "lion" (Nah. 2:11-12); Daniel called four successive empires "beasts" (Dan. 7:1ff.); Isaiah called his own people "oxen, asses, dogs" (Isa. 1:3; 56:9-12). Jesus told his disciples not to cast their "pearls" before "swine and dogs"; Jesus called the Pharisees, "sons of snakes"; Jesus called Herod "that fox"; Jesus called false teachers, "wolves." Paul called the Judaizers, "dogs" (Phil. 3:2). Peter called false teachers "irrational animals" (II Pet. 2:12). When men and societies accept the evolutionary philosophy that they are nothing more than beasts, they begin to act like beasts and should be called "beasts."

The Beasts (13:1-18)

13 And I saw a beast rising out of the sea, with ten horns and seven heads, with ten diadems upon its horns and a blasphemous name upon its heads. ²And the beast that I saw was like a leopard, its feet were like a bear's, and its mouth was like a lion's mouth. And to it the dragon gave his power and his throne and great authority. ³One of its heads seemed to have a mortal wound, but its mortal wound was healed, and the whole earth followed the beast with wonder. ⁴Men worshiped the dragon, for he had given his authority to the beast, and they worshiped the beast, saying, "Who is like the beast, and who can fight against it?"

5 And the beast was given a mouth uttering haughty and blasphemous words, and it was allowed to exercise authority for forty-two months; ⁶It opened its mouth to utter blasphemies against God, blaspheming his name and his dwelling, that is, those who dwell in heaven. ⁷Also it was allowed to make war on the saints and to conquer them. And authority was given it over every tribe and people and tongue and nation, ⁸and all who dwell on earth will worship it, every one whose name has not been written before the foundation of the world in the book of life of the Lamb that was slain. ⁹If any one has an ear, let him hear:
¹⁰If any one is to be taken captive, to captivity he goes;
If any one slays with the sword, with the sword must he be slain.
Here is a call for the endurance and faith of the saints.

11 Then I saw another beast which rose out of the earth; it had two horns like a lamb and it spoke like a dragon. ¹²It exercises all the authority of the first beast in its presence, and makes the earth and its inhabitants worship the first beast, whose mortal wound was healed. ¹³It works great signs, even making fire come down from heaven to earth in the sight of men; ¹⁴and by the signs which it is allowed to work in the

presence of the beast, it deceives those who dwell on earth, bidding them make an image for the beast which was wounded by the sword and yet lived; [15]and it was allowed to give breath to the image of the beast so that the image of the beast should even speak, and to cause those who would not worship the image of the beast to be slain. [16]Also it causes all, both small and great, both rich and poor, both free and slave, to be marked on the right hand or the forehead, [17]so that no one can buy or sell unless he has the mark, that is, the name of the beast or the number of its name. [18]This calls for wisdom: let him who has understanding reckon the number of the beast, for it is a human number, its number is six hundred and sixty-six.

vv. 1-2 And I saw a beast rising out of the sea — The imagery of this chapter is not only comparable to Daniel 7:1ff., it is *directly connected to* Daniel's prophecy. Revelation 13 takes up and continues predicting the history of the fourth beast of Daniel 7. Daniel's fourth beast can be none other than Rome (see comments, *Daniel*, by Butler, College Press).

John sees this beast rising out of the sea—so does Daniel (Dan. 7:3). "Sea" or "waters" symbolizes the mass of humanity in constant motion, or commotion, and especially the heathen masses in hostility toward God (cf. Isa. 8:7ff.; Jer. 46:7-9; 47:2; Isa. 17:2ff.; 57:20-21; Rev. 17:1, 15, etc.). The devil is the original anarchist and rebel. He is the source of all that in human government which sets itself against God's sovereignty in creation. Human government opposed to God is, therefore, beastly and animalistic in character. Each of Daniel's empires were symbolized by beasts. Human governments opposing God are (a) cruel, (b) concerned almost totally with animalistic aspects of men, (c) victimizers of mankind preying on man's weaknesses, (d) rule and dominate by "red tooth and claw" methods of animals. Human governments and rulers do not see themselves as God sees them. They dream about themselves as great images (Dan. 2) made of precious and enduring "metals." They dream about themselves as huge trees (Dan. 4) reaching to heaven providing sustenance and protection for the whole human race. They see themselves as "queens" in regal splendor adored by the world, (Isa. 47:5-9; Rev. 18:7). God sees them as hated *beasts* and despised *harlots*. They rend and tear; they seduce and prostitute.

The beast John saw had ten horns and seven heads, with ten crowns upon its horns and a blasphemous name upon its heads. Seven heads and ten horns identifies this beast as the same beast upon which the harlot rides in Revelation 17:3-18. The ten horns and ten crowns represent ten emperors who made emperor-worship (blasphemous name) popular—only seven of the ten were really "heads" of any significance; three of them were "barracks emperors" who ruled a total of 18 months among them: (see comments Rev. 17:3ff.).

14

1. Tiberius (14-37 A.D.) (begin with Tiberius because he was emperor
2. Caligula (37-41 A.D.) when Christ preached, died, and rose again
3. Claudius (41-54 A.D.) to found His church).
4. Nero (54-68 A.D.)
   Galba, Otho and Vitellius (18 months)
5. Vespasian (69-79 A.D.)
6. Titus (79-81 A.D.)
7. Domitian (81-96 A.D.)

Ten horns symbolize great power; seven heads symbolize a septumvirate of mentality; ten diadems symbolize a totality of human authority. And although this beast (and the one of Rev. 17) may be identified with the above emperors, it probably symbolizes the Roman empire in its continued beastliness from Domitian to Diocletian. The "blasphemous name" represents deification these emperors heaped to themselves, calling themselves "Lord, God, and Savior," and decreeing that they should be worshiped by their subjects.

The beast John saw was a composite of a leopard, a bear and a lion. This is in exact agreement with Daniel 7:12. There, the fourth beast is pictured as destined to be slain and burned with fire. That is exactly what happened to Rome (cf. Rev. 19:20-21). But *before* it was slain, the first three beasts of Daniel 7:1-6 (the lion, bear and leopard) had their lives and characters "prolonged for a season" in the fourth beast (Rome). Rome, so long as she lasts, perpetuates the beastliness of the first three great universal empires (Babylon, Persia and Greece) in herself. She becomes the tool of the devil for one last hope in universal heathenism to stamp out the universal reign of righteousness in God's church. Revelation 13:2 plugs right in to Daniel 7:12. All the characteristics of wild beastliness is resident in this fourth beast (Rome)—cruelty, viciousness, rapaciousness, cunning and predatoriness.

The dragon *gave* (Gr. *edoken,* aorist, already *gave* at some point in time past) the beast his power, throne and authority. Again we must emphasize the devil's power, throne and authority is only *pretended.* The devil creates nothing, he owns nothing, and whatever deception he exercises he does so within the sovereign limitations imposed on him by God. Whatever promises he may make to give power (cf. Mt. 4:8-10) are only empty promises he may make to give power (cf. Mt. 4:8-10) are only empty promises for God alone reigns sovereign over all the kingdoms of the world (cf. Isa. 10:5ff.; Jer 27:5ff., etc.). Whatever power the devil may have is in his ability to deceive through lying. The power he gave the beast did not last long for God overthrew the beast (cf. Rev. 19:20-21). (See Lesson Thirteen: "Questions About Whether the Devil Can Actually Perform Supernatural Deeds or Not.") Rome allowed itself to be deceived by the devil and willingly perpetuated that deception by persuading the whole empire (except Christians) that it should "exchange the glory of the immortal God for images resembling mortal man or birds or animals or reptiles" (Rom. 1:22-23). Rome broadcast the devil's original lie that man could become as god (Gen. 3:4). Rome used persecution, false religions and carnality to perpetuate the devil's "power." The devil's second great lie is that the flesh should take priority. This was Rome's motto. Engraved on the pavement of a Roman forum in Timgad, North Africa, is a checkerboard with the words, *Venari, lavari, ludere, ridere, hoc est vivere*—"to hunt, bathe, play, and laugh, this is to live." Thus Rome capitulated to become the devil's instrument for the seduction of a civilization.

vv. 3-4 One of its heads seemed to have a mortal wound . . . — One of the beastly heads had a mortal wound and died, but that did not kill the beast for the wound was healed and the beast went right on terrifying the world and seducing the world to worship it.

This is an apparent reference by John the apostle to the *Nero redivivus* legend. Nero (54-68) was a monster of wickedness and cruelty. When he killed himself in 68 A.D., people actually danced in the streets. A few mourned his death because their positions and fortunes had depended on his patronage. These "friends" perpetrated a legend that Nero had not really died; that he had gone to Parthia in the far east; and that he would return, incarnate in another ruler, leading the dreaded hordes of Parthia, and take up his power again. Suetonius mentions this legend. There were some who believed Domitian (because of the similarity of character) was the reincarnated Nero (see comments Rev. 17:3-14). The beastliness of Nero was not only perpetuated by Domitian but by others following him (e.g. Septimius Severus, Decius, Diocletian). John the apostle did not believe in reincarnation, but he used this myth about Nero to identify in cryptic (secretive) language who the "beast" was. Writing this Revelation during the reign of Domitian John was suggesting that in Domitian Christians were faced with a "reincarnation" of Nero. These "friends" propagated the idea that Nero was somehow immortal in his wickedness—having the power of the devil. The Romans could not rid themselves of this idea; and even as late as A.D. 80 a pretender arose in Parthia, claiming that he was Nero; and he very nearly succeeded in persuading the Parthians to invade Europe under him.

Satan-worship or demon worship was widespread in the Roman empire of the first century (and succeeding centuries) (cf. I Cor. 10:20ff.). The gods of the underworld were believed by the Romans (borrowed from the Greeks) to have powers to make those who worshiped them immortal. Men worshiped the dragon (Satan) for it *appeared* to men he had given his power and authority for immortality to the beast. It appeared Nero had been reincarnated in Domitian and his successors. The beast seemed invincible, immortal, with supernatural powers. Nero, the devil incarnate, had died— or had he? In Domitian the demonic power and viciousness is perpetuated.

Rome's beastliness seems unassailable, unconquerable. That kind of power (unless one believes there is Higher power) clamors to be worshiped. So men began to clamor for deification of their emperors. Most of the emperors gloried in such flattery—some more publicly than others. Popular adoration for and self-acclamation of the deification of political tyrants was nothing new to the world. It had been practiced as far back as ancient Egypt, Assyria, Babylon, Persia, and Greece. It is practiced in the modern world (e.g. Hitler, Lenin, et al.). But the beast is not invincible (13:18)—he is human, not divine.

vv. 5-6   **And the beast was given a mouth uttering haughty and blapshemous words . . .** — The same thing is said of the fourth beast (Rome) in Daniel's prophecy (cf. Dan. 7:8, 11, 20, 25). John is probably referring immediately to Domitian's *edictum domini deique nostri* ("Our Lord and God decrees"). Domitian commanded that he be addressed as deity; he promoted the practice of all bowing before him and embracing his feet. He was not the only emperor to assume such blasphemous arrogance. Caligula (37-41 A.D.) ordered that an image of himself be set up in the Holy of Holies in the Jewish temple in Jerusalem. Caligula believed he was a god; he once struck the English Channel with a rod believing he could whip it into submission to his deity. Diocletian declared himself to be Jupiter (the god) in the flesh, and required all visitors to kneel and kiss the hem of his robe. Not only did most of the Roman emperors think of themselves as gods, they made blasphemous utterances (depraved, defamatory, despicable words) against Christians and their Christ. Nero accused Christians of burning down the city of Rome. Other Romans accused them of cannibalism, sedition, and atheism.

Once again the time-limit of forty-two months (and its equivalent of 3-1/2 years or 1260 days) is decreed by heaven to be the extent of the Roman "blasphemy." This time-limit is the same mentioned in Rev. 11:3, 12:6 and 12:14. It covers, symbolically and generally, the time from Domitian to Diocletian (81-310 A.D.). With the coming of Constantine and the Edict of Toleration (312 A.D.), the beastliness and blasphemousness of Rome was conquered.

vv. 7-8   **Also it was allowed to make war on the saints and to conquer them. . . .** — Again we have exactly the same phraseology of Daniel (Dan. 7:21, 25). The beast of Revelation 13 is the fourth beast (and "little horn") of Daniel 7—it is Rome (and Domitian to Diocletian, specifically). Rome would not have had the power to bring such a severe test upon the church of Christ had not God "allowed" it. Permission from God for severe testing of his people is not strange to Biblical history. The covenant people of the Old Testament were put in the crucibles of Egypt, the Judges-period, Assyrian-Babylonian-Persian captivity, and the severest test of all during the days of Antiochus IV ("the contemptible one") predicted by Daniel, chapters 8 and 11. God will not have an untested, unpurged, uncommitted people. He allows his saints to be attacked, to struggle, to fight because they have need of endurance that they may do the will of God and receive what is promised them (cf. Heb. 10:32-39; 12:1-11; I Pet. 4:12-19; II Cor. 12:7-10, etc.). The first sentence of verse 7 is omitted in some less significant minuscule manuscripts of the Greek New Testament but in none of the more important manuscripts.

Authority over the whole civilized world was given to this beast (Rome). It is apocalyptic hyperbole. It is prophetic symbolism. It is not the intention of the writer to mean that Rome had authority over every single individual human being on the face of the earth (American Indians, South Africans, etc.). Nor is it the intention of the writer to predict some time future to the present when one "beast" will be given authority over every single human being living on the face of the earth. John is describing the power and authority of the Roman empire of the first four centuries A.D. Its authority extended over the known civilized world. It is apparent Rome is the beast with this authority when one compares the same symbolism being applied to the same "beast" in Rev. 17:1-18.

All who dwelled in the civilized world under Rome's authority would do obeisance to Rome and worship the emperor by compulsion. Only those who took their redemption in Christ seriously would not do so. These are distinguished as those "who had their names written before the foundation of the world in the book of life of the Lamb that was slain" (cf. also 17:8). It was not enough to have merely embraced Christianity. When the imperial edict forced Christians to decide about emperor-worship, many capitulated to idolatry rather than suffer persecution. Only those Christians deeply committed to Christ ("those who loved not their lives even unto death" 12:11) were written in the Lamb's book of life. Only these refused to worship the beast.

vv. 9-10 If anyone has an ear, let him hear: . . . — Having painted a realistic picture of what Rome is going to do to the world and to the saints, John now calls for endurance (Gr. *hupomone,* steadfastness, lit. remaining under) and faith from the saints. When this great war and trial comes the saints will simply have to trust Christ enough to remain and not seek to get out from under the trial by renouncing their faith. If they must go to prison and death, they must go. This call for endurance is not any less than God asked of his saints in the Old Testament. Especially is this imagery taken from the time of the captivities of the Jews by the Babylonians in Jeremiah's time (cf. Jer. 14:12; 15:2; 24:10; 43:11; Ezek. 5:2, 12). Jeremiah told his people to surrender to God's chastening through Babylonian captivity (Jer. 27:1-15) and make the most of it (Jer. 29:1-9) and God would deliver them after 70 years (Jer. 29:10ff.). Jeremiah expected those who trusted God to believe his prediction and obey it as the word of God no matter what they had to suffer. That is exactly what John is telling the Christians of Asia Minor.

John is telling the Christians, further, that those who slay them with the sword will themselves be slain through the judgments of God. Those who live by the sword will die by the sword. Jeremiah (and all the prophets) promised God's saints of old that their persecutors and executioners would die by the same violence they perpetrated on others. Rome will receive her *dues* (cf. Rev. 16:15-16; 18:6-8; 18:21-24). Rome lived by violence and that is the way she died! That principle has been repeated in history more than a thousand times, and the world does not repent!

vv. 11-12   Then I saw another beast . . . — The first beast was war-like. The first beast represents Roman military and political power in opposition to God's saints. The second beast is lamb-like, although it speaks the same as the devil (the old dragon). The second beast represents the powers delegated to Roman *concilia* to enforce emperor worship throughout the Roman provinces. *Concilia* (councils) or sometimes called *commune* were organized from politicians and heathen priests nominated from the provinces of the empire. They were charged with administering Roman law, judging in local civil disputes, and enforcing loyalty to the emperor by requiring an annual burning of incense to the emperor as god. Many of the members of these *concilia* were priests of the pagan religions and temples. The president of the *concilia* was usually called *archiereus* (chief priest) or *Asiasrches* in Asia Minor which means, "Chief officers of Asia" and probably refers to the high priests of the temples of the Imperial worship in the various cities of Asia Minor.

Pliny the Younger (62-113 A.D.), appointed governor of Bithynia (a province of Asia Minor) wrote in a letter to Trajan, emperor of Rome, concerning the prosecution of people for the crime of following Christ:

". . . the methods I have observed toward those who have been brought before me as Christians is this: I asked them whether they were Christians; if they admitted it, I repeated the question twice, and threatened them with punishment; if they persisted, I ordered them to be at once punished. . . . An anonymous information was laid before me, containing a charge against several persons, who upon examination denied they were Christians or had ever been so. They repeated after me an invocation to the gods, and offered religious rites with wine and incense before your statue (which for that purpose I had ordered to be brought, together with those of the gods), and even reviled the name of Christ. . . . They all worshiped your statue and the images of the gods, uttering imprecations at the same time against the name of Christ."

The second beast exercises all the authority of the first beast in the very presence of the image of the emperor. The second beast (the *concilia*) gets its power to enforce idolatry from the emperor himself. It was after the death of Octavian (Caesar Augustus) that the Senate decreed his *genius* (or soul) was to be worshiped as one of the official divinities of Rome. But it was not until Domitian that an official edict was issued for all the subjects of the empire to annually worship the image of the emperor. Throughout the provinces, each *concilia* appointed *inquisitores* (secret investigators) to ferret out the identity of all persons refusing to burn incense to the emperor and to bring them to trial. Many Christians were tortured and slain because they would not burn incense to the emperor. Many declared publicly their allegiance to Christ and became "martyrs" for their faith. Thousands of others, Christian in name only, denied their faith and saved their lives by worshiping the image of the emperor and cursing Christ.

vv. 13-15 It works great signs . . . it deceives those who dwell on earth . . .— This second beast, presenting itself as a benefactor of man in the form of religion, works pseudo-signs. Notice John carefully designates all these "signs" by the second beast *deceptive* (Gr. *plana,* erroneous, wrong) signs. They are not true signs proving deity at all. They deceive people because people *want* to be deceived—not because they are authentic signs (cf. II Thess. 2:9-12). The student should read Lesson Thirteen at the end of this volume entitled, "Questions About Whether the Devil can Actually Perform Supernatural Deeds or Not."

The Roman world of the first four centuries was a polyglot of pagan cultism. Every religion of the world found its way to Rome and thence to the provinces. Priests and priestesses, prophets and prophetesses of every cult were allowed to practice their "religions" so long as they did obeisance to the emperor. Sorcery, magic, witchcraft, augurism, mystery-cultism, occultism of every kind was popular. Rome had long believed in and proclaimed a "sacred flame" which had fallen from heaven and had instituted an order of Vestal Virgins who were keepers of this flame. Priests were magicians skilled in sleight-of-hand amazing the worshipers and deceiving them into believing their tricks were supernatural miracles. Pagan priests often claimed natural phenomena such as falling meteorites as their own magic (cf. Acts 19:35). This alleged ability of the second beast to make fire come down from heaven to earth in the sight of men is in no way genuinely miraculous. As Homer Hailey puts it, "If God allowed Satan to deceive by genuine miracles He would thereby nullify His own witness to truth." It is clear from Acts 8:5-13 that the signs done by priests and sorcerers then were pseudo-signs, for even the sorcerer (Simon) recognized the true miracles when he saw them. If modern "magicians" may work illusions on television which mystify the modern mind, how much more might sorcerers do so with the superstitious and those subject to political pressure.

All these "magical" signs were done by the priests and augurs at the annual festivals, celebrating the births of emperors and at the worship of the souls of the deceased emperors as gods. Roman officials and members of the *concilia* were present to represent the emperor (the beast). Worshipers were amazed and awed by all the pomp, power and magic displayed. They were all deceived into making images (Gr. *eikoni,* icon, idol) of the Roman emperor (specifically Domitian) and worshiping them.

The ancient pagan priests had for centuries practiced deceiving superstitious worshipers into believing images made of stone, metal and wood could talk. Many of them used drugs or self-hypnosis to induce a trance in which they claimed to be speaking oracles from the gods or images. One such was the "oracle at Delphi," a Greek temple inhabited by priestesses and from which Alexander the Great demanded a revelation. Ventriloquism was a highly skilled and widely practiced art in heathen idolatry. Eurycles of Athens was the most celebrated of Greek ventriloquists. They were called *engastrimanteis,* or "belly prophets" because the ancients believed the voices of these "gods" came from the bellies of the oracles. Priests of ancient pagan religions were masters of this art and to ventriloquism may be ascribed the alleged miracles of the "speaking statues" of the Egyptians, Greeks and Romans. Alexander of Abonoteichus trained a serpent to hide its head under his arm and allow a half-human mask to be affixed to its tail; he announced that the serpent was the god Asclepius come to earth to serve as an oracle; and he amassed a fortune by interpreting the sounds made by reeds inserted in the false head. Modern archaeologists have found devices used for secretly piping the human voice beneath the altars bearing the statues of pagan gods. Caligula had a contrivance made by which he could produce a fiery reply to Jove's thunder and lightning stroke for stroke. He claimed that the moon-goddess had come down amd embraced him. Vespasian was alleged to have healed blind men with his spittle and lame people with the touch of his foot.

If the *concilia* (second beast) had the skill to deceive millions of gullible and superstitious people into believing the statues of Rome's emperor could speak, they would believe the emperor was indeed a god. Whatever the *concilia* or Rome wished to be carried out by its subjects would be obeyed with fear. The *concilia* also had delegated power to execute all who would not worship the beast (the emperor).

vv. 16-17 Also it causes all . . . to be marked on the right hand or the forehead . . . — The Greek word translated *mark* is *charagma* and is the same word from which we get the English word *character*. The "mark" of the beast probably has to do with the stamp of heathen character manifested in life rather than some literal, physical mark.

Some think this figure of speech concerning a "mark" has reference to the requirement that all legal documents for ownership of property, purchasing rights for food, etc., had to bear the stamp of the emperor. Some refer to the fact that it was actually true that among pagan religions in many cases the devotees were branded with the sign of their gods (cf. III Macc. 2:29).

Decius issued an edict in 250 A.D. that demanded an annual offering of sacrifice at the Roman altars to the gods and the *genius* of the emperor. Those who offered such sacrifices were given a certificate called a *libellus*. A copy of such a document from that era is extant today and reads:

"To the superintendents of offerings and sacrifices at the city from Aurelius . . . thion son of Theodorus and Pantonymis, of the said city. It has ever been my custom to make sacrifices and libations to the gods and now also I have in your presence in accordance with the command poured libations and sacrificed and tasted the offerings together with my son Aurelius Dioscorus and my daughter Aurelia Lais. I therefore request you to certify my statement. The 1st year of the Emperor Caesar Gaius Messius Quintus Trajanus Decius Pius Felix Augustus, Pauni 20."

Cyprian (200-258 A.D.), a Christian, writes that the imperial edict to worship the emperor or be arrested as an *atheotes* (atheist) struck terror to the hearts of all whose faith was weak. Many did not even leave it to be said for them that they seemed to sacrifice to idols unwillingly so anxious were they to escape arrest. Cyprian pictures many half-hearted Christians as running to the market place to burn incense to the emperor. Many were so impatient to deny their faith that they could hardly wait their turn. Many who would neither flee nor sacrifice suffered the most terrible tortures and died in prison, or were sent to labor in Roman mines until they died, or were cruelly executed without delay. Some by bribing the officials procured certificates of having sacrificed without committing the overt act. Some allowed others to say that they had sacrificed or to procure certificates for them. Holders of these fraudulent certificates were called *libellatici* and were despised as much as those who openly denied their faith. Some weak Christians who possessed precious copies of the Scriptures gave, under threat, these scrolls to be burned and destroyed—they were called *traditores* (traitors).

Whatever the "mark" was that distinguished one as loyal to the beast, it was apparently necessary to survive in the economic life of the empire. Anyone not loyal to the emperor and Rome would be banned from the business world and might even be deprived of the fundamental necessities of livelihood such as food, clothing and shelter. This form of persecution on Christians who refused to burn incense to the emperor may explain in part the scarcity of food symbolized in the third seal (Rev. 6:5-6). We know for a fact that some Christians were persecuted this way by Jewish authorities (cf. Heb. 10:32ff.). Even contemporary Christians are starved and discriminated against in employment and economics by modern "beasts."

We believe John's "mark of the beast" is symbolic, not literal. It is probably the figurative counterpart of the "seal" of God on Christians (7:1-3). Nowhere in history do we find God literally putting a brand or tattoo on the hands or foreheads of Christians (Rev. 3:12; 22:4). God stamps his image (mark) on Christians through the character of the Holy Spirit living in and through them. The devil and the beast mark those who belong to them in the same manner. Those who have the mark of the beast are those who think like and live like the beast. The mark of the beast is the stamp of paganism impressed upon the character and conduct of idolaters. Men become like that which they worship (cf. Hosea 9:10; Psa. 115:8). Christians are "conformed to the image of God's Son" (Rom. 8:29; II Cor. 3:18) and non-Christians are conformed to the image of their father, the devil (John 8:42-47; Acts 13:10; I Jn. 3:8-10; 3:15).

v. 18 . . . **it is a human number, its number is six hundred and sixty-six.** — John intends readers and believers of this book to understand what this number means. He does not intend it to be misunderstood or mis-applied. The Christian who has thus far understood the purpose and message of Revelation should have no trouble understanding the "number of the beast's name."

First, we must understand that had John written out the literal name of the beast it could have meant John's death warrant and anyone who possessed a copy of the scroll. So John identifies the beast in apocalyptic numerology—666. The ancient people had no figures for numbers so the letters of their alphabets did duty for numbers. The following, based on numbers for letters in alphabets, are some theories as to the identity of 666:

a. Hebrew consonants have numerical value as follows: N = 50; R = 200; O = 6; N = 50; K = 100; S = 60; R = 200; total—666 thus NRON KSR or *Nero Caesar*

b. Greek letters have numerical value as follows: L = 30; A = 1; T = 300; E = 5; I = 10; N = 50; O = 70; S = 200; total—666 thus LATEINDS, or Rome (others interpret as Roman Catholic Church).

c. Someone in 1941 applied an English numerology to it as follows: A = 100; B = 101; C = 102; etc. through Z = 126. H = 107; I = 108; T = 119; L = 111; E = 104; R = 117; total—666 thus HITLER. But the English alphabet was unknown in John's day; the English alphabet has no numerical value; why start at A = 100—why not A = 1?

d. Roman letters have numerical value (where there is no numerical value, zero is the equivalent) thus: V = 5; I = 1; C = 100; A = 0; R = 0; I = 1; V(U) = 5; S = 0; F = 0; I = 1; L = 50; I = 1; D = 500; E = 0; I = 1; total—666 thus the Latin expression, *vicarius filii dei,* "in place of the Son of God." Roman emperor.

e. Another suggestion uses Greek alphabet thus:
T = 300; E = 5; I = 10; T = 300; A = 1; N = 50; total—666 thus *Teitan.*
Teitan could refer in Greek mythology to the Titans who were great rebels against God; or it could refer to the family name, *Titus,* of Vespasian, Titus and Domitian.

f. All sorts of modern hypotheses have applied the number 666 to a multitude of persons, nations, things or ideologies.
One man suggests that by using three six-digital units the entire world could be assigned a working credit card number programmed through a universally-centralized computer all of mankind could be controlled. This is the "beast." Others have appealed to license plates on cars in the Arab countries bearing the number 666 as an indication that the "beast" (or as they think, The Antichirst) is arising there.
Some have shown clothing labels from Red China bearing the number 666 as an indication that Red China is the "beast."

While there may be some credence to the idea that 666 may symbolize Domitian as the reincarnation of Nero, we believe the idea to be symbolized is more general than specific. Seven is the number of perfection or infinitude. Six is short of seven and denotes incompleteness, imperfection or finiteness. A trinity of sixes (666) means fully human, fully evil and fully conquerable. The focus for understanding the number is in the phrase, "for it is a *human* number." John is answering the question asked in 13:4, "Who is like the beast, and who can fight against it?" By pomp, power and sorcery the beast appeared *invincible;* he appeared supernatural; he claimed and tried to prove he was god. But John has his number! The beast is not invincible; the beast is not supernatural; he is not god—he is human! We do not think John means to identify a specific person so much as he is identifying the Roman emperorship from Domitian to Diocletian in all its beastliness but in its vincibility also. Emperors are not gods! They are human and are not to be worshiped no matter how deceptive their "signs" may be.

There can be no credence given to the interpretation that this number 666 refers to The Antichrist, some very wicked ruler to appear during the 7 years of tribulation, after the rapture, just prior to the establishment of the millennium. In the first place, the term *The Antichrist* does not appear in Revelation and is not even, by itself, a Biblical term. There had been many antichrists already gone out into the world before John wrote Revelation (I Jn. 2:18, 22; II Jn. 7). Second, none of the ideas concerning a tribulation, a rapture or a literal millennium are to be found in Revelation. Third, the idea of a very wicked ruler 2000 years subsequent to the time of John would have little, if any, relevance or meaning to the churches of Asia Minor.

John could not have more clearly identified the Roman emperorship nor exposed its facetious claims to supernaturalness than by using the number 666. Had John simply said, "the beast is the heathen Roman emperor" it would have been fatal to him and many others. But in a cryptic symbol (666), hidden to unbelievers, but known to Christians, he got his message through. His message was, do not fear the Roman emperor's attempt to declare himself god—he is not, he is human.

APPREHENSION AND APPLICATION:

1. How does the vision of chapter 13 connect Rome to the devil? Is all human government vulnerable to be used as a tool of the devil?
2. Is the Roman government the only one called "beast" in the Bible? Did Jesus ever call rulers and wicked men beasts?
3. Why are human governments symbolized as beasts in the Bible? Can you think of governments today which might earn the name, "beast"?
4. How does John's beast of chapter 13 fit into Daniel's four beasts (Dan. 7)?
5. What authority did the devil give to the beast? How much authority does the devil have? Do you think the devil is god of this world? In what way?
6. How did one of the heads of John's visionary beast become healed of a mortal wound? Why would this beast seem invincible?
7. In what way did the beast blaspheme? How long was his blasphemy to last?
8. Why would God allow the beast to make war on the saints and dominate them? Would God do that to his saints today? What were the saints to do when the beast conquered them? What was to happen to the beast who lived by the sword?
9. Who is the second beast? Can you think of governmental religious powers today, or world religious organizations, which might earn the name "beast"?
10. How did the second beast deceive the world then? Does the devil work miracles?
11. What is the mark of the beast? What is the meaning of the number 666?

Lesson Three
(14:1-20)

THE LAMB AND THE SPIRITUAL CONFRONTATION

Once again John is given a vision of the protection and blessedness of God's saints before a vision of judgment upon the Roman empire is given. This follows the pattern of chapters 4 and 5, 7, and 10 and 11, (see the Climactic Parallelism Chart at the beginning of Vol. I). Chapter 14 also provides a vision of victory to follow the vision of the war upon the saints by the devil and his cohorts, the two beasts.

While all the Roman empire trembles at the apparent invincibility of the beast and prostitutes itself to a lifestyle like that of the beast, Christians may rejoice and sing the song of redemption for they are secure in the citadel (Zion) of God. The scene which just closed in chapter 13 did not give much hope, from an earthly perspective, for those who would refuse to worship the beast. Refusal to worship the beast was going to bring war, captivity, starvation and death. Would refusal be worth it? Would faithfulness to death be vindicated? The answer is in chapter 14.

The theme of this chapter is the same as that of chapters 4 and 5—Throne perspective. The great tribulation of the Roman empire must be seen by Christians through the perspective of heaven. Heaven is in control. The Lamb is the Victor, not Domitian. The persecuted saints of earth are in direct contact with heaven—they are just a breath away from final and complete victory. If they die "in the Lord" they will be ushered immediately into rest and reward. Some may be terrified by the first beast, some may be seduced by the second beast, but not the Christian.

The Blessed (14:1-20)

14 Then I looked, and lo, on Mount Zion stood the Lamb, and with him a hundred and forty-four thousand who had his name and his Father's name written on their foreheads. ²And I heard a voice from heaven like the sound of many waters and like the sound of loud thunder; the voice I heard was like the sound of harpers playing on their harps, ³and they sing a new song before the throne and before the living creatures and before the elders. No one could learn that song except the hundred and forty-four thousand who had been redeemed from the earth. ⁴It is these who have not defiled themselves with women, for they are chaste; it is these who follow the Lamb wherever he goes; these have been redeemed from mankind as first fruits for God and the Lamb, ⁵and in their mouth no lie was found, for they are spotless.

6 Then I saw another angel flying in midheaven, with an eternal gospel to proclaim to those who dwell on earth, to every nation and tribe and tongue and people; ⁷and he said with a loud voice, "Fear God and give him glory, for the hour of his judgment has come; and worship him who made heaven and earth, the sea and the fountains of water."

8 Another angel, a second, followed, saying, "Fallen, fallen is Babylon the great, she who made all nations drink the wine of her impure passion."

9 And another angel, a third, followed them, saying with a loud voice, "If any one worships the beast and its image, and receives a mark on his fore head or on his hand, ¹⁰he also shall drink the wine of God's wrath, poured unmixed into the cup of his anger, and he shall be tormented with fire and sulphur in the presence of the holy angels and in the presence of the Lamb. ¹¹And the smoke of their torment goes up for ever and ever; and they have no rest, day or night, these worshipers of the beast and its image, and whoever receives the mark of its name."

12 Here is a call for the endurance of the saints, those who keep the commandments of God and the faith of Jesus.

13 And I heard a voice from heaven saying, "Write this: Blessed are the dead who die in the Lord henceforth." "Blessed indeed," says the Spirit, "that they may rest from their labors, for their deeds follow them!"

14 Then I looked, and lo, a white cloud, and seated on the cloud one like a son of man, with a golden crown on his head, and a sharp sickle in his hand. [15]And another angel came out of the temple, calling with a loud voice to him who sat upon the cloud, "Put in your sickle, and reap, for the hour to reap has come, for the harvest of the earth is fully ripe." [16]So he who sat upon the cloud swung his sickle on the earth, and the earth was reaped.

17 And another angel came out of the temple in heaven, and he too had a sharp sickle. [18]Then another angel came out from the altar, the angel who has power over fire, and he called with a loud voice to him who had the sharp sickle, "Put in your sickle, and gather the clusters of the vine of the earth, for its grapes are ripe." [19]So the angel swung his sickle on the earth and gathered the vintage of the earth, and threw it into the great wine press of the wrath of God; [20]and the wine press was trodden outside the city, and blood flowed from the wine press, as high as a horse's bridle, for one thousand six hundred stadia.

vv. 1-5 . . . on Mount Zion stood the Lamb, and with him a hundred and forty-four thousand . . . — The 144,000 with the Lamb on Mount Zion are the same 144,000 as those in 7:1-8. They are the redeemed still on the earth, numbered and sealed (marked) by God, with Christ in their midst as he was portrayed walking among the seven lampstands (1:13; 2:1).

First, Mt. Zion is without question symbolic of the church on earth. It is plainly taught in the Old Testament prophets that Zion is the church of Christ to be established at the first advent of the Messiah (cf. Psa. 2:6; 110:2, 6; Isa. 2:2ff.; 35:10; 61:3; 66:7-9; Joel 2:32; Micah 4:7—5:2, etc.). Jesus and the apostles confirmed that the church was the fulfillment of the prophecies concerning Zion (cf. Zech. 9:9 with Mt. 21:5; Jn. 12:15; Isa. 62:11; cf. Isa. 28:16 with Rom. 9:33; I Pet. 2:6; Isa. 59:20; Rom. 11:26). But the most significant confirmation of this is found in Hebrews 12:22-28. There the apostle Paul informs Hebrew Christians that they should not be tempted to return to Judaism (which is symbolized by Mt. Sinai Heb. 12:18-21) *because* they had, by becoming Christians, arrived at the Zion predicted in the Old Testament prophets. Paul uses the perfect tense verb in Heb. 12:22 which would be interpreted, "But you have come and are coming to Mount Zion . . ." indicating that Mount Zion was not future but *present* in the first century A.D.

The Father's name "written on their foreheads" is the same name written on those of the church of Philadelphia who kept the faith (Rev. 3:12); it is the seal of God upon the foreheads of the "new Israel" (Rev. 7:3) the church on earth; it is the mark in contrast to the mark of the beast (cf. Rev. 13:16-18; 14:9-11; 19:20-21; 20:4). It is not a literal mark or name. It has to do with character, spiritual kinship. The Jews Jesus called sons of the devil had no literal mark on their foreheads but their spiritual kinship was recognizable in their character and their deeds (cf. Jn. 8:44-47)—they did not have to have 666 tattooed with a laser beam literally on their flesh. Christians do not have to wear gold or wooden crosses around their necks to be recognized as belonging to Jesus. The world will know them as citizens of Zion by their character and deeds (cf. Jn. 13:35; Acts 4:13).

Next John's attention is directed away from Zion (the church on earth) to heaven. From heaven he hears a sound like the sound of many waters and like loud thunder. The sound he heard was like harpers playing on their harps. It was a sound like that of a roaring, crashing orchestra of musical instruments (harps). He hears from heaven majesty, power, sovereignty and praise. "They" sing a new song. "They" cannot be the 144,000 of "new Israel" on earth; "they" cannot be the four living creatures and 24 elders because "they" sing this new song *before* (to an audience of) the creatures and elders; "they" cannot be angels because angels cannot learn this song (cf. I Pet. 1:12; Heb. 2:16); "they" must be the innumerable multitude which had, at the time John was writing, come out of the great tribulation and were before the throne in heaven (cf. notes on 7:9-17).

Now John's attention is directed back to earth, to the 144,000. They are learning that song of redemption by presently going through the great tribulation. They were in the process of redemption. They were being purchased (Gr. *egorasmenoi*, perfect participle) from the world. It is through tribulation that people become Christians and enter the kingdom of God (Acts 14:21-23; Heb. 10:32-39; etc.). These Christians, the 144,000 safe in the citadel of Zion, had not defiled (Gr. *emolunthesan*, besmeared, filthied, fouled) themselves with the filthy woman (Rome). The 144,000 are spiritually pure and chaste (Gr. *parthenoi*, virginal). This probably refers primarily to the fact that the 144,000 have not committed spiritual adultery by worshiping idols. They have not bowed to emperor worship. The Old Testament constantly symbolizes idolatry as spiritual adultery (cf. Hosea 1:2; 2:1, 5; Ezek. 16:1-63; etc.). The idea of spiritual harlotry is emphatic in Revelation 17:1, 2, 4, 5; 18:3, 9; 19:2. That the church of Christ on earth should keep herself pure and undefiled from "fornication" with Rome is also emphatic in Revelation 18:4, 20; 19:6-6. These scriptures portray economic, political and religious intercourse with Rome as "fornication" with her because such intercourse demanded emperor-worship (idolatry). Complicity in any form of idolatry is spiritual whoremongering. Christians are to keep themselves pure from all forms of idolatry (I Cor. 10:14-22; II Cor. 11:2-3; I Jn. 5:21). Covetousness is idolatry; worship of political systems of potentates is idolatry; trust in non-Biblical religious systems is idolatry. Anything or anyone, other than God the Father and God the Son, to whom man gives first loyalty and love is idolatry. Being a Christian is being *married* to Christ (Eph. 5:21-33). Unfaithfulness to Christ's standards is spiritual adutlery.

THIRTEEN LESSONS ON REVELATION

The 144,000 were learning the new song (the song of Moses and the Lamb, Rev. 15:3-4) as they went through the great tribulation, because that is the song Moses and the Lamb both had to sing themselves. Both Moses and the Lamb were redeemed or purchased out of the earth *through* tribulation by *faith.* It is a song learned by experience. The 144,000 (the church on earth in the Roman empire) followed the Lamb wherever he went. Jesus told his disciples when he was on earth, "If any one serves me, he must follow me; and where I am, there shall my servant be also. . . ." (Jn. 12:26). Jesus said that in a context of talking about his death on the cross. The 144,000 followed Jesus in "hating his life in this world" (cf. Rev. 12:11). Whatever Jesus did when he was in the world—whatever "road" walked— his "marked ones" expected to follow. If Jesus was persecuted, His disciples must be willing to follow (Jn. 15:18-27); if Jesus was willing to lay down his life for the word of God and for the sheep of God's flock, His 144,000 must follow; if Jesus was willing to renounce all the world's fame, fortune and pleasure for the kingdom's sake, so must those who wish to sing his song! Wherever Jesus goes (I Pet. 2:21) and wherever Jesus calls (Jn. 10:27-28) the citizens of Zion will go.

In verse 3 John says the 144,000 had been and were continuing to be purchased from the world; he uses the perfect tense participle *egorasmenoi.* In verse 4 John says the 144,000 had been purchased from mankind; he uses the aorist tense verb *egorasthesan.* John emphatically declares this 144,000 had been purchased at some point in the past and was continuing in the redemption process. This 144,000 was not, therefore, in heaven when John wrote; this 144,000 was not to be redeemed 2000 years after John wrote Revelation. John further indicates this 144,000 was of the first century A.D. by calling them "first fruits" for God and the Lamb. John uses the Greek word *aparche* which is related to the word *aparchomai,* meaning, "to make a beginning." Paul applies the word *aparche* to his first converts in Asia and Achai (Rom. 16:5; I Cor. 16:15). This 144,000 was abiding in the truth. In their mouth no deceit or falsehood (Gr. *dolos*) was to be found. They would not say the Roman emperor was a god because that would be to acknowledge deception and falsehood. They would not renounce Christ as the Son of God, even at the sacrifice of their lives, because that would be to lie. Truth is more important than physical life. This 144,000 had been purified and purged of all deceitfulness and compromising of the truth by declaring their loyalty to Christ who is the Way, the Truth and the Life. In Christ by faith they had their past sin forgiven and had present power to overcome the temptation to live in sin. They were spotless (Gr. *amomoi*); the word literally means, "unmarked, without blemish." This 144,000 had no mark of having been deceived by the devil or beguiled by the beast on them. It was apparent to all they did not belong to the kingdom of darkness and falsehood. They could not be carried about by the cunning of men (Eph. 4:14ff.) but spoke the truth in love (Eph. 4:15, 25, 29, 30, 31).

vv. 6-7 . . . **another angel flying in midheaven, with an eternal gospel to proclaim to those who dwell on earth** . . . — Still another angel (cf. 7:2; 8:3; 10:1) comes with a vision. This angel was flying in midheaven (Gr. *mesouranema*)—the point at which the sun reaches its apex or directly overhead. This gives the angel maximum visibility by all on earth. This angel had a gospel-everlasting (Gr. *euaggelion aionion*) with which he evangelized (Gr. *euaggelisai*) those dwelling on the earth. What is this gospel? Some commentators have speculated that this was different than the gospel of salvation by grace through faith proclaimed by Jesus and the apostles elsewhere in the New Testament. They think it is a special announcement of judgment for the "end times." But, as Homer Hailey points out succinctly in his commentary on Revelation, this must be the very same gospel preached by Jesus and the apostles elsewhere for the New Testament says plainly there is only one gospel to be preached for all time. The faith was once for all delivered to the saints (Jude 3) and any one (even an angel) preaching any other gospel than that which was first delivered was to be anathema (Gal. 1:8). The gospel Christ accomplished and commissioned to be preached was to be proclaimed to every creature in the whole creation (Mt. 28:19; Mk. 16:15f.). Besides, it is doubtful that God would literally send heavenly beings to preach the gospel to human beings. In the first place, the gospel was a treasure deposited in "earthen vessels" (II Cor. 4:7); in the second place, the gospel of human redemption is something in which angels have only limited knowledge (cf. Heb. 2:16; I Pet. 1:10-12). This angel symbolizes human messengers much the same way the angels of the seven churches symbolized preachers or elders who were messengers for the seven churches of Asia.

What is interesting about this gospel ("good news") is the terminology by which it is capsulated. One would not ordinarily think of "fearing God" and "judgment to come" as "good news"! Yet, reverence for God, obeying God (giving God glory), worshiping God, and preparing for judgment by trusting in Christ's atonement is the very essence of the good news. This gospel of God was to be proclaimed to every nation and tribe and tongue and people—to the whole civilization of the Roman world. All who willingly follow the Lamb wherever he goes will be redeemed out of a lost and doomed Roman civilization. In the process of their redemption they will be numbered among the "144,000" and be protected by the Lamb in God's citadel, Zion. They will learn the new song of Moses and the Lamb which those already finished with their redemption are singing around the throne.

v. 8   Another angel, a second, followed, saying, "Fallen, fallen is Babylon the great. . . ." — The Greek verbs, *epesen epesen,* are aroist tense and signify something that has happened. It seems strange that John would not use the future tense *pesoumai* and say, "Shall fall, shall fall, Babylon the great." But when God declares something shall be, it is as good as done already (cf. Isa. 46:10; 48:3). God decreed the fall of ancient Babylon and its king in the Old Testament decades before it happened as if it had already happened (cf. Isa. 13:1—14:21; Jer. 51:8; etc.). There is no question in the mind of heaven that the "Babylon" of John's day will fall. This is part of the good news to be proclaimed. The "judgment" announced in 14:7 is not the final judgment but "Babylon's" justment. The question is: Who is "Babylon"? That is settled in chapters 17 and 18 of this Revelation. It can be none other than ancient Rome. Rome is symbolized by the first beast (political opposition), the second beast (idolatrous emperor-worship), and Babylon, the mistress or harlot (carnal materialism and sensualism). These are the three main pressures (tribulations) brought to bear on Christians and others during the age of the Roman empire.

Babylon's (Rome's) judgment from God was the result of her wickedness and making the whole Roman world "drink the wine of her impure passion." The term wine is not to be limited to literal alcoholic beverage but is symbolic of everything that intoxicated Rome to attempt the usurpation of the sovereignty of God and the Lamb. Political, religious and economic power is intoxicating. Most men become drunk with power. They lose all reason and perspective with power. They are incapable of facing the reality that the power does not really belong to them. That is the way a drunkard sees things—irrationally and unrealistically. The drunkard, to control others, must intice them to become drunk with the same "wine." Rome inticed the whole world (except faithful Christians) to indulge in political oppression of Christ's church, emperor-worship and suppression of the truth of Christianity, and abandonment to carnal, fleshly, materialistic life-style.

The words *impure passion* are a translation of the Greek word *porneias* which is usually translated *evil* or *wickedness;* sometimes it is translated *fornication.* It is a word related to *ponos* which means, *labor, toil, pain* or *sorrow;* thus *porneias* denotes evil that causes pain, labor or sorrow and is therefore *worthless* and *grievous.*

The imagery of drinking the wine of wickedness is undoubtedly taken from the Old Testament (cf. Jer. 51:7). Rome is pictured again intoxicated with the wine of her wickedness (Rev. 17:2, 6; 18:3). God does not allow those drunk on the wine of wickedness to escape reality long. Soon the "piper must be paid."

vv. 9-11 If anyone worship the beast . . . he also shall drink the wine of God's wrath . . . for ever and ever — A third angel had a message for the whole Roman world also, so he cried with a loud voice announcing the judgment upon all who worshiped the beast and its image (see comments on chapter 13 for emperor-worship).

God has a cup of wine for all who intoxicate themselves with wickedness. God's cup is filled with divine wrath *unmixed* (Gr. *akratou,* untempered, undiluted). In ancient times (as well as modern) The juice of the grape (wine) was often mixed with water and spices for taste and economic reasons. Diluted wine would not have full effect, but undiluted would cause those who drank it to stagger and reel and become incapacitated. God's undiluted and untempered wrath incapacitated his enemies. The imagery of God's cup of wrath is taken from the Old Testament prophets (cf. Psa. 75:8; Isa. 51:22; Jer. 25:15, 27; 49:12; Ezek. 23:31-32; Obadiah 16; Hab. 2:15-16). When God decides to make an enemy drink His cup of wrath the enemy cannot refuse it! When Rome's time came, she inexorably drank the cup of God's wrath (cf. Rev. 17:17; 18:6-10).

The warning is that all who have worshiped the beast and its image and have not repented are to be *tormented* (Gr. *basanisthesetai,* rubbed, abraded, chaffed torturiously—tortured) in fire and brimstone while they must cringe in guilt in the presence of the holy angels and the Lamb. Brimstone (Gr. *theion,* sulphurous, explosive, lightning) and fire as an agent of God's wrath and torture upon the wicked is as old as Genesis 19:24 and Sodom and Gomorrah. It is also referred to in the prophets (cf. Isa. 30:27-33; 34:9; Ezek. 38:22). John is trying to picture the doom of the impenitent in the most terrifying terms available in the human language. But even human language is incapable of communicating the excruciating torture of eternal punishment by an infinitely just, holy and powerful God. The rich man who died and went to Hades experienced the torments of the wrath of God (cf. Lk. 16:19-31). And the punishment of those who have the mark of the beast and do not repent will be eternal. The Greek phrase here is *aionas aionon* which literally means, "for ages of ages," or "ages without end." Matthew used the same word for *eternal* punishment as he did for *eternal* life (Gr. *aionion*) in reporting Jesus' statement in Matthew 25:46. In the statement of Jesus, recorded by Mark (9:43-48), we understand also that the punishment of the wicked will be without end (eternal). Mark says Jesus described the fires of hell as *unquenchable* (Gr. *asbeston,* asbestos) where the "worm" (Gr. *skolex,* used metaphorically of the devouring process) has *no end* (Gr. *ou teleuta,* no finish, no completion). Jesus told the account of Lazarus and the rich man (Lk. 16:19-31) and said there was an impassable chasm between the place of torment and the place of blessedness. None can pass from one to the other. Man's destiny is *eternally* fixed after death! The impenitent and unbelieving are forever tormented!

Since the torment of the impenitent is in the *presence* (Gr. *enopoion,* in the face of, or, in the eye of) the holy angels and the Lamb, it will also be in the presence of the redeemed for the redeemed are in the presence of the Lamb. We may think of this idea as repugnant; but that is because we do not understand, and may not believe, the utter horridness of wickedness. We may not comprehend or believe the absoluteness of the Lord's justice and righteousness. Whatever we may think, it is definitely the teaching of scripture that in eternity the divine justice of heaven will *demonstrate* to the saints the vindication of their faith and suffering. Abraham went to see with his own eyes the holocaust which had destroyed Sodom and Gomorrah (Gen. 19:27-28). Isaiah predicts that the progeny of the faithful remnant will witness with their own eyes the destruction of apostate Judaism and the birth of the Messianic kingdom (the church) (Isa. 66:1-24) as a vindication of the faith and suffering of the remnant. In torments the rich man saw Lazarus in Abraham's bosom (Lk. 16:19-31) and we assume Lazarus saw the rich man in torments—Abraham certainly did. Christians were told to rejoice over the catastrophic judgment of the Lamb upon the Roman empire (Rev. 18:20). As Barclay puts it: "Many a time the heathen had looked down from the crowded seats of the tiers of the arena on the sufferings of the Christians, and the Christians looked for the day when the spectators would be the saints and the hosts of heaven, and when the victims would be the erstwhile persecutors, and when the roles on earth would be reversed in heaven." Our attitude about God's right to send impenitent people to be tormented forever, must be brought into conformity with God's revealed Word, no matter what our feelings may be. John's vision here revealed no cessation of the torment—not even for a moment in eternity. They have no rest day or night from the torment. If the saints are called to be aware of God's judgments here on earth as vindication of their faith, why not in eternity?

v. 12   Here is a call for the endurance of the saints — This is the second "call" for the endurance of the saints. The first "call" was in 13:10. Actually, the word "call" in the English version is a supplied word—it is not in the Greek text. The Greek text reads literally, "Here is the endurance of the saints who keep the commandments of God and their faith in Jesus." In 13:10 the endurance or perseverence of the saints is found in accepting death or captivity for their faith. In 14:12 their perseverance is found in trusting God's word that he will vindicate them by his wrath upon those who have the mark of the beast and by taking the saints through death to blessedness (14:13). The saint develops perseverance in two ways: (a) trusting God's promises; (b) experiencing godly trials and tribulations. This is the teaching of Hebrews 10:32-39 and I Peter 4:12-19. John is not just "calling" for perseverance, he is giving the formula for developing it.

v. 13   . . . Blessed are the dead who die in the Lord henceforth . . . — Everything in the Roman world of that day was manipulated by the devil in an attempt to separate Christians from Christ. The power of evil applied political persecution, false religious teaching and practice, and moral seduction to deceive believers into abandoning Christ and the church. John is told to *write* (permanency) the promise of God's Holy Spirit. Those saints who endure by keeping the commandments of God and the faith of Jesus will fly immediately to a state of blessedness at the time of their physical death. They must not allow themselves to be deceived by the beast or those who have the mark of the beast. They must not abandon Christ.

This is a promise of God as old as the Old Testament. "Precious in the sight of the Lord is the death of his saints" (Psa. 116:15). Dying in the Lord means going to the blessed presence of the Lord in the New Testament also (cf. I Cor. 15:18-23; I Thess. 4:13-18). Paul was so eager to "gain" Christ, he could hardly decide whether he preferred to stay alive or die (Phil. 1:21-23). Jesus told the believing thief on the cross, "Today shalt thou be with me in Paradise" (Lk. 23:43). The beggar Lazarus when he died, was carried by the angels immediately to the presence of Abraham where he was comforted, (Lk. 16:25).

Those who die *in* the Lord find rest from the tribulation (pressure and testing) they had to endure in the world. These do not shrink back from the pressures and tensions of trusting in Jesus, nor do they give up when tested. They love Christ and trust Him even to death. But when they die they are pressured no more, they are tested no more, they find their "Sabbath rest" (Heb. 4:1ff.) where they may serve the Lord and do good and enjoy God's joyful presence forever. And their works go with them. John does not mean to say, of course, that some sort of balance sheet of good works in such quantity or quality as to outweigh evil works will accompany us so that the Lord may justify us by our works. The New Testament is plain that "by the works of the law shall no flesh be justified" (Gal. 2:16). But it is by doing the works of Christ we develop the character or Spirit of Christ in us. John is really saying here that when the Christian dies he takes with him to the presence of Christ a character made over into the image of Christ by the works of Christ done in the body. This cannot be confined strictly to the idea that good deeds are left behind after the death of believers as testimonies to their goodness on earth. This promise is for the blessedness of the saints in heaven in direct connection to their deeds. What the believer does on earth in assimilating the will and character of Christ will follow him to the next life and enhance his happiness there.

vv. 14-20 . . . Put in your sickle and reap . . . — John's next vision is a prediction, in symbolic form, of the imminent judgment of the Lamb upon the Roman empire. The imagery of the Son of man coming on a cloud does not necessarily have to be restricted to the Second Coming (see comments on Rev. 1:7). In fact, what John sees here may not be Christ on a cloud at all. The one on the cloud was *like* a son of man. Furthermore, an angel shouted with a loud voice to the one on the cloud giving him orders— Christ would not be taking orders from an angel. Finally, the one having the sickle is said to be an *angel* (14:19). This angel had a crown. That is not unusual since the 24 elders also had crowns.

The imagery of God's judgment falling upon nations in the form of "reaping with a sickle" is from the Old Testament prophets (see Joel 3:13).

Jesus told a parable about "reapers" at harvest time (Mt. 13:24-30; 13:36-43; Mk. 4:29).

The angel with the sickle is told to gather the *clusters* (Gr. *botruas*) of the *vine* (Gr. *ampelou*) of the earth because its *grapes* (Gr. *staphulai*) were *ripe* (Gr. *ekuasan,* aorist, "had ripened"). It appears the word *vine* is to be understood as *vintage* (a season's produce of grapes) and not as the whole vine. The *earth* is the whole vine, but *only* the clusters of the vine are to be gathered. In other words, God is not going to reap the whole earth in this context—only vintage of pagan Rome. The angel gathered pagan Rome and threw it into the great wine press of the wrath of God. Wine presses (Gr. *lenos,* trough or vat) were usually dug out in the soil or excavated in a rock. Clusters of grapes were poured into these round or square excavations and men and women climbed into them bare-footed and squeezed the juice from the grapes by treading back and forth upon the ripened grapes (see Rev. 19:15).

This is apocalyptic hyperbole. It is figurative and exaggerated. The winepress was trodden *outside the city*. The "city" of God is the church. They had the seal of God upon them and were protected (cf. 7:1ff.; 11:1-2; etc.). But those "outside" the church were to be trodden in God's wine-press of wrath. That which flows from the wine-press is blood, not grape juice. This is a figurative scene. It could never be literally fulfilled—certainly not in Palestine for there is no place for a river 200 miles long (1600 stadia) there, especially not in the plain of Meggido. If the river of blood is intended to be understood literally, so must the sickle and the winepress. This is the kind of apocalyptic imagery used by other prophets (cf. Isa. 34:5-7; Ezek. 38:19-23; 39:17-24; etc.). It describes the awful carnage which will attend the destruction of the Roman empire. Jesus used such apocalyptic language to describe the fall of Judaism in Matthew 24 and Luke 21. The essence of chapter fourteen is in its contrast to chapter thirteen. The forces of evil are strong. They seem invincible (13:4). But the forces of righteousness are stronger (14:17-20). Now that the persecuted saints are reassured of their relationship to the Lamb and their destiny of blessedness, it is time for the Lamb to unleash His wrath upon Babylon, the harlot (also known as the beast and false prophet) which is Rome.

APPREHENSION AND APPLICATION:

1. How is the theme of chapter 14 the same as that of chapters 4 and 5? Do you think the Christians of those early centuries were strengthened by these words of John's revelation? Would you have been? Are you?
2. What is Mt. Zion? Why is Zion used by John in the Revelation? What kind of glorious picture is painted of Zion in the Old Testament prophets? Do you think of yourself as a resident of Zion?

3. What is the "new song"? Have you learned it? How does one learn it?
4. Who is following the Lamb? Where? Why do some not follow the Lamb? Will you follow the Lamb *wherever* He goes?
5. What is the eternal gospel the angel had to proclaim? Is God's wrath and judgment a part of the good news of Christ? Should it be preached that way today?
6. Who is Babylon? How could she be fallen before she fell? How did she make all nations drink of her wine?
7. Are unbelievers tormented by God in fire and brimstone *forever*? Are there other scriptures to substantiate this? Would Jesus say this? Will the saints be aware of the punishment of the wicked? Won't that make them sad?
8. What does the call for endurance and obedience and faith of the saints have to do with the preceding questions? With the following question?
9. What is the "rest" of the dead saint? How does his "works" follow after him? What sort of character (works) are you building up to take with you?
10. What "reaping" is being commanded here? Is it the end of the world? Why would the language be so gory if it is only the fall of Rome? Does the Bible use gory language about other empires falling?

A Parallel Comparison of the Seven Seals, Seven Trumpets and Seven Bowls

	SEALS	TRUMPETS	BOWLS
1	White horse. Rider with bow and crown who went out conquering and to conquer.	Hail and fire mixed with blood fell on the earth and burnt up 1/3 of the earth, trees and grass.	Foul and evil sores came when men who bore the mark of the beast and worshiped its image. Poured on the earth.
2	Bright red horse. Rider with sword was permitted to take peace from the the earth so that men should slay one another.	Something like a great fiery mountain thrown into the sea, and 1/3 of the sea became blood, and 1/3 of the sea creatures died, and 1/3 of the ships were destroyed.	Poured on the sea which became like dead men's blood, and everything in the sea died.
3	Black horse. Rider with balance in hand. Voice apparently from midst of 4 living creatures, saying, "A qt. of wheat and 3 qts. of barley for a denarius but don't harm the oil and wine.	A great blazing star fell from heaven on 1/3 of the rivers and fountains of water. The star's name was Wormwood and a third of the waters became bitter and many died.	Poured on the rivers and fountains of water which became blood, and the angel of water says that God is just to give men who have shed blood blood to drink.
4	Pale horse. Rider named death with hades following, given power over 1/4 of the earth to kill with sword, famine, pestilence and wild beasts.	1/3 of the sun, moon and stars were struck so that a 1/3 of their light was darkened so that a 1/3 of the day and night was kept from shining.	Poured on the sun which is allowed to scorch men with a fierce heat, and they curse God's name but did not repent and give him glory.
5	Sons of slain for God's word and witness born under a trask-ing when the Lord would judge and revenge their blood. Given white robes and told to rest until the others who were to be killed had been.	Star fell from heaven and given key to bottomless pit which he opened releasing smoke that darkened the sun. Locusts came from the smoke with scorpion-like power to harm all mankind not sealed of God, to torture them 5 months. Men will seek death but not find it. Locusts look like battle horses and make chariot-like noise. Their king is the angel Abaddon or Apollyon of the bottomless pit.	Poured on the throne of the beast and its throne was in darkness where men gnawed their tongues in anguish, cursed God for their pain and sores but did not repent of their deeds.
6	Earthquake, sun blackened, moon blood red, stars fall, sky rolled up, mountains and islands removed, all men seek to hide from the wrath of Him who is seated on the throne and the Lamb.	Voice from golden altar commands release of 4 angels bound at Euphrates river to kill 1/3 of man. 200,000,000 man army with fire, smoke and sulphur coming from mouths to kill, riding horses with tails like serpents who wound with their mouths. The rest of mankind did not repent of their idolatry and immorality.	Poured on Euphrates river which dried up to prepare way for eastern kings. From the mouths of the dragon, beast and false prophet frog-like foul spirits, which are demonic, doing signs and assembling the world's kings for battle on the great day of God at Armageddon. (Christ is coming like a thief, so keep alert and ready.)
7	Silence in heaven for about 1/2 hour. 7 angels with 7 trumpets come forth.	A voice in heaven declares that the kingdom is the Lord's, and the 24 elders worship God. The heavenly temple is opened to reveal the Ark of the Covenant, lightning, loud noises, thunder, earthquake and heavy hail. Then came the war in heaven and the beast of the sea.	Poured into the air and a voice came out of the temple saying, "It is done." Great lightning, noises, thunder, earthquake follow causing Babylon to split in thirds, nations' cities to fall as God's wrath is fully vented. Every mountain and island is destroyed and 100 lb. hailstones fall on men till they curse God for the plague of hail.

Lesson Four
(15:1-8, 16:1-21)

THE LAMB AND THE SPIRITUAL CONFLICT

In 14:1-5 the Lamb stands in Zion and receives the worship of the saints in heaven already "out" of the great tribulation, and the worship of the saints on earth "in" the great tribulation. Let a petty emperor of the earth in a little decade or even in a century or two assert his deity. He is nothing compared with the Christ of the ages! An emperor's enforced worship is a cheap sacrilege when viewed against the worship of God; his required formulas are nothing compared with the new song of the redeemed.

And in 14:6-20 the purpose of the eternal God is set over against that of an earthly pretender. An angel proclaims the purpose of God in an eternal gospel to every tribe under heaven. Men and nations are warned to worship not an impotent earthly creature but Him who made the heavens and the earth and all that is in them. Those who do not will suffer judgment in torments forever in the presence of the holy angels and the Lamb. Many will not heed the warning. The Babylon (Rome) of John's day had caused the nations to follow after lies and to reject God. Babylon, the seat of Satan's rebellion, must therefore be judged by the gospel Babylon rejected. Jesus came with the eternal gospel to save. However, His coming became a judgment upon those who refused the truth because their deeds were evil (cf. Jn. 3:19-21; 9:39-41). All judgment has been given to the Lamb (cf. Jn. 5:22ff.).

The judgment of the Lamb upon Babylon (Rome) has been building up to the crescendo of the seven *last* (Gr. *eschatas,* eschatological) plagues. This has been in process since the beginning of the seven seals (ch. 6) and the seven trumpets (ch. 8-9). Now the final judgment on Rome is about to break upon her. Chapter 15 pictures the temple in heaven (God's residence) opened and God's agents (angels) being sent to finish Rome's judgment. Chapter 15 is so directly and inseparably tied to chapter 16, we have chosen to make them into one lesson.

Pronouncement of Final Judgment: (15:1-8)

15 Then I saw another portent in heaven, great and wonderful, seven angels with seven plagues, which are the last, for with them the wrath of God is ended.

2 And I saw what appeared to be a sea of glass mingled with fire, and those who had conquered the beast and its image and the number of its me, standing beside the sea of glass with harps of God in their hands. ³And they sing the song of Moses, the servant of God, and the song of the Lamb, saying,

"Great and wonderful are thy deeds,
O Lord God the Almighty!
Just and true are thy ways,
O King of the ages!
⁴Who shall not fear and glorify thy name, O Lord?
For thou alone art holy.
All nations shall come and worship thee,
for thy judgments have been revealed."

5 After this I looked, and the temple of the tent of witness in heaven was opened, ⁶and out of the temple came the seven angels with the seven plagues, robed in pure bright linen, and their breasts girded with golden girdles. ⁷And one of the four living creatures gave the seven angels seven golden bowls full of the wrath of God who lives for ever and ever; ⁸and the temple was filled with smoke from the glory of God and from his power, and no one could enter the temple until the seven plagues of the seven angels were ended.

v. 1 . . . seven angels with seven plagues . . . — John saw these seven plagues in the form of a *portent* (Gr. *semeion,* sign) from heaven. The Greek word *plegas* (plague) literally means, "a stripe, or a wound" and is from the root word *plesso,* "to smite." It is used metaphorically of any calamity. These "plagues" will be termed "bowls of the wrath of God" in chapter 16.

These seven plagues are called the *last* (Gr. *eschatas,* eschatological). The word *eschatos* does not necessarily have to mean the end of all time; it is used frequently in the New Testament to signify that God has reached some goal, in time, in his redemptive program (cf. I Cor. 15:45; Acts 2:17; Heb. 1:2; I Jn. 2:18; I Pet. 1:20; etc.). Last (*exchatas*) days in the New Testament often means the end of the Jewish dispensation and the beginning of the Christian dispensation. These *last* plagues signify God has reached the *goal* of judgment he put into operation with the seals and the trumpets upon the Roman empire. In these plagues the wrath of God was finished. The Greek word *etelesthe* is aorist tense and should be translated *was* finished—not shall be finished. The word is from *teleo* which means consummated, completed, reached the goal intended, or perfected.

vv. 2-4 **... those who had conquered the beast ...** — John saw through the same crystal-clear sea, or sea of glass, he had seen earlier (4:6). This time the crystal-clearness surrounding the throne of God reveals the *fire* of God's judgment ready to fall in the form of the seven plagues upon Rome. John saw standing *beside* this fiery sea those conquering the beast and its image. The Greek participle *nikontas* (conquering) is in the present tense indicating John is being given a vision of the saints presently *in* the tribulation on earth as if they had already conquered the beast and were in heaven around the throne of God. This vision is a "sign" that those Christians who die during the pouring out of God's judgments upon Rome will go immediately to surround the throne of heaven with harps and songs of praise for the justness of God's judgments and the mercies of their redemption.

What are the harps? Are they literally instruments of music being used in the next life to praise God, or are they merely symbolical of praise being made with the voices of the saints in the next life? Harps are mentioned in 5:8 and 14:2. In 5:8 each of the twenty-four elders is said to be "holding a harp"; it would be difficult to be *holding* a symbol. In 14:2 a voice was heard *like* the *sound* of harpers—this does not necessarily specify an instrument. Here, in 15:2, the conquerors stand beside the sea *with harps of God in their hands.* Granted, this could be all a symbolic picture, symbolizing praise. But then the singing, the song and the voices of the saints should also be only symbolic and not real. We think it is not fair to the grammar, the context and the rest of the Bible to symbolize these harps in order to sustain an opinion that musical instruments are not to be used in the praise of God. A human voice is an instrument made of "clay"! The vocal chords of the human body will return to matter just as surely as the bronze of a trumpet or the steel of a harp-string. The archangel will signal the end of time with a blast from a trumpet (I Thess. 4:16)—perhaps this trumpet, too, is a symbol. Jesus worshiped in a Jewish temple where musical instruments were used; the apostles and early Christians worshiped God in the temple where musical instruments were played

(Acts 2:46; 3:1; 5:12, 20, 42; 21:26; etc.). If musical instruments are heaven's symbols, then the literal instruments should be acceptable for use in the early church. Nowhere in the New Testament is there a plain command that Christians should refrain from the use of musical instruments in praising God. If one should say the New Testament infers or implies non-use of instrumental music in worship, then one must also say the New Testament infers or implies non-construction of church buildings for God does not dwell in temples made with hands (cf. Acts 7:48; 17:24; Eph. 2:19-22).

The lyrics for the song of Moses are found in Exodus ch. 15. It is a psalm of praise for Israel's redemption from Egyptian bondage. This song was sung at every Sabbath evening service in the synagogue. At every Jewish service the recital of the *Shema* (Deut. 6:4-9) is followed by two prayers, one of which refers to the song of Moses. The Christian saints have the song of Moses plus a new song—the song of the Lamb. The song of the Lamb, however, is a combination of praises compiled from the Psalms, the Prophets and the writings of Moses! You may find all the phrases in the following passages (Psa. 92:5; 111:2; 98:1; 139:14; 145:17; 86:9; I Sam. 2:2; Psa. 99:3; 111:9; 86:9; 98:2; Jer. 10:7). What better place to find words with which to praise God and the Lamb than in the scriptures!

Barclay makes a timely comment: "But there is another thing which must strike anyone about the song of the triumphant martyrs. There is not one single word in it about their own victory and their own achievement; there is not a single mention in it of their triumph; from beginning to end the whole song is a lyric outburst on the greatness of God." In light of so much modern "Christian" music making its focus on the personal victories and experiences of people, it is refreshing to read that in heaven hymns are total, complete, unadulterated praise of God and his deeds. In heaven, in the unobscured knowledge of God's nature and his redemptive grace, man forgets himself and all his achievements and even his trials. In heaven man will realize the greatness of God so fully and totally he will remember that nothing matters except God and the Lamb. "Heaven is heaven because in it at last all self, and self-importance, are lost in the presence of the greatness and the glory of God," (Barclay).

This paean of praise is interesting also from the fact that so much is said about God's judgments in it. First, the statement, "Just and true are thy ways. . . ." The judgments of God upon impenitent, rebellious, wicked and blasphemous sinners is just. God is not to be blamed, contradicted or disbelieved when he reveals his judgments about what is right and what is wrong (in his word). God is not to be declared unfair, injust, or immoral when he executes his judgments in history through whatever secondary agents he may wish to serve him. It is only when the judgments of God are revealed that men of all nations come and worship Him. When God's judgments are in the earth, the inhabitatns of the world learn righteousness (Isa. 26:9). If favor is shown to the wicked, he does not learn righteousness . . . for he does not see the majesty of the Lord (Isa. 26:10). How many Christians on earth praise God today for his judgments? Yet that is the song of heaven! More than half of modern Christendom believes that God's judgments (especially those revealed in the Bible) are mythological and allegorical— for if they were real they would consider them unfair, injust and immoral.

vv. 5-6   . . . **the temple of the tent of witness in heaven was opened.** . . . — This phrase might well be translated, "the sanctuary of the tabernacle of the testimony was opened." The Greek word *naos* (temple) is used in Mt. 23:35 to designate the inner part of the Temple in Jerusalem. The Greek word *skenes* is often translated *tabernacle;* the Greek word *marturiou* is translated *testimony.* The "tent of testimony" is a common title for the Old Testament tabernacle (cf. Num. 9:15; 17:7; 18:2). John sees in a vision God's angelic servants coming out from the presence of God's written Law. The most important thing in the tabernacle was the ark of the covenant and the most significant thing in the ark was the Decalogue (the Ten Commandments). The tables of Stone symbolized the whole Law (or Will) of God. Rome, the beast, has defied the Law of God and blasphemed the Law-Giver. Rome has mocked and disobeyed every one of the Commandments. Now God must vindicate his law for his law is his character. He *must* be faithful to his word. The angels in procession, receiving the bowls of God's wrath to pour out, symbolize that God is about to uphold his word, verify his Law, and sustain his faithfulness. The whole Roman world is about to know that it cannot disobey the Law of God, remain impenitent, and escape the justice of God. These angels were dressed in priestly garments (pure white linen, and golden girdles). Priests of the Old Testament were charged with administering God's Law and executing punishments for disobedience to it.

vv. 7-8   . . . **seven golden bowls full of the wrath of God** . . . — One of the four living creatures gaves the seven angels their bowls of wrath from God. That is appropriate imagery to symbolize that God will execute his wrath on Rome through secondary agencies of creation—through living nature and living people (see Rev. 4:6ff. for symbolism of four living creatures). The Greek word for *full* here is *gemousas* and is most often used to describe a ship *heavily* laden with cargo or passengers. These bowls are heavily laden with God's wrath.

The temple (or sanctuary) was seen to be filled with smoke from the glory of God and from his power, and no one could enter until the seven plagues were *finished* (Gr. *telesthosin,* reached their goal, perfected, completed). The smoke filling the sanctuary and making it inaccessible symbolizes God's refusal to hear any intercession for impenitent Rome. As others have pointed out, this imagery is from the Old Testament also. When the tabernacle was first erected, the glory of God filled it, and Moses was not able to enter it (Exodus 40:34ff.); when Solomon had completed the Temple the glory of God filled the house so that the priests could not minister (II Kings 8:10ff.). All this was to typify that man, the sinner and rebel, could not, on his own merit, come into the presence of God. Atonement had to be made and accepted in faith and obedience. Until that was done, no one could have intercession from God.

Here, the message is that Rome, sinful, rebellious and impenitent, has no intercession which God will accept. The sanctuary is closed. No approach of man to God on behalf of Rome will be heard because Rome has chosen to continue in rebellion against God. The righteousness of God must be upheld; his name must be avenged and vindicated; there is nothing that can be done to halt it or turn it back until it is done! The rebellious, impenitent and wicked Jews of Jeremiah's day were beyond intercession. God commanded Jeremiah that he must pray for them (cf. Jer. 7:16; 11:14; 14:11; 15:1; 16:5; 17:1). Jesus sorrowfully had to pronounce upon the Jews of his day the inexorable judgment of God (Mt. 23:37-39). Not even Jesus could intercede for a people who rejected his interecession. When the Jews refused to know the "day of their visitation" (Lk. 19:41-44) there was nothing Jesus could do but weep.

Plagues Poured Out (16:1-21)

16 Then I heard a loud voice from the temple telling the seven angels, "Go and pour out on the earth the seven bowls of the wrath of God."

2 So the first angel went and poured his bowl on the earth, and foul and evil sores came upon the men who bore the mark of the beast and worshiped its image.

3 The second angel poured his bowl into the sea, and it became like the blood of a dead man, and every living thing died that was in the sea.

4 The third angel poured his bowl into the rivers and the fountains of water, and they became blood. ⁵And I heard the angel of water say,

"Just art thou in these thy judgments,
thou who art and wast, O Holy One.
⁶For men have shed the blood of saints and prophets,
and thou hast given them blood to drink.
It is their due!"
⁷And I heard the altar cry,
"Yea, Lord God the Almighty,
true and just are thy judgments!"

8 The fourth angel poured his bowl on the sun, and it was allowed to scorch men with fire; ⁹men were scorched by the fierce heat, and they

cursed the name of God who had power over these plagues, and they did not repent and give him glory.

10 The fifth angel poured his bowl on the throne of the beast, and its kingdom was in darkness; men gnawed their tongues in anguish [11]and cursed the God of heaven for their pain and sores, and did not repent of their deeds.

12 The sixth angel poured his bowl on the great river Euphrates, and its water was dried up, to prepare the way for the kings from the east. [13]And I saw, issuing from the mouth of the dragon and from the mouth of the beast and from the mouth of the false prophet, three foul spirits like frogs; [14]for they are demonic spirits, performing signs, who go abroad to the kings of the whole world, to assemble them for battle on the great day of God the Almighty. [15]("Lo, I am coming like a thief! Blessed is he who is awake, keeping his garments that he may not go naked and be seen exposed!") [16]And they assembled them at the place which is called in Hebrew Armageddon.

17 The seventh angel poured his bowl into the air, and a loud voice came out of the temple, from the throne, saying, "It is done!" [18]And there were flashes of lightning, voices, peals of thunder, and a great earthquake such as had never been since men were on the earth, so great was that earthquake. [19]The great city was split into three parts, and the cities of the nations fell, and God remembered great Babylon, to make her drain the cup of the fury of his wrath. [20]And every island fled away, and no mountains were to be found; [21]and great hailstones, heavy as a hundredweight, dropped on men from heaven, till men cursed God for the plague of the hail, so fearful was that plague.

vv. 1-2   . . . foul and evil sores came upon the men who bore the mark of the beast. . . . — Lenski summarizes succinctly that the seven *seals reveal,* the seven *trumpets announce* and *warn,* and the seven *bowls execute.* The bowls are the final series of judgments; they complete God's conflict with Rome. They are the final judgments and are presented as in process and as God's direct action in defense of his saints, and the vindication of his honor and faithfulness. The loud voice from the sanctuary commanding the angels to pour out the bowls is God's voice. Orders come for Rome's destruction from none less than the Omnipotent Creator and Judge of all that is. The Greek word *phialas* is sometimes translated *vial* and is the word from which the English word *phial* comes; however, the Greek word really means a broad, shallow vessel or large, deep saucer; the word is suggestive of rapidity in the emptying of the contents. The number seven, as we have seen, represents completeness or perfection. When God's wrath is poured out on Rome, it will not need to be poured out on her again—she will have come to an end.

The *destruction* of Rome has God's approval. We know this is referring to Rome because people are left alive, refusing to repent, *after* the bowls are poured out which would be the case at the end of time (cf. 16:6, 9, 10,

11, 12, 19). We also know this is Rome from chapters 17-19. The bowls (plagues) signify that Rome will go through a process of pestilence, mourning, famine, and violence (18:8, 20, 21). The violence will include internal revolution (the people who had listened to Rome and followed her policies will hate her and revolt against her, 17:15, 16); this is the disaster that befalls Rome for opposing the sovereignty of God and the Lamb and for refusing to repent.

These plagues are the natural consequences of sin (cf. Rom. 1:18-32). They represent the wrath of God inherent in sin. Sin has these plagues inherent within it. They are the result of defying God's moral Laws. God uses nature and uses history to destroy that which opposes his redemptive kingdom in the world.

The bowls (plagues) are to be understood as hyperbolic, apocalyptic and symbolic. They do not need to be interpreted as supernatural events. The prediction in 17:16-17 indicates that the "city" will be laid low by traitorous friends, by the beast itself turning on itself, and by the puppet allies (the 10 horns) of the beast. John clearly represents Christians as being present on earth, within the Roman empire, as the plagues (bowls) are descending upon the "harlot," (18:4). Just as in the case of the impenitent Pharaoh and the Egyptians, the bowls fail to work repentance in the hearts of the enemies of God in Rome. Since Rome was at the peak of her power in John's day, and evidently in no danger of falling, the bowls *predict* the yet undiscovered future destruction of Rome.

If we seek for some illustration in our time of the certain and continuous operation of the wrath of God in history against a people who turned from God to deify its own rulers, we may find that illustration in the case of Germany. If there be any doubt that the wrath of God as illustrated in the pouring out of the bowls could be expressed in history by natural means, let the terrible destruction and carnage visited upon Nazi Germany and the downfall of this once proud state serve as the answer to the doubt. Nazi Germany deified Hitler and made Nazism a religion, paralleling rather closely the action of the ancient Roman Empire in deifying the emperor and making a religion out of emperor worship. This is not to place upon Germany all the blame for World War II, nor is it to solve all the mysteries connected with the suffering of the innocent as a result of that conflict. It seems significant, however, that no nations in that conflict, Germany and Japan, which deified their rulers lost their sovereignty as nations. It might be pointed out here that there has been no sovereignty in history which has successfully challenged the sovereignty of God in Jesus Christ. Might this not be considered a token of the fact that there never will be in history a nation which will successfully challenge that sovereignty?

—E.A. McDowell, *The Meaning and Message of the Book of Revelation,*
pp. 164-165

The first bowl was poured out upon the earth and foul and evil sores came upon those who bore the mark (character, identity) of the beast and who worshiped the beast's image. *Foul* (Gr. *kakos,* noisome) may be defined as troublesome, injurious, woeful, distressing, whether physically or mentally. *Evil* (Gr. *poneron,* abominable, wicked) may be defined as painful, virulent, serious, or grievous. *Sore* (Gr. *helkos,* abscess) may also be translated, ulcerous or angry. Some understand this bowl of wrath to be predicting literal diseases which came upon the Roman empire as a consequence of its insatiable lust to conquer other nations (contagious diseases) and its decadent sexual immoralities. Others interpret this symbolically to represent the breaking out of corruption in the whole diseased social, economic, educational and political world of Rome where ungodliness and unbelief has been willingly exchanged for the truth of God (cf. Rom. 1:18ff.). It may predict both! Both were certainly used as instruments of God to bring about Rome's fall.

vv. 3-4 **. . . the sea . . . became like the blood of a dead man . . . the rivers and fountains of water . . . became blood.** — "Sea" is often used to symbolize the whole mass of humanity (Isa. 8:7ff.; Jer. 46:7-9; 47:2; Isa. 17:2ff.; 57:20-21; Rev. 17:1, 15; see comments Rev. 13:1). The second and third bowls are definitely connected to the parenthetical statement in 16:5-7. It is apparent that John is predicting judgment upon the Roman empire in such a blood-bath as to permeate the whole mass of humankind as to be symbolized by all the "waters" on the face of the earth becoming blood. The "blood of a dead man" is life poured out. It signifies death! The life of the flesh is in the blood (Lev. 17:11) and when it is the blood of a dead man it has been poured out of the man. Rome shed the blood of the saints and prophets in terrible persecutions, and soon God would pour out her blood all over the empire in retribution. The assassinations by paranoid emperors and subordinate rulers (like Tiberius, Caligula, Nero, Domitian, the Herods, and others) contributed to the blood-bath of the empire; the wars of aggression, the invasions of barbarian hordes, crime, disease, famine, natural disasters and the like also poured the blood of mankind out until the "sea" of humanity became blood!

These two bowls might also signify God's use of the sea and rivers as destructive forces of nature to pour out the life-blood of Rome until she was dead. That would parallel second and third trumpets.

vv. 5-7 **Just art thou in these thy judgments . . .** — God is just and righteous in all his judgments (Psa. 119:137; 145:17; Deut. 32:4; Dan. 9:14; Hosea 14:11; etc.). See comments on Rev. 15:3. When man disobeys the laws or commandments of God it is just and fair and right that he receive a commensurate punishment or reward for such violation. God is Creator and Sustainer—he is Absolute. He cannot be blamed. The creature who willfully rebels is to blame. God offers a merciful way, through belief of his Son, for man to repent. If man deliberately and knowingly refuses

THIRTEEN LESSONS ON REVELATION

God's mercy, he must suffer the penalty. God, by his very nature, must execute the penalty of his law or he cannot be trusted to be Absolute. Rome was warned (Rom. 1:18ff.) by nature and by the revealed Word of God, but she refused the offer of mercy and would not change her mind (repent). God must execute his promised penalty or his sovereignty is invalid.

Verse 6 indicates that the "sea" or "waters" symbolizes pagan humanity of the Roman empire—those who worshiped the beast—because they are the "men" who shed the blood of saints and prophets. The harlot (Rome) is the one seated on many waters (17:1ff.) and she is the one whose judgment the saints and apostles and prophets were to rejoice (18:20). Rome shall be paid back with blood to such an extent that she will have nothing to drink but blood! Rome must reap what she has sown. God is not mocked— God is just (Gal. 6:7-8). The word *due* is the Greek word *axioi* from which we get the English word, *axiomatic, axiology,* and means "due, lawful, equal, value-received." It is axiomatic (moral, fundamental, truism) that rebellion against the Absolute God will be judged and punished. There is no escaping this principle—it is a law of the Creator. The Creator has written it in nature, on human conscience, and in his propositional revelation, the Bible. It is impossible for man to gainsay it. Man may attempt to refuse to acknowledge it, but he cannot.

The angel of water (each instrument of judgment in the bowls has its "angel") cried out that God was just in these judgments. The "altar" (the souls under the altar of the martyred saints, 6:9-11) gave the antiphonal reply, "Yea, Lord God Almighty, true and just are thy judgments!" These persecuted saints had prayed for vindication of their faith and suffering (6:9-11; 8:1-5) and now it is about to be answered. The student should turn to Isaiah ch. 13 & 14, to Jeremaih ch. 50 & 51 and read again God's statements about his vengeance upon ancient Babylon.

vv. 8-9 . . . the sun, and it was allowed to scorch men with fire . . . — The pouring out of the fourth bowl produced a "fierce heat" which "scorched" men. The Greek words used are *kaumatisai* (from *kausis,* English *caustic*) and *puri* (from *puros,* English *pyre*); men were burned acutely, crisply, severely on a pyre. The picture is one of immolation, self-destruction in a consuming fire. This "sun" was *allowed* (not forced) to scorch men with fire; they brought it on themselves. Those who play with fire will be burned (cf. Psa. 97:3, 7; Isa. 47:13ff.; Isa. 50:11). These deceiving pagans had tried to imitate "fire from heaven" (Rev. 13:13), now they will have the real thing.

This great "fire" could be God's use of the natural elements (as in the darkening of the celestial lights in the fourth trumpet (8:12). In the case of the fourth bowl God may have used the sun to produce droughts and radiation to destroy life, just as he does today. This fourth bowl could also refer to some sort of psychological torment symbolized by fire (cf. Lk.

48

16:24-31) such as guilt, conscience and anticipation of judgment (cf. Heb. 10:26-31; 12:25-29). Conscience is certainly a tormenting "fire" for the sinner (cf. Psa. 38:1-10; Dan. 6:16-18; etc.). It is possible that the fourth and fifth bowl are both symbolizing spiritual suffering and mental anguish of Rome's heathenism. The pathos of it all is that rather than being moved to repent through this fiery judgment (whether physical or spiritual) those who worshiped the beast blasphemed (cursed) the name of the God who had authority (power) over this destruction. Pharaoh would not allow the plagues of Egypt to soften his heart—but he hardened his heart against all efforts to get him to change his mind. That is the very nature of ultimate truth— it is never forced upon anyone. It may be accepted and trusted, or distrusted and disobeyed, but it will stand inflexibly, relentlessly and uncompromisingly. All truth is moral for all truth is from God and is designed to stamp the image of God's nature upon his creatures. But his image (seal) can be rejected in favor of the image of the beast if man chooses. Actually, God is going to give every man what that man chooses.

vv. 10-11 . . . the throne of the beast, and its kingdom was in darkness . . . — The fifth bowl parallels the fifth trumpet. In the fifth trumpet the bottomless pit was opened (9:1-11) and a cloud of stinging locusts belched forth like a cloud of black smoke; men with the mark of the beast were tortured until they sought death (which they were unable to find). In the fifth bowl the throne of the beast (Rome's imperial leadership) was in darkness. This symbolizes the fact that Rome, although "claiming to be wise, they became fools" (Rom. 1:22) and they "became futile in their thinking and the senseless minds were darkened" (Rom. 1:21). They exchanged the truth of God for a lie (Rom. 1:25) and were without God and without hope in the world (Eph. 1:12). The wisdom that comes from God, the only wisdom there is, they did not have because they did not *want* to have it. All that is left for them is the darkness of wickedness, superstition, falsehood, rebellion and sin. Rome's imperial leadership could not lead the empire out of darkness and chaos because they were blinded by their own deceitfulness—can the blind lead the blind? They would not acknowledge and follow the truth of God and the Lamb because they arrogantly enthroned themselves as gods, (Rom. 1:18-22). They said, "We see!" therefore, they could not see (cf. Jn. 9:39-41).

When this black cloud of smoke (9:1ff.) darkened the throne and kingdom of the beast now with the fifth bowl in judgment, men *gnawed* (Gr. *emassonto,* from *massaomai* meaning to chew, eat, consume, used only here in the New Testament) their tongues from the torment or anguish. This picture is just like that of the fifth trumpet but with great intensification. In the fifth trumpet they were tormented only five months and not killed. Here they *consume* (meaning of the Greek word *massaomai*) themselves from the anguish.

THIRTEEN LESSONS ON REVELATION

Once again men blaspheme God and blame Him for their judgment and refuse to repent. Men who refuse to acknowledge their own moral turpitude will inevitably blame God or someone else for their sufferings. The failure of men to repent when these bowls are poured out shows that these plagues are not the final judgment. At the *final* judgment there is no opportunity even presented for repentance. The *final* judgment is not intended to bring men to repentance but to everlasting punishment. These bowls were intended to bring men to repentance but did not.

vv. 12-16 . . . the great river Euphrates . . . was dried up . . . they assembled . . . at . . . Armageddon — The sixth bowl parallels the sixth trumpet (9:13ff.). Both symbolize invasion of the Roman empire by the barbarian Partians, Goths, Ostrogoths, Visogoths and Huns (see comments Rev. 9:13-19). In the sixth trumpet only a third of mankind was hurt, but in the sixth bowl the whole world is assembled to do battle with the kings from the *east* (Gr. *anatolon heliou,* where the sun rises). These barbarian invasions eventually brought Rome's complete destruction.

Out of the mouth of the dragon (Satan), the beast (emperor), and the false prophet (second beast, pagan religion), John saw three *unclean* (Gr. *akatharta*) *spirits* (Gr. *pneumata*). These had the symbolic appearance of frogs, but they were demonical. A frog is, of course, "unclean" or illegal (Lev. 11:9ff.) to a Jew. That has some significance. In Egyptian mythology the frog represented supernatural life-giving power. The frog was the symbol of the goddess Hekt, who was believed to blow the breath of life into the nostrils of the bodies of men that Hekt's husband (Khnum) had fashioned on the potter's wheel from the dust of the death. Hekt supposedly assisted women in childbirth, and was a symbol of the resurrection and fertility. Each September after the summer overflowing of the Nile had gone down, frogs would become numerous in ponds of water all over Egypt. Their croaking was a reminder that the gods had done their duty again and another fruitful year lay before them.

The "frogs" John sees perform lying signs and wonders throughout the Roman world to assemble all the kings of that world for battle with God on His great day of judgment on Rome. We believe the unclean, demonic breathings (spirits) represent the "river" of lies issuing from the dragon, the first beast, and the second beast (false prophet) designed to deceive all those who dwell on earth (see comments Rev. 13:13-15). Rome assimilated false religions from all over the world, including Egypt. Men supposedly made reptiles speak oracles of truth and prophecy for guidance. False prophets of heathen religions kept predicting another fruitful year for Rome or that Rome would never die. False prophets are characterized by Peter as irrational animals (II Pet. 2:10ff.). The false prophets of Rome kept deceiving the whole Roman world with their "signs" of Rome's invincibility and eternality so that all the subordinate "kings" of Rome aligned themselves or assembled themselves with Rome. Then God judged them *with* Rome.

To say that frogs came out of the mouths of the dragon, the beast and the false prophet is to say, symbolically, their words were like plagues, that they were unclean, that they were empty "croaking" and meaningless. False, ungodly, immoral emperor-worship and pagan cultism brought a plague of heartlessness and ruthlessness upon the Roman world (cf. Rom. 1:18-32).

The "battle" on the great day of God the Almighty is the battle the Lamb is to have with the Roman empire for sovereignty. It is the same battle described in Daniel 2:44-45 and 7:7-27 between the saints of the Most High and the fourth beast (Rome). It is not specifically predicting or referring to the end of time (certainly not to some alleged "seven years of tribulation" either preceding an alleged literal earthly reign of Christ or following one). This victory of the Lamb and the saints over the Roman empire may symbolize the end of time and the consummation of everything (just as Old Testament victories symbolized the messianic conquest—the church), but is not predicting any battle between Russia and the present nation of Israel. If ancient Rome's conquest by Christ and the church symbolizes anything, it prefigures the complete and final destruction of *all* human, earthly governments—American, Israeli, Russian and Chinese, and the establishment of a new heaven and a new earth (II Pet. 3:10; I Cor. 15:24ff.).

The Revelation is here using the same terminology and symbolism used by the Old Testament prophets on so many occasions. It is the seminal idea that is important. That idea is the faithfulness of God to keep his promises of deliverance and eternal perpetuation of his church (the kingdom of God). What God accomplished for Old Testament Israel by bringing "great days" of judgment upon Assyria, Babylon, Egypt, Edom, et al., he accomplished for new Israel (the church) by bringing down "great days" of judgment upon Rome. The Bible is not as concerned to give man chronological timetables when it speaks of God's faithfulness in history, as it is to emphasize the *fact* of God's faithfulness and absolute sovereignty. Two clear examples of God's apocalyptic judgments on the enemies of God's covenant people are in the Old Testament—Ezekiel chs. 38-39, Gog and Magog, and Joel chs. 2-3, the Valley of Jehoshaphat. It will be apparent to the reader of those passages that a literal fulfillment is impossible: *all* nations could not be gathered in the Valley of Johoshaphat; the number of enemies necessary to leave behind weapons for seven years of fires and dead corpses for more than seven months of solid burying (approximately 360,000,000) could not possibly fit into and subsist in the land of Palestine, literally. These Old Testament "Armageddons" are probably referring to the *complete defeat* of the ultimate attack on God's redemptive program—the devil's attempt to devour the "male-child" (see Rev. 12:1ff.)—when Christ

THIRTEEN LESSONS ON REVELATION

arose from the dead, ascended to heaven, and established his church on Pentecost. The Old Testament "Armageddons" may, in fact, be predicting not only the *establishment* of the church of Christ but its victory over the last (fourth) beast of Daniel (Rome).

The word *Armageddon* in Greek is *Harmageddon* and is a combination of two words, *har* (meaning, mountain) and **megiddo** (a city overlooking the plain of Esdraelon). It was a famous battlefield in Hebrew history. Gideon and his 300 defeated the Midianites here; Saul was defeated by the Philistines here; Barak and Deborah overthrew the hosts of the Canaanite king, Jabin, here; Ahaziah died of Jehu's arrows here; Pharaoh-Neco overthrew Josiah here. Armageddon, the mountains and valleys of Meggido, aptly symbolizes the forces of righteousness and evil engaged in deadly struggle. In the days of Deborah Sisera had 900 chariots of iron (Judges 4:13), but in Israel there was scarce a shield or spear among 40,000 (Judges 5:8). Israel's situation seemed completely hopeless, but God delivered!

Armageddon represents the decisive conflict between the worship of Caesar and the worship of the Lamb. Contrary to every theory involving a literal interpretation of Revelation, it should be clear that the book involves in its whole context a battle of opposing cultures (pagan and Christian) waged by opposing ideologies. Human language could not give a clearer picture of humanism (Caesar-worship) than the Apocalypse does. Humanism is the deceptive propaganda which gathers all who bear the character of the beast for the ideological and moral battle against God's forces of righteousness. The Roman empire was the apex of humanism. If humanism was ever to control all of mankind that was when it would have been done. But, just as Daniel predicted, and as John predicts in Revelation, humanism came to its Armageddon.

Armageddon as John sees it has no location on the maps of the world; it is spiritual, not spatial. The battle is not one in which material, physical armaments will decide the issue; the battle was really decided at the cross of Christ, at the empty tomb, and at the fall of the last world-dominating empire of humanism (Rome). Rome's Armageddon came when Diocletian lost his battle to eradicate Christians and their Bibles. It came when Constantine declared Christianity no longer an illegal religion and the gospel began to be carried to the far reaches of mankind (see comments Rev. 11:11-13).

Christ's defeat of the threat of universal humanism by the fall of Rome took the world unawares—just as a thief slips up on his victim. The world was "holding a party" (Rev. 11:7-10) celebrating its victory over Christianity and suddenly, with simply the change from one emperor to another, the beast was slain. Christ encouraged Christians who read in Asia Minor to guard against being caught without their robes or righteousness in Him when He judges the beast.

52

vv. 17-21 ... **a great voice** ... **from the throne, saying, "It is done!"** — This is the seventh bowl of wrath. It is poured into the air to symbolize its permeation of the realm of the "prince of the power of the air" (Eph. 2:22). It also symbolizes that it comes from the throne of heaven. The fact that there was a *great* voice, from the *temple*, from the *throne*, emphasizes the finality and absoluteness of this seventh bowl. The Greek verb, *gegone,* is perfect tense, translated, "It is done," and means literally, "it has been done and will continue with its results." That is, when the seventh bowl was poured out, Rome fell and the results continued. It was done, just as the predictions of Daniel and John foretold, and the "kingdom and dominion . . . were given to the people of the saints of the Most High." And there will never be another kingdom of universal humanism posing such a threat to the church's existence. When the seventh bowl was poured out into the devil's sphere, the devil was bound (cf. comments on Rev. 20:1-6).

The visions of the Throne (4:5), the Seven Seals (8:5) and the Seven Trumpets (11:19) were attended by visions of cosmic phenomena (lightning, thunder, hail and earthquakes). Now, at the conclusion of the Seven Bowls, the cosmic phenomena are *great.* This passage is symbolic in nature. It does not mean there had to be a literal earthquake which measured on the seismograph the highest ever. It symbolizes the fall of Rome and the spiritual forces behind her (the devil) in such a devastating degree that there had never been such a fall before. There had never been a greater force displayed against God's kingdom before Rome ("the great city") (see Daniel chs. 2 and 7). The "great city" was earlier introduced by John (11:8; 14:8). Now, with the final bowl of wrath, the great city is split into three parts—divided for destruction (cf. Ezek. 5:2ff.; Rev. 18:8).

The great city (Rome) does not go down alone. All the cities of the nations fall with her. All the people of the Roman world seduced into drinking the "wine of the wrath of her fornication" (see comments 14:8), those who have the mark of the beast, are doomed with her. With the pouring out of the seventh bowl Rome is made to drain the cup of the fury of God's wrath. "Islands and mountains" (their inhabitants) which have joined in the "fornication" of the great city also attempt to flee from the wrath of God but to no avail. They, too, fall and there is no vestige of the beast's dominion left. This is normal apocalyptic, symbolic language (see Ezek. 26:18). Hail (approximately 100 lbs. in weight) is also symbolizing divine judgment (cf. Ex. 9:18-26; Psa. 78:47; 105:32; Josh. 10:11; Isa. 28:15-18; Ezek. 38:22).

Although these seven bowls represent the final and complete judgment of the Roman empire, we see again that they do not predict the end of time and the judgment at the Second Coming of Christ. After the huge "hailstones" did their work there were still men cursing God for the "plagues" sent upon that world, and not repenting.

THIRTEEN LESSONS ON REVELATION

The seven bowls of God's wrath symbolize the final judgment of God upon the Roman empire. They represent natural and historical forces used by the Sovereign God to execute His wrath. That is not at all unusual. It is a principle revealed repeatedly in the Bible from the flood of Noah through the destruction of Jerusalem in 70 A.D. and substantiated in Acts and the Epistles. Any challenge to God's sovereignty as wicked and pervasive as that of the Roman empire's cannot go unanswered. God must vindicate his holiness and absoluteness (see Ezek. chs. 20, 33, 34, 35, etc.). The demonstration of God's sovereignty cannot await the final judgment if man is to be given a visible warning to repent. So God executes his judgments continuously upon a world doomed to destruction through natural and historical and psychological tribulations. If God has dealings at all with man—if there is action and reaction in history in which God is involved—the relationship between God and man and history must exhibit God as he is. God is absolutely sovereign and absolutely just. God must, therefore, exhibit Himself in history as sovereignty knowing and directing history; He must exhibit Himself in time and space, while history proceeds, as just, punishing rebellion and sin by His wrath. The necessity for God to thus exhibit Himself is fulfilled in His moral governing of history. God's moral government continually expresses itself in "the things that are made" (cf. Rom. 1:18-32; 2:4; Acts 14:15-18; Gal. 6:7-8; Lk. 13:1-9; etc.). God's will that those who rebel against Him shall reap what they have sown is not reserved in its entirety until the final judgment.

A contextual and Biblical interpretation of the seven bowls is that they symbolize the effects of the wrath of God executed through historical and natural conditions and human events to bring about the disintegration and downfall of the heathen world power which challenged the sovereignty of the Lamb through imperial Rome. Such an interpretation does not exclude the truth that the historical manifestation of the truth of God upon Rome *prefigures* the consummation of his wrath in the final end of the world. The wrath of God displayed continually in history (from the Flood to today) is to be accepted by Bible believers as *prefiguring* the final judgment (cf. II Pet. 3:1-18). Every exhibition of God's wrath in history is a foretaste of the wrath to come at the end of time (cf. Mt. 24:36-44).

Executions of God's wrath continually in history are also a vindication of the faithful endurance of God's suffering saints. In breaking of the fifth seal there was a cry from underneath the altar, "How long . . ." When the third bowl is poured out we have the dramatic sequel to this cry, "And I heard the altar saying, Yea, O Lord God, the Almighty, true and righteous are thy judgments." The sacrifices of God's people *are* vindicated. Their vindication does not have to await the final judgment. Those who have eyes of faith will see such vindications continually in history!

APPREHENSION AND APPLICATION:

1. Does the word *last* (Gr. *eschatos*) always have to mean the absolute, final, end of all things in the Bible? What else can it mean? If these seven plagues do not mean the end of the world, what do they mean?
2. What do you think about musical instruments being played in worship of God? in heaven? on earth? Can you worship God without them? with them?
3. What is the song of Moses? What is it all about? Why is it sung by Christians? What is the song of the Lamb? How is it different from that of Moses? How are they both different from much of modern "Christian" music? Do you give most attention to lyrics or beat or melody?
4. Do you praise God for His judgments? Do you question God's fairness, ever, in any of his judgments? What about his ordering the Jews to kill *all* the Amalekites (I Sam. ch. 14 & 15)? What about judgment on Rome?
5. What was the point in giving John a vision of the "sanctuary of the tabernacle of testimony"? You have often thanked God that He keeps His word to redeem, deliver and bless—have you thanked Him that He keeps His promise to judge and destroy the wicked?
6. What do the bowls represent? Is it necessary to think of them as supernatural judgments at the end of time? Do these bowls parallel the seals and trumpets in any fashion? Are there any parallels to bowls of wrath in modern history?
7. What are the possibilities for interpreting the meaning of the "foul and evil sores" of the first bowl? What about the second bowl? The third, and the fourth? Do you see any pattern on the *agency* used by God in the first four bowls? Does this pattern follow, generally, the first four seals and first four trumpets?
8. Why do you think so much emphasis is placed in these later chapters (15, 16, 18, 19) on the *justice* of God's judgments on Rome? Did you realize it was that emphatic in the New Testament?
9. How does the fifth bowl parallel that of the fifth trumpet? How is it different?
10. How does the sixth bowl parallel the sixth trumpet? What are the three frogs? How do they gather the kings of the whole world for battle? What is the battle of Armageddon? What do you think of much modern eschatology today which makes Armageddon a literal war in the 20th or 21st century between Russia and Israel with nuclear weapons?
11. Why is the seventh bowl poured "into the air"? Why does the great voice say, "It is finished"? What Old Testament imagery divides into three parts for destruction? Who goes down to destruction with the great city?
12. How are the bowls the answer to the cry of the martyred saints under the altar "How long, O lord. . . .?"

THE SEVEN BOWLS OF THE WRATH OF GOD
Revelation 16

Bowl 1: Foul and evil sores came upon the men who bore the mark of the beast and worshiped its image. Contagious disease in plague proportions; a "natural" result of wicked lust to conquer and social immoralities.

Bowl 2: A "blood-bath" falls upon the masses of heathen humanity ("the sea") in the Roman empire until there is wide-spread death. This "blood-bath" is due to natural disasters, pestilence, famines, war.

Bowl 3: The same "blood-bath" as the second bowl. Both these bowls are judgments which are "due" the Roman empire for its vicious blood-letting upon God's saints and prophets.

Bowl 4: An acute fire is allowed to "burn" Rome to a crisp. They "played with fire" and now they must be burned. It could be natural "fires" in drought, radiation, or forest fires. It could be psychological "fires" in the conscience in anticipation of judgment.

Bowl 5: Darkness upon the throne of Rome. The darkened minds of Rome's political leaders resulted in great suffering to her citizens. Their senseless hurt they blamed on God and his people.

Bowl 6: Preparations are completed for the permission of the invasion of Rome by her enemies. All the kings of the world are propagandized to join her in battle against God where God will have a great victory.

Bowl 7: Judgment is completed on Rome. Every region of her empire is judged. No one, on island or mountain, is able to keep her from falling. Even the capital city itself is divided up for judgment. The empire which bragged it was eternal is no more!

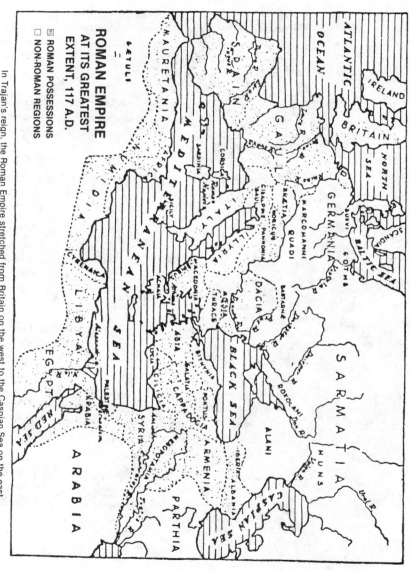

ROMAN EMPIRE
AT ITS GREATEST
EXTENT, 117 A.D.

⊠ ROMAN POSSESSIONS
☐ NON-ROMAN REGIONS

In Trajan's reign, the Roman Empire stretched from Britain on the west to the Caspian Sea on the east.

57

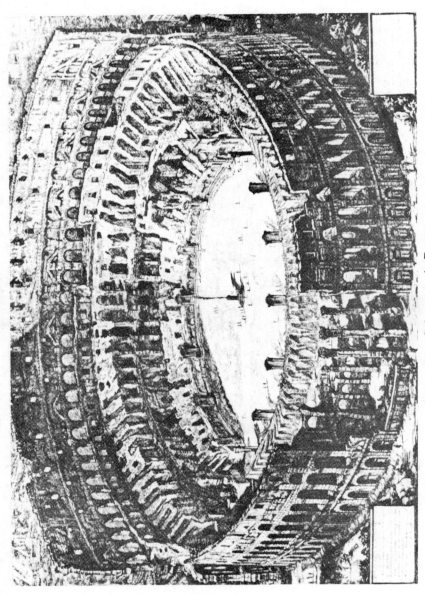

The Colosseum in Rome

Lesson Five
(17:1-18)

THE LAMB AND THE SPIRITUAL CONFLICT

Such great importance is attached to the city of Rome as the center of forces opposing God and profaning all of that civilization, three chapters (17-18-19) are given to portray her doom. Rome's seduction of mankind into paganism and her declared intention to obliterate the kingdom of God made it appropriate for her to be symbolized as "Babylon." In connection with this lesson the student should read Isaiah, chapters 13 and 14, Jeremiah, chapters 50 and 51, and Daniel, chapters 1 through 5. It would be well, too, to read Habakkuk's prophecy against Babylon in the Old Testament.

It is a well established fact of history that a nation, civilization or empire will be as godly or ungodly as its leadership. The Old Testament prophet Micah (Micah 1:5) said the sin of Israel (ten northern tribes) was Samaria (Israel's capitol city) and the sin of Judah was Jerusalem (Judah's capitol). The wickedness of national leaders inevitably infects those who look to them for guidance. Revelation 17, 18 and 19 portrays the evil throughout the Roman empire as having issued from the capitol—from the throne of the emperor.

The seventeenth chapter focuses on identifying the great harlot (or, "Babylon"). A number of symbols are given in detail for the benefit of the early

59

church (the church of the first four centuries). They were *expected* to understand the "mystery of the woman" (Rev. 17:7). As the Roman empire's disintegration began to unfold in history there could be no doubt in the minds of those living through it that John's Revelation had forseen it. In fact, John's symbolism is so clear, the immediate readers of the Revelation would have had no problem identifying the "woman" as Rome.

Prostitute "Babylon" (17:1-18)

17 Then one of the seven angels who had the seven bowls came and said to me, "Come, I will show you the judgment of the great harlot who is seated upon many waters, ²with whom the kings of the earth have committed fornication, and with the wine of whose fornication the dwellers on earth have become drunk." ³And he carried me away in the Spirit into a wilderness, and I saw a woman sitting on a scarlet beast which was full of blasphemous names, and it had seven heads and ten horns. ⁴The woman was arrayed in purple and scarlet, and bedecked with gold and jewels and pearls, holding in her hand a golden cup full of abominations and the impurities of her fornication; ⁵and on her forehead was written a name of mystery: "Babylon the great, mother of harlots and of earth's abominations." ⁶And I saw the woman, drunk with the blood of the saints and the blood of the martyrs of Jesus.

When I saw her I marveled greatly. ⁷But the angel said to me, "Why marvel? I will tell you the mystery of the woman, and of the beast with seven heads and ten horns that carries her. ⁸The beast that you saw was, and is not, and is to ascend from the bottomless pit and go to perdition; and the dwellers on earth whose names have not been written in the book of life from the foundation of the world, will marvel to behold the beast, because it was and is not and is to come. ⁹This calls for a mind with wisdom: the seven heads are seven mountains on which the woman is seated; ¹⁰they are also seven kings five of whom have fallen, one is, the other has not yet come, and when he comes he must remain only a little while. ¹¹As for the beast that was and is not, it is an eighth but it belongs to the seven, and it goes to perdition. ¹²And the ten horns that you saw are ten kings who have not yet received royal power, but they are to receive authority as kings for one hour, together with the beast. ¹³These are of one mind and give over their power and authority to the beast; ¹⁴they will make war on the Lamb, and the Lamb will conquer them, for he is Lord of lords and King of kings, and those with him are called and chosen and faithful."

15 And he said to me, "The waters that you saw, where the harlot is seated, are peoples and multitudes and nations and tongues. ¹⁶And the

ten horns that you saw, they and the beast will hate the harlot; they will make her desolate and naked, and devour her flesh and burn her up with fire, [17]for God has put it into their hearts to carry out his purpose by being of one mind and giving over their royal power to the beast, until the words of God shall be fulfilled. [18]And the woman that you saw is the great city which has dominion over the kings of the earth."

vv. 1-2   . . . I will show you the judgment of the great harlot . . . — It is appropriate that one of the seven angels having the seven bowls should explain the judgment on "Babylon." That ties the seven "last" plagues (or bowls) directly to the city to be identified in chapters 17 and 18. The seven "last" plagues are not, therefore, for the end of the world. The Greek word *porne* (from which we get the English word, *pornography*) means prostitute, harlot, or whore. The awful judgment of God predicted and portrayed to fall upon the "beast" is the same judgment to fall upon the "harlot" because they are one and the same entity. The beast, the false prophet, and the harlot are all the Roman empire, seen from the perspective of Rome's three-sided attack upon Christ's church. Rome attempted to destroy the church by militant, political persecution, by idolatrous emperor worship and pagan cultism, and by carnal, hedonistic worldliness. Rome is portrayed as a "harlot" because of the seductive attractiveness of her appeal to the whole world to consort with her in promiscuous carnality. While Rome's worldliness may have been appealing, it was a prostitution, a perversion, of everything Almighty God had created for good. In the Old Testament three cities are symbolized as harlots: (a) Nineveh (Nahum 3:1, 4); (b) Tyre (Isa. 23:15-17); (c) Jerusalem (Isa. 1:21; Jer. 2:20); and (d) Babylon portrayed as a great "mistress" of pleasure (Isa. 45:5-15). John is probably characterizing Rome as a composite of all these: the cruelty of Nineveh, the riches of Tyre, the religious whoredom of Jerusalem, and the arrogance and indulgence of Babylon.

The great harlot, Rome, is seated upon many waters, which we are told are "peoples and multitudes and nations and tongues" (17:15). Rome ruled over a *sea* of humanity. This "sea" protected her, enriched her and entertained her. It should be noted that the "woman" is *sitting* (Gr. *kathemenes,* present participle) indicating she *was sitting* when John wrote the Revelation and not that she would sit in the future. Rome is the one with whom the kings of the earth fornicated. "Fornication" is used here, of course, metaphorically to picture all kinds of intercourse other rulers of the world carried on with Rome perverting and exploiting God's creation especially as they joined Rome in attempting to seduce the Bride of Christ, the church. Not only had the kings of the earth consorted with Rome's debauchery, the ones then dwelling on the earth (Gr. *katoikountes,* present participle) had intoxicated themselves with the heady "wine" of the woman's depravity. Arrogant rebellion against Almighty God and his redemptive kingdom in the world has always "intoxicated" unbelievers. Rebellion inebriates, but it also stupifies—just like wine. Rebellion is the cup of deception Satan offered Eve and Adam in Eden. Sin distorts the spiritual brain and those who imbibe make themselves incapable of seeing or understanding spiritual truth realistically (cf. Lk. 11:33-36; 12:54-56).

v. 3 . . . I saw a woman sitting on a scarlet beast . . . — In visionary form, under the divine power and direction of the Holy Spirit, John was transported into wilderness circumstances. The definite article is missing before "wilderness" so there is no specific wilderness intended—just wilderness in general. Wilderness symbolizes the Gentile, pagan world of depravity, contrasted over against the heavenly place (Judaism) (see comments on Rev. 12:6, 14). John was transported spiritually, by the Spirit, from Patmos and given a vision of the whole depraved, debauched Roman world—and especially a vision of the harlot herself, the city of Rome.

The harlot was sitting on a *scarlet beast* (Gr. *kokkinon therion*). The *scarlet* color allies the beast to the *red* dragon (the devil) of Rev. 12. They are not the same person but they are affiliated. Scarlet may also symbolize the blood of the martyrs upon which the beast fed itself.

The beast is Rome, seen from her political and military aspect, already described (see our comments, chapter 13). This identification is also clearly symbolized in Rev. 17:7-14. The depraved carnality of Rome (the harlot) is represented as being supported and carried along ("sitting upon") the political power (the beast). The beast was full of blasphemous names picturing the many divine titles the Roman emperors had arrogated to themselves (e.g. *Kurios,* Lord; *Theos,* God; *Soter,* Savior). It would also symbolize the blasphemous decrees of the emperors that they should be worshiped. The seven heads and ten horns are interpreted in 17:7-14.

vv. 4-6 The woman was arrayed in purple and scarlet . . . — The harlot is dressed royally (purple) and alluringly (scarlet). She intices with riches (gold and jewels and pearls) and mesmerizes by offering others a drink from the golden cup in her hand (full of abominations and impurities of her carnality). On her forehead was written *Musterion, Babulon He Megale, He Meter Ton Pornon kai Ton Bdelugmaton Tes Ges.* Translated, it reads, "Mystery, Babylon The Great, The Mother of The Harlots and of The Abominations of The Earth." *Mystery,* as used in New Testament Greek, is not something that *cannot* be known at all. It means something which may be known to the initiated. In the New Testament it denotes information outside the range of human knowledge but which *is made known by divine revelation* (apostolic preaching and writing) (cf. Eph. 1:9; 5:32; 6:19; Rom. 16:25; Col. 1:27, etc.). Rome's identity as the seductress of the world was a reality that most of the world, because of sin, was unable to know.

Rome's beastliness and rottenness was as clear to Christians as if she had a written sign across her forehead because the Holy Spirit was revealing it to them through John's Revelation. Rome's alliance with the devil and God's imminent wrath upon her was a reality to those who believed John's message. Those who did not believe John would scoff at the very idea that Rome was headed for destruction. Those who believed would understand by faith, not by human calculation, and they would be wise (17:9). Daniel said the same of those who would believe his prophecies of the holocaust upon the Jewish people for their rejection of the Messiah (Dan. ch. 7-12).

This is not the geographical Babylon situated on the Euphrates River to be restored once more; Isaiah 13:19-22 predicts that ancient Babylon would be destroyed by the Medes and never exist again as a powerful empire. The "Babylon" John sees is the city of Rome, mother of a world-wide brood of harlotrous capitols and countries. Rome is also the mother of all the *abominations* (Gr. *bdelugmaton*, disgusting, loathsome, vile, perverted things) in that world.

Rome gorged itself on pride, arrogance, and opposition to the kingdom of God. She sated herself on the blood of the saints and witnesses (martyrs) of Jesus until she was "drunk." Intoxicated with what she thought was absolute power and eternal perpetuity, she lost all ability to function realistically and became as Paul described her in Romans 1:18-32. Power corrupts and absolute power corrupts absolutely. Suetonius quotes an anonymous satirist in his *Lives of the Twelve Caesars,* regarding the emperor Tiberius:

> He is not thirsty for neat wine
> As he was thirsty then,
> But warm him up a tastier cup—
> The blood of murdered men.

When John saw this vision he "marvelled with a great marvel." Apparently he was not prepared for what he saw. The statement of the angel (17:7) indicates John was having difficulty identifying the "harlot." Perhaps John was even trying to identify the harlot with *ancient* Babylon. Whatever the problem, the angel set him straight. The "harlot," or "Babylon" was Rome. It certainly cannot be Jerusalem. The "woman" is the great city which has dominion over the kings of the earth (17:18). That has to be Rome.

vv. 7-8   The beast that you saw was, and is not, and is to ascend from the bottomless pit and go to perdition . . . — The woman and the beast are one. John will identify them both as one. This symbolic identification of the beast coincides with that of Rev. 13:3ff. (see comments there). It adapts the Nero redivivus (reincarnation) myth just as chapter 13 did. It is a warning that imperial Rome's power in Domitian, and those to follow him, is to become Nero incarnate. The beast John saw is the reincarnation, symbolically speaking, of an emperor who was, is not, is to ascend from the abyss, and then go to perdition.

The earth-dwellers whose names are not in the book of life are amazed and seduced into following the beast because of the invincibility the beast appears to have. The beast appears to be able to perpetuate itself and its absolute power from one emperor to another. But the saints know better—they know the beast is not divine and not invincible for Christ has revealed the beast's "number" to John and it is a human number (see comments 13:4, 18).

vv. 9-11 . . . the seven heads are seven hills . . . also seven kings . . . — The fact that the city of Rome was built on the seven hills bordering the Tiber River was an ever recurring theme of Roman poets and historians. John's readers would immediately think of the imperial city and its occupant —the emperor. But even the seven hills (mountains) symbolized seven heads of the empire. We think seven specific emperors are symbolized. We begin with *Tiberius* (14-37 A.D.), the emperor when Christ died, rose from the dead, and established the church so viciously opposed by the empire; the six following "kings" (emperors) were: *Caligula* (37-41 A.D.), *Claudius* (41-54 A.D.), *Nero* (54-68 A.D.), *Vespasian* (69-79 A.D.), *Titus* (79-81 A.D.), and *Domitian* (81-96 A.D.) who was ruling when John wrote Revelation. Five of these had fallen when John wrote this: Tiberius, Caligula, Claudius, Vespasian and Titus. Nero, although one of the seven, is *not* one of the five because he is regarded as "coming alive" in the adaptation of the redivivus (re-incarnation) myth and thus he is *not* "fallen." "One *is,*" refers to Domitian who was the only one of the seven then living. "The other has not yet come" is the symbolic personality of Nero revived in Domitian (which Domitian did display in his last years). The "Nero personality" that came in Domitian lasted only a "little while." There were three "barracks emperors" (military generals hailed into the office by their troops, but not really of the "royal" line of Caesars). They are not to be considered in the conglomerate of seven kings. Their combined rule lasted less than 18 months. Their names were Galba, Otho and Vitellius. They were never fully recognized by the whole empire as emperors.

The beast that was and is not is an *eighth.* He *belongs* to the seven and goes to perdition with all the rest. The reincarnated personality of *Nero* in Domitian was "an eighth" while being, at the same time, belonging to the original "seven." He was not one of the five "fallen" because he was to live as an "eighth" in Domitian; see below:

1. Tiberius — fallen
2. Caligula — fallen
3. Claudius — fallen
4. Nero — one who was, is not, is to come for a little while, is an eighth, is of the seven

5. Vespasian — fallen
6. Titus - fallen
7. Domitian - One *is* ————————— Nero, an eighth,
8. *NERO*————————   symbolically reincarnated in Domitian.

There is another possibility. Perhaps the number seven is simply symbolic of completeness and symbolizes all the "kings" (emperors) of Rome who opposed the kingdom of God. Each would be a part of the seven. Each continued for a little while and then went to perdition.

vv. 12-14   And the ten horns that you saw are ten kings . . . — There are two possibilities here also. The number ten probably symbolizes fullness of power. The ten kings may be symbolizing a totality of future puppet "kings" throughout the empire (such as the Herods were) who would at first swear allegiance to Rome ("be of one mind") but would later cannibalize the empire (17:16ff.). Or, the ten kings may be symbolizing a totality of future Roman emperors who would yet receive royal power and, aligning themselves with the beastliness of other elements of the empire, cannibalize it themselves. We prefer the first possibility.

These future "kings" will be united in purpose with the beast (Rome) and surrender their sovereignty to Rome. Their appointment as "kings" will probably be conditioned upon their complete subservience to Rome's imperial opposition to any rivalry. That opposition will include the church of Christ. Thus, these "kings" will join the beast (Roman empire) in making war on the Lamb and those with the Lamb. Rome allowed absolutely no competition to her sovereignty or glory. She demanded her emperors be worshiped as gods by all peoples. She demanded all her subjects to be ready to die in battle against any form of sedition or revolution. Rome considered the kingdom of Christ seditious.

But the Lamb and those with him will conquer the beast and its "kings." The Lamb's conquest of the beast has been predicted from the beginning of John's Revelation. It will be vividly symbolized in chapter 19. The Lamb is Lord of lords and King of kings. He is the absolute Sovereign—not the beast!

Those with the Lamb will conquer with Him. They have been called into His kingdom by the proclamation of the gospel (Mt. 22:1-13; II Thess. 2:14); they have been chosen by God because they have aligned themselves with Christ and that is where God has chosen to make men citizens of His kingdom (Eph. 1:4); they are loyal and faithful, not perfect, but faithful to Christ following Him wherever He leads (Rev. 12:11; 14:4ff.).

vv. 15-18   . . . And the ten horns that you saw, they and the beast will hate the harlot . . . — In the Old Testament "waters" is used as a symbol for "people" (cf. Isa. 8:7; Jer. 47:2). Here the whole Roman empire is symbolized which would comprise many ethnic groups, cultures and languages. The harlot sits upon this world, seducing it and exploiting it for her own profit. But just as in real life, many a person who has seduced others and exploited them for profit and has paid for it with his/her life, at the hands of complicitors, so Rome will be devoured by her former lovers. Wickedness inevitably leads to self-destruction. The Old Testament rulers cannibalized their own nation (Micah 3:2-3; Ezek. 22:27; Ezek. 34:1-6; Micah 7:2).

Rome's cannibalism of itself is well attested in history. Will Durant writes in *Caesar and Christ, The Story of Civilization, Vol. III,* pg. 669:

The armies of Rome were no longer Roman armies; they were composed chiefly of provincials, largely of barbarians; they fought not for their altars and their homes, but for their wages, their donatives, and their loot. They attacked and plundered the cities of the Empire with more relish than they showed in facing the enemy; most of them were the sons of peasants who hated the rich and the cities as exploiters of the poor and the countryside; and as civil strife provided opportunity, they sacked such towns with a thoroughness that left little for alien barbarism to destroy. . . . In this awful drama of a great state breaking into pieces, the internal causes were the unseen protagonists; the invading barbarians merely entered where weakness had opened the door, and where the failure of biological, moral, economic, and political statesmanship had left the stage to chaos, despondency, and decay.

This very picture of self-destruction, incredible as it may have seemed in John's day (the glory days of Rome), was revealed by God 150 years before it began.

That is because God is Sovereign of all history. All of history is subject to God's eternal purpose. This does not mean that God is responsible for the wickedness and cannibalism of Rome, but it does mean that in all the wicked and rebellious acts of men and nations he is able to use them to serve his purposes. These evil powers thought they were serving and working out their own goals, but they were, in fact, serving the purposes of God. Even the wrath of men is made to praise God. God never loses control of human affairs. Even those who are rebelling against him are ultimately working out his purposes as they work out their own destruction.

Precisely how God did this we are at a loss to even know, let alone to understand. The Greek text says: God *gave* (*edoken*) into the hearts of them to do the *mind* or *purpose* (*gnomen*) of him, and to do one *mind* or *purpose* (*gnomen*) and to *give* (*dounai*) the kingdom of them to the beast, until shall be *completed* (*telesthe*) the words of God. The Greek verb *telesthe* means fulfillment, completion, finish. This self-destruction, this cannibalism, would bring to *completion* the prophecies of John's Revelation concerning the desstruction of the beast. This process of self-destruction would take another 200 years (until about 450 A.D.), but it came, inexorably and irrevocably. God has built this moral judgment of self-destruction into his moral creation. It is an undeniable doctrine of revelation and an unimpeachable fact of history (cf. Judges 7:22; I Sam. 14:20; II Chron. 20:23). The angel has identified the beast. It is Rome. Now, in one terse sentence he identifies the woman. She is Rome. Babylon, the harlot, the woman is that great city which had dominion over the kings of the earth. It *cannot* an apostate Roman Catholic Church—it is Rome, the mistress of nations.

Although the devil was severely bound when Rome fell, and his accomplices (the beast, the false prophet, and the harlot) were destroyed, he still tries to deceive those who refuse to come to the glorious light of the gospel through the same three agencies. The beastliness of ungodly political power still persecutes; the masquerading of the false prophet in the religion of humanism still subtly leads astray; the attractiveness of worldliness and carnality still seduces millions into spiritual prostitution. Thanks be to God life and immortality has been brought to light through the gospel. Christ destroyed the power of the devil, the fear of death, and the devil's power to deceive has been forever broken. Though there may be the pressures of persecution, false teaching and carnality, through the gospel men may now know beyond any reasonable doubt that this slight momentary affliction is preparing for an eternal weight of glory beyond all comparison. The hope of a better life in heaven forever is no longer a thing unseen; it has now been demonstrated in time and in history by the resurrection of Jesus Christ from the dead. By his precious and very great promises men may now escape the corruption that is in the world and become partakers of the divine nature. Now we know that the things of earth which are seen are transitory; but the things of Christ, by his absolutely faithful word, are eternal. Do not be deceived!

APPREHENSION AND APPLICATION:

1. Why are three chapters devoted to the judgment upon the city of Rome itself? Why would capitol cities of nations and empires be responsible for national depravity? Could they produce national righteousness?
2. Why is Rome portrayed as a "harlot"? Could any modern capitol city become a "harlot"? How?
3. What made the "harlot" drunk? Do you see how rebellion intoxicates? What else does the incarnation of sin do?
4. Why is the beast scarlet colored? What relationship does the beast have to the "harlot"? Is this true of most political structures?
5. Does the name "Mystery" mean the identity of the "harlot" was not to be known? What are Bible "mysteries"? How are they to be known?
6. How do we know John is not referring to a revival of ancient Babylon? or could John's "Babylon" be Jerusalem?

7. Why does John identify the beast as the one who "was, is not, and is to ascend from the bottomless pit"? Who is he? Who are the seven "kings"?
8. Who were the 10 horns? Why did they hate the harlot? How did they make her desolate? Is this a recurring principle of history?
9. How could God put this into their hearts? How could their wicked deeds fulfill the purpose of God? Does men's wickedness still serve God?

Lesson Six
(18:1-24)

The Lamb and the Spiritual Conflict

This chapter portrays, in symbolic terms, the devastating prostration of the city of Rome. It will be many years future to the time John is writing, but it is so certain John speaks of it as an accomplished fact! The glory of ancient Rome did disappear from the earth in exactly the manner John predicted it would.

Chapter eighteen presents a vivid picture of the contrast between heaven's attitude and the world's attitude when the judgments of God fall on wicked worldliness. Heaven and the saints rejoice; the worldly-minded mourn. To some people it may seem out of character for heaven to call for rejoicing over the devastation of Rome (18:20). But heaven knows that the life of the godly on earth is one of persecution, deprivation and injustice (Jn. 15:18-21; 16:33; II Tim. 3:12). Christians cannot always expect to have injustices vindicated in this life. They are not permitted to carry out any personal vengeance (Rom. 12:14). Christians must trust God to punish wickedness in the ultimate sense and they may rejoice at every clear judgment of wickedness in history.

It is clearly a distinguishing mark of Christian character to hate evil and love good. Christian character insists on a demand for justice and an uncompromising call for an end to evil. Righteous men will rejoice when wickedness is brought to an end, either by conversion or judgment. But

69

they will let God accomplish both through the faithfulness of his word. Moses and the Israelites sang for joy at the fall of Pharaoh's army. The Old Testament prophets repeatedly exhort the believing "remnant" to rejoice at the promised destruction of their enemies. The Christian is not to love the world or anything in it. He must be ready and willing to rejoice at its destruction! Because that is how it is in heaven, forever!

Prostrate "Babylon" (18:1-24)

18 After this I saw another angel coming down from heaven, having great authority; and the earth was made bright with his splendor. ²And he called out with a mighty voice,

"Fallen, fallen is Babylon the great! It has become a dwelling place
of demons,
a haunt of every foul spirit,
a haunt of every foul and hateful bird;
³for all nations have drunk the wine of her impure passion,
and the kings of the earth have committed fornication with her.
and the merchants of the earth have grown rich with the wealth of
her wantonness."
⁴Then I heard another voice from heaven saying,
"Come out of her my people,
lest you take part in her sins,
lest you share in her plagues;
⁵for her sins are heaped high as heaven,
and God has remembered her iniquities.
⁶Render to her as she herself has rendered,
and repay her double for her deeds;
mix a double draught for her in the cup she mixed.
⁷As she glorified herself and played the wanton,
so give her a like measure of torment and mourning.
Since in her heart she says, 'A queen I sit,
I am no widow, mourning I shall never see,'
⁸so shall her plagues come in a single day,
pestilence and mourning and famine,
and she shall be burned with fire;
for mighty is the Lord God who judges her."
9 And the kings of the earth, who committed fornication and were wanted with her, will weep and wail over her when they see the smoke of her burning; ¹⁰they will stand far off, in fear of her torment, and say,
"Alas! alas! thou great city,
thou mighty city, Babylon!
In one hour has thy judgment come."
11 And the merchants of the earth weep and mourn for her, since no

one buys their cargo any more, [12]cargo of gold, silver, jewels and pearls, fine linen, purple, silk and scarlet, all kinds of scented wood, all articles of ivory, all articles of costly wood, bronze, iron and marble, [13]cinnamon, spice, incense, myrrh, frankincense, wine, oil, fine flour and wheat, cattle and sheep, horses and chariots, and slaves, that is, human souls.

[14]"The fruit for which thy soul longed has gone from thee,
 and all thy dainties and thy splendor are lost to thee,
  never to be found again!"

[15]The merchants of these wares, who gained wealth from her, will stand far off, in fear of her torment, weeping and mourning aloud,

[16]"Alas, alas, for the great city
 that was clothed in fine linen,
  in purple and scarlet,
  bedecked with gold, with jewels, and with pearls!

[17]In one hour all this wealth has been laid waste."

And all shipmasters and seafaring men, sailors and all whose trade is on the sea, stood far off [18]and cried out as they saw the smoke of her burning,

"What city was like the great city?" [19]And they threw dust on their heads, as they wept and mourned, crying out,

"Alas, alas, for the great city
 where all who had ships at sea grew rich by her wealth!
In one hour she has been laid waste.

[20]Rejoice over her, O heaven,
 O saints and apostles and prophets,
  for God has given judgment for you against her!"

21 Then a mighty angel took up a stone like a great millstone and threw it into the sea, saying,

"So shall Babylon the great city be thrown down with violence.
 and shall be found no more;

[22]and the sound of harpers and ministrels, of flute players and
  trumpeters,
  shall be heard in thee no more;
and a craftsman of any craft
  shall be found in thee no more;
and the sound of the millstone
  shall be heard in thee no more;

[23]and the light of the lamp
  shall shine in thee no more;
and the voice of the bridegroom and bride
  shall be heard in thee no more;
for thy merchants were the great men of the earth,

and all nations were deceived by thy sorcery.
²⁴And in her was found the blood of prophets and of saints,
and of all who have been slain on earth."

vv. 1-3 . . . Fallen, fallen is Babylon the great . . . — "After this" does
not mean chronologically. It is a phrase used in Revelation to distinguish
one vision from another, but not necessarily in time. Chapter 18 is merely
a continuation or an amplification of the subject matter of chapter 15, 16
and 17—the judgment of God upon Rome. The angel now coming down
from heaven is apparently not one of the seven who had the bowls. This
angel is one of great power and authority and probably directly from the
presence of the glory of God; the earth was made *bright* (Gr. *ephotisthe*)
with his glory. He cried with a *mighty* (Gr. *ischui,* "boisterous"), *great*
(Gr. *megale,* "mega-") *voice* (Gr. *phone*). What he said thundered; it
roared; it was ear-splitting.

"*Fell, fell* Babylon the great," is a literal translation of the Greek aorist
verb, *epesen, epesen.* Rome's fall, though not for another 350 years after
John, is so *certain* it may be said, from heaven's perspective to have already taken place! Rome, and all her consorts, may not see herself as ever
to fall (18:7), but from heaven's vantage point her doom is sealed.

"And she *became,*" is a literal translation of the Greek aorist verb,
egeneto. The fall will result in the once proud, rich, arrogant and splendid
buildings of Rome becoming the haunts or "*cages*" (Gr. *phulake,* "prison")
of demons, unclean spirits and unclean, hated birds. It is doubtful that
John meant the ruins of ancient Rome would become haunts of actual
demons. There is no evidence that evil spirits are living in the ruins of the
ancient Coliseum. John is merely symbolizing the devastation of ancient
Rome and the contempt with which history shall hold it for its arrogance,
its injustices done to Christians, and its insane depravity which brought
self-destruction. In a figurative way the ruins of Rome are today haunted
by the ghosts (spirits) of demon-worship, uncleanness of the human spirits
long gone, and every foulness ever hated by God-fearing men. No civilization
or culture has ever been able to outdo Rome in depravity. Many have
imitated her, but none have exceeded her. And why should Rome escape
total devastation when "Babylons" which had preceded her suffered it
(cf. Isa. 13:19-22; 34:11-15; Jer. 50:39; 51:37; Zeph. 2:15).

All the world (nations) known to civilized man was made by Rome to
participate in her ungodliness. Rome built her empire by military conquest
and economic extravagance. Practically all the cultures and races of the
world willingly joined in political and military alliance with Rome, following her depraved ways, to gain powers and favors from her. Puppet kings
and influential men (like the Herods) grew rich through political and
business advantages granted them by Rome. By fawning to the indulgent

whims of the Caesars, even when it meant exploitation and treason against their own people, the politicians and merchants grew rich. By imposing exorbitant taxes upon their subjects, by selling many of their own peoples into slavery, and by exporting to the lascivious and insatiable Rome all their best national products, these provincial kings and traders engaged in intercourse with the "harlot" and became as guilty as she. *Wantonness* is "insolent, insatiable, luxuriating." The Greek word *strenous* is translated wantonness and means "to run riot, to indulge voraciously." Kings and merchants sacrificed truth and kindness to grow rich with Rome. International dealings today which compromise principle for mammon are as wanton as those who "fornicated" with Rome. God wants his creation to be administered by nations upholding truth and justice even if it means the loss of economic gain. Nations making efforts to trade and negotiate on the basis of fundamentally revealed truth will be supplied with power and prosperity. That is what Rome and her consorts did *not* do.

vv. 4-6 . . . **Come out of her, my people, lest you take part in her sins** . . . — The voice saying this is not identified. We assume it was God's voice since it said, ". . . my people." The Greek verb *exelthete* is aorist imperative. God does not merely suggest Christians should "come out" of the world, he *commands* it. John is not ordering Christians to make a geographical exodus from the city limits of Rome. Even if they came out of the city they would still have been in "Rome." Neither does John mean that Christians of his day should withdraw from the world into monastic societies. Paul made it plain in I Cor. 5:9-13 that while Christians must associate with the ungodly because they cannot take themselves away from the world, they do not have to allow the ungodly to join in the fellowship of the saints. John is enjoining Christians to "have no fellowship with the unfruitful works of darkness . . ." as Paul did in Eph. 5:11. God called the righteous from fellowship with the ungodly all through the Old Testament (cf. Gen. 12:1; 19:12-14; Isa. 48:20; 52:11; Jer. 50:8; 51:6, 9, 45). The saints of the New Testament are not to be partakers of other men's sins (cf. I Tim. 5:22; II Cor. 6:14-15; II Jn. 11). Christians may be in the world but they are not to be of the world (Jn. 17:11, 16; Rom. 12:1-2). The person who chooses the world is an enemy of God (Jas. 4:4).

Many of the Christians to whom John wrote would have to make great sacrifices to live their lives separated from Rome's idolatry and depravity. Some would have pagan family members turn against them. Others would be accused of treason against the emperor and slain. Some would be deprived of employment, food and property. But whatever the cost, the separated life would eventually lead to glory—for if God was for them, who could be against them? (cf. Rom. 8:31-39). Nothing Rome could do to them could separate them from the love of God. Those who share in Rome's sins will also share in her plagues (see Rev. 15:1—16:21) and eventually be cast into the lake of fire and brimstone (Rev. 19:20-21).

THIRTEEN LESSONS ON REVELATION

The Greek verb *ekollethesan* is from *kollao* and means literally, "glued."
It is translated "heaped" or "reached." Sin after sin had been glued together until a huge mountain of wickedness had reached even up to heaven.
It was a vile, black, mountain of rebellion, profligacy and depravity. God
reached the limit of her mercy. The longsuffering of God mercifully gives
nations and men opportunity after opportunity to make choices, but eventually those who stubbornly and deliberately amass records of continued
sin must suffer the limits of God's toleration. God will not forever bear
rebellion against his sovereign will. No nation or people on the face of
the earth can long postpone the wrath of God if it continues to pile up sins
against him (cf. II Chron. 28:9; Jer. 51:9; Ezra 9:6, etc.), and does not
repent.

Men may forget some of their sins (Mt. 25:44-46) but God will not—
except those covered by the blood of Christ. Men may think God forgets,
but he does not (Hosea 7:2). The idea that God forgets the sins of the
impenitent is one of the most subtle of the devil's deceptions. God is love,
but he is also just (Rev. 2:23; 22:12). Jehovah would be no better than the
idol-gods made by the hands of men if he should be incapable of remembering and dealing with impenitent sin. If he cannot or will not judge, he
cannot save.

After calling his people "out" of Babylon, God calls those who will
execute his wrath (angels) upon her. They are to give her what she has
given. God is evenhanded in his justice. Rome is not to suffer twice as much
as she handed out, but the phrase "Double unto her double according to
her works" (as it would be translated literally) means that since Rome was
generous and gave double portions of evil to the world, so she shall receive
double portions of God's wrath. The same idea is in "mix for her what she
has mixed-double." God has operated on this principle of justice always
(cf. Psa. 137:8; Jer. 16:18; 17:18; 50:15, 29), and any man or nation that
thinks he will not continue to do so (Gal. 6:7-8) is deceived. We think of
nations and governments which have been doubly cruel to the saints of
God in our own century and wonder if God remembers. God remembers!
When their crimes against God and his church have reached heaven he
will execute his justice, double wrath for double wickedness.

vv. 7-8 As she glorified herself and played the wanton . . . — Rome
exalted herself and ran riot in luxurious indulgence of the flesh (Gr. *estreniase,*
played the wanton). Just as proud and irresponsible as Rome bragged she
could get by with, so she is to be *equally* humiliated and punished. The
higher one flies, the farther one has to fall! The Prodigal Son flew high,
wasted all his inheritance in riotous living, and wound up living with the
pigs.

But Rome does not see herself as a profligate or derelict. She tells herself she is enthroned as the queen of the world. The Greek word translated

sit is *kathemai,* a derivative of the Greek word *kathedra,* from which we get the English word, *cathedral,* which means "a seat of authority, a throne." Isaiah portrayed ancient Babylon saying the same thing of herself—". . . who say in your heart, I am and there is no besides me; I shall not sit as a widow or know the loss of children"; (Isa. 47:7ff.). Ancient Nineveh said the same of herself (Zeph. 2:15). So did Tyre (Ezek. 28:2); and so have scores of other great world-capitals, both ancient and modern! Many emperors and nations have boasted they would last forever—Cyrus the Great's Persia; Alexander the Great's Greek empire; the British empire; Hitler's Third Reich. None of these were as powerful and rich as the Roman empire of the first century, but they are all gone, including Rome! The Roman Forum which was the seat of her power is today only ruins visited by tourists. Rome's power and grandeur is only a cadaver of the past upon which historians pronounce *post mortems.*

It is a temptation for Americans to look at their mighty nation—"the most powerful and richest nation that ever existed" some say—and think, "It may have happened to ancient empires but it could never happen to us." Americans would do well to look at Rome—or at Berlin after World War II. It can happen anywhere, anytime, where nations and people continue in rebellion against God!

Rome says she shall *never* mourn. God says, "in one day" her plagues and destruction come. One, twenty-four day is not meant to be understood literally. It is figurative language, poetic in style, symbolizing the suddenness and unexpectedness of Rome's fall. In 410 A.D. the entire world was stunned by the news that the once proud city of emperors had been sacked, looted and burned by the barbarian Visigoths (see comments on Rev. 9:13-19, Vol. I, pgs. 108-113). That was just the beginning of the plundering of Rome, but it was sudden and unexpected and signaled her demise. God is equal to the challenge of Rome for eternal sovereignty of the world. She boasts she will never relinquish her hold on the world. But God is mighty. Rome's predicted fall is guaranteed on the basis of God's power and character (faithfulness and justice). What God says will surely come to pass. Nebuchadnezzar learned that (see Daniel chs. 1-4).

vv. 9-10   And the kings of the earth . . . will weep and wail over her . . . — What a strange paradox! The kings of the earth who had turned in hate upon the harlot and joined in making her desolate, now weep and wail over her as she is being destroyed. But that is the way of worldliness. These "kings" were not weeping out of compassion for the harlot, they were mourning their own loss. When the harlot passed away, what they had enjoyed by her power was gone. There is no "rhyme or reason" for the actions of most unbelievers. The unbelieving mind does not think logically, for it is a mind in rebellion against the Source of Logic and Reason. It is a mind in anarchy—a mind gone mad. That is why Paul wrote to the

THIRTEEN LESSONS ON REVELATION

Corinthians, "Come to your right mind and sin no more" (I Cor. 15:34). A mind that deliberately chooses falsehood over truth is an unbalanced, irrational mind. That does not relieve such a mind of culpability. Lenski says, "The lover of a whore strangles her and then weeps like a fool." But that does not mean the "lover" is not guilty.

These "allies" of Rome stand afar off as she burns. They cannot help her and are careful to stay their distance to avoid sharing in her doom. Such are "fair-weather-friends." The citizen of the country where the Prodigal Son spent all his money gave the prodigal room and board with his herd of hogs! The worldly-minded always looks out for himself above everyone else. That is why the Christian must have a transformed mind— for he must always look not only to his own interests, but also to the interests of others (Phil. 2:4).

vv. 11-13   And the merchants of the earth weep and mourn for her . . . — The city of Rome was like a voracious and insatiable wild animal. Roman aristocrats and the new-rich spent money in unbelievable quantities. Modern man's most extravagant luxury is poverty compared with the riotous extravagance of ancient Rome. One of Nero's "freemen" was so rich he regarded a man with a fortune of $12 million dollars a pauper. Apicius squandered a fortune of $2 million in refined debauchery, and then committed suicide when he had only $250,000 left because he could not live on such pittance. In one day Caligula the emperor squandered the taxes of three provinces amounting to $250,000, and in a single year boasted of spending $40 million dollars. There was an insanity of wanton extravagance in first century Rome without parallel in history. (See comments on Lesson 1, Vol. I, for more information).

John's list of the goods no longer being sold in Rome is an amazingly detailed inventory of first century merchandize. It shows the indulgent luxury of Rome and how widespread Rome's commercial empire was. Gold and silver came from Egypt and Spain. Pliny the Elder writes of hydraulic mining for gold in that age which would put recent operations to shame. Roman aristocrats and emperors used gold and silver in building and crafts like we would use steel and marble today. Jewels and pearls and the various spices all suggest the Orient. Silk and cinnamon apparently came from China. Silk was usually purchased to make clothing for the rich. One pound of silk was sold for one pound of gold (worth approximately $8000 today). Thyine wood was from a special citrus tree which grew in North Africa, prized for its coloring which was like a peacock's tail or the stripes of a tiger. The grain in the wood made it valuable for tables. One table made from this wood could cost anywhere from $8000 to $30,000. Ivory would be shipped from India and Africa and was very costly. It was used to make furniture and decorative pieces. Fine linen (made of flax or hemp) came mainly from Egypt and only the very rich could afford it. Purple and scarlet cloth was dyed in Asia Minor and transported to Rome for making clothing for Roman emperors, senators, and their wives. Wine was a universal table drink in that age. Water was usually unfit to drink. Italy could not supply enough wine for her own people so Rome paid high prices to have wine from other countries shipped in. Oil, used for lamps, medicine, cooking and a number of other things, was also in short supply and therefore very expensive. Metals and lumber, mined and harvested all over the world, were voraciously consumed by Rome in her world-wide public works programs and in extravagant beautification of the city of Rome. Agricultural products and animals were imported by the ton to be consumed as food and offered daily by the hundreds as sacrifices to the gods. Horses and chariots were imported by the rich to become part of the stables of the aristocrats as well as resupply for the massive Roman military complex.

The Greek word *somaton* is translated *slaves* in verse 13, but literally means, *bodies*. The slave markets were called *somatemporos,* "body-emporiums." The Greek word translated *human souls* is *psuchas,* from which we get the English word, *psyche.* In this context *psuchas* means *life.* Slaves were sold and owned, body and soul. The slave was no more than the livestock on the farm. There were over 60 million slaves in the Roman empire. In the city of Rome alone there were 400,000 slaves, half the population of the city. It was no unusual thing for a man to own 500 slaves. One Roman left in his will 4116 slaves. Emperors often had households of at least 20,000 slaves. People from every nation and culture were sold into slavery (even Hebrews). Those who owned slaves held over them the power of life and death. Slaves might be legally killed by an owner on the slightest whim or set free. Slavery was a world-wide industry and many became rich by trading and selling human beings.

The Roman empire of John's day had an astoundingly well organized passenger, freight, and express system. For the transport of goods, there were *mansiones,* which in English means waiting-places. These *mansiones* maintained riders, drivers, conductors, doctors, blacksmiths, wheelwrights, and about forty beasts and the appropriate amount of rolling stock. In this way the trade of the empire could be kept moving. Where in our world there are scores of obstacles to free trade, in that Roman world there were no such obstacles. From the Great Wall in Britain to the Sudan in Africa, and to Mesopotamia and China there was one huge trading unit. There was such an immense volume of trade and prosperity banking and credit capitalism were well advanced. Checks were used, letters of credit were common, and Roman currency was valid anywhere. The Roman empire was a paradise for businessmen. Commerce was frenzied. Only a very few ever cried warnings of the dangers of inflation and commercial crash. But the crash came. And it was one of the contributing factors to the death of the empire.

THIRTEEN LESSONS ON REVELATION

v. 14   The fruit for which thy soul longed has gone from thee . . . —
The *merchants* (Gr. *emporoi,* those of the emporium or market) all over
the Roman empire and even those in countries not under Roman rule like
China, Africa and the Orient, would mourn and wail because the luxurious
"fruits" of their commercial traffic with Rome was gone when she fell.
The Greek word *opora* means ripe and juicy *fruit;* the word *epithumias*
translated *longed* means *lusted;* the word *lipara* translated *dainties* means
literally, *anointed with oil* signifying luxurious or costly; and the word
lampra translated *splendor,* means literally, bright, shiny, *radiant.* The
idea is that the sumptuous and luxurious life merchants of the empire were
making for themselves by selling to Rome was all over with Rome's fall.
**vv. 15-16   The merchants . . . will stand afar off . . . weeping and
mourning . . . —** Like the kings, the merchants will not try to come to
Rome's rescue but will stand afar, afraid for themselves. Like the kings,
they do not care for Rome—only for their own loss. The merchants do
not think of Rome as "mighty" as the kings did—the merchants think
of her as "wealth," clothed in fineness and bedecked with precious jewels.
Their market had collapsed! Suddenly, completely, and disastrously they
lost everything. One is reminded of the stock-market crash of 1929 in
America. Many businessmen were so psychologically devastated by that
they committed suicide. The stock-market of the Roman empire was as
sensitive to international events as is Wall Street today.
**vv. 17-19   . . . And all shipmasters and seafaring men . . . stood afar
off . . . —** Every *helmsman (Gr. kubernetes,* shipmaster, helmsman), all
the *ship's company* (Gr. *ploion ho homilos*), and *sailors* (Gr. *nautai,* nautical
ones), and as many as *work the sea* (Gr. *thalassan ergazontai,* make a
living from the sea) mourned Rome's fall. Throwing dust on the head was
a sign of great grief in that civilization. But again, the grief is selfish. There
is no pity for Rome, only pity for self. The world of sea-faring men had
also become *plutocrats* (Gr. *eploutesan,* rich) through Rome's *value* (Gr.
timiotetos, price, cost). Homer Hailey writes: "Trade and commerce of
themselves are not wicked; they are good when used for the welfare of
humanity. However, when used for selfish luxury and the gratifying of
fleshly lusts, they become unrighteous, profane and wicked." To make
mammon one's god is to make oneself vulnerable to destruction when
mammon's impotence is exposed.
**v. 20   Rejoice over her, O heaven . . . for God has given judgment for
you against her! —** The martyred saints in heaven, under the altar, had
cried out for God's justice to be done upon their murderers (Rev. 6:9-11).
The Lord told them to rest a little while longer. Now heaven (including
the saints and apostles and prophets) is *commanded* (Gr. *euphrainou*
present imperative, "rejoice") to be glad about Rome's devastating death.
We have already discussed the ethical aspect of believers rejoicing in the

judgment of wickedness (see introductory comments to this chapter). Those that dwelt upon the earth had rejoiced at the apparent death of the "two witnesses" (ch. 11:10), but now the witnesses rejoice at the judgment of the wicked earth. When Satan was defeated in the heavenly place and cast to the "earth," heaven was told to rejoice (Rev. 12:12ff.), because God knew (as well as the devil) that Satan's time to use the "earth" (Roman empire) was short. Now the time is up. Rome falls (prophetically). Heaven may now rejoice (prophetically). God gives judgment for his saints. God keeps his word. His judgments are faithful, just, and perfect. Believers need not fret that those who persecute them and oppose them will not receive justice—God will take care of that. Christians must have faith and leave vengeance to God. Even the Lord Jesus when reviled on earth left justice up to the Father (I Pet. 2:22-23).

vv. 21-22   **So shall Babylon the great city be thrown down with violence** . . . — Throwing a millstone into the sea symbolized a punishment of severity for extreme wickedness or perversion. Jesus said anyone who caused a child to stumble should be executed this way (Mt. 18:6). Jeremiah was told to symbolize the destruction of ancient Babylon in this manner (Jer. 51:63-64). Such a punishment also pictured that the one punished was never to rise again. Rome's death will be with passion, impulsively, violently. The Greek word *hormemati* means, with haste, suddenly, violently. Her fall will not be pleasant. She will not just fade away peacefully. There will be bloodshed, misery and surprise at her end.

The Greek reads, *ou me*, (No, no) and is a double negative emphasizing total obliteration. Never again would the empire of Rome be found. This is exactly what Daniel predicted. Daniel said the fourth world empire (Rome) would be the last universal human empire. The fifth universal kingdom would be God's kingdom (the church). This double negative occurs six times in these final verses of chapter 18! Ancient Rome will never rise again. There is an interesting progression to Rome's fall in John's prophecies which parallels the historical reality; first the beast (the political structure of the empire), then Rome's allies (kings and merchants), and last the harlot (the capitol city itself).

The total death of the city is pictured in three ways. First, there never again would be seen or heard the licentious revelry and sinful gaiety which characterized the city of Rome. The wild orgies, the bloody contests in the arenas, the gluttonous feasts, the indecent and blasphemous theater productions and the pomp and extravagance of the royal processions, all attended with music and trumpets, would *not ever* be experienced in Rome again. Second, industry would cease. No more would there be found craftsmen plying their trades—no more would there be found mills grinding their produce. Rome's great commercial capitol was to die. Third, all vestiges of family and home-life was to disappear. No more lighted homes, no more marriages, no more Rome! Some interpreters of Daniel and Revelation (including other Old Testament prophecies) have envisioned a resurrected and restored Roman empire prior to what they call "the end of the age." Some are declaring the European Common Market is the "new Rome." During World War II a number of books on prophecy were written which announced that Benito Mussolini was about to resurrect the Roman empire as prophesied in Revelation. Adolph Hitler was supposed to be "The Antichrist" and, together with Mussolini, he would usher in the seven years of tribulation before which Jesus Christ would "rapture" the church and after which Jesus would come to earth and set up his millennial kingdom and he would rule the nations "with a rod of iron" from the city of Jerusalem. Needless to say, those books are now obsolete and out of print! Rome, a universal power of wickedness, is never to be again! When Jesus comes the next time, it is not to deal with sin (cf. Heb. 9:27-28). Sin has been dealt with once for all! God has established his *kingdom* on earth—it is the *church*. Because ancient Rome was destroyed, and Satan was bound, the church has become a universal kingdom. It is composed of citizens from all nations, races, tongues and cultures. When Christ comes the second time, for the last time, this cosmos will melt with a fervent heat and he will create a new heavens and a new earth in which will dwell righteousness only (cf. II Pet. 2:8-13).

In the last two verses of this chapter we are reminded of the three reasons God judged Rome and obliterated her. First, she made wealth and worldliness her chief ambition—"thy merchants were the great men of the earth." When materialism becomes supreme in a nation it ceases to acknowledge and practice spiritual and moral values which are the very fiber of society and of human stability. Second, Rome deceived and exploited the whole world with her "sorceries." This would symbolize all the idolatrous and blasphemous religions (including particularly deification of the emperors) Rome advocated. Idolatry and paganism have their origin and source straight from hell. They are false and in direct rebellion against the God of truth! And Rome led the whole world (except Christians) into complicity with hell. Third, Rome is accused by God of the murder of prophets and of saints. These are the millions (some estimate 2 million martyrs) slain in persecutions or dying from forced starvation because they would not worship the emperor but rather called Jesus their king. But Rome's guilt does not stop there. She is also accused of the blood of all who have been slain on earth. In her greed to conquer and luxuriate herself, she killed and destroyed and deprived until many more millions of victims were added to her crimes. It is interesting to note that the Greek verb *esphagmenon* is a perfect tense participle and would literally be translated, "having been slain and are continuing to be slain." Perhaps God intends Rome to be *symbolically* guilty of all the blood shed on earth from the beginning of time until the end of time! Rome (figuratively called, Babylon) did unite in itself the symbolic nature of worldliness and wickedness for all generations (cf. Rev. 13:2). Rome did give the ultimate order to crucify the Son of God (cf. Rev. 11:8). Jesus pronounced the Pharisees guilty of all the blood shed from Abel to Zechariah because of their duplicity in crucifying the Messiah (Mt. 23:29-39). The universal pagan sovereignty Rome enjoyed is gone, never to be revived. But the triad of forces opposing the church of Christ which were so powerful in Rome live on with less concentration and in subdued influence in the present world—political persecution, humanistic idolatry, and materialistic indulgence. The subduing of these powers is the result of the missionary thrust of the gospel into the far reaches of civilization. Truth sets people and nations free from ignorance and falsehood and Satan's powers are bound to a greater degree than they were when Rome controlled the world.

APPREHENSION AND APPLICATION:

1. What contrast in perspectives on the fall of Rome does chapter 18 present? Is it all right to rejoice when wickedness on earth is destroyed?
2. Why does John say Rome had already fallen when he wrote Revelation? Do you believe the words of the Bible will come to pass so certainly that you can consider them as good as done? What about your forgiveness?
3. Do evil spirits live in the ruins of ancient Rome today? What did John mean by such a statement in 18:2? When you look at the ruins of ancient Rome today, what do you think about?
4. Why did all the nations of the world join Rome in her depraved opposition to the kingdom of God? Do nations still join one another opposing the kingdom of God for the same reasons?
5. Could Christians have remained residents of the city of Rome and still obeyed God's command, "Come out of her, my people . . ."? Could Christians in Moscow, Washington, D.C., or Tokyo obey the same command today? What about you—are you "coming out of your Rome"?
6. How many sins does a nation have to commit to heap up a pile to heaven? Will nations which have persecuted Christians in our generation ever be punished? How do you know? When?
7. God saw Rome destroyed. How did Rome see herself? How many nations have seen themselves as Rome did? Do Americans?
8. Why would those kings who had joined in destroying the harlot (17:16) wail when she was destroyed? Have you observed people or countries acting this way in your experience? What would cure such irrational behavior?

9. Where did these merchants who were mourning Rome's fall come from? Why did they weep and wail? Do you think the world which hates America today would weep and wail if she were suddenly destroyed? Why?
10. Why are slaves mentioned in connection with commerce? What does the Bible say about slavery? Why didn't Jesus demand an end to it when he was preaching? Did the Old Testament permit the Hebrews to have slaves? Do you think America would be here today had it allowed slavery to continue?
11. Could you rejoice today if certain nations which are persecuting God's saints and making trouble for the rest of the world were destroyed? What about great religious organizations which oppose Biblical belief or lead millions into falsehood? How many ways does God have to deal with such opposition to his kingdom?
12. Does the proclamation of the gospel and its belief by a majority of a nation affect that nation's behavior toward mankind? How? Why? Can you name some examples of nations, both pro and con?

Lesson Seven
(19:1-21—20:1-6)

THE LAMB AND THE SPIRITUAL CONQUEST

The apocalyptic drama of the sovereignty of God in Christ versus the pretended sovereignty of the devil and his allies (the beast, the false prophet, and the harlot—Rome) has come to its grand climax. The opposing characters have all been clearly defined. From the moment of the birth of the Man Child, it was apparent that the old dragon, the devil, was raging to devour the Child. But he could not do it—God brought the Child back to life and caught him up to heaven. So the dragon gave his deceptive authority to the beast, the false prophet and the harlot. They set upon the Woman (the church) in the wilderness (the world of pagan sin). But God pronounces his final judgment upon Rome (especially the prostitute-city itself). Rome's doom is sealed. Her death is inevitable. She will even be an instrument to bring about her own fall. There will be none to help her.

But the real reason behind her doom is that God, through the Lamb, is going to defeat Rome and throw her into the lake of fire and brimstone. The Lamb will become the Warrior-King (Messiah) and completely defeat his enemies. The Lamb will prove his sovereignty by dramatically saving His church (His Bride) on earth and by destroying that fourth great world empire of which Daniel prophesied and which the world believed to be invincible.

83

John is going to be given an apocalyptic, highly symbolic vision of victory. The vision will be in the form of a glorious contrast between the defeat of "the city of the world" (Rome) and the revealing of the Perfect City of God coming down out of heaven from God. John will skip from Rome's fall to the end of all time without telling us what is to transpire between. First, the climactic battle between the King of kings and the devil and his allies (beast, false prophet and harlot) Revelation 19:1 through 20:6.

The Bride (19:1-10)

19 After this I heard what seemed to be the loud voice of a great multitude in heaven, crying,

"Hallelujah! Salvation and glory and power belong to our God,
²for his judgments are true and just; he has judged the great harlot who
corrupted the earth with her fornication,
and he has avenged on her the blood of his servants."
³Once more they cried,
"Hallelujah! The smoke from her goes up for ever and ever."
⁴And the twenty-four elders and the four living creatures fell down and worshiped God who is seated on the throne, saying, "Amen. Hallelujah!" ⁵And from the throne came a voice crying,
"Praise our God, all you his servants,
you who fear him, small and great."
⁶Then I heard what seemed to be the voice of a great multitude, like the sound of many waters and like the sound of mighty thunderpeals, crying,
"Hallelujah! For the Lord our God the Almighty reigns.
⁷Let us rejoice and exult and give him the glory,
for the marriage of the Lamb has come,
and his Bride has made herself ready;
⁸it was granted her to be clothed with fine linen, bright and pure"—
for the fine linen is the righteous deeds of the saints.
9 And the angel said to me, "Write this: Blessed are those who are invited to the marriage supper of the Lamb." And he said to me, "These are true words of God." ¹⁰Then I fell down at his feet to worship him, but he said to me, "You must not do that! I am a fellow servant with you and your brethren who hold the testimony of Jesus. Worship God." For the testimony of Jesus is the spirit of prophecy.

vv. 1-3 . . . I heard what seemed to be the mighty voice of a great multitude in heaven . . . — This multitude is probably all the angels, the living creatures and the martyred saints together in heaven. All heaven was commanded to rejoice at the revealed fall of the harlot (18:20) and now heaven's corridors are ringing with shouts of Hallelujah and praise to the name of God for victory. The rejoicing of heaven is in sharp contrast to the weeping and wailing on earth over Rome's fall! The world sees Rome's fall as detrimental (especially will opportunities for fleshly indulgence and carnal exploitation be lost). Heaven sees Rome's fall as beneficial. Now the power of Satan will be bound. Now the good news of salvation will be able to go to the farthest reaches of human habitation on earth.

Furthermore, God has proved himself true to his word and just and fair. He has kept his promises to avenge wickedness done to those who trust Him. The Greek text makes it emphatic that *the* salvation and *the* glory and *the* power belong to God by placing the Greek article before each noun. When Rome fell according to God's word it was apparent that all sovereignty belong to God and none to Rome. That is still true today! All salvation, glory and power still belongs to Jehovah who manifested himself in the incarnate Christ.

God judged (Gr. *ekrine*) the great harlot who corrupted the whole world with her fornication. The Greek word *ephtheire* is translated *corrupted* but literally means, "to destroy by bringing to a state of moral rottenness" (cf. Eph. 4:22). Moral decadence is destructive! Individuals, one by one, make up a society or civilization. When individuals throw off the absolutes of divinely revealed morality, the society becomes corrupt and is destroyed. Individual freedom is not to be equated with individual moral license. "No man is an island. . . ." No man lives or dies to himself (cf. Rom. 14:7ff.). Each man is morally responsible to the whole of his society or civilization. The decadence of Roman aristocracy soon permeated the whole of Roman society and killed it.

God *avenged* (Gr. *exedikese,* "proceeding from justice; vindicating"). There was no vindictiveness in God's vengeance—it was simply the fair, deserved, right and proper result of Rome's wickedness. It is simply God giving them up to eat the fruit of their deeds. Rome wanted to stamp out the saints of God, to stamp out all that stood for goodness, righteousness and truth, that she might have the opposite, so God gave it to her. God made all His creation to function on the principles of right, justice, faith and love. Creation fulfills its purpose only when it willingly agrees and practices those principles. God also built into His creation a constant revelation of these principles, as well as consequences for obeying and disobeying them. The realm of the spiritual was made to function on the same principles. All God had to do was simply give mankind its choice and it received either the consequence of blessedness or cursedness. All God has to do with an impenitent, rebellious society is give it what it wants and it is judged. So God gave Rome up to the lusts of their hearts, to dishonorable passions, to a base mind and improper conduct (cf. Rom. 1:18-32).

A second time this great multitude in heaven cried, "Hallelujah!" Hallelujah is a Hebrew word, *Alleluia,* transliterated into Greek and English, and means, "Praise Jehovah." Heaven's multitude observed the smoke (destruction) of Rome going up forever. Rome will never be built again as in the days of the Empire. And for that, heaven praises God!

v. 4   And the twenty-four elders and the four living creatures . . . — From the time of the order to pour out the seven bowls of wrath upon the earth, the throne has been hidden. No one was able to find or approach the throne of God to intercede on Rome's behalf. Her judgment was inevitable. Now that the judgment is sealed by prophetic certainty, once again the throne is seen. Once again are seen the symbolic creatures representing all of God's obedient creation paying homage and praise to his righteousness and justice. "So be it!" (Amen) they said, in perfect agreement with God's final word on Rome.

v. 5   . . . Praise our God, all you his servants . . . — It is not only heaven's hosts that are expected to be in harmony with God's judgments on Rome, but all who claim to be God's servants are exhorted to praise him. God's ways are beyond man's comprehension (Isa. 55:8-9). He does not ask us to evaluate whether his judgments are right or wrong. He does not even give us the prerogative of criticizing his methods. God leaves us free to simply acknowledge his sovereignty, on the basis of his actions, and then to accept them by faith. Habakkuk the prophet fretted because he could not understand or agree with the methods of God's dealing with the Israelites. God told Habakkuk that he did not require the prophet to understand or agree—only to believe, (Hab. 2:2-4). All those servants of God upon the earth—unable to see from heaven's perspective as yet—must trust God's judgment's on Rome even though they may not understand. Jesus had to face this problem when he predicted the destruction of Judaism (Mt. 24). Even Jesus' Jewish disciples could not understand or agree with what he was predicting—but he expected them to accept his predictions by faith and thus save themselves from the holocaust to come in 70 A.D. Many did (see Lesson 11). Some would say this sounds like fatalism. But there is a world of difference between fatalism and faith. In faith, the Christian looks beyond this world to the next and thus lives by hope. In fatalism, the unbeliever's highest expectation is a resignation to oblivion or annihilation. While he lives he is forced to surrender to injustices, frustrations, losses and death.

vv. 6-8   . . . for the marriage of the Lamb has come . . . — The next voice John heard from heaven was awesome! It was roaring and booming. It demanded attention. It symbolized urgency and importance and power. Anyone who has stood at Niagara Falls, or heard the cannon-like boom of thunder in a violent storm, knows what this means. It means that all sound of man's talking is to be drowned out and imperative attention is to be given to the voice from heaven. "The Lord is in his holy temple; let all the earth keep silence before him" (Hab. 2:20). God is about to reveal something extremely significant.

What is significant is that the harlot (Rome) had brought ultimate pressure upon the Bride of Christ, to seduce her, but the Bride remained faithful to her Husband. It might have seemed that the whole world had been deceived and had committed fornication with the harlot, but not Christ's Bride. She married Him and adorned herself in the righteousness Christ had provided for her. She did not dirty her garments with compromise or strip them off by unfaithfulness. The Greek verbs, *elthen* (came) and *etoimasen* (made herself) are aorist tense and, in light of other New Testament statements, indicate the "marriage" pictured here has already happened in the past.

In order to understand this passage the reader must remember Jewish marriage customs. The betrothal (engagement) was considered as binding as marriage. Joseph was told that he should not fear to take Mary his wife when it was found she was with child by the Holy Spirit, and Mary was *called* Joseph's *wife* even in the betrothal period (Mt. 2:20, 24). Therefore, people who were betrothed were considered to be married even before the ceremonies, the wedding suppers and before the sexual consummation. The time lapse between the betrothal and the ceremonies (including the feast) is pictured for us in Jesus' parable of the ten virgins (Mt. 25:1-13). In other words, marriage was considered to have taken place long before any feast might be given.

It is evident from many scriptures that the church on earth is married to Christ. In the Old Testament the relation of Jehovah to his covenant people is portrayed as a marriage (cf. Hosea 2:1ff.; Isa. 50:1; Jer. 2:32; Ezek. 16:1ff.; Isa. 62:4ff.). Actually, Isaiah 62:4-5 is a prophecy that when the Messiah comes in His *first* advent, those who believe and follow him will be "Married." It is clearly revealed in the New Testament that the church in the earth is the Bride of Christ (cf. Jn. 3:29-30; Eph. 5:22f.; Rom. 7:4; II Cor. 11:2). So, the "marriage of the Lamb" in our text here is not speaking of some future event. It is past. It took place at the *first* advent of Christ when the church was established on earth. But the *consummation* of the marriage (not the "supper") is yet to take place at Christ's *second* advent, (Rev. 21:2).

As a result of her faithfulness through the great tribulation of Rome's attempt to seduce her, the Bride of Christ "has made herself ready." She allowed Christ, through His Word, to sanctify her. John had already written letters to seven of the churches of Asia Minor (Rev. ch. 2-3) warning them to purify themselves by repentance. They had done so (cf. comments Rev. 14:1ff.). They had remained pure and chaste (cf. II Cor. 7:1; I Jn. 3:2-3; Jude 21) following the Lamb wherever He led them. They had not joined

87

the "harlot" in her fornications. God declares the Bride (by grace) to be dressed in fine linen, bright and pure (holy). The reason God *declares* the Bride to be holy is the righteous deeds of the saints. We have here the gospel in brief. God, in the redemptive work of Christ, made it possible for sinful man to be cleansed (dressed in fine linen). But man, is cleansed (dressed in fine linen) only when he appropriates it by faith expressed in obedience to the Gospel.

v. 9 Blessed are those who are invited to the marriage supper of the Lamb — First, the Greek word *keklemenoi,* translated "invited," is a perfect tense verb, meaning, "having been and continuing to be called." Perfect tense means an action in the past with a continuing result. This means the "marriage supper" had already come when John wrote Revelation and people were continually being invited to it (as they would become Christians), or it means those who had become Christians when John wrote were continuing to enjoy it as a feast. John would surely *not* have used the perfect tense verb to predict some *future* "marriage supper" of the Lamb. The consummation of the marriage comes after the feast.

The whole Christian age is depicted in the New Testament as a festival. Jesus likened the kingdom of God unto a "feast" many times (cf. Mt. 22:1ff.; Lk. 14:15ff.; Lk. 15:1-32; Rev. 3:20). The New Testament indicates the feasts of the Mosaic dispensation were types of the New Testament experience (cf. I Cor. 5:8; Heb. 13:10; et. al.). The Old Testament prophets pictured the Christian age as a "feast" (cf. Isa. 55:1-3; 65:13; et. al.). As we have noted earlier, the Old Testament prophets (Isa. 62:4-5) predicted the re-marriage of God with his Bride when the messianic kingdom would be established (the church) at Christ's first coming.

It appears, therefore, that both the "marriage" of the Lamb and the "marriage supper" of the Lamb have already begun and are continuing to take place as men and women are becoming Christians on earth and becoming a part of Christ's "Bride." The Spirit and the Bride are *still* saying, "Come," and inviting whosoever will to come (Rev. 22:17). To say that the marriage and the marriage supper have already come does not imply the marriage has already been consummated. The ultimate union of the "Bride" (the church) and her "Husband" (Christ) will take place at Christ's second coming (Rev. 21:2).

The contrast is the wretchedness and doom upon those who have answered the call of the harlot to fornicate with her (Rome), and the blessedness and happiness of those who have answered (and those who will continue to answer) the call of the Father to the marriage and marriage feast of his Son (the Lamb). Smoke (destruction and torment) goes up forever and ever from the judgment upon the harlot. Hallelujahs and praises and blessings forever are the experiences of those married to Christ.

v. 10 Then I fell down at his feet to worship him . . . — For some reason John thought the one speaking to him should be worshiped. Was it because John did not see clearly who was speaking; was it because John did not know the difference between an angel and God; or was John carried away with the emotional impact of the message and moved to worship the messenger? Whatever the reason, John was quickly corrected. Angels, as spiritual and supernatural as they may be, are *not* to be worshiped (cf. Col. 2:18-19; Rev. 22:8). This should be a constant warning for all Christians about the insidious tendency of the human heart toward idolatry. No one but the Godhead deserves to be worshiped. Everyone else (including angels) and everything else is a *servant* of the Godhead.

The testimony of Jesus is the *spirit* (Gr. *pneuma*, "life") of prophecy. John was probably moved to worship the angel speaking these prophecies to him because of the awesomeness of what was being said. So the angel corrected John by telling him that what Jesus testified to (when he was on earth) was the very life (spirit) of all the prophecies of Revelation (and, of course, of every prophecy in the Bible). The awesomeness of the message of Revelation should make John focus his worship on the *Lamb* instead of the servant delivering the message. The testimony of Jesus was that he was the Son of God—God incarnate (Jn. 1:1ff., et. al.). The statement here by the angel confirms the declaration in Revelation 5:11-14 that the *Lamb is worthy* to receive honor, power, glory, and to open the scroll. Whoever does not honor the Son does not honor the Father (Jn. 5:23). The deity of Jesus is the very life of the book of Revelation, and of the whole Bible! Jesus declared unequivocally that all the Old Testament prophecies were fulfilled in him (Lk. 24:25, 26, 27, 44, 45, 46, 47). The testimony of Jesus, that He is Sovereign God, is the very point of the book of Revelation. Caesar is not sovereign—Jesus, the Lamb, is!

The Bridegroom: (19:11-16)

11 Then I saw heaven opened, and behold, a white horse! He who sat upon it is called Faithful and True, and in righteousness he judges and makes war. [12]His eyes are like a flame of fire, and on his head are many diadems; and he has a name inscribed which no one knows but himself. [13]He is clad in a robe dipped in blood, and the name by which he is called is The Word of God. [14]And the armies of heaven, arrayed in fine linen, white and pure, followed him on white horses. [15]From his mouth issues a sharp sword with which to smite the nations, and he will rule them with a rod of iron; he will tread the wine press of the fury of the wrath of God the Almighty. [16]On his robe and on his thigh he has a name inscribed, King of kings and Lord of lords.

89

THIRTEEN LESSONS ON REVELATION

vv. 11-12 . . . and behold, a white horse . . . — The Groom (Christ) appears, not to consummate the marriage (that is predicted in 21:2-9), but to *rescue* his Bride by destroying the beast and the false prophet. Heaven is opened and Christ, the Warrior-King (Messiah), rides forth on a white horse (symbolizing conquest). Poellot says: "If someone could accurately and infallibly predict the tides of battle in civil and international war, the world would beat a path to his door. There is one conflict, however, of which we can say with complete assurance what the outcome will be. That is the warfare between God and all that are God's, on the one hand, and Satan and all that are Satan's, on the other." The book of Revelation accurately and infallibly predicts *that* battle. God conquers!

This Warrior-King is called "Faithful and True"! Jesus Christ is called the "faithful witness" in Rev. 1:4-5. Christ's words and actions are ultimate truth. There is no other truth except that it relates to Christ. In Him are all the treasures of wisdom and knowledge (Col. 1:15-20; 2:1-5). His teaching and his life are the ultimate reality. Everything else is transitory. Furthermore, Christ's word is faithful. It has always proved to be faithful in the past and we may trust everything He says about the future to be fulfilled precisely as he says it. What he revealed to John about the conflict between the Roman empire and the early church was absolutely true and faithful. To millions of unbelievers Rome was no "beast." To them she was man's beneficent god! To millions of unbelievers Rome was eternal. She was invincible. But the true and faithful Revelation of Christ declared Rome was a beast and she would be destroyed.

The Warrior-King judges Rome in righteousness. His judgments are according to facts, not according to appearances (cf. Jn. 7:24). He is not fooled by hypocrisy. Man cannot even hide the thoughts and intents of the human heart from Christ—he knows even these and is therefore able to judge correctly. He makes no mistakes in His judgments. It is interesting to note that the Warrior-King rides forth from heaven to *make war* upon the beast and false prophet as they *are upon the earth*. This context is, therefore, speaking of action to take place before the second advent of Christ, for at His second coming He does not come to make war but to reward and punish for all eternity.

The Warrior-King has eyes like a flame of fire (cf. comments 1:12-16) and He is crowned with many crowns. All sovereignty belongs to Him. And He has a name which no one knows but Himself. If He alone knows it, it seems useless for us to speculate. Perhaps it has something to do with the nature of the three-persons-in-One! Who understands that? In Him dwelt all the fulness of the *Godhead* (Gr. *theotetos*) bodily (Col. 2:9). That also is incomprehensible to man. Man cannot understand that—he simply believes it! Man's belief is, of course, based on evidence to substantiate the claim. When Moses wanted to know who was sending him to Pharaoh,

God replied, "I Am, That I Am!" or YHWH. The English word "God" is simply a human symbol to describe the Being who is above and beyond human experience. Full comprehension of the name and nature of God and Christ is impossible for man.

v. 13   **He is clad in a robe dipped in blood** . . . — Some ancient manuscripts have the Greek word for "sprinkled" rather than "dipped" to describe the blood on the robe of the Warrior-King. The imagery is unquestionably following that of Isaiah 63:1-6 where the Lord Jehovah is seen in vision form coming from the destruction of enemies to his redemptive program in the Old Testament. After God destroyed Edom, as he said he would in the prophet Obadiah, Isaiah the prophet sees a vision of the Lord, symbolically, with blood-spattered garments from having tread the winepress of his wrath. Isaiah was given this vision to relay to the Old Testament "remnant" God's promise that He would judge and defeat all (even the most secure) enemies of his messianic program.

The Lamb has revealed to John that He is going to tread the awful winepress of God's wrath upon Rome (Rev. 14:17-20) and that He is going to assemble all the world of Rome for the battle at Har-Meggido (Armageddon) (Rev. 16:14-16). Awesome defeat and judgment upon the world of Rome has been predicted numerous times in Revelation. Now the Lamb (seen as the great Warrior-King) is seen with his robe spattered by the blood of his enemies. The context and the similar vision in Isaiah would preclude this blood being that of the Lamb or of the saints. It is the life-blood of His enemies.

This Warrior-King is called "The Word of God." The use of *Logos* (Greek, *Word*) was a favorite title of John for Jesus Christ (cf. Jn. 1:1, 14; I Jn. 1:1). A person's *word* is himself. A person's word reveals what a person is, who a person is and relates him to other persons. The fleshly body of a person is not really the person. The body is merely an instrument through which a person (word) functions. Thus, Jesus was the Word of God (the Person of God) in a fleshly body. Jesus demonstrated in space and time that the Word of God (Person of God) is powerful, loving faithful, omniscient, just, righteous and eternal. Jesus is God's Word to mankind. He is the final Word of God to mankind. Who is appearing to John with blood-sprinkled garments? The Word of God! The Logos is God's Messiah. The Logos is God's judge of the world. The Logos is God!

vv. 14-16   **And the armies of heaven . . . followed him on white horses** . . . — The armies of heaven do not necessarily have to come from heaven. This undoubtedly refers to the church on earth and its spiritual victory over the Roman empire. It most certainly does not refer to some battle at the end of time and Christ's second coming. There will be no battle at His second advent—only judgment and salvation (cf. Heb. 9:27-28). It is not intended to portray a literal battle of swords, spears, chariots and horses. It is symbolism. The Christians of the first century were told their war was a spiritual war—not one of flesh and blood (cf. Eph. 6:10-20). Christians were even told that the weapons of their warfare were not fleshly (II Cor. 10:3-5) but were spiritual weapons taking thoughts and imaginations captive for obedience to Christ.

The sword issuing from the mouth of the Warrior-King is symbolism and so is the "rod of iron." Therefore, the weapon by which the church overcomes the world is the Word of God. Armies-sword-rod-of-iron are all symbolic of the sovereignty of the Word of God. The sovereign, faithful, Word of God will rule the world—not Caesar (cf. Psa. 2:9; Isa. 11:4). Whatever God's Word says about the world will come to pass—not what human rulers say. This parallels the clear teaching of the book of Daniel (see Dan. 2:20-23; 2:46; 3:28-30; 4:34-37; 6:25-28). God allows men to choose and act in this world as they wish—but He still rules. He may intervene or He may not intervene—but He still rules. His rule in the hearts of believers (see Col. 3:15) is established by persuasion, not by force. God will never *force* anyone (not even with a rod of iron) to be good. Whatever the battle and whatever the rule John is describing here, it is not a rule of force with a literal rod of iron. Righteousness and faith and love cannot be wrought by force. Hell is God's prison for all who will not believe and love and obey by choice. There they shall have forever to be wicked (cf. Rev. 22:11). Unbelief and falsehood cannot be wiped out by force—only overcome by truth and faith. Actually, the word translated "rule" is, in the Greek texts, the word *poimanei* which would more accurately be translated "shepherd" them. The nations will be smitten and shepherded with the indestructible and sovereign Word of God. The Warrior-King (also known as the Lamb) will do the work of fulfilling God's wrath. The Messiah (whom Rome thought they had crucified) will squash Rome and all her influence like grapes in a winepress (see comments on Rev. 14:17-20).

This One whom Pontius Pilate (on behalf of Caesar) scorned and crucified for claiming to be "king of the Jews" is seen by John as having the title, "King of kings and Lord of lords." Every knee on earth is obligated to bow before Him, and every tongue on earth and in heaven is obligated to confess that Jesus, the Lamb, is King of kings and Lord of lords. This title is inscribed on His thigh—plain enough, now that He has been historically proved to be Sovereign, for all men to acknowledge it.

The Battle (19:17-21)

17 Then I saw an angel standing in the sun, and with a loud voice he called to all the birds that fly in midheaven, "Come, gather for the great supper of God, 18to eat the flesh of kings, the flesh of captains, the flesh of mighty men, the flesh of horses and their riders, and the

flesh of all men, both free and slave, both small and great.'' ¹⁹And I saw the beast and the kings of the earth with their armies gathered to make war against him who sits upon the horse and against his army. ²⁰And the beast was captured, and with it the false prophet who in its presence had worked the signs by which he deceived those who had received the mark of the beast and those who worshiped its image. These two were thrown alive into the lake of fire that burns with sulphur. ²¹And the rest were slain by the sword of him who sits upon the horse, the sword that issues from his mouth; and all the birds were gorged with their flesh.

vv. 17-18   Come, gather for the great supper of God . . . — Now the fall of Rome is pictured as a great, gory feast for the carrion-eating birds of the earth. A messenger (angel) from heaven is giving the invitation to this feast. Once again the imagery is from the Old Testament prophets. They, too, describe great victories of God over the forces opposing His redemptive work as feasts for the vultures (cf. Isa. 34:6; Jer. 46:10; Ezek. 39:17-20).

The fallen and dead are from every spectrum of humankind. Mighty men, kings, princes, and men of all categories of life, both slave and free, joined the army (Rome) opposing God's kingdom. Satan does not discriminate when he seeks to deceive people into joining him fight against God. He takes his wicked helpers wherever he can seduce them. And his helpers may be found in every vocation and stratum of life. Some of them even pretend to be angels of light (II Cor. 11:14-15).

The imagery of this great devastation and death is borrowed from Ezekiel's symbolic battle between God and the forces of Gog and Magog (Ezek. ch. 38-39). Just as Ezekiel's vision was described symbolically, so John's vision of this war is not intended to be literal but symbolic—spiritual. The reason Ezekiel and John used such symbolism was to impress the minds of their readers with the *complete* defeat of the Lord's enemies. God does not have to slay people and leave rotting cadavers strewn on a battle field in order to defeat His enemies and rescue His chosen remnant—neither in Old Testament times or New Testament times! God delivered the Old Testament remnant from Persia, "not by might nor by power, but by his Spirit . . ." (Zech. 4:6). God merely "stirred up the spirit of Cyrus" and the remnant was delivered (II Chron. 36:22-23; Ezra 1:1-4). He did not march great armies into Persia and kill thousands of Persians. But He led His prophets to describe this deliverance as gory battles with thousands of dead corpses! The whole world of mankind was not slain when Rome fell. Many of those individuals who had worshipped the Caesars and opposed the church went right on living when Rome fell. But God had John describe it symbolically as an enormous slaughter for the sake of impression.

THIRTEEN LESSONS ON REVELATION

vv. 19-20   And the beast was captured, and with it the false prophet... — The beast and false prophet are the two beasts of Revelation 13:1-10. They are Rome's political-military power and Rome's idolatrous religion of Caesar-worship arrayed against the church. They are willing tools of Satan. Earlier the beast had called the kings of the world together at Har-Meggido (Armageddon) to do battle against the Lamb and His followers (see Rev. 16:13-16; 17:12-14). But the battle is never described—only the outcome is always total defeat for the beast and his allies and total victory for God and His kingdom.

Now, for the third time, only the consequences of the great spiritual struggle for the allegiance of mankind and sovereignty over the world are described. Total defeat for the forces of Caesar—total victory for the forces of Christ. The beast was *seized* (Gr. *epiasthe,* apprehend, arrest, take, lay hands on). God did not have to chase the beast down, he simply seized the beast and the false prophet. This false prophet was the one (Rev. 13:11-18) who, in the presence of the beast, had worked the *signs* (Gr. *semeia,* not necessarily miracles) by which he *misled* (Gr. *eplanese*) those who were willing to receive the mark of the beast and worship the image of the beast. The "signs" of the false prophet were pseudo-miracles—not real ones (see comments on Rev. 13:11-18). The reason so many were deceived was because they *wanted* to be deceived. It had to do with character. The Greek word translated "mark" is *charagma,* from which we get the English word *character.* Those who had the *mark* of the beast had the *character* of the beast (see comments Rev. 13:16-17). People *become* what they worship (cf. Hosea 9:10).

The beast (politico-military power) and the false prophet (idolatrous influence) were thrown into the lake of fire that burns with brimstone. This is the second consequence of the battle-not-described. These two forces (not specific individuals) are forever overcome. They are banished to the eternal prison. They will never rise again to the extent they enjoyed in the Roman empire. That does not mean the devil does not continue to oppose God and His kingdom. The devil is not banished forever until the great judgment (Rev. 20:10). But with Rome's fall, the devil is bound—his sphere or power is limited since he no longer has a universal carnal power dominating civilization as Rome did. The statement that the beast and false prophet were cast *alive* into the lake of fire merely symbolizes that the "life" of Rome's power to oppose the church of Christ was no more. It symbolizes that ". . . the wrath of God is revealed from heaven against all ungodliness and wickedness of men who by their wickedness suppress the truth" (Rom. 1:18ff.). Not even universal paganism with all the accumulated wealth and power of the Roman empire can thwart God's redemptive program in the world. God is in the process of destroying every rule and every authority and power (I Cor. 15:24-26). The "life" of paganism is consigned to eternal banishment in the lake of fire and brimstone. These are the "rest" of the dead who did not come to life during the thousand years (see comments on 20:5).

v. 21 And the rest were slain by the sword of him who sits upon the horse . . . — "The rest" probably refers to all opposers of God's kingdom who die during the Roman empire having exerted their wickedness attempting to supress the truth. They will be cast into the lake of fire and brimstone along with the beast and the false prophet and the devil in due time (cf. Rev. 20:15) because they have the mark (character) of the beast.

All these are also slain by the sword (Word of God) issuing from the mouth of the Warrior-King (Messiah). God's word is powerful. It will accomplish that for which it is spoken and will not return unto him void. God's word saves, or it judges (Jn. 12:44-50).

Homer Hailey has an excellent summary of this section:

> The victory is won, and the defeat of the beast and his ally, the false prophet, is complete. The Roman power and the paganism which it supported are now destroyed forever. The vision of Daniel is fulfilled (Dan. 7:11), and in this defeat and destruction is revealed the destiny of all such powers that should ever arise to fight against God and His kingdom. This is God's guarantee of victory to the saints who lived then and to all who would come after them, even until the end of time . . . Not a vestige of the anti-Christian forces was left; the destruction was complete. The sword of truth and judgment prevailed over the sword of political force and human wisdom in false worship (*Revelation*, pg. 388).

The Binding (20:1-6)

20 Then I saw an angel coming down from heaven, holding in his hand the key of the bottomless pit and a great chain. ²And he seized the dragon, that ancient serpent, who is the Devil and Satan, and bound him for a thousand years, ³and threw him into the pit, and shut it and sealed it over him, that he should deceive the nations no more, till the thousand years were ended. After that he must be loosed for a little while.

4 Then I saw thrones, and seated on them were those to whom judgment was committed. Also I saw the souls of those who had been beheaded for their testimony to Jesus and for the word of God, and who had not worshiped the beast or its image and had not received its mark on their foreheads or in their hands. They came to life, and reigned with Christ a thousand years. ⁵The rest of the dead did not come to life until the thousand years were ended. This is the first

resurrection. ⁶Blessed and holy is he who shares in the first resurrection! Over such the second death has no power, but they shall be priests of God and of Christ, and they shall reign with him a thousand years.

v. 1 . . . an angel . . . holding in his hand the key of the bottomless pit and a great chain . . . — Chapter and verse numbers are not inspired! The earliest Greek manuscripts of the New Testament have no numbers for chapters or verses; in fact, they have no paragraphs or punctuation. Although the English versions begin a new chapter here, we believe these first six verses are an inseparable part of the preceding context which deals with the defeat of the beast and false prophet. Since they are specifically and intimately allied with Satan in the last half of the Revelation (from chapter 12 through 20) as his tools to suppress the truth, their total defeat would unquestionably produce a devastating limitation on Satan's sphere of influence.

Revelation 20 is undoubtedly the most talked about chapter of the Bible. Many people, although they know *about* the chapter, have never analyzed the actual words of the chapter itself, in its context. Numerous books have been written on eschatology taking Revelation 20 out of its context and casting it into a conglomeration of texts from the Old Testament and New Testament. This chapter has been used as a basis for various theories of a literal thousand-year reign of Christ on the earth. The general theory, with variations among different eschatological schools, is briefly this:

1. Within a generation (40 years) from the time the Jews reoccupy the land of Palestine, Christ will begin His 1000-year reign.
2. At this time, the saved, both living and dead, will be "raptured" (caught up in the heavens to meet with Christ).
3. There will be seven years of tribulation on earth, while the "raptured" will be enjoying the "marriage supper of the Lamb."
4. After the seven years tribulation, Christ and His saints will come to earth and set up the kingdom of God. Christ will sit on the throne of David in the literal city of Jerusalem.
5. This will begin His 1000-year (exactly) millennial reign. The Jews will be converted to Christ; Old Testament worship (with modifications) will be restored; there will be peace, prosperity and an idealistic society. Those who do not wish to join this ideal society will be ruled over with a rod of iron, so that the tranquility of the millennium will not be disturbed.
6. At the end of exactly 1000 years, Satan will be loosed for a little while and make furious war upon the saints on earth. But Christ and His armies, engaging in literal combat against their foes, will defeat them at the literal site of Har-Meggido.

7. Following this, the wicked dead will be raised and, with the wicked remaining alive, judged and sent to hell, forever, while all the righteous will go to heaven forever.

We should note *carefully* the following about *this* text:

a. There is no mention whatever of the second coming of Christ.
b. There is no mention of a *bodily* resurrection. The New Testament, in other places, provides for the possibility of a resurrection other than and prior to the bodily resurrection.
c. There is no mention in this text of a literal reign of Christ on earth.
d. There is no mention in this text of a literal throne of David.
e. There is no mention in this text of literal Jerusalem or Palestine.
f. There is no mention in this text of the conversion of the Jews.
g. There is no mention in this text of the church being "raptured."

This vision begins as John sees an angel coming *down* from heaven. Whatever is to happen in this vision, is to connect immediately to what has happened in 19:1-21. It is not Christ coming down, but an angel sent down. This angel holds in his hand the key of the bottomless pit (Gr. *abussou,* abyss) and a great chain. This is symbolic language. Literally, in human experience, there is no such thing as a "bottomless pit." It could not be a pit if it had no bottom! Furthermore, how does one bind the spiritual, non-physical being Satan with a literal chain? If the thousand years are literal, so should the bottomless pit and the chain be literal. Evidently, the bottomless pit (abyss) is not the final destiny of Satan (the lake of fire and brimstone, 20:10). It is probably to be equated with *Hades* (Lk. 16:23), the *abyss* to which Jesus could send demons (Lk. 8:31), or *Tartarus, the nether darkness* (II Pet. 2:4; Jude 6) where demons reside. Peter says sinning angels are kept until judgment in *Tartarus* (not hell) in *chains* (the best Greek texts have the word for chains rather than pit), in *darkness.* Jude says the angels who abandoned their own (or proper) dwelling-place are kept in eternal *bonds* under *darkness for* the great day of judgment. This is the *abyss* to which the angel had the key—not the lake of fire and brimstone.

v. 2   And he seized the . . . Devil . . . and bound him for a thousand years . . . — The Greek word *ekratese* (from *krateo*) is translated *seized;* it has the idea in it of laying hold of in order to restrain, hinder, repress or keep under reserve (cf. its use in Mark 9:10; Lk. 24:16; Rev. 7:1). The angel laid hold of Satan in order to repress him, to bind him, and not, at this point to destroy him. It is interesting, to say the least, that God gave an angel power to lay hold of and bind Satan. Satan was "allowed" to make war on the saints through the beast (13:7)—now he is "bound."

That leads us to discuss the meaning of the word *bind* as it is used in this context respecting Satan. The Greek word is *edesen,* from *deo,* the same word used in Jude 6. We believe this text refers to a binding of Satan, to some extent, *as a result of the fall of the Roman empire* which took place in the fourth and fifth centuries, A.D. These are our reasons:

1. The very terms "binding" and "loosing" in the Bible are relative terms.
   a. God is Almighty. He is the only almighty being in existence.
   b. Satan, therefore, is *always bound* to some degree or other.
   c. Any "binding" or "loosing" Satan has is by God's sovereign permission, and according to God's purposed limitations.
   d. The record of Job's experience (Job ch. 1 and 2) shows God kept Satan in check ("bound") to some degree even in Old Testament times. God allowed certain freedoms with Job that Satan could not have otherwise taken (see also Zech. 3:1-5).

2. Revelation ch. 20 is *only one* of a number of passages in the Bible that deal with the "binding" of Satan and his hosts. Thus the passage must be interpreted in the light of the consistent teaching of these other scriptures. Revelation 20 must not be used to outweigh or contradict the cumulative statements on this subject from all other passages.
   a. Mk. 3:27; Mt. 12:25-29; Lk. 11:17-22 make it plain that Jesus claimed to be "binding" or restricting Satan's sphere of influence at His first coming, incarnate, into the world. Jesus proved His claim by casting out demons.
   b. Jesus claimed that His death and resurrection would "throw" (Gr. *ekblethesetai,* cast) out (Jn. 12:31) the pretended "ruler" of this world. In other words, Jesus' redemptive accomplishment at His first advent placed severe limitations on Satan's sphere of influence.
   c. Discussing the work to be accomplished by His death, resurrection, and return as the Holy Spirit, Jesus said (Jn. 16:11), "the ruler of this world (Satan) has been, and is being (Gr. *kekritai,* perfect tense verb), judged." When Satan was judged, he was handcuffed and restrained, but not then consigned to eternal incarceration.
   d. Paul writes in Hebrews 2:14-15 that Jesus shared the flesh and blood experience of humankind, died and rose again, that He "might cause to cease to operate the one having the power of death, that is the devil." The Greek verb *katargese* in this text means "to deprive of force, influence or power." Compare its use in I Cor. 2:6; II Tim. 1:10; I Cor. 15:24.
   e. Jesus said (Lk. 10:18) He *saw* (Gr. *etheoroun,* imperfect tense, meaning, "I was seeing") Satan as lightning (brilliant and instantaneous) falling out of heaven." This was said in connection with Jesus having given miraculous power over demons to the seventy disciples.

f. John writes (I Jn. 3:8) that the Son of God was revealed at his first advent to *undo* (Gr. *luse*) the works of the devil.

g. Paul writes (Col. 2:13-15) that Jesus' death and resurrection *disarmed* the rulers and authorities (spiritual hosts of wickedness) and triumphed over them publicly (historically).

h. Jesus, when He ascended, took *captivity* captive (Eph. 4:8-9).

i. Peter preached that the devil *could not hold* Jesus in the bonds of death (Acts 2:24).

j. Christians *overcome* the devil in the blood of Christ (Rev. 12:11).

3. From these passages it is clear that the "binding" of Satan was initiated at the onset of Jesus' earthly ministry and was *finished at the downfall of Rome.* Rome was the last of the four great empires which Daniel predicted would exert *all possible* human and Satanic power to erase Jehovah's work of redemption from the face of the earth. But Daniel also predicted that "during the days of those kings" (the fourth empire) God would establish a fifth universal kingdom (the church) which would overcome the last universal humanistic empire and continue forever (Dan. 2:44-45). Rome's military-politico, religio-idolatrous, and materialistic stranglehold (as the tool of Satan) on civilization is a classic example of what it was like before Satan was "bound" or limited by the ascendency of the Gospel (the spread of Christianity to the ends of the earth). The very fact that God could rescue His covenant people from the worst that men could do (Isa. 49:24-25) and from the worst that demonic powers could do (Dan. 10:13, 20) is proof even in the Old Testament that *God keeps Satan bound all the time* to the extent He wishes to have it so in order to carry out His redemptive work. The binding of Satan in Revelation 20 is *relative* to the needs of God's redemptive work in the New Testament age which is the last of the ages (I Cor. 10:11). Satan's final incarceration takes place at the end of the world and the final judgment.

To help us understand the relative binding of Satan someone has suggested we think of Satan as a vicious animal on a chain tied to a tree. In Old Testament times, the chain binding Satan to the tree was extended to great lengths and his sphere of influence to deceive and destroy was wide. In New Testament times, because sin has been atoned for historically, because forgiveness has been wrought, because life and immortality have been brought to light historically, God, through the Gospel of Christ, has *shortened* the chain binding the devil and has severely restricted the power the devil has to deceive the world. The devil is still active, like a roaring lion seeking whom he may devour. And though his chain (sphere of influence) is less than it was, anyone who steps within that sphere of influence will be deceived and devoured.

THIRTEEN LESSONS ON REVELATION

Another way to help understand the relative nature of Satan's present binding is to contemplate what widespread area of influence the devil had when the only verbal revelation of God before Christ was to a small nation of Jews surrounded by many nations of paganism. The whole world (except for isolated and exclusivistic Judaism) was held hostage by Satan in ignorance, superstition and fear. Most of ancient civilization was controlled, life and death, by one-world government. We introduce the following charts as aids to understanding this concept.

LIMITATIONS ("BINDING") IMPOSED UPON SATAN BY THE FORCE OF GOD'S TRUTH AND MERCY THROUGH THE HISTORICALLY-ACCOMPLISHED REDEMPTIVE WORK OF CHRIST, WRITTEN IN THE NEW TESTAMENT AND ESTABLISHED ALL OVER THE WORLD AFTER THE FALL OF THE ROMAN EMPIRE.

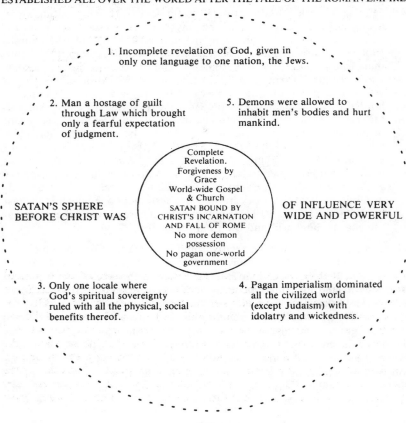

1. Incomplete revelation of God, given in only one language to one nation, the Jews.

2. Man a hostage of guilt through Law which brought only a fearful expectation of judgment.

5. Demons were allowed to inhabit men's bodies and hurt mankind.

Complete Revelation.
Forgiveness by Grace
World-wide Gospel & Church
SATAN BOUND BY CHRIST'S INCARNATION AND FALL OF ROME
No more demon possession
No pagan one-world government

SATAN'S SPHERE BEFORE CHRIST WAS

OF INFLUENCE VERY WIDE AND POWERFUL

3. Only one locale where God's spiritual sovereignty ruled with all the physical, social benefits thereof.

4. Pagan imperialism dominated all the civilized world (except Judaism) with idolatry and wickedness.

ANOTHER VIEW OF THE "BINDING" OF SATAN BY THE POWER OF GOD ACCOMPLISHED THROUGH CHRIST AND THE FALL OF THE ROMAN EMPIRE.

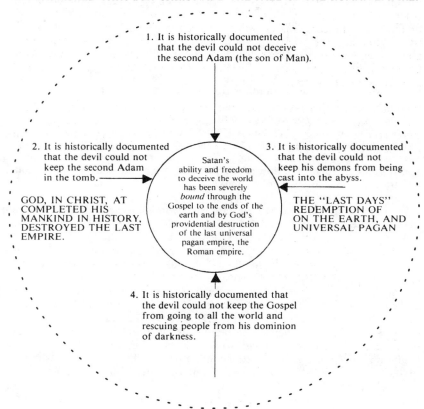

1. It is historically documented that the devil could not deceive the second Adam (the son of Man).

2. It is historically documented that the devil could not keep the second Adam in the tomb.

GOD, IN CHRIST, AT COMPLETED HIS MANKIND IN HISTORY, DESTROYED THE LAST EMPIRE.

Satan's ability and freedom to deceive the world has been severely *bound* through the Gospel to the ends of the earth and by God's providential destruction of the last universal pagan empire, the Roman empire.

3. It is historically documented that the devil could not keep his demons from being cast into the abyss.

THE "LAST DAYS" REDEMPTION OF ON THE EARTH, AND UNIVERSAL PAGAN

4. It is historically documented that the devil could not keep the Gospel from going to all the world and rescuing people from his dominion of darkness.

v. 3 . . . that he should deceive the nations no more, till the thousand years were ended . . . — We believe the thousand years during which Satan is "bound" symbolize the Christian age following the victory of God for His saints over Rome until the "little while" of Satan's loosing and the end of time. The thousand years started *after* the "time, times and half a time" of the near death of the two witnesses (see Rev. 11:3-13) and after the "time, times and half a time" of the woman's nourishing in the wilderness (see Rev. 12:13-17). The beast, false prophet and harlot (prompted by the old dragon, the devil), bring great tribulation upon the woman and her offspring for three and one half times. That comes to an end when these wicked forces are defeated and the devil is bound. Then begins the thousand year reign of the saints.

It is clear that the Bible often uses the number thousand (as well as many other numbers) in a figurative, symbolic sense. Surely, more than all the cattle on a thousand hills belong to God (cf. Psa. 50:10). Did the Lord multiply Israel exactly, or figuratively, a thousand times more than they are at the time of the exodus (see Deut. 1:10-11)? For other figurative uses of the number thousand see Job 9:3; 33:23; Psa. 90:4; Eccl. 6:6; 7:28; II Pet. 3:8. John's use of numbers throughout this Revelation is altogether figurative and symbolic—why should he suddenly select such a "round number" to predict something literal.

The "little while" when Satan is to be loosed here is the same as the loosing of Satan in 20:7. It is not the same as the "short time" of Rev. 12:12. The "short time" of 12:12 is the same as the three and one half times of 11:3-13 and 12:13-17, the time when Satan knows he has only a limited time left to use Rome as his tool to make war upon the woman and her offspring.

How does one account for the fact that Rome has been dead for *more* than one thousand years and yet Revelation 20 seems to indicate the final judgment follows immediately after the thousand-year binding of Satan and the death of Rome? The thousand years is simply symbolic of a vast, indeterminate, yet complete time known literally only to God. Why doesn't John tell us in detail what will transpire during this "thousand-year" binding of Satan, if it is predicting the time-span between the death of Rome and the end of time? Because it is not necessary for the faithfulness of any saint to have that information (Acts 1:7). The Old Testament prophets left centuries of blanks in their eschatology, just as John does here. Many of them jumped, eschatologically, from their own times (700 B.C.) to the beginning of the messianic age (the coming of the Christ and establishment of the church) with hardly any details of the intervening centuries being revealed at all.

This is a unique vehicle of prophetic, apocalyptic literature and is sometimes called "Shortened Perspective." It is the same perspective one gets as he approaches a mountain range on the horizon head-on. The mountains appear to be jammed up against one another without any space or valleys between them. Once the traveler arrives along side the mountain range, he sees that there are valleys in between. The prophet Joel furnishes us a classic illustration of shortened perspective. In Joel 2:27 the prophet is speaking of the blessings God gave the land after the locust plague of Joel's day. In Joel 2:28, the prophet leaps some 800 years into the future (from one verse to another) and predicts the messianic age and the establishment of the church. We have that on divine authority. Peter interpreted Joel 2:28 for us in Acts 2:16ff. Joel sums up what will happen in the messianic age from the establishment of the church until the "great and terrible day of the Lord" comes (final judgment) by saying there will be "signs in the heavens and on the earth" and whoever calls upon the name of the Lord during that time will be saved. Joel goes on, in chapter 3, to explain that what he has prophesied about the messianic age will be God's defeat of all the forces of worldliness and wickedness. All of Joel's prophecy from 2:28 through 3:21 is figurative and symbolic of the messianic age. But the important point is to see clearly how the prophet shortened the eschatological perspective by jumping over 800 years from one verse to the next.

This is precisely what John does in Revelation. He jumps over centuries and centuries of time (now more than 1500 centuries) from 20:6 to 20:7. The two charts at the end of this chapter will aid in understanding the "Shortened Perspective" concept.

The devil is caged (thrown into the abyss with the opening shut and sealed) so that he may *deceive* (Gr. *planese,* lead astray) the *nations* (Gr. *ethne,* ethnic groups) no more until the thousand years are ended. The devil's only power is that of falsehood (deception). He has no real authority. Jesus said the devil has "nothing to do with the truth and there is no truth in him . . . he is a liar and the father of lies" (Jn. 8:44). The devil's primary goal is to deceive the world into believing that he is the ruler of this world. The recurring theme of this book of Revelation centers in Satan's false claim to sovereignty in the universe. Deception is really the only power Satan has. This whole book of Revelation is a refutation of that deception. That claim is totally and empirically refuted in the historical work of Christ's redemption. Essentially, Satan was bound when Christ was raised from the dead and proved that "all authority was given to him in heaven and on earth" (Mt. 28:18).

John uses the term "nations" in the sense of whole nations. After the fall of the Roman empire with her military and economic powers broken, whole nations could no longer be deceived and led into idolatry because the Gospel freed many people in every nation, tribe, tongue and race. Satan no longer had the awesome, apparently invincible power of Rome to use to deceive the whole world into believing that demons and idols and emperors should be worshiped as sovereign. Once the eyewitnessed testimony that Jesus Christ had conquered death permeated the world, people from every nation turned away from allegiance to satanic falsehood unto the truth of God. This principle is still true today. Because there is no universal imperialism ruling the whole world today, Satan cannot use such a tool to deceive the nations. Large segments of the world are free today only because the Word of God is believed and honored there. In many nations today truth has the upper hand and not falsehood. And even in nations today ruled by unbelieving dictators, there are millions who refuse to be deceived by the lie of Satan that he rules the world. Of course, in every nation after the fall of Rome, as well as today, millions of individuals believed the lie of the devil. They were, and are, willingly deceived (cf. II Thess. 2:11ff.). But the whole world is not deceived as it was during the unchallenged rule of the Roman empire.

It should be noted that this text never says that the church of Christ was deceived. Before Christ came and instituted his kingdom of truth, practically the whole world had joined Rome in idolatry. The church remained for a while confined, with a few exceptions, to the land of Palestine. The "nations," therefore, were being deceived by Satan. Then the great apostle to the Gentiles began invading the "nations" (Asia Minor, Greece and Italy) with the truth of God. Thousands of Paul's converts also took the Gospel to the ends of civilization. Eventually, the veil of Satanic deception began to fall away from the eyes of those in the "nations" and the empire of darkness began to crumble. When Rome fell Satan's power to deceive the whole world was severely restricted—Satan was bound.

E.A. McDowell says succinctly in, *The Meaning and Message of Revelation,* pg. 190, "Let it be repeated that this is not the termination of Satan's power; he has not been cast into the lake of fire; he is confined for a 'thousand years' to the abyss, the home of the demons. In the vision John teaches that with the failure of the Caesars to make Christianity subordinate to the imperial rule, the reign of Christ as King of kings and Lord of lords in history was confirmed. . . . So far as the span of history which stretches from the triumph of Christianity in the first and second centuries to our time is concerned, we may say that no instance is on record of a general challenge to the rule of Christ paralleling the challenge made to that rule by the empire of Rome which ruled almost all the civilized world."

v. 4 Then I saw thrones, and seated on them . . . the souls of those who had been beheaded . . . — This describes only one group of people; believers who had been martyred during Rome's attempt to stamp out Christianity. They are *such as* (Gr. *hoitines,* a relative pronoun) those who had not worshiped the beast or its image. The Greek perfect participle *pepelekismenon,* from *pelekus,* "axe," indicates a continual slaughter of Christians. These are the "two witnesses" Satan and Rome believed they had eradicated (Rev. 11:7-10), but God raised them up (Rev. 11:11-13)! Rome died but these saints came to life! The visionary, figurative (*not* bodily) "resurrection" of the martyred saints symbolized the resurrection of the kingdom of Christ (the church) on earth and its sovereignty rather than Rome's. John does not see Christians in bodies living and reigning— he sees souls. It is a vision—it is symbolic—it represents a principle. At Rome's defeat, the sovereignty of Christ as King of kings and Lord of lords was proven, and those martyrs seen in John's vision as coming to life and judging symbolized that Christ's kingdom would come to life, defeat and judge Rome.

The Greek phrase, *kai ezesan* in verse 4, literally, reads, "and they lived." Satan and Rome tried to deceive the world into believing that martyred Christians and Christianity were dead forever, while the Empire would live and be enthroned forever. Christ is revealing, through John, that those martyred Christians, faithful unto death, had not died but had really come to life and, furthermore, the kingdom to which they belonged reigned and judged the world—not the empire of Rome. This revelation of the martyred saints alive and reigning is not intended to single them out as a group holier than other Christians or as a group appointed to positions higher than others. The vision is designed to make a sharp distinction or contrast to "the rest of the dead."

The "rest of the dead" (the pagan contemporaries of the Christian martyrs) were those *unbelievers* who had died during the same tribulations of empire in which the Christians died. The unbelieving dead did not live during the thousand years—they remained forever dead. The second death claimed them.

v.5   The rest of the dead did not come to life . . . — The sentence here in Greek reads, *oi loipoi ton nekron ouk ezesan achri telesthe ta chilia ete.* The Greek word *achri* is usually translated *until,* but may be translated *during.* The Greek word *telesthe* is usually translated *ended,* but may also be translated *completion.* The rest of the dead, during the 1000 years, did not come to life. This would emphasize the absolute difference between the martyred Christians and dead pagans who worshiped the beast and the false prophet. If "the rest of the dead" is to refer to Christians, we must assume that John visualizes a "special" resurrection for a favored class, and at the same time assume that hosts of Christians who did not experience martyrdom by Rome are to be exposed to the possibility of suffering the "second death."

Contrary to the devil's lie, those *faithful* to Christ and slain came to life and reigned. The "rest of the dead" never did. They came to the "second death." The Greek word translated "rest" is *loipos.* It may also be translated "other" (cf. Lk. 8:11; Acts 17:9; Rom. 1:13; II Cor. 12:13; 13:2; Gal. 2:13; Phil. 1:13; 4:3). The "other" dead are the dead of another kind— they are the pagan dead. The "rest" of Rev. 19:21 slain by the Word of God. These apparently went with the beast and false prophet to the lake of fire.

That which the Christian martyrs experienced is called symbolically "the first resurrection." It is *not* the bodily resurrection. There will be only one bodily resurrection. That is the plain teaching of the rest of the New Testament. John's vision of these "resurrected" *souls* may be explained as that which takes place when the soul of every faithful believer departs the dead body and goes to be with the Lord. When the Christian's body dies, the soul of the Christian is "raised" to be with Christ, and is conscious and alive

THIRTEEN LESSONS ON REVELATION

with the Lord (cf. Phil. 1:21-23; Lk. 23:43; Lk. 16:19-31). When the unforgiven sinner's body dies, his soul dies the "second death" and is eternally separated from the Lord in torments.

While this "first resurrection" must, according to sound hermeneutical principles and the immediate context, apply primarily to the saints martyred during the Roman empire, it reveals and symbolizes that the gates of Hades (death) never prevails over the Lord's church. The New Testament also speaks of the act of becoming a Christian as a "resurrection" from being dead in sin (cf. Jn. 5:24-25; Jn. 5:26-29; Rom. 6:12-13; Eph. 2:4-7; Col. 2:13; I Jn. 3:14). When people believe and obey Christ they "have passed from death unto life." Jesus talked about a "first" and "second" resurrection in John 5:24-25 and 5:26-29, respectively. The "resurrection" spoken of in John 5:24-25 is present tense and takes place at belief and baptism into Christ (the new birth). The "resurrection" spoken of in John 5:26-29 is future and takes place at the resurrection of the physical body from the grave.

Nowhere in the New Testament are we led to believe there will be more than one bodily resurrection. This "first resurrection" of the martyred saints must, therefore, be only of the soul and revealed simply to symbolize the never-dying nature of Christ's kingdom. "First resurrection" and "they came to life" are simply synonymous terms. The vision is graphic symbolism —it is not declaring some complex, detailed eschatological schedule for multiple bodily resurrections and multiple judgments. Symbolic "resurrections" are not uncommon to Scripture. The Old Testament prophets symbolized Israel's return from the captivities as a "resurrection" (cf. Isa. 26:19; Hosea 13:14; Ezek. 37:1-14). Daniel was told that during the troubled times of Antiochus IV there would be a "resurrection" of many Jews to faith and loyalty to God's word (Dan. 12:1-4). The seemingly dead "witnesses" were "raised up" by God (Rev. 11:11-13). Mothers, during the Syrian persecutions under Antiochus Epiphanes, "received" their dead sons in symbolic resurrection because of their faith in God (Heb. 11:35).

The saints martyred by Rome not only symbolized the perpetual life of God's kingdom, they also symbolized its perpetual reign. Daniel had predicted that at the death of the "fourth beast" (Rome), the warred-upon saints would reign and judge (Dan. 7:19-27). John's vision is a fulfillment of Daniel's prophecy. Christians are said to reign with Christ as they remain faithful to him on this earth (cf. Eph. 2:6; II Tim. 2:12; Rom. 5:17; Rev. 5:10). They are also said to have certain judgments committed to them (cf. Mt. 7:1-20; I Cor. 5:9-13; Heb. 11:7; I Cor. 6:1-6).

v. 6   Blessed and holy is he who shares in the first resurrection . . . — Those Christians who were slain for their faith by Rome are completely and finally separated from the wickedness and pain and trials they endured so faithfully. They are alive where everything is happiness and holiness. Over these the "second death" has no authority (power). The second death is defined as "being thrown in the lake of fire" (Rev. 20:14; see also Rev. 2:11; 21:8). The "second death" is eternal separation from God and incarceration in eternal torments—it is hell. The Bible does not teach annihilation of the wicked dead (cf. Mt. 25:46), but *eternal* (Gr. *aionion,* everlasting) punishment. But condemnation and punishment has no authority to claim the Christian. The authoritative Word of God claims the Christian for blessedness and holiness (cf. Rom. 8:31-39; II Cor. 4:16-18; I Pet. 1:3-9). These Christians who came to life by coming out of the great tribulation are also declared to be ministering to God as priests. Again, that is an experience to be shared in an anticipatory way by Christians even while they are on earth (cf. I Pet. 2:4, 5, 9; Rev. 1:6; 5:10; etc.).

Careful contextual analysis of this highly symbolic and figurative passage, and studied comparison with what the rest of the New Testament teaches on resurrection and judgment, should bring the reader to a sensible and harmonious interpretation. It goes without saying that the Holy Spirit would not contradict himself. He would not reveal a doctrine of *multiple bodily* resurrections in Revelation 20:1-6 and then contradict that by declaring in the rest of the New Tesatment that there is *only one bodily* resurrection. We are constrained to quote at length here from *Worthy Is The Lamb,* by Ray Summers, pgs. 205-206:

No basis is found in the symbolism (of this passage) for a literal reign of a thousand-year reign of the saints with Christ on earth either before or after this second coming. No basis is found in the symbolism for multiple resurrections and judgments. Theological systems which have majored on a literal interpretation of these verses and have interpreted the clear teachings of the New Testament in the light of the obscure have found several resurrections and several judgments taught. They find a resurrection of believers at what they call the "rapture," when Christ comes to call his people out of the earth before the great tribulation which is also interpreted as future. Seven years later, at the "revelation" (the second stage of the program of the Lord's second coming), they find a resurrection for those who have become believers and died during the period between the "rapture" and the "revelation." According to their system, people are converted and die during the millennium which is set up at the "revelation." So there must be a resurrection of this group at the close of the earthly millennium when the heavenly order is set up. If the wicked dead are raised at a separate judgment, the system has at least four (perhaps more) resurrections. In similar fashion they find multiple judgments ranging from two (one before and one after the millennium) to seven, according to the particular interpreter.

This is pure fantasy read into a literal interpretation of these highly symbolical verses. By the "proof-text" approach one can prove practically any proposition by perverted use of Scripture passages. When the entire New Testament is studied, it teaches *one* general resurrection (of both good and evil) and *one* general judgment (of both good and evil), both of which are directly related to the second coming of Christ which brings to an end this world order and ushers in the eternal heavenly order.

The "resurrection" of the souls of the martyrs not only symbolizes that the kingdom of Christ defeats Rome and reigns in sovereignty, it also guarantees, symbolically, the perpetuation of their "priestly" work in mediating the messianic blessings of salvation throughout the world during the "thousand years" (Gospel age) (see Rom. 15:16).

The Bridegroom (Messiah-Warrior) has ridden forth into the arena of history to defend his Bride against the beast, the false prophet, and the harlot. John sees these enemies of the Bride captured and thrown into the lake of fire, along with the "rest" of the pagan dead. Satan, with his most powerful allies ever destroyed, is "bound" for a thousand years; his power to deceive is severely restricted. The martyred church is "resurrected" to life, reigns and minsters for the "thousand years." Death cannot prevail against it. Others (pagans) who died did not come to life; they came to the second death. This is John's answer to the challenge of the Caesars to the sovereignty of the Lamb—the defeat of the Roman empire and the victory of the church. Rome did fall! The church did live on and spread throughout a larger world than the Caesars ever dreamed existed. God won—as he always has!

APPREHENSION AND APPLICATION:

1. Why was heaven so joyful about the fall of the harlot? Would heaven rejoice today if the political powers persecuting the church fell? Would you?
2. Do you understand why God acts the way the Bible portrays him acting? What do you do about it?
3. When did "the marriage of the Lamb" take place? Do you think of your relationship to Christ as intimate and binding as a marriage? What does that require of you?
4. When does the "marriage supper of the Lamb" take place? Is the Christian experience like a festivity to you—or is it more like being in prison?
5. Whom should you worship in light of the prophecies of Revelation? Would you worship an angel if one appeared suddenly in your congregation?

6. Who is the rider on the white horse? What does he ride forth to do? What kind of warfare does he fight? Are you in his army? What is your weapon? Is it powerful enough to do the job?
7. Is the scene depicting vultures eating the flesh of dead bodies to be understood literally or figuratively? Would Christ ever lead an army to such a literal slaughter?
8. Who was the "beast" and the "false prophet"? Where were they thrown? Who else was slain with them? What is having "the mark" of the beast?
9. Why should Revelation 20:1-6 be tied inseparably to the end of chapter 19?
10. Name some events, said to be taught in 20:1-6, which are not there. Where do you think material comes from for the many millennial theories?
11. When was the devil "bound"? How was he "bound"? Do you think the devil is "bound" now more than he was in ancient times?
12. Is the devil completely inoperative today? How do you resist him?
13. What are the "thousand years"? Why doesn't John tell us what is to happen during the "thousand years"? What is "shortened perspective"?
14. What did the devil deceive the nations about? Just how much power does the devil have? Is he really the god of this world?
15. Who are those beheaded souls John saw? Why was he given a vision of them? Does John's vision mean anything to you?
16. Who were the "rest of the dead"? Why didn't they come to life?
17. What is the "first" resurrection? Is there another resurrection? What? When? Who will participate in it?
18. Does the "second death" have any power over those believers not martyred during the Roman empire? What is the "second death"?
19. Has all this apocalyptic imagery done anything for your faith and Christian growth? Should it have? Didn't John begin the book by saying, "blessed are those who read and keep the words of this prophecy"?

THE BINDING OF SATAN AND THE "THOUSAND YEARS" IN PERSPECTIVE

by Paul T. Butler

The "nations" deceived
by the lie of the devil that
he rules the universe.

30 A.D. Christ crucified and risen from
the dead. The devil's lie proven false.
Satan "judged," "cast out," "power
destroyed."

The "binding of Satan" in process. The Gospel beginning to
free people out of every "nation" from the devil's lie and
bring about the fall of pagan Rome.

100 A.D. The book of Revelation completed.

Pagan Rome's deception (the tool of
Satan) increasingly being overcome by the
Gospel.

Revelation
1:1 through
20:6 decribes
symbolically
the "1000
years."

313 A.D. Constantine; Edict of Toleration.
The "beast" (Rome) essentially defeated.
Christianity no longer an illegal religion.
Gospel reaching to the ends of civilization.
The "thousand years" begin. It includes the
whole Gospel age until the end of time.

Satan is bound. The "thousand years" continue. Martyred
saints reign with Christ, symbolically raised to life in the
"first resurrection." These martyrs, judged by Rome, now
become judges. These martyrs, killed for not worshiping the
emperor, become priests serving the true God.

Apocalyptic method of
"Shortened Perspective."
Two widely separated
points of eschatological
time noted in succeeding
verses of Scripture with
no detailed revelation of
the chronological interval.

Revelation
20:7 through
22:21

End of the "thousand years" Date unknown!
The "little season" when Satan is loosed. Length unknown!
The second coming of Christ. Final judgment
of the world. Eternal heaven and hell.

110

APOCALPTIC METHOD OF
"SHORTENED PERSPECTIVE" AS APPLIED TO
REVELATION 1:1—20:6 AND 20:7—22:21

by Paul T. Butler

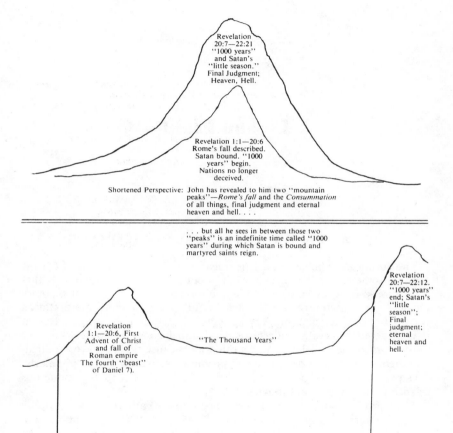

Revelation
20:7—22:21
"1000 years"
and Satan's
"little season."
Final Judgment;
Heaven, Hell.

Revelation 1:1—20:6
Rome's fall described.
Satan bound. "1000
years" begin.
Nations no longer
deceived.

Shortened Perspective: John has revealed to him two "mountain peaks"—*Rome's fall* and the *Consummation* of all things, final judgment and eternal heaven and hell. . . .

. . . but all he sees in between those two "peaks" is an indefinite time called "1000 years" during which Satan is bound and martyred saints reign.

Revelation
20:7—22:12.
"1000 years"
end; Satan's
"little
season";
Final
judgment;
eternal
heaven and
hell.

Revelation
1:1—20:6, First
Advent of Christ
and fall of
Roman empire
The fourth "beast"
of Daniel 7).

"The Thousand Years"

Satan bound for "1000
years," the nations no
longer deceived.

Lesson Eight
(20:7-15)

THE LAMB AND THE SPIRITUAL CONSUMMATION

The author *does* believe in an historical, literal, second advent of Christ. Perhaps some readers had begun, to this point, to wonder. But, you see, that is because so many eschatological presuppositions and so much contemporary eschatological literature insists on a literal, pre-millennial interpretation for the book of Revelation. Any hermeneutical approach contrary to that is considered "liberal, modernistic, and unbelieving." People who have *never studied* the Revelation think this way because the literal, pre-millennial theory has been propogated and promoted so widely and so popularly. The pre-millennial view has provided a fertile seed-crop for numerous science-fiction books and movies.

The Lord is coming again. But not according to any schedule set up by a literal interpretation of Revelation 20:1-6 (plus "X" amount of data from Old Testament and the rest of the New Testament thrown together). As noted in the previous lesson, John leaps over more than one thousand years from Revelation 20:6 to 20:7. From one verse to the next there is a "gap" of a symbolic "thousand years." With Revelation 20:7, therefore, we begin from a whole new reference point in time. The prophet has "shortened his perspective." From the victory of the church over the

Roman empire (beginning of the "thousand years"), he focuses immediately down to the future to the second coming of Christ and the final judgment. But does the Bible tell us any times or signs as to when that will be? No! Who knows when the Lord will come again? No one—not even the angels nor the Son! The emphasis we look for, then, in the remainder of the book is not on times or seasons, but on meaning and application for our lives now.

Destiny of Satan (20:7-10)

7 And when the thousand years are ended, Satan will be loosed from his prison ⁸and will come out to deceive the nations which are at the four corners of the earth, that is, Gog and Magog, to gather them for battle; their number is like the sand of the sea. ⁹And they marched up over the broad earth and surrounded the camp of the saints and the beloved city; but fire came down from heaven and consumed them, ¹⁰and the devil who had deceived them was thrown into the lake of fire and sulphur where the beast and the false prophet were, and they will be tormented day and night for ever and ever.

v. 7 And when the thousand years are ended . . . — As noted in the previous lesson, we believe the "thousand years" not to be intended literally. It represents a long, complete (as long as God's purposes need) time beginning with the victory of the Lamb over Rome. Since the Lamb's victory over Rome is already more than a thousand years old, we should not understand the number to be literal. The main concern of this passage is not time anyway, but the *revelation* of Satan's ultimate defeat and the absolute victory of the saints of God. If the Lamb reveals victory, who needs a time schedule? It is as good as done! He is the Faithful and True Word of God.

When the purpose of God no longer needs severe restrictions upon Satan (completion of a "thousand years") God will loose Satan to some extent. It is clear, as we have already noted, that Satan is *always bound* in some relative sense; Satan is never completely free from the sovereignty of God and able to stand as an equal to God. So, whatever "loosing" Satan may enjoy, it is not complete or full. In Rev. 20:3 it was stated Satan would be loosed for "a little while" (Gr. *mikron chronon,* micro-time). What is a "little time"? Looked at from God's perspective, it may involve centuries of man's time. In Revelation 12:7-12, after the devil's defeat in "the heavenly" and his being cast down upon the "earth," we learned the devil came in great wrath for he knew his time was "short." The "short time" there meant the 350 years (more or less) the devil still had to use the Roman empire against the church of the Lamb, (see comments there). The devil learned that from Daniel's prophecies. It must be frustrating for him to know that God holds the "times" of the devil in his sovereign hands so completely. Whatever the devil does and when he does it are all permitted by God. And when God gets ready to imprison the devil forever, he will be imprisoned—no matter how wide his influence in the world and no matter how circumstances may appear to the world.

v. 8 . . . will come out to deceive the nations . . . — The spirit of Christian martyrdom and missions overcame Satan and he was bound by the Word of God. The church survived and conquered Rome, (Satan's greatest tool), through the spirit of faithfulness to the Lamb that caused them to "love not their lives even unto death" (12:11). When such a spirit of devotion and discipleship no longer distinguishes God's people, the restraining power of Satan is gone; Satan is loosed (relatively) once more; his work of *deception* (Gr. *planesai* to lead astray) will have room once again to flourish. It is significant to note that the fundamental attack of Satan is to deceive. He has no other power. More deception is accomplished by lies and false teachings than by brute physical force.

Satan will find himself loosed apparently at some point in time future to today. A time will come, apparently, when the whole world will appear to be on the side of Satan and the church about to be surrounded or besieged by a world in the throes of deception. Satan no longer has one great political power to use, but he does deceive millions to his cause from all sources, from nations all over the globe ("four corners of the earth"). This is *not* Armageddon—that was Rome's fall (see comments 16:14-16). It is the same war, but a different battle. It is the war that started before Eden when the devil and other angels, trapped by pride, left their appointed places. For purposes known only to God, he has allowed that war to rage through the historical centuries of mankind. The spiritual perfection of man is undoubtedly one reason God has allowed the war to continue. But during the war God has accomplished so many undeniable and unimpeachable victories over his adversary that ultimate conquest is a foregone conclusion. The most emphatic of these victories (and the one to which all others point) is the victory of God's Son at the cross and the empty tomb.

John appropriates the imagery for this great struggle from the Old Testament prophet Ezekiel (ch. 38-39). The battle of God's people with "Gog and Magog" is symbolic in the prophet Ezekiel and not literal. Although Ezekiel's prophecy is predicting an actual struggle between the forces of evil and God's covenant people, the *language* used must be symbolic because a literal interpretation of Ezekiel's language would involve physical impossibilities. Ezekiel shows that "Gog and Magog" symbolized all the heathen enemies of God's people from the time of the former prophets to the Roman empire by identifying "God and Magog" as ". . . he of whom I (God) spake in old time by my servants the prophets of Israel, that prophesied in those days for many years that I would bring these against them . . ." (Ezek. 38:17). No prophet before Ezekiel ever named "Gog and Magog" but they did speak of enemies from different "corners" of the world coming against Israel and they predicted God would defeat them. We believe that although the initial aim of Ezekiel's "Gog and Magog" prophecy may be predicting the struggle of faithful Jews against Antiochus IV (171-165 B.C.) and their victory over him, the ultimate goal of Ezekiel's prophecy is the victory of the Messianic kingdom over the worst attack that all the combined forces of evil and the world could bring against it. That would be the assassination of the Messiah himself and the attempt to stamp out his church. That is "Gog and Magog" of Ezekiel! This interpretation would fit into the whole symbolic Messianic picture portrayed by Ezekiel's glorious Temple, glorious land, glorious "terumah," glorious priesthood and kingdom (Ezek. ch. 40-48).

We believe John is using "Gog and Magog" simply as symbols to give his readers some idea (from the Old Testament imagery) of how wide spread and intense this last assault of the forces of evil will be. John's use of Old Testament imagery would be like a secret code to the "uninitiated" (heathen who did not know the Old Testament), but would certainly provide a graphic picture for the believers. The main point John wishes to communicate is the complete *victory* of God over the devil on behalf of his covenant people (the church). That is exactly what Ezekiel was portraying for the Old Covenant people in his vision of "Gog and Magog." The two prophecies form an interesting parallel. That is because the Old Testament is typical, in practically all its historical events, of the New Testament. This parallel is best seen in the chart below:

"Gog and Magog" symbolizing all enemies of God's covenant people making one final drive to stamp them out in Antiochus IV . . . but God defeats in the miracle of the Cross and Resurrection and establishment of the church.

| Captivity of Jews in Babylon | Release from captivity, long period of relative peacefulness while God's forces "patrol" the earth (cf. Zech. 1:11ff.). Satan rebuked (Zech. 3:1-10) etc. | First Advent of Christ |
| Church under tribulation of "Babylon" Rome | Fall of Rome. Binding of Satan. Church given relative peacefulness while God keeps Satan in check, and the Gospel makes it impossible for Satan to deceive the nations to the extent he had before. | Second Advent of Christ |

Satan and power of deception allowed to make one final, short drive to seduce the church. Satan uses "Gog and Magog" (unbelieving men from all over the world). God defeats this attempt with miraculous power.

THIRTEEN LESSONS ON REVELATION

This is definitely a spiritual battle. It is a battle of the mind. There is not one word of any physical weaponry being used here. The devil is smart enough to know that making martyrs of Christians by force, persecution and bloodshed is definitely a losing battle. He knows that the only sure way to conquer men is to deceive them. The Christian's warfare is mental and spiritual (cf. Eph. 6:10ff.; II Cor. 10:3ff.). This is a great mass of mankind scattered all over the world ("Gog and Magog") and not just one "antichrist" located in the Middle East or Russia. And they do not, of their own planning, call upon the devil to help them—they are, in fact, *deceived* by the devil into assisting him. Just how and when this is done John does not elaborate.

vv. 9-10   And they . . . surrounded the camp of the saints . . . but fire came down from heaven and consumed them . . . — John does not mean to say that all the Christians from all over the world will be gathered at one geographical location and physically surrounded by the devil and those he has deceived to assist him. He simply means to say the church-universal will be *besieged by deception.* The "camp of the saints" is another way of saying "the church" (cf. Heb. 13:11, 13). The "beloved city" is also the church ("Zion," see Heb. 12:22; Gal. 4:26). The church of Christ could very well find itself at this time (whenever it is to be) existing in a society much like that described in Romans 1:18-32! What the church (individual Christians) must guard against are the powers of deception—false teaching, carnality and pride.

Whenever and whatever the nature of the struggle, God is set to deliver his church. And, as he destroyed the enemy Anitochus IV "without human hand" (Dan. 8:25), so he will deliver his church by divine intervention. Heaven consumes the enemies of God's saints. The divine hand of God defeated the world and delivered his redemptive nation in the death and resurrection of Christ. Power from on high established the church and protects the church even now. The gates of death cannot prevail against it. So, in the last analysis, God will consummate that deliverance by divine action direct from heaven. The church need not fear the worst the devil and his deceived millions may do; the church needs only to be faithful and God will deliver her just as surely as he delivered Jesus Christ from the tomb.

At the same time God delivers his church by direct divine action, he will also banish the devil (with those he has deceived) completely and forever into the lake of fire and brimstone. The devil will never again be released or loosed—not even relatively! The devil's incarceration in hell (where the beast and false prophet and those with their mark have already gone) is *forever* (Gr. *eis tous aionas ton aionon,* or, "unto the ages of the ages"). The word for *torment* in Greek is *basanizo* and means abrasiveness, struggle, torture. The words *aionas* and *aionon* are used to describe the existence of God (forever) and the duration of the saints in heaven (forever). We

116

assume the torment of the devil and the unsaved will last as long as God lasts. If there is to be a complete annihilation of the wicked, we cannot find it in the Bible.

Contrary to popular opinion, Satan does not rule over hell! He is an inmate and is to be tortured right along with all those deceived by him. He is no longer a *pretended* ruler; he never was a real ruler. He is now pictured as an eternal rebel-sufferer. He controls nothing, but is himself controlled. God created and reserved this eternal prison for the devil and his angels (cf. II Pet. 2:17; Jude 13; Mt. 25:41). It is the devil's inevitable destiny, and the destiny of all those who choose to trust his deceptions against God.

Destiny of Sinners (20:11-15)

11 Then I saw a great white throne and him who sat upon it; from his presence earth and sky fled away, and no place was found for them. ¹²And I saw the dead, great and small, standing before the throne, and books were opened. Also another booktwas opened, which is the book of life. And the dead were judged by what was written in the books, by what they had done. ¹³And the sea gave up the dead in it, Death and Hades gave up the dead in them, and all were judged by what they had done. ¹⁴Then Death and Hades were thrown into the lake of fire. This is the second death, the lake of fire; ¹⁵and if any one's name was not found written in the book of life, he was thrown into the lake of fire.

v. 11   **Then I saw a great white throne and him who sat upon it . . .** — Remember, this is a vision. There is no literal throne in heaven made of wood or gold. It is simply John describing spiritual realities in terms of the limitations of human experience. The throne was "great" and "white" to symbolize Absolute Sovereignty and Absolute Wisdom and Righteousness. This is the throne of God; it is not the throne of any human judge whether it be Caesar or some other human potentate. Any judgments issuing from this "great white" throne will be omnipotent and omniscient. There will be no mistakes, no deviations and no appeals from it. This judgment will be perfect, final and forever.

We have already dealt with the telescope-effect John is placing on history in this section. We have called it "shortened perspective." All earlier judgments in the book of Revelation dealt with the fall of the Roman empire. All through history God judges and destroys nations and forces which oppose his redemptive program in time and history. At the consummation of time and history God will judge each individual who has ever lived on earth. That is the judgment here depicted. John skips in time from the fall of Rome (20:1-6) to the second coming of Christ, the incarceration of

Satan, and the final judgment (20:7-15) without telling what transpires between these two events except for the "loosing of Satan for a little while." Apparently John is expecting his readers to be encouraged by the fall of the seemingly invincible Rome that the consummation of all history was just as certain. Most certainly John is given this revelation of the consummation to encourage the saints of all ages that eventually and inexorably, justice will be done: wickedness will be eternally punished and righteousness eternally rewarded.

Who is sitting upon this great white throne? John does not say. Scriptures could be cited for both God and Jesus (the Lamb) (see the following verses: Rev. 16:5, 7; 18:8, 20; 19:2; 19:11; John 5:22, 27; Matt. 25:31ff.; Acts 17:31; Rom. 2:16; 14:10; II Cor. 5:10; Rev. 22:1). Perhaps it is both the Father and Son in One Person (see Jn. 10:30; 14:10). Whatever the case the judgment will be that in which both Father and Son are participating and agreeing.

Creation will disappear when God appears to confront it. The Greek word *ephugen* is translated *fled* away (the English word *fugutive* comes from that Greek word). Physical matter has no power to exist in the presence of pure spirituality. Physical matter is transitory, temporary, and when its Creator decides it is no longer useful to him, it takes its leave. This corrupted creation will not stand in the awful presence of perfect holiness. When it comes to a "face down" corrupted creation must disappear. The Greek word *prosopou* is translated *presence* but literally means *face*. God told Moses no man could see God's face and live (Ex. 33:20). Peter writes that at the great judgment day of God the heavens will pass away with a great rushing sound, and the *elements* (Gr. *stoicheion,* the rudimentary elements of matter) will be dissolved with fire and the earth and the works that are upon it will be burned up (II Pet. 3:10). This present creation was declared futile by God (Rom. 8:18-25) so God's plan is to destroy it immediately at the time of judgment and to create a new place for spiritually minded followers of the Lamb.

v. 12   And the dead were judged by what was written in the books . . . — John now sees in a vision the dead standing before the throne of God for final judgment. This is all the dead from Adam to the end of the world (cf. Jn. 5:28; Acts 24:15; Ro. 2:6, 16; II Cor. 5:10). It is both small (non-celebrities) and great (celebrities). It will include the supposed powerful dead of the world (Caesars, Hitlers, Stalins) and the weak. Those who are alive at the coming of Christ in judgment will be there too for the living will not go to eternity before the dead go (cf. I Thess. 4:15-18) or vice versa. John's vision of this mass of total humanity "standing" is to be understood of figurative terms. Perhaps God will have already given all humanity celestial or immortal bodies designed to fit their specific destinies. Will God judge all humanity in one huge audience or will he have all human beings stand or appear before him one by one? We do not know for sure, but the latter seems to fit II Cor. 5:10.

What are the books? God does not need literal "books" or ledgers to keep a record of men's deeds. His mind is omniscient and infallible. "Books" is a word of human language to symbolize that every deed, every thought, every secret (Rom. 2:16) of every man is known and remembered by God. Now the Bible is clear that God can and will forget some things. God will "blot out" and "remember no more" the sins of men who have trusted in the atoning death of Jesus Christ on their behalf (cf. Psa. 51:1, 9; Micah 7:19; Isa. 43:25; 44:22; Acts 3:19; Heb. 8:12). Those who are in the book of life, also known as the Lamb's book of life, will not be judged by what is in the same "books" in which sinner's deeds are recorded. The sinner, who stubbornly insists on attempting to be justified by some law of human works, will be judged by that criterion. All who are will be weighed and found wanting (Dan. 5:24-28; Rom. 2:12; James 2:10). There is none righteous without the substitution of Christ's death (Rom. 3:10-31); all have sinned. And by law, shall no flesh be justified (Gal. 2:16). The sinful dead will be judged (sentenced and executed) according to what they have done—and what they have not done (James 4:17). The standard God will use is perfection. Anyone not found perfect, sinless, justified, will be unfit to abide in the presence of a perfect, sinless Father. Anyone who has refused the gracious offer of sinlessness through faith in Christ will be declared in rebellion and not eligible for citizenship under the rule of Christ.

Those who have accepted the atonement and justification provided by Christ through an exercise of their faith, will be found written in the book of life. This book of life is mentioned a number of times in the Bible (cf. Ex. 32:32ff.; Psa. 69:28; Isa. 4:3; Mal. 3:16; Lk. 10:20; Phil. 4:3; Rev. 3:5; 13:8; 17:8; 21:27). The ones who have washed their sins away by accepting God's gracious offer of the death of His Son in their place will be judged according to the good they have done. And although they will have forgotten some of the good things they have done (Mt. 25:37-40), the Lord will not forget (Heb. 6:10). There is some indication that the Lord will reward His servants according to the exercise of their faithfulness in managing what he entrusted to them on earth (cf. Lk. 16:10-12; 19:11-27; Matt. 25:14-30; I Cor. 3:10-15). All people who have ever lived will appear before the judgment throne of God, saint and sinner. The saint will appear to hear the acclaim of the God who promised him vindication for his faithfulness in suffering, his trust in Christ's merit for him, and his willingness to obey the revealed will of God when it seemed impossible, unpopular and costly. There it will be declared of the saint, by the Great Creator and Redeemer, "well done, you good and faithful servant, enter into the joys of your rest." The saint will appear at judgment to receive the inheritance Christ has for him which is beyond all comparison (II Cor. 4:16-18).

v. 13   . . . Death and Hades gave up the dead in them . . . — The sea, Death and Hades (Hades is the intermediate state of the dead, whether in peace or torments, see Lk. 16:19-31). The "sea" may be symbolic of the total mass of living humanity (see comments on Rev. 13:1), or it may be speaking literally of the oceans of the earth. It appears John added these phrases simply to emphasize that wherever men may be, disembodied or in the body, they will be called forth to appear at the final judgment of God. None shall escape; none shall be overlooked. Now the final judgment will not determine whether one will go to heaven or hell. That will have been determined according to one's spiritual relationship at death (Jn. 3:18, etc.). The final judgment is to declare it, vindicate it, and finalize it. The final solution to sin and rebellion will be executed; the eternal and perfect circumstances for development of righteousness and love will be established.

v. 14   Then Death and Hades were thrown into the lake of fire — The experience known as Death and the experience known as Hades can have no part in eternal bliss. The only place left for those experiences is hell. Death is the experience of separation, alienation, irreconciliation, dissolution and disorder. The second death is the eternal experience of all the preceding torments. Hades is the experience of disembodiment and there can be no place for that in heaven. It is cast into hell to be part of the cumulative experience of all rebel sinners. This is God's final statement that he has given the Lamb power over these forces which frustrate and torment men in this life. The Lamb does as he pleases with them and it is his pleasure to ban them from the experience of the saved forever in hell. Alford writes, "As there is a second higher life, so there is also a second and deeper death. And as after that life there is no more death, so after that death there is no more life."

v. 15   and if any one's name was not found written in the book of life, he was thrown into the lake of fire — At the final judgment there will be only two classes of humanity; the saved and the lost. Human beings will be either cast into the lake of fire or they will be found written in the book of life and *not* cast into the lake of fire. There will be no "in-between" categories. It is no wonder Jesus told the seventy disciples that they should not rejoice over supernatural powers exercised through them, but rejoice simply that their names were written in heaven (Lk. 10:20). Not all who exercise miraculous powers will go to heaven (Mt. 7:21-23). One does not have his name written in heaven by the mere fact that he is religious, does religious deeds, even miraclulous religious deeds. One's name is written in heaven by "having the Son of God." The same apostle given this vision of the final judgment wrote: "And this is the testimony, that God gave us eternal life, and this life is in his Son. He who has the Son has life; he who has not the Son of God has not life" (I Jn. 5:11). Now this same epistle, called First John, tells us very plainly how we "have the Son"! (see I Jn. 2:3, 5, 6, 24; 3:19-24; 4:6-15).

APPREHENSION AND APPLICATION:

1. Why do some people think the whole book of Revelation is about the second coming of Christ?
2. Is the second coming of Christ mentioned in Revelation? Where?
3. When are the "thousand years" ended?
4. What is to happen when the thousand years end?
5. How long will Satan be loosed?
6. How "loose" will Satan be?
7. What will Satan attempt to do during his "little time"?
8. Why does God allow the devil to go on making war against the saints?
9. What do you think you will do if Satan's "loosing" comes while you are alive? Will you be deceived? Is there any way to withstand Satan's little time?
10. Why does John mention "Gog and Magog" in his Revelation?
11. What will God do about Satan's surrounding the camp of the saints?
12. What is going to be Satan's experience in hell? Will he be in charge?
13. Who will be judged by God at the great white throne?
14. Why does earth and sky flee from God's presence?
15. Why are all the dead judged by what is written in the "books"?
16. Will believers appear at judgment? Why?
17. How does one have his name written in the book of life?
18. What happens to those whose names are not written there? Do you really believe that?
19. Do you have any friends or relatives whose names are not written there? Have you talked with them about it?

Lesson Nine
(21:1-27—22:1-5)

THE LAMB AND THE SPIRITUAL CONSUMMATION

Actually, this lesson will include the first five verses of chapter 22 also. As we have said before, those who originally assigned chapter numbers seem to have made a few errors in judging contextual connections. This is one of the classic examples of that. The context of chapter 21 decidedly continues through 22:1-5.

The Revelation has, to this point, pictorialized the defeat of all forces opposed to God. Final judgment will consummate the victory of God. Satan and his hosts will be confined to the lake of fire. God will reign on his throne in undisputed sovereignty.

But what is the state of the redeemed? This question was of imminent interest to the persecuted saints in Asia Minor. It is a question of utmost relevance to saints through all the ages. The final vision given to John deals with this issue.

The "Babylon" which was described in chapter 18 (Rome) as having been completely destroyed was an earthly empire with a humanistic and antitheistic spirit, a self-appointed substitute for the eternal God and the kingdom of God on earth. The symbolic unity of the Revelation would not be completed without a picture of the ideal kingdom of God which in some way united heaven and earth. As a means of doing this John is given a vision of the new Jerusalem "coming down out of heaven from God." No carnal kingdom can accomplish God's purposes for man. God has instituted a heavenly kingdom, even on this present earth, to serve his ultimate purposes for man. This heavenly kingdom, even while on this present earth, is the ideal and should be functioning, as nearly as circumstances will allow, in all respects as God has revealed his ideal (cf. Mt. 6:10). One day, in the sovereign time schedule of God, the ideal kingdom will be taken out of this world order (which is to be destroyed) and placed in a new world order, with all new blessed circumstances. This is what the last vision of Revelation is all about. The two world orders are only the "twinkling of an eye" apart.

Destiny of the Saved (21:1—22:5)

21 Then I saw a new heaven and a new earth; for the first heaven and the first earth had passed away, and the sea was no more. ²And I saw the holy city, new Jerusalem, coming down out of heaven from God, prepared as a bride adorned for her husband; ³and I heard a loud voice from the throne saying, "Behold, the dwelling of God is with men. He will dwell with them, and they shall be his people, and God himself will be with them; ⁴he will wipe away every tear from their eyes, and death shall be no more, neither shall there be mourning nor crying nor pain any more, for the former things have passed away."

5 And he who sat upon the throne said, "Behold, I make all things new." Also he said, "Write this, for these words are trustworthy and true." ⁶And he said to me, "It is done! I am the Alpha and the Omega, the beginning and the end. To the thirsty I will give from the fountain of the water of life without payment. ⁷He who conquers shall have this heritage, and I will be his God and he shall be my son. ⁹But as for the cowardly, the faithless, the polluted, as for murderers, fornicators, sorcerers, idolaters, and all liars, their lot shall be in the lake that burns with fire and sulphur, which is the second death."

9 Then came one of the seven angels who had the seven bowls full of the seven last plagues, and spoke to me, saying, "Come, I will show you the Bride, the wife of the Lamb." ¹⁰And in the Spirit he carried me away to a great, high mountain, and showed me the holy city Jerusalem coming down out of heaven from God, ¹¹having the glory of God, its radiance like a most rare jewel, like a jasper, clear as crystal. ¹²It had a great, high wall, with twelve gates, and at the gates twelve angels, and on the gates the names of the twelve tribes of the sons of Israel were inscribed; ¹³on the east three gates, on the north three gates, on the south three gates, and on the west three gates. ¹⁴And the wall of the city had twelve foundations, and on them the twelve names of the twelve apostles of the Lamb.

15 And he who talked to me had a measuring rod of gold to measure the city and its gates and walls. [16]The city lies foursquare, its length the same as its breadth; and he measured the city with his rod, twelve thousand stadia; its length and breadth and height are equal. [17]He also measured its wall, a hundred and forty-four cubits by a man's measure, that is, an angel's. [18]The wall was built of jasper, while the city was pure gold, clear as glass. [19]The foundations of the wall of the city were adorned with every jewel; the first was jasper, the second sapphire, the third agate, the fourth emerald, [20]the fifth onyx, the sixth carnelian, the seventh chrysolite, the eighth beryl, the ninth topaz, the tenth chrysoprase, the eleventh jacinth, the twelfth amethyst. [21]And the twelve gates were twelve pearls, each of the gates made of a single pearl, and the street of the city was pure gold, transparent as glass.

22 And I saw no temple in the city, for its temple is the Lord God the Almighty and the Lamb. [23]And the city has no need of sun or moon to shine upon it, for the glory of God is its light, and its lamp is the Lamb. [24]By its light shall the nations walk; and the kings of the earth shall bring their glory into it, [25]and its gates shall never be shut by day —and there shall be no night there; [26]they shall bring into it the glory and the honor of the nations. [27]But nothing unclean shall enter it, nor any one who practices abomination or falsehood, but only those who are written in the Lamb's book of life.

22 Then he showed me the river of the water of life, bright as crystal, flowing from the throne of God and of the Lamb [2]through the middle of the street of the city; also, on either side of the river, the tree of life with its twelve kinds of fruit, yielding its fruit each month; and the leaves of the tree were for the healing of the nations. [3]There shall no more be anything accursed, but the throne of God and of the Lamb shall be in it, and his servants shall worship him; [4]they shall see his face, and his name shall be on their foreheads. [5]And night shall be no more; they need no light of lamp or sun, for the Lord God will be their light, and they shall reign for ever and ever.

vv. 1-4   Then I saw a new heaven and a new earth . . . — The imagery of a new heaven and earth may be taken from Isaiah 65:17 and 66:22, but Isaiah is speaking of the New Testament age verses the Old Testament system and John is speaking primarily of the consummation of all the ages. John's vision of the new heaven and earth follows chronologically his vision of the present earth and sky "fleeing from the presence of" God and their disappearance (20:11). John's vision is the same revelation as that given by Peter (II Pet. 3:7-10).

It may be that this vision of John is to serve a twofold function: first, to picture the Christian fellowship of this age set ideally in the "new" Jerusalem; second, to give as near a picture of the life hereafter as can be given

124

in human language. The new Jerusalem is the exact opposite of "Babylon" (Rome). Babylon, the seat of Satan's power, is finally destroyed; "new Jerusalem," the seat of God's power in a spiritual sense, is eternally established and victorious. And the "new Jerusalem" must look forward to glorified circumstances after the consummation of all the ages, for it is through this hope of the eternal experience that the saint is able to endure and purify himself (I Jn. 3:1-3).

This corrupted and cursed cosmos (world order) will pass away. With it will pass away all circumstances hindering the unity and fellowship of all believers as one. There will be no more "sea." Homer Hailey thinks the "sea" symbolizes the mass of pagan humanity standing opposed to God's redemptive society and writes, ". . . this phrase indicates the removal or passing of the body of society, the great sea in which the restless upheavals of men have cast up their mire as the nations rage against God."

The "holy city, new Jerusalem," coming down out of heaven from God, should be understood as synonymous with "kingdom" of God or "the Israel of God"—the whole number of the redeemed. The emphasis, in the Greek text, is on who it comes from, not where. The Greek text would literally be translated, "And I John, saw the city, the holy one, Jerusalem, new, coming down from God out of heaven. . . ." The eternal residence of the faithful saints is from God, not from man. It is heavenly, not earthly, therefore, abides forever.

New Jerusalem is made ready and adorned like a bride for her husband. The Greek word *hetoimasmenen means "readied" or "prepared." Nothing is lacking. Infinite love has made it perfect! The word adorned* is translated from the Greek word *kekosmemenen;* it is a perfect tense form of the word *cosmos,* from which we get the English word *cosmetics.* When the consummation of the ages comes, when time is no more, the church will have been readied in every respect, and perfectly beautified in every characteristic to be at home with its Husband, God. The perfect tense indicates the New Jerusalem had been adorning itself resulting in a continuing beauty. This does not mean that the church by its own merit beautified itself for its Husband. The New Testament plainly teaches that the church is beautified by accepting the merit of Christ. But the church must adorn itself with "robes washed pure in the blood of the Lamb" on the terms of acceptance dictated by the One who offers the adornment.

A great voice from the throne (God) announced, "Behold, the dwelling of God is with men. . . ." The Greek word *skene* is literally, *tabernacle* or *tent,* but means metaphorically, *dwelling place.* It is the same word used in John 1:14 speaking of the incarnation of the Son of God. Jesus was God dwelling in a fleshly "tabernacle" among men. It means that God will abide in the very presence of redeemed mankind in the New Jerusalem. God will associate Himself with men in a person-to-person relationship.

THIRTEEN LESSONS ON REVELATION

This is the essence of this passage. Redeemed man's destiny is to be present with God in circumstances unbounded and not hindered by matter, flesh and blood, or anything else opposing spiritual blessedness. This is the ultimate experience of the people of God. It is the goal of all spirituality, the end of all righteousness—the complete mastery of all that would rebell against God. This is the Life beyond death, beyond resurrection, beyond judgment.

The central dynamic of this existence is the glorious presence of the eternal God. No more separation for man from his Creator and Father. God will put up his "tent" right in the midst of our "tents." Beyond history in heaven there is no suffering, no pain, no sorrow and no parting. There will be no wrong there, no falsehood—nothing ugly or defeating or temporary. All is freely given to those who have proved their right to it by faithfulness, love and loyalty to Christ and his Word. Heaven is for those who want it and prepare themselves to live in it.

This universe is to be subjected to a glorious process of transformation or redemption and all things will be new, for the former things will have passed away. In the next life (except in hell) every vestige of human rebellion and wickedness and every trace of God's curse will be gone (II Pet. 3:7, 11, 12). This new universe, whatever its composition, will be fitted to parallel the "glorious liberty of the children of God" (Rom. 8:18-23). At the present, in this cursed universe, creation cannot attain the full potential for which God created it in the beginning. Man sinned and God cursed creation under the sentence of *futility.* It is futile for man to think this present cosmos can ever satisfy its Creator or reach the potential man needs. The liberty to attain its highest possibility is constrained—it has been subjected to arrested development. It is out of harmony with the Perfectly Harmonious God. One of the great promises of the Old Tesatment prophets is that the Messianic redemption will accomplish, in prospect, the restoration of the harmony between God, man, and the universe. The consummation of the Messianic work will be a restored Eden, (see Heb. 2:5-18).

"The eternal God is your dwelling place, and underneath are the everlasting arms . . ." (Deut. 33:27). Heaven will be *home* for the child of God. It is interesting to note that our text (Rev. 21:4) does *not* say God will simply take away all crying, but that "he will *wipe* away every tear from their eyes. . . ." The tender touch of a Father! How the tender touch from Jesus (God in the flesh) dispelled sorrow and hurt from those seeking mercy! Heaven will be like that a millionfold. William Hendriksen, in his book, *The Bible on The Life Hereafter,* pg. 210, characterizes our heavenly home as the place of perfect safety and security, the place of perfect rest or satisfaction, the place of perfect understanding and love, and the place of everlasting permanence.

vv. 5-7 . . . **these words are trustworthy and true** . . . **It is done!** — The throne Occupant (God) instructed John to *write*. Perhaps God's statement that he would make *everything new* (Gr. *kaina panta*) overwhelmed John so that he stopped writing momentarily. But God wants this promise repeated and repeated and verified. So God vows again that his words are true and faithful. The present heaven and earth may pass away but God's word will be fulfilled precisely as he says it will; God's word will never pass away!

The Greek word *gegone* is the perfect tense of *ginomai*, to become, to occur, to exist. Perfect tense means, it (whatever *it* may be) has existed and is continuing to exist. That coincides with the next statement characterizing God's nature as "Alpha and Omega, the beginning and the end." "Forever, O Lord, thy word is firmly fixed in the heavens. Thy faithfulness endures to all generations; thou hast established the earth, and it stands fast" (Psa. 119:89-90). "The sum of thy word is truth; and every one of thy righteous ordinances endures forever" (Psa. 119:160). "For He (God) spoke, and it came to be; he commanded, and it stood forth" (Psa. 33:9). God is not merely the beginning and end of history, he is history's goal and sustainer. Seen, by faith, from the perspective of God, the glorious consummation of all things has always been immediately present with God. God did not create this world order and then temporarily absent himself from it, leaving it to destroy itself or find its own redemption. He is daily, hourly, constantly in control. The consummation and redemption of this creation is as constant as God himself. It is there, where he is. It is now. Those yet alive in the time-space frame of reference do not yet experience it because God is not willing that any should perish but that all should have opportunity to repent and prepare themselves to enter into it.

The "water of life" is Christ (Jn. 4:13-14; 7:37-39)—his grace, his love, his holy nature. The promises of Isaiah (55:1ff.) and Zechariah (14:8) were predicted to be fulfilled in the work of the Messiah. And that is what Jesus promised Himself to be—the source of complete spiritual fullness and satisfaction. Like the thirsting desert wanderer finds his life saved and satisfied at the clear oasis pool, so the sinner realizes the salvation of his spirit and its satisfaction in Jesus' promises and way of life. Only the "thirsty" find it. Those who have deep yearnings for God and spiritual contentment will be given it (cf. Psa. 42:1; 63:1; Mt. 5:6, etc.). And it cannot be produced by the one thirsting—it is given without price by the grace of God to those who continually thirst. It is *thirsting* that qualifies one for being given the water of life. The one thirsting is the one depending on and trusting God to supply; that is faith. There is a pseudo-slaking of the thirst for life; it is called self-righteousness. It does not *really* thirst believing it has no need.

The one *conquering* (Gr. *nikon*, Eng. *Nike*) will receive the satisfaction of his spiritual thirst as his heritage. The Greek word for *heritage* is *kleronomesei* and is "that into the possession of which one enters in virtue of sonship, not because of a price paid or of a task accomplished" (cf. Gal. 4:30; Heb. 1:4; 12:17). Our heritage (inheritance) depends upon *whose* we are! Whose we are depends upon whose we *choose* to be!

v. 8   But as for the cowardly . . . their lot shall be in the lake that burns with fire and brimstone . . . — These unpleasant words in the midst of glory, serve to remind us there is a definite relationship between the life to come and the life that now is! We are to conduct our pilgrimage here in this life in the light of this fact—*we are becoming what we shall be!* And what we are becoming is the result of that to which we consecrate ourselves (cf. Hosea 9:10; Psa. 115:1-8; I Pet. 2:21-25). If we wish to go to "Abraham's bosom" (Lk. 16:22) when we die, we must "share the faith of Abraham" (Rom. 4:16; 9:6-8; Gal. 3:26-29).

The Greek word *deilois* is translated *cowardly;* it means *fright, timidity.* In II Tim. 1:7 we are told that sons of God are given *not* the spirit of cowardice (Gr. *deilois*) but they *are* given the spirit of power, love and self-control; cowardice here is connected with being *ashamed* of the testimony of the Lord. The Christian must not let anything in this world intimidate his trust in the Lord—not a storm at sea (cf. Mt. 8:26; Mk. 4:40) or persecution (Jn. 14:27; Heb. 10:38f.). The verb *deiliao* was used in early Christian writings to testify that Polycarp (bishop of Smyrna, 69-156 A.D.) was not *intimidated* at the threat of martyrdom before the wild beasts in the Roman arena.

The *faithless* (Gr. *apistois,* unbelieving) are those who have been disobedient and untrustworthy stewards of the Master's trust (see Lk. 12:46). They have taken the Master's property (their lives, their earthly goods, the gospel of Christ) and stolen it for themselves, misused it and acted in rebellion against the Master. They are not fit to be trusted with the Master's property in the next life (Lk. 16:10-13).

The *polluted* (Gr. *ebdelugmenois,* foul, stinking, detestable, abominable) are not necessarily those who are sexual perverts. The word is constantly associated with idolatry in both the Old Testament and New Testament. Jesus used it to characterize the Pharisees who "were lovers of money" (Lk. 16:14-15). What is highly esteemed among carnal-minded men (wealth, honor of men) is disgusting in the sight of God because men have made such things their gods. The attitudes Peter expressed in refusing to accept the atoning death of the Messiah (cf. Mt. 16:21-23) was satanic and abominable in the sight of God. Peter, while unquestionably a moral upright man, was, in his worldly attitude toward the Messiah, an abomination before God!

The *murderers* (Gr. *phoneusi,* murder) are those who individually kill others outside the provisions of the civil law. Capital punishment is *not* murder. The Bible makes provision for the taking of human life as a means of maintaining civil order and justice (cf. Gen. 9:6; Rom. 13:1-7). Individuals are not to kill other individuals except as they may be executing civil laws (which may also include laws of defense against international aggression, better known as "war"). Murderers are those who have no respect for human life, no respect for the laws of God and men, and no intention of living within the moral boundaries of social order. They will take a human life to suit any whim of their selfishness. There are many Greek words used in the general sense of *killing* (e.g. *apokteino, anaireo, thuo, thanatoo, sphazo*), but the word *phoneuo* is specifically used to mean *murder* (see Mt. 19:18; 23:35; Lk. 18:20; Rom. 13:9, etc.).

Fornicators (Gr. *pornois*) means those practicing illicit sexual intercourse (see I Cor. 5:1; 6:13, 18; 7:2; Mt. 5:32, etc.). Illicit sexual practices are *not* what society forbids, but what *God* forbids in his Word! An illicit sexual life-style manifests a carnal (worldly) mind in rebellion against God's demand for a spiritual mindedness; rebellion is idolatry (I Sam. 15:23; Gal. 5:20; Col. 3:5).

Sorcerers (Gr. *pharmakeusi,* English *pharmacology*) means those "devoted to the magical arts, especially those who use drugs, potions, spells, enchantments." Vine's Expository Dictionary says, "In sorcery, the use of drugs, whether simple or potent, was generally accompanied by incantations and appeals to occult powers, with the provision of various charms, amulets, etc., professedly designed to keep the applicant or patient from the attention and power of demons, but actually to impress the applicant with the mysterious resources and powers of the sorcerer." Sorcery is mentioned as one of the "works of the flesh" (cf. Gal. 5:20; see also Rev. 9:21; 18:23; 22:15; in the LXX see Ex. 7:11, 22; 8:7, 18; Isa. 47:9, 12). Men may dismiss sorcery, witchcraft and the occult as harmless nonsense, but God has sentenced all who practice it to the lake of fire and brimstone forever!

Idolaters (Gr. *eidololatres,* idol-hireling or idol-server) are those who worship or serve images and false gods for what they can get from them. Idolatry is traced directly to the attitude of *ingratitude* toward the true God (Rom. 1:18-23; see also Hosea 2:5-13; Isa. 1:3; Ezek. 16:19; Hosea 8:4). Men worship money because of what they think they can *get.* The "what can I get out of it" life-style is destined to wind up in hell (see Lk. 12:13-21; 16:19-31).

Liars (Gr. *pseudesi,* pseudo-ones) are those who speak and live contrary to the truth (see Jn. 8:44, 55; Rom. 3:4; I Tim. 1:10; Titus 1:12; I Jn. 1:10; 2:4, 22; 4:20; 5:10). In Romans 1:25 the word is used as a metonymy for an idol. An idol is a lie! The belief that man is a god is a lie (see II Thess. 2:4-12). Those who refuse to love the truth will be deluded and believe a lie. To deny that Jesus is the Anointed One of God (the Christ) is to lie (I Jn. 2:21, 22). Lying is the very nature of the devil (Jn. 8:44), and those who continue to speak and live what is false (pseudo, make-believe) are sons of the devil; their destiny is the lake of fire and brimstone, the second death. Heaven is the inheritance of those who are lovers of truth, those who are honest, and those who speak and live what God's Word says is real as opposed to what is false. The Messiah's eternal kingdom cannot abide anyone who wants to deceive God or his fellow man. A kingdom of liars would be a kingdom in rebellion against the King of Truth.

It is of utmost significance that spiritual character is emphasized prior to the description of the New Jerusalem. Life upon earth is preparatory to life in heaven. Here character is formed; there character is savored.

vv. 9-27 . . . and he showed me the holy city Jerusalem . . . — The "Bride of the Lamb" and the New Jerusalem are one and the same. The "Bride" of Christ is the church (cf. Eph. 5:21ff.). One of the seven angels who revealed to John the final destruction of the harlot (Rome) was commissioned by God to reveal to John the final victory of the saints. John was carried in spirit (the definite article is absent in the Greek text indicating John was to be given a *spiritual*, or symbolic, vision of the of the consummated church) to a great, high mountain and shown the holy city coming down out of heaven from God (see comments 21:2). We must constantly remember that human language (composed of words which may only describe that which falls within human experience) is inadequate to describe any thing beyond human experience. When God condescends to using human language to describe heaven, we must admit such human language is, of necessity, being used only in a figurative, symbolic sense.

The city was glorious because of God's presence there. God's presence radiated (Gr. *phoster,* luminous, light-giving) his glory there. And it is God's *character* (absolute faithfulness, love, justice, righteousness) that radiates glory. The city is not glorious because of what it is but because of who God is. Those who want heaven without the character of God present, really do not want heaven but hell. The radiance of God's character is *like* (as nearly as human language can describe it) a most rare jewel (Gr. *timiotato,* very costly), *like* a jasper (Gr. *iaspidi,* diamond) clear as crystal. "Diamonds are forever" and God is eternal. There is nothing lacking in God. Like the diamond, God is pure, enduring, worthy, most valuable (see Rev. 4:3).

The main idea symbolized by the details of this highly figurative vision of the heavenly city is *perfection.* While the harlot (Babylon, the wicked city of Rome) has her decadance and vileness exposed and her destiny determined as destruction, the Bride of the Lamb (the city of God, the church) is promised glory and eternality. The harlot is punished forever; the Bride is perfected forever.

Suggested Symbolism of the New Jerusalem

Symbol	Meaning
1. A great high wall	1. Perfect "inclusion" showing a clear separation between those within and those without, Rev. 22:14-15
2. Twelve gates	2. Perfect and abundant access, Heb. 10:19-21
3. Twelve foundations	3. Perfect security; it will never be shaken from where it is, Heb. 12:25-29
4. The city foursquare (a 1500-mile cube)	4. Perfect spaciousness, room for all the redeemed, II Pet. 3:9
5. Walls and foundations built out of every precious jewel imaginable and pure gold	5. Perfect or infinite purity, infinite costliness, infinite beauty, no flaws or imperfections at all, Rev. 22:3
6. No Temple but the Lord	6. Perfect, completely satisfying, worship and service in the actual presence of the Lord, Heb. 9:11ff.
7. No sun or moon	7. Perfect knowledge or insight; nothing hidden; perfect guidance; perfect reality—no shadows or images, cf. Isa. 60:19-20; Psa. 36:10.
8. Into it comes the glory and honor of the nations.	8. Perfect universality of redeemed mankind; no more racial or cultural or social hostilities, Jn. 17:20ff.; Eph. 2:11-22.
9. Nothing unclean entering.	9. Perfect holiness, righteousness and goodness. Nothing bad or false there.

Again, it is clearly the intent of God to emphasize that heaven is heaven principally because of spiritual character or quality rather than because of circumstances. Clearly, men must choose where they want to spend eternity on the basis of their preference for quality of life-style. Getting people to heaven involves more than ritual and regimentation. It can be done only by persuading them to change their choices and desires and their way of living.

THIRTEEN LESSONS ON REVELATION

vv. 22:1-5 Then he showed me the river of the water of life . . . — The antithetical relationship of this passage to the Genesis account of Eden is readily apparent. In Eden there was a river, the tree of life, innocence, fellowship between man and God, and man serving his Creator. *But,* in Eden man chose to rebel against God's will and was banished from the tree of life and brought God's curse upon creation.

The New Jerusalem will be, essentially, Eden redeemed. The great difference will be that man, the occupant of Eden redeemed, will be immortal. In Eden man's body was of the dust of the earth, mortal. In new Eden man's body will be immortal (I Cor. 15:35-58). In the new Eden, the river and tree will be the spiritual reality of which the first Eden was only a material shadow and type. Old Eden was temporary—new Eden is eternal. New Eden provides a life of perfect enjoyment for those who have chosen it as their immortal home. In it is perfect sustenance, perfect longevity, perfect blessedness, perfect service and perfect knowledge. There is nothing that is *accursed* (Gr. *katanathema,* anathema, marked for destruction). Everything there pleases God and has his favor. If that is so, it will all certainly please man.

John's imagery here is anticipated in Ezekiel's new land, city and temple (Ezek. 40:1—48:35) especially in Ezek. 47:1-12. Ezekiel's vision was of the Messianic age (the church). John's vision is of the *consummation* of the Messianic age (eternal life in heaven). Ezekiel's river flowed from the threshold of the temple and emptied into the Dead Sea making it fit for life. John's river flows from the throne of God, through the midst of the eternal city, with no apparent emptying place. Both apparently symbolize the grace of God in giving penitent man his divine Spirit to dwell in man, imputing the righteous nature of God to man (cf. Jn. 4:7-15; 7:37-39; Mt. 5:6; Rom. 8:1-17; Acts 2:38; 3:17-26; II Pet. 1:3-4). The "river" is common apocalyptic imagery (see Joel 3:18; Psa. 46:4; 42:1-2; 63:1-4; 143:6; Isa. 55:1ff.; Zech. 14:8) for designating God, the Redeemer, as the gracious source of new spiritual life through the Messiah.

The "tree of life" on either side (both sides) of the "river" is also similar to Ezekiel's Messianic vision. The "tree" probably symbolizes the sustaining and deepening of spiritual life (cf. Psa. 1:1-3; Jer. 17:7-8; Prov. 3:18; 11:30; 12:28; 15:4). The Lord Jesus Christ, on the "tree" of substitutionary atonement, becomes our source, sustenance and maturation of eternal life (Jn. 3:14-15; 6:51-71; Acts 5:30; 10:39; 13:29; Gal. 3:13; I Pet. 2:24). These "trees" of life are also for the *healing* (Gr. *therapeian*) or therapy of the nations (Gr. *ethnon,* ethnics). Through the cross ("tree") Jesus reconciled all ethnics in one body, bringing hostility of man toward God and man toward man to an end (Eph. 2:11-22). All the hostilities of ethnic prejudices find therapy or healing in the grace of God. There are no more divisions estranging one man from another. In the eternal kingdom of God

132

each man pleases his neighbor for his good, to edify him (Rom. 15:2). This kingdom will be composed of people from every culture, tribe, tongue and "class"; all will be *servants* (Gr. *douloi,* slaves) of God and one another.

In the heavenly city there will be no more anything accursed. Because of man's rebellion in Eden, God cursed (sentence to eternal destruction) all creation—including man. To be banished forever from the presence (face) of God is eternal destruction. But the Son of God became man and suffered the curse of God for all creation (cf. Gal. 3:13). In him there is no condemnation (Rom. 8:1ff.). Under his rule and in his kingdom it was promised, ". . . there shall be no more curse . . ." (Zech. 14:11). In the new city of God, the servants of God shall dwell forever in God's presence (see his face) and worship him. This perfected service and worship will undoubtedly be man's involvement in carrying out God's will for man from the beginning. That would be conforming to and producing in themselves the nature (image) of God's Son, Jesus Christ (cf. Rom. 8:28-29; 12:1-2; II Cor. 3:18; Gal. 4:19; Eph. 3:16-19; 4:13; Phil. 2:1-11; Col. 1:27-28).

Those who love truth and righteousness and desire to have it, also desire to see God face to face and abide in his immediate presence (cf. Jn. 14:8). In the redeemed city of eternity, that longing becomes a reality. And those there are sons of God (they have his name on their foreheads; symbolizes kinship) for they are like him (cf. Eph. 5:1-2; Mt. 5:48; I Jn. 3:1-3) they imitate him, they are partaking of his nature by doing his will (Jn. 6:63; II Pet. 1:1-4). They are his children because he loves them and they love him (cf. Jn. 14:21, 23; 15:7-10, etc.).

Those who have overcome by the grace of Christ and their faithfulness to him now have their reign extended from the "thousand years" with Christ in this age (cf. Rev. 20:4) to a reign forever and ever, ages without end. The dominion man lost in Eden by rebelling against God's will for his life is restored in New Jerusalem by man's repentance and surrender to the will of God for his life as accomplished by Jesus (cf. Heb. 2:1-14; Eph. 1:3-23; 2:6, etc.).

It is important that the reader of Christ's Revelation to John return to the letters to the seven churches at this point and re-read the promises to those struggling Christians who overcame their world by faith. They were promised: (a) To him who conquers I will grant to eat of the tree of life which is in the paradise of God (2:7); (b) He who conquers shall not be hurt by the second death (2:11); (c) To him who conquers Christ will give some of the hidden manna, a white stone, with a new name written on it (2:17); (d) He who conquers will be given power over the nations to rule over them with a rod of iron, and given the morning star (2:26-27); (e) He who conquers will be clad in white garments and will not have his name blotted out of the book of life and will be confessed before God by Jesus Christ (3:5); (f) He who conquers will become a pillar in the temple of God, shall never go out of the temple, shall have the name of God and the city of God and Christ's own new name written on him (3:12); (g) He who conquers will be granted to sit with Christ upon his throne (3:21).

What Christ promised the faithful saints of Asia Minor, God allowed John to look down the corridors of time and see fulfilled when time is transferred to eternity, when the mortal takes on immortality. What glory! What blessedness! What fulfillment! Let those who belong to Christ and are overcoming by the power of their faith in him say, "even so, come Lord Jesus!" Let those who do not belong to him yet, but wish to, say, "What must I do to inherit eternal life" and turn to his Word to find their answer and obey it!

APPREHENSION AND APPLICATION:

1. Should the kingdom of God on earth now be attempting to function, as nearly as circumstances permit, like the picture of the kingdom in heaven? (see Mt. 6:10). Is it? What needs to be done?
2. Why must the kingdom of God find its consummation in glorified circumstances? Does the hope of heavenly circumstances help you? How?
3. Why is redeemed man's destiny essentially to be present with God? Is that what you look forward to? Would you like to see God face to face at this very moment? What's the alternative?
4. Do you think of heaven as home? If you do not, what do you think the reason might be?
5. What qualifies a person to receive the free gift of the water of life? Do you qualify?
6. Why the unpleasant description of those whose lot is the second death in the midst of the glories of heaven? Do you believe you are becoming what you shall be? Are you ready for heaven in your attitudes and desires?
7. Define cowardly, polluted, sorcerers, idolaters, liars; is there any change you need to make in any of these areas?
8. What is emphasized in all the symbolism of heaven's description? What makes heaven such a glorious place?
9. How is the New Jerusalem like Eden? How is it different?
10. What or who is the river of life? the tree of life? How does a person partake of each of these?
11. In what way will people most likely be serving God in heaven? Are you serving God this way now?
12. What is symbolized by the name written on the foreheads of people in heaven? Do you imitate your heavenly Father now? How do you know how to?

Lesson Ten
(22:6-21)

THE LAMB'S SUMMARY CONCLUSION

Most people who study the book of Revelation give chapter twenty-two only cursory treatment. They are intrigued with the fast-moving, highly symbolic drama of the middle portion of the book and especially chapter twenty.

The very idea that chapter twenty-two probably contains the last words, the last revelation, to be spoken by God to man before the second coming of Christ, make these words take on tremendous importance. These last words were declared by the Revealer, God, to be soon fulfilled and would, therefore, be important to every believer of every age as an aid to understanding the early church's confrontation with the Roman Empire.

This closing chapter of the last Word of God to man is a beautiful recapitulation of the purpose of the whole Bible. It is:

    a. A message of divine authority
    b. A message of immediate importance
    c. A message of divine invitation
    d. A message of divine warning
    e. A message of divine hope

135

Dear student, do not neglect this lesson for in this last chapter of Christ's Revelation to the churches of Asia Minor, the Lord commissions *you* to use the information you have gained from it to invite all who are thirsty for the water of life to come to Jesus.

A Message of Divine Authority (22:6-9)

6 And he said to me, "These words are trustworthy and true. And the Lord, the God of the spirits of the prophets, has sent his angel to show his servants what must soon take place. ⁷And behold, I am coming soon."

Blessed is he who keeps the words of the prophecy of his book.

8 I John am he who heard and saw these things. And when I heard and saw them, I fell down to worship at the feet of the angel who showed them to me; ⁹but he said to me, "You must not do that! I am a fellow servant with you and your brethren the prophets, and with those who keep the words of this book. Worship of God."

vv. 6-7   And the Lord . . . has sent his angel to show his servants what must soon take place . . . — The Lamb himself affirmed the Revelation John had seen (the whole revelation) was trustworthy (faithful) and true. The Lamb, whose every word and deed when he was on the earth came to pass, whose resurrection from the dead confirms his every promise, is the One who attests the certainty of this Revelation. The conquest of the "beast" and the fall of "Babylon" is confirmed by its fulfillment in history (the fall of the Roman Empire). The future consummation of all things in universal judgment and eternal life we may know by faith in the word of the Lamb who is always and absolutely true and faithful.

The Lamb affirms that what John had seen and heard was from the same God whose Spirit was in the prophets (both Old and New Testament prophets). The message of Revelation is part of the fulfillment of the plans and purposes that God revealed in the prophets (especially in Daniel 7:1-27). Revelation directly plugs into Daniel, chapter seven, and shows its fulfillment (see comments Rev. 10:7). The message of the prophets is that nothing in this world or in any other world can thwart the program of God to offer redemption to mankind. The Messiah would come to earth, the kingdom of God would be established forever, and no human being or human kingdom would stop this program—not even the most "beastly" that might be envisioned. The God of the spirits of the prophets sent his angel to reveal to John that what the churches of Asia Minor were soon to undergo was all in accordance with the revelations given to the prophets of old. The great tribulation coming upon the church during the rise and fall of the Roman Empire was shown to fit into the plan of God's redemptive program.

The timing of this great tribulation facing the church is important to the Revelation and the understanding of it. It was to be soon. Actually the Greek words, *en tachei,* literally mean, "with speed." The Greek word *tacheos* is the word from which we get the English *tachometer,* and other words related to *speed.* This Greek word is used in verse 6 and verse 7. Whatever was to take place "soon" was to coincide with the "soon" coming of the Lamb. Some commentators think the Lamb's "soon" coming of verse 7 refers exclusively to the Second Coming of Christ at the end of time. However, it seems more reasonable to expect it to apply primarily to the Lamb's "coming soon" in judgment upon the Roman Empire, and to apply, perhaps, as a prophetic type of his "coming soon" at the end of time. The Lord certainly referred to his "coming" in a symbolic way to judge and destroy apostate Judaism (Mt. 26:64; Heb. 10:25; Mt. 22:7). The Old Testament is filled with statements of the "Lord's coming" in judgment upon the idolatrous Hebrews. The student should study the notes in chapter twenty-four (especially Daniel 7:13), and chapter twenty-five (Mt. 24-26) for further discussions of the symbolic use of the phrase, "the coming of the Lord."

The immediate promise of his "soon coming" was to the saints in Asia Minor. He was coming to their aid speedily. Domitian died just one year after (A.D. 96) John received the Revelation in A.D. 95! See comments on Rev. 1:4, 7; 16:15, etc. At the same time, we must remember Jesus taught very clearly that believers should expect his Second Coming at any moment so the coming of the Lord in judgment *suddenly* or *unexpectedly* upon Rome may be considered a prophetic type of His Second Coming. Time is no problem with the eternal God. All *time* is the *present* with God. He is the eternal *I AM!* One day is as a thousand years and a thousand years is as a day with him. Peter dealt with those who scoff at the idea of His imminent return to consummate all things (II Pet. 3:1-18). The writers of the New Testament made *no mistake* when they wrote to their first century readers to expect the Lord's return at any moment! We would make no mistake today to tell people to expect his "coming" at any moment. The mistake would be to *not* expect it momentarily.

The Lamb is promising *quick* relief to the beleagured saints of Asia Minor. That relief, while beginning within a year at the death of Domitian, will proceed slowly and take two more centuries to be completed (Constantine's edict of toleration, 313 A.D.). Suffering saints of every age have felt that Christ's intervention on their behalf has been slow in coming. But the Lord says those who cry out for vindication should always pray and not lose heart (cf. Lk. 18:1-8) for he will "vindicate them speedily" (see also Rev. 6:9-11). Therefore, blessing comes from the Lord to those who keep the words of the prophecy of Revelation. And what is there to *keep* in Revelation? There are words like "endurance," "repentance," "come out of her, my people," "conquer," "overcome," "open the door," to keep.

vv. 8-9   And when I heard and saw them, I fell down to worship at the feet of the angel . . . — John was once again overwhelmed by the presence of a supernatural being—an angel (see comments, Rev. 19:10). The angel who was sent to transmit this Revelation (Rev. 1:1) apparently was manifested along with the Lamb at this time. This angel, having spoken much of this Revelation directly to John, appeared to have great authority. John was ready to accord the angel equal authority with the Lamb and God. But the angel quickly corrected John. As authoritative as the message is, the messenger (whether angel, apostle or other human being) accrues no divine authority himself (cf. Gal. 1:8-9). It is the *Author* of the message who must be worshiped and served. *All* others are servants, be they angels or archangels or men. This Revelation to John, though it came through an angel, is divinely authoritative because it is *from* God—the angel is merely a messenger. Angels are *fellow-slaves* (Gr. *sundoulos*) with men and *brothers* (Gr. *adelphon*) of the prophets. They also *keep* the words of Revelation! Angels who serve God deliberately choose to trust, love and obey God. If angels *keep* the book of Revelation, men should make every effort to do so!

A Message of Immediate Importance (22:10-15)

10 And he said to me, "Do not seal up the words of the prophecy of this book, for the time is near. ¹¹Let the evil-doer still do evil, and the filthy still be filthy, and the righteous still do right, and the holy still be holy."

12 "Behold, I am coming soon, bringing my recompense, to repay everyone for what he has done. ¹³I am the Alpha and the Omega, the first and the last, the beginning and the end."

14 Blessed are those who wash their robes, that they may have the right to the tree of life and that they may enter the city by the gates. ¹⁵Outside are the dogs and sorcerers and fornicators and murderers and idolaters, and every one who loves and practices falsehood.

vv. 10-11   . . . Do not seal up the words of the prophecy of this book . . . — The Greek word for *seal* (Gr. *sphragises*) is aorist subjunctive. This means the action has not taken place as a fact yet, but it is desirable because of some contingency. John was told not to shut the scroll upon which he was writing the Revelation with seals (like the scroll of Rev. chapters 5-6) but to leave it accessible because of the contingency of *time*. The time when its message was needed was *then* at hand! The churches of Asia Minor needed it, primarily. It was *not* a message to be fulfilled two thousand years or more *after* John wrote it—it was for that great tribulation. The churches of Asia Minor were being exhorted to "conquer" and "endure." Of course, the principles of God's sovereignty and the church's ultimate triumph are relevant for all ages. The consummation of all things, the judgment of Satan and the wicked, and the restoration of Paradise for the faithful is also relevant for saints of all time. But the Greek word *engus* ("near") is often translated, *at hand.* The Lord meant for this message to be read, understood, obeyed and fulfilled (for the most part) immediately after it was given.

The Greek word *adikon* is translated in the RSV, *evildoer,* but more literally means, *unjust.* The Greek word *hrupon* is translated in the RSV, *filthy,* but is translated *shabby* in James 2:2 and *dirt* in I Pet. 3:21. There are other Greek words for the human idea of filth—*perikatharma* (see I Cor. 4:13) means "scum, rubbish, despicable," and still another Greek word (*skubalon*) for human excrement or garbage (Phil. 3:8). What we have in Rev. 22:11 is inward evil and inward filth—unseen and often discounted by man as less condemning than outward filth. A man may clean off his outward filth and dress up his body, be accepted by the world, and still be inwardly filthy. But not with God. To be acceptable with God man must wash away the inward filth of the mind and the conscience (Mt. 15:1-20; 23:25-26; I Pet. 3:21).

The Greek word *eit* is translated, *still,* but may be translated *yet more.* In other words, God allows men to choose the kind of character they want to *develop.* And character is an *ever-developing* capacity of human nature. Paul wrote, "Evil men and impostors shall wax (develop) worse and worse, deceiving and being deceived" (II Tim. 3:13). The impenitent, unjust and morally-filthy people of the Roman Empire were called to repent by the plagues God sent upon them but they did not repent! The sufferings they endured on earth did not bring repentance. But there is no repentance in the next life, only remorse, torment, and continued rejection of the Word of God (see Lk. 16:19-31). Men will continue to develop what their hearts have chosen in this life, whether evil or righteousness. One either grows in grace and stature as a Christian or sinks deeper into hardness and indifference as a sinner; there is no standing still. There is no in-between. Of course, God wants all unjust and filthy people to choose the cleansing he has provided in the blood (atoning death) of Christ in this life. God is not willing that any should perish (II Pet. 3:9). But God will not force any person to become a Christian—neither should the church attempt to do so. A person convinced against his will is of the same opinion still! The Lamb gave this dramatic Revelation to John and the churches of Asia Minor as an instrument of edification for the persecuted saints and an instrument of evangelism for the impenitent Roman Empire. Warnings and invitations are repeated throughout the Revelation. Both Christians and unbelievers must make their choice for or against the *last* revealed word from God. This urgency applies not only to the world of the days of the Roman Empire, but to our world of the twentieth century as well. The parable of the Tares in Matthew 13:24-30 is an excellent commentary on Revelation 22:10-11.

vv. 12-13 Behold I am coming soon, bringing my recompense . . . — The Lamb warns about his *speedy* (Gr. *tachu*) "coming" again (see comments on 22:6-7)! This time the Lamb announces he is coming rapidly to *reward* (Gr. *misthos,* wages, honorarium, recompense) each according to his works. This is a divine promise repeated throughout the Bible (cf. Isa. 40:10; Prov. 24:12; Mt. 16:27; II Tim. 4:14; II Cor. 11:15; Rev. 14:13; 20:12, 13). To the saints in Asia Minor this promise of the Lamb meant reward for their persecution and martyrdom; to the unbelievers of the Roman Empire who chose the mark of the beast, it meant judgment for their impenitence. Jesus taught many parables about rewards according to work (Gr. *ergon*) (see Mt. 20:1-15; 21:28-32; 21:33-43; 22:1-14; 25:1-46; Lk. 12:35-40; 12:41-48; 16:1-13; 16:19-31; 18:1-8; 19:11-27, etc.). The Lord does not save us *because* of our works, but he will reward us *according* to our faithfulness in doing his work.

The Lamb referring to himself as the "Alpha and the Omega" is repeated three times, Revelation 1:8; 21:6; 22:13. The statement that God is "first and last and there is none other" is a favorite phrase of Isaiah (see Isa. 43:10; 44:6, 8; 45:5, 6, 12; 48:12). The emperor of Rome may claim to be a god, but he is not. There is only one God and he is eternal. Everything from beginning to end, first, last and always, owes its existence sustenance and destiny to God and his Son, the Lamb. He is the uncreated Creator, the uncaused Cause, the only Redeemer of a cursed universe. He is the only Imperative of man the moral being. It is of absolute importance that men give their total allegiance to the Lamb.

vv. 14-15 Blessed are those who wash their robes . . . — The KJV reads, "Blessed are they that do his commandments . . ." in place of the RSV reading "Blessed are those who wash their robes. . . ." Bruce Metzger, in his *Textual Commentary on The Greek New Testament,* believes the phrase as it is in the RSV is correct and the KJV reading appears to be a scribal emmendation. The Codex Sinaiticus, Codex Alexandrinus and fifteen minuscules (cursive style manuscripts from 700 A.D. on) read, "Blessed are those who wash their robes. . . ." The KJV reading is not found in the most ancient manuscripts but only in later minuscules. Of course, the promise of blessedness for keeping the commandments of Christ is certainly a principle well stated in differing phraseology throughout the book of Revelation. But here, the *right* (or *authority,* Gr. *exousia*) to partake of the tree of life is conditioned upon having washed one's robes in the blood of the Lamb (Rev. 7:14). There are commandments of instructions from the Lord as to the attitudes and actions required of man in order to wash his "robes" in the blood of the Lamb (cf. Titus 3:4-8; I Pet. 1:22-25; 3:21; I Cor. 6:11; Acts 2:38; 22:16; Col. 2:11-12; Gal. 3:26-27; Heb. 10:22; see also comments on Rev. 7:14). This washing is not something done apart from an obedience in faith to the ordinance of immersion in water. God's Word declares that this obedience accomplishes the uniting of sinful man to the atoning death of Jesus Christ (cf. Rom. 6:3-5), provided for man solely by the grace of God. The "washed" ones are able to partake of the tree of eternal life by the *power* (Gr. *exousia*) of the meritorious perfection of Christ imputed to them by his grace and appropriated by them in loving obedience to his ordinance of baptism (immersion) (cf. Mt. 28:18-20; Acts 2:38; 8:12-13; 8:36; 10:47; 16:15; 16:33; 18:8; 19:5, et al). These also have the authority or right to enter the eternal city of God.

Outside the eternal dwelling place of God, separated from him forever, are the dogs, sorcerers, fornicators, murderers and idolaters, and everyone who loves and practices falsehood. The word "dogs" is often applied in Scripture to morally vicious people who behave like such animals (cf. Mt. 7:6; Phil. 3:2; II Pet. 2:10-22). Others who have forfeited the opportunity to partake of the tree of life and enter the holy city are discussed earlier in 21:8 (see comments there). Here, the added dimension is given to lying (Gr. *pseudos*) or falsehood that it is something one *does* as well as speaks. Falsehood is a life-style, a fundamental and basic character trait (cf. I Jn. 1:6; II Thess. 2:10-12) acquired by choice and desire. It is possible for man to love and live according to the truth, but it is also possible for man to love and live according to falsehood (cf. Jn. 3:19-21; 8:42-47, etc.). There is no place in heaven for those who do not love the truth and devote all their energies to living according to it. They have no right to be there. The *truth* is God's Word, the Bible. Those who wish to live in the eternal city of God must live according to the Bible, specifically, the New Testament!

A Message of Divine Invitation (22:16-17)

16 "I Jesus have sent my angel to you with this testimony for the churches. I am the root and the offspring of David, the bright morning star."

17 The Spirit and the Bride say, "Come." And let him who hears say, "Come." And let him who is thirsty come, let him who desires take the water of life without price.

v. 16   I Jesus have sent my angel to you with this testimony for the churches. — The Revelation opened with the claim that it was the revelation of Jesus Christ. Now the very voice of Jesus attests that he is the Author of the Revelation. He undoubtedly uses the name Jesus in this final invitation to emphasize his Saviorhood. Jesus is the "Lord, the God of the spirits of the prophets . . ." (22:6). Jesus, the root and offspring of David, born a true human being is also truly God. The Greek preposition *epi* is translated *for* the churches, but more precisely means *in regard to* or *concerning* the churches. The "churches" are specifically the seven churches of Asia Minor. But this Revelation is as relevant to the twentieth century church as the First Epistle to the Corinthians. The significance in stressing that the Revelation was "in regard to the churches" (of Asia Minor) is that it must be interpreted and understood from that particular historical background.

The title "root and offspring of David" is Messianic and identifies the Author of Revelation as the Promised One of the Old Testament prophets; it identifies him not only as David's son but as David's Lord (Mt. 22:41-46; Mk. 12:35-37; Lk. 20:41-44); it testifies to his incarnation (see comments on Rev. 5:5).

The "bright morning star" is a title prophesied by Balaam (Num. 23:17). Apocryphal literature applied this title to the Messiah (Testament of Levi 18:3; Testament of Judas 24:1ff.). The "morning star" is a metaphor of the well-known star of the morning, brighter than all the rest, heralding the dawning of a new day. Ancient shepherds, keeping watch over their flocks by night, seeing the silent procession of the stars through the hours of darkness, knew without clock or timepiece when the dawn of the new day was near. The "morning star" became a guide for them, revealing what they needed to know to make preparations for the next day (see II Pet. 1:19).

The Savior of all mankind gave the Revelation through John in regard to what the churches must do to be prepared for the dawn of a new day. He is the Messiah predicted in the prophets, son of David and Lord of David, who came incarnate to this world and was the "morning star" who enlightens all who will give heed to him.

v. 17   The Spirit and the Bride say, "Come." — The Greek verb *legousin* is present active indicative and denotes continuous action. In other words, the Spirit and the Bride *are continuing to say,* "Come." Who is the object of this plea? The Lord Jesus! The Spirit, by the revealed Word continues to state to the church (the Bride) that Jesus is coming very soon. The *Bride* (Gr. *nymphe*), which is the church, continues to pray that Jesus will come and vindicate her (cf. II Tim. 4:8; Titus 2:13; II Pet. 3:15; I Cor. 16:22; Rev. 22:20). *Everyone* hearing and believing the message of the Spirit and the pleading of the church should make the coming of the Lord Jesus his constant and personal prayer.

The Spirit, the Bride and every individual Christian must also plead with the whole world to partake of the water of life without price (cf. Isa. 55:1; Jn. 4:14; Rev. 21:6), and thus join the blessed anticipation of the Lord's coming at the consummation of all things. The invitation to join in expectation of the coming of Christ is to those who *thirst* (Gr. *dipsao,* English derivative, *dipsomania*). And those who partake must be willing to do so. Those who really anticipate the coming of our Lord are those who need him as much as the human body needs water! When a person realizes he needs the life of the Spirit of God that much, he will *willingly* come for his "handout"; he will do whatever the Spirit reveals in his Word must be done to receive this free gift of spiritual life. It is up to the church (the Bride), by conveying the Word of the Spirit, and living the life of the Spirit, to create in all men this *need.* Most of Christendom has so thoroughly misrepresented life in Christ, the world has said, "I don't need that"! Therefore, most of the world is unwilling to anticipate the coming of the Lord.

A Message of Divine Warning (22:18-19)

18 I warn every one who hears the words of the prophecy of this book: if any one adds to them, God will add to him the plagues described in this book, ¹⁹and if any one takes away from the words of the book of this prophecy, God will take away his share in the tree of life and in the holy city, which are described in this book.

v. 18   . . . if any one adds to them . . . — Everyone who hears the words of the prophecy of this book is warned against tampering with it. This warning is made a number of times in God's Word (see Deut. 4:2; 12:32; Prov. 30:5ff.; Mt. 15:6; II Cor. 4:2; Gal. 1:6-9). The principle applies to all the Word of God, but here, particularly, it refers to the book of Revelation.

Homer Hailey says, "The words of the prophecy are the thoughts, principles, judgments and messages of the book. The Lord is not speaking of an honest error in judgment and interpretation, even though this is serious. Rather he condemns the presumptuous and all who manifest a careless or flippant attitude toward the Word. As Lenski intimates, this makes writing about the book a serious and sublime matter to be pursued with the deepest of reverence for God and his truth." The same could be said of honest errors in translating from the original language. But men must not "peddle" Revelation (II Cor. 2:17). Some today have commercialized on this book for their own mercenary purposes. Men must not "tamper" with the Word of God in disgraceful, underhanded, cunning ways (II Cor. 4:2). And yet, many bizarre and impossible eschatological systems have been imposed upon this book in disgraceful and underhanded ways until there is widespread confusion among believers as to the fundamental message and meaning of Revelation.

v. 19   . . . and if any one takes away . . . — Anyone taking away from the words of the prophecy of Revelation will have his name blotted from the book of life and his right to the tree of life and the blessings of the eternal city removed. Sincere mistakes about the book will be forgiven, but indifference toward it result in eternal condemnation! Every letter to every church of Asia Minor ends with the admonition: "He who has an ear, let him hear what the Spirit says to the churches." People who would never literally omit an English word or a Greek word from the printed text of Revelation will neglect to read the book and especially refuse to allow the book to be studied in church assemblies. In our opinion, this comes dangerously close to "taking away from the words of this book"! *Christian people must not neglect this book!* That is a divine warning! One of the reasons for lukewarm Christian discipleship is that the church has neglected the *real* message of the book of Revelation: the *imperative* need of the church to *repent,* to *endure,* and to have *faith,* because the Lamb is Sovereign *in* and *over* all heaven and earth (Rev. 11:15).

A Message of Divine Hope (22:20-21)

20 He who testifies to these things says, "Surely I am coming soon." Amen. Come, Lord Jesus!
21 The grace of the Lord Jesus be with all the saints. Amen.

The last Word from Christ is a promise. He is coming soon! That elicits a prayer from John who represents all who are loving Christ's imminent appearing—"Even so, Come, Lord Jesus!" The benediction, "The grace of the Lord Jesus be with all the saints" exudes hope for sinful, penitent men. The long struggle which began in Eden is shown to be resolved. Satan's pseudo claim to sovereignty is exposed for what it is—a lie. He will be cast into eternal hell along with all who believed his lie and joined his rebellion against the true Sovereign, Jesus Christ. God and the Lamb are on the throne. They are coming soon to take all who have faithfully worshiped them to eternal joy in the new kingdom of God. These who are to dwell in God's presence forever do so by the grace of God which provided the atoning death of His Son to wash away their sin. They have trusted all to Him!

After living with this book of Revelation with the intensity of a researcher and teacher for ten years, and as a writer for two years, it is nearly impossible to bring these notes to a close. But we must, and so we close (by the gracious permission of Homer Hailey) with these incomparable words:

"As the vision fades from our view and the last word spoken echoes in our souls, our hearts are wrapped in awe at the majestic sight and sounds which we have beheld and to which we have listened. Surely our faith in God and His Christ has been strengthened, our hope for victory and heaven made more precious, our love for the spiritual and eternal made to abound beyond all previous measure, our will given a permanent determination to succeed, and our whole aim and goal of life become more fixed.

"Now that we have advanced with John from glory to glory in this drama of spiritual history, conflict, and victory, we feel that we are more than excited spectators of a divine cinema—we are a part of the drama! We continue to share with those early Christians the pressures of political power and intrigue, the subtlety of false religious appeal through human wisdom, philosophy, and tradition, and the seduction of the world of lust. Also we share with them the strength, power, and help that come from our heavenly Father through faith in the blood of the Lamb. And we shall share with them the eternal reward of victory and an inheritance in God's celestial city as the bride of the Lamb. And so with the voice of all creation, let us join the song as they sing:

> Unto him that sitteth on the throne,
> and unto the Lamb, be the blessing,
> and the honor, and the glory,
> and the dominion, for ever and ever."

APPREHENSION AND APPLICATION:

1. Why is the last chapter of Revelation important? Does it impress you as containing personal obligations? What are you doing about them?
2. How does the soon-to-take-place events of Revelation connect to what all the prophets of the Bible predicted? Does this help you understand Old Testment prophecies?
3. How did the "soon" coming events coincide with the "soon" coming of the Lord? Should Christ's coming in judgment on Rome tell us anything? What?
4. Did the writers of the New Testament make a mistake by expecting Christ's Second Coming in their own life-time? Why?
5. What is meant by, "Let the filthy *still* be filthy . . ."? Do you think we are becoming what we shall be? Is character development an eternal capacity of man?
6. What has the Lord said about rewarding according to works? What is the Lord's criterion of rewarding?
7. How does one "wash his robes" so that he has the right to the tree of life? Is baptism all that important?
8. Is lying only done with words? How does one "practice" a lie? Do you know anyone "practicing" a lie? Have you tried to warn them?
9. To whom is the Spirit and the Bride saying, "Come"?

10. Would you like Christ to come back for the consummation of all things *today*? Would you be more ready if it were one year from today? Why?
11. What is "adding" to the words of the prophecy of this book? Are there some doing so today?
12. What is "taking away" from the words of the prophecy of this book? Do you know anyone who might be doing this?
13. After studying this magnificent revelation from God do you feel like you are more than a spectator? Why?

Lesson Eleven
(Daniel 7—12)

DANIEL, CHAPTERS 7 THROUGH 12

A great many eschatological theories mix the prophecies of Daniel with those of other Old Testament apocalyptic prophecies with the book of Revelation and construct a conglomerated, self-contradicting jumble purporting to be "signs of the end-times."

We believe the prophecies of Daniel are clearly fulfilled in the first coming of Christ, the establishment of the church, and the destruction of Judaism. The following notes on Daniel are incorporated into this study-book on Revelation in hopes it may be clearly seen that Daniel and Revelation are not to be eschatologically mixed, but that one (Revelation) is the continuation of the other (Daniel).

George Washington said in his inaugural address to Congress, April 30, 1789: "It would be peculiarly improper to omit, in this first offical act, my fervent supplication to that Almighty Being, who rules over the universe, who presides in the councils of nations, and whose providential aids can supply every human defect, that His benediction may consecrate to the liberties and happiness of the people of the United States. . . . No people can be bound to acknowledge and adore the invisible hand which conducts the affairs of men more than the people of the United States. Every step by which they have advanced to the character of an independent nation seems to have been distinguished by some token of providential agency. . . . We ought to be no less persuaded that the propitious smiles of Heaven can never be expected on a nation that disregards the eternal rules of order and right, which Heaven itself has ordained." Benjamin Franklin said it even *more* eloquently before the Constitutional Convention of 1787.

In Daniel ch. 1-6 we see how God rules in the lives of *individuals*—both believers and unbelievers. In chapters 7-12 we see incontrovertible evidence (fulfilled prophecy) that Almighty God, the God of the Bible, rules in affairs of *nations* and in all of *history*. We see:

a. God's control of 600 years of history in minute detail, ch. 7-8
b. All for the purpose of redemption by Christ (Messiah), ch. 9-10
c. God's plan is to carry this out through Jews who would be faithful in great suffering until he brings the Old Testament dispensation to an end, ch. 11-12

We will be discussing subjects you hear a great deal about in "prophecy preaching" today:

a. The "fourth beast"; b. the "little horns"; c. the 2300 days; d. the "contemptible one"; e. the 70 7s; f. the "anointed prince"; g. the "time of the end"; h. the 1290 days and the 1335 days; i. the "latter end of the indignation."

DANIEL

SEVENTY SEVENS

BEAUTY AND THE BEASTS

by Paul T. Butler

Daniel 7:1—8:27

INTRODUCTION

Why do the nations conspire, and the people plot in vain? The kings of the earth set themselves, and the rulers take counsel together, against the Lord and his anointed, saying, Let us burst their bonds asunder, and cast their cords from us.

He who sits in the heavens laughs; the Lord has them in derision. Then he will speak to them in his wrath, and terrify them in his fury, saying, I have set my king on Zion, my holy hill.

BEAUTY AND THE BEASTS

I will tell of the decree of the Lord: He said to me, You are my son, today I have begotten you. Ask of me, and I will make the nations your heritage, and the ends of the earth your possession. You shall break them with a rod of iron, and dash them in pieces like a potter's vessel.

Now therefore, O kings, be wise; be warned, O rulers of the earth. Serve the Lord with fear, with trembling kiss the feet, lest he be angry, and you perish in the way; for his wrath is quickly kindled.

Blessed are all who take refuse in him.

—Psalm 2:1-11

This is a prophecy about the Messiah (Christ) and His kingdom—there can be no doubt about that for it is applied this way in the New Testament (cf. Acts 13:33; Heb. 5:5). Essentially it is predicting the futility of humanistic government in rebellion against God. There is only *one* kingdom adequate for man's ultimate needs and which will last forever—the kingdom of God, the church. Those who are wise will embrace God's kingdom because everything that exists belong to it. All that is not in harmony with it is to be destroyed.

This is the idea to be taught in the remaining chapters of Daniel (7-12). Out of the raging tumult of man in rebellion against God, man setting up one "kingdom" after another, God is going to quietly but inexorably establish His kingdom on earth through His Son. The *kingdom* (dominion, sovereignty) is to be given to the "saints" (sanctified ones) (Dan. 7:18, 22, 27). GOD KEEPS HIS PROMISES . . . NOTHING MAN CAN DEVISE WILL STOP HIM FROM FULFILLING HIS WORD!

Daniel 7 and 8 were written some 50 years after chapter 2 (about 555 B.C.). In the interim of those years Daniel has seen not only the persecution of his people but also the fragile favors of reigning monarchs. Babylon is now about to fall, and the period of the captivity foretold (70 yrs.) by Jeremiah is about 3/4 past. What awaits the people of God? In this following section (Dan. 7-12) the prophet must warn his people to expect renewed antagonism from the worldly powers. Daniel's experience in chapter 6 (which in time follows chapter 7 by about 15 years or more) emphasizes continued antagonism from the world for God's redemptive program.

Discussion

I. MALEVOLENT BEASTLINESS, 7:1-8

    A. Origin

        1. Daniel's revelation shows where human governments come from.

The Four Symbolic Beasts

150

2. "Sea" or "waters" symbolize the mass of humanity in constant motion, commotion and especially the Gentile masses in hostility toward God (cf. Isa. 8:7ff.; Jer. 46:7-9; 47:2; Isa. 17:2ff.; Rev. 13:1, 11; 17:1, 15; Isa. 57:20, 21).
3. "Winds" stand for the passions of men that lash the "seas of humanity" into an angry mob in revolution or drives them into great conflict. Winds of anger, greed, pride and all emotions or false teachings that stir humanity into social and civil strife and war.
4. The devil is the original anarchist and rebel. He is usually the source of all in human governments that sets itself against God's sovereignty over man in the church! (cf. Rev. 13:2). Therefore humanism expressed in human governmental structures, is beastly and animalistic in character.

B. Character
 1. Daniel saw four great beasts coming up out of the sea, different from one another in some instances, and succeeding one another. These empires are *beastly* because:
   a. They are cruel
   b. They are animalistic—they have as their only concern the fleshly aspects of man
   c. They victimize mankind by preying upon weaker
   d. They dominate by "tooth and claw" methods like animals
 2. Human government and rulers do not see themselves as God does!
   a. They dream about themselves as great images (Dan. 2) made of precious and enduring "metals."
   b. They dream about themselves as huge trees (Dan. 4) reaching to heaven, providing sustenance and protection for the whole world.
   c. They see themselves as "queens" (Isa. 47:5-9; Rev. 18:7).
   d. God sees them as *beasts* and *harlots*. They rend and tear; they seduce and prostitute.

C. Symbolism
 1. Lion, with eagle's wings, Babylon
   a. she is spoken of as a lion in Scripture (Jer. 49:19; 50:17, 44); and an eagle (Jer. 48:40; 49:22; Ezek. 17:3, 12). See also Jer. 4:7.
   b. Babylon was a majestic "king of beasts," pouncing on smaller and weaker nations, grinding them in its teeth, swift and powerful also as an eagle, "king of birds."

151

c. Wings plucked, turned into more human form, even given mind of human. This undoubtedly refers to humiliation of Nebuchadnezzar (ch. 4) when he became more humane (as Daniel tells his grandson Belshazzar in ch. 5).

2. Bear, Medo-Persia

a. slow-plodding nature of bear represents distinction between Persia and other animals listed.
b. raised up one side represents raising up of Persians over Medes in later history of empire.
c. three ribs in its mouth represents the three empires it devoured: Babylon, Asia Minor (or Lydia), and Egypt.
d. told to rise and devour much flesh—represents its leading by God (cf. Isa. 44:28—45:7; Jer. 50:3, 9; 51:11, 28). Persia was much more voracious in its lust to devour and conquered much more territory than Babylon. It tried even to devour Macedonia and Greece.

3. Leopard, Greece

a. four wings, extreme swiftness is symbolized by leopard— then more emphatically, with four wings.
   Alexander the Great conquered his world, clear to India, in less than 10 years!
b. four heads represent the four-way-division of Alexander's empire which eventuated after his untimely death at age 32; Cassander received Greece; Lysimachus received Macedonia and part of Asia Minor; Seleucus received Asia Minor and Persia and Syria; Ptolemy received Egypt.
   Later wars between the Seleucids and Ptolemies for control of Palestine ("the glorious land") will be predicted im Daniel ch. 11-12.
c. "dominion was given to it," represents clearly that what Alexander accomplished, he did so by the permission of Almighty God, to serve God's purposes (probably to spread Greek culture and language into the world anticipating the coming of Christ and the New Testament). The Jewish high priest, when Alexander came through Palestine, showed Alexander this prophecy of Daniel about him and Alexander asked the Jews to make a sacrifice in their temple for him.

4. Beast, Terrible, Dreadful, Exceedingly Strong, Rome

a. No beast in all the animal-world sufficiently fierce and powerful to symbolize this fourth beast.
b. iron teeth and grinding feet appropriate to represent Rome

because it ground up all other cultures and stamped them into submission to Roman way-of-life.

   c. 10 horns represent first ten recognized emperors of Rome beginning with Augustus (Octavian), Tiberius, Caligula, Claudius, Nero, Galba, Otho, Vitellius, Vespasian, and Titus

   d. The little horn (not the same as little horn in ch. 8) arises out of the 10 of this 4th empire—it is Domitian.

   d. Three plucked up by roots may be: 3 "barracks emperors" not in royal Julian line (Galba, Otho, Vitellius) assassinated; or, 3 later conspirators to Domitian's throne (Senecio, Rusticus, and Priscus—all slain by order of Domitian); or three uprisings put down by Domitian (Sarmatians, Chatti, Dacians).

   e. eyes like man, mouth speaking great things, represents that Domitian was a man, not a god and not invincible (see Rev. 13) no matter how blasphemous his claims to be Lord and God, (see Dan. 7:24-25).

   f. Domitian (81-96 A.D.) was emperor when John wrote Revelation and is undoubtedly the "beast" (plus his successors) of whom John writes.

II. MAGNIFICENT BEAUTY, 7:9-18

  A. Throne

1. Ferocious as the fourth beast is, it is the throne of God that reigns as sovereign over all creation.

    This same idea is portrayed in the book of Revelation.

2. "Thrones," plural, probably refers to thrones for Father, Son and Holy Spirit; or to the 24 thrones of the 24 elders (Rev. 4:4). These thrones, however, are not important except to draw attention to the *one supreme* throne.

3. Ancient of Days is lit. "the one from eternity," God the Father (see Micah 5:2), the one who lives forever, the mighty Creator (Rev. 4:10, 11).

4. Raiment white as snow—absolute purity and holiness

5. Hair like pure wool—wisdom (eternal)

6. Fiery flames—judgment, consuming power

7. Wheels burning fire—omnipresence of God "riding" through earth dispensing judgment through secondary agents (Ezek. 1:15-21; 10:1-22; Zech. 6:1-8), bringing "rest" to the earth that God's redemptive program may be carried on.

8. Thousand-thousands, ten thousand times ten thousand—all the creatures at God's command to carry out His orders.

    While God only needs one angel to slay 185,000 Assyrian soldiers in one night (Isa. 37:36), He has millions and millions of angels to do His will.

9. Court sits in judgment—all that is gathered around the one throne of God will execute His judgment on the fourth beast and the little horn.
10. Books opened—God records actions of all men, esp. His enemies (Isa. 65:6; Jer. 17:1; Mal. 3:16; Lk. 10:20). (See Rev. 20:12ff.).

B. The One like a Son of man

1. The little horn spoke "great words" (7:25) (Rev. 13:5-6)—Domitian proclaiming himself Lord and God, ordering the world to worship him.
2. This "beast" is slain—Domitian and his empire (Rome) are destroyed and burned with fire (thrown into lake of fire and brimstone, Rev. 19:20-21).
3. Before it is slain, it is apparent that the first three beasts had their lives and character "prolonged for a season" in the fourth beast, Rome. This is in exact agreement with Revelation 13:1-2 which shows Rome as a composite of Daniel's four beasts!
4. In connection with the fall of the fourth beast and little horn the Son of man enters the scene—this is none other than Christ, the Lamb, the incarnate Lion of David.
5. Son of man comes to the Throne-occupant (Ancient of Days) and is given dominion. This coincides exactly with the Lamb being given the scroll (Rev. 5:1-14) and dominion over history and redemption, because the Son is worthy having obtained salvation by incarnation.
6. Son of man given universal dominion over a universal kingdom—this is the church universal made of every nation, tribe, people tongue (cf. Rev. 1:5-6; 5:9-14; 7:9-12).

   The beast's (Rome) reign is not nearly so universal and everlasting as that of the Son of man's kingdom!
7. The saints of the Most High shall receive the kingdom and possess it for ever and ever. THIS IS THE MAIN POINT OF THE WHOLE VISION!

   That is precisely what God did when He established the church in the days of the fourth beast (Rome) by the work of Christ (see Lk. 12:32; 22:29, etc.). That kingdom, the church, will abide forever—it will never die, for even death cannot prevail against it. The kingdom is the church—not some 1000 year millennial reign of Jesus and the Jews in Palestine.

III. MEANING BESTOWED, 7:19-28

A. Testing the Saints

1. Daniel was alarmed when he first received this revelation

154

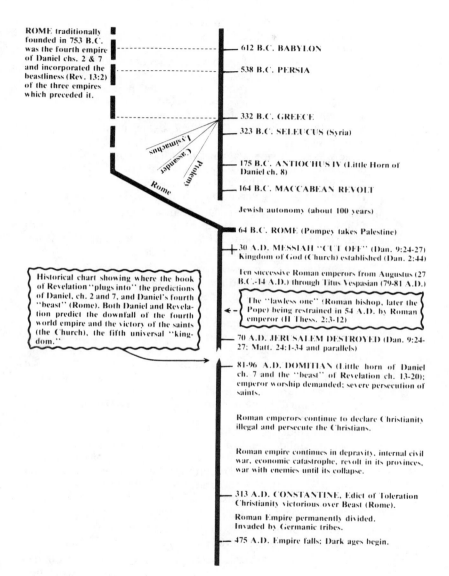

ROME traditionally founded in 753 B.C. was the fourth empire of Daniel chs. 2 & 7 and incorporated the beastliness (Rev. 13:2) of the three empires which preceded it.

Lysimachus

Cassander

Ptolemy

Rome

612 B.C. BABYLON

538 B.C. PERSIA

332 B.C. GREECE

323 B.C. SELEUCUS (Syria)

175 B.C. ANTIOCHUS IV (Little Horn of Daniel ch. 8)

164 B.C. MACCABEAN REVOLT

Jewish autonomy (about 100 years)

64 B.C. ROME (Pompey takes Palestine)

30 A.D. MESSIAH "CUT OFF" (Dan. 9:24-27) Kingdom of God (Church) established (Dan. 2:44)

Ten successive Roman emperors from Augustus (27 B.C.-14 A.D.) through Titus Vespasian (79-81 A.D.)

The "lawless one" (Roman bishop, later the Pope) being restrained in 54 A.D. by Roman emperor (II Thess. 2:3-12)

Historical chart showing where the book of Revelation "plugs into" the predictions of Daniel, ch. 2 and 7, and Daniel's fourth "beast" (Rome). Both Daniel and Revelation predict the downfall of the fourth world empire and the victory of the saints (the Church), the fifth universal "kingdom."

70 A.D. JERUSALEM DESTROYED (Dan. 9:24-27; Matt. 24:1-34 and parallels)

81-96 A.D. DOMITIAN (Little horn of Daniel ch. 7 and the "beast" of Revelation ch. 13-20); emperor worship demanded; severe persecution of saints.

Roman emperors continue to declare Christianity illegal and persecute the Christians.

Roman empire continues in depravity, internal civil war, economic catastrophe, revolt in its provinces, war with enemies until its collapse.

313 A.D. CONSTANTINE, Edict of Toleration Christianity victorious over Beast (Rome).

Roman Empire permanently divided. Invaded by Germanic tribes.

475 A.D. Empire falls; Dark ages begin.

155

(7:15) because it appeared there was going to be a great struggle. Perhaps the messianic destiny of God's program was even in doubt.

2. God was revealing that there were, in fact, going to be *centuries* of struggle for the messianic kingdom.
3. The little horn of the fourth kingdom has more revealed about himself in the following verses.
   a. he will seem greater than his fellows
   b. he will seem to prevail over the saints, until the judgment of God falls
   c. he will speak words against the Most High
   d. he will think to change times and the law
   e. he will wear out the saints of the Most High
   f. saints will be "given into his hand" for 3-1/2 times
4. This graphically describes Domitian and those emperors who followed him up to the death of Diocletian—the era from 81 A.D. to 312 A.D. (about 231 years) in which it appeared Rome would wipe out the church by persecution.

   a. Domitian became censor (one who determines whether a law is right or wrong) and the first to openly renounce and disregard the republican aspect of the state in favor of dictatorial.
   b. He changed many Roman laws, and assumed the right of first vote in the Senate so that voting differently from him endangered his life.
   c. He issued his letters and edicts with the salutation: "Our Lord God Domitian instructs you . . ." and demanded that anyone addressing him call him Lord God.
   d. He renamed September and October as Germanicus and Domitianus.
   e. He demanded to be hailed as Jupiter's son and heir, the earthly embodiment of the "king of the universe."
   f. His profligacy and cruelty were greater than Nero's.
   g. One historian says: "Domitian is the emperor who has gone down in history as the one who bathed the empire in the blood of the Christians."
5. The most crucial time for the infant church of Christ (especially in Asia Minor because most Christians were there) was during the reign of Domitian through the reign of Diocletian.

   a. That is why God reveals this crucial time to Daniel of Domitian
   b. That is why Christ revealed the visions to John in Revelation and addressed it mainly to the churches of Asia Minor.

c. From Domitian for about 231 more years it appeared as if the fourth beast (esp. the "little horn") was invincible (Rev. 13:4) and could not be withstood even by God.

d. Thus Daniel is shown the eventual rise of the Roman empire; that its great universal and complete power for an extended, but not eternal time, would eventually be brought to an end.

e. Daniel is shown that the kingdom of God will prevail against the ultimate power the world can bring to bear against it. It is significant that the Son of God was put to death during the Roman empire, by a Roman procurator—and that was the very ultimate that could be done to stop God's redemptive program. But God caught his Son up. God, in fact, used the death of His Son to accomplish man's redemption, raised him from the dead, and exalted him to have control (the scroll, Rev. 5) over the destiny of the world and his church.

f. When God caught his Son up, the devil began to try to swallow up the church with a "flood" of persecution (Rev. 12:13-17) but the church is rescued—however the devil did not give up his attempt to make war on the church.

5. These verses are the crucial section of Daniel (7:19-28). They must be interpreted in the light of *Daniel's* purpose.

a. His aim is to reveal to people of his day and those Jews who will come after him until the Messiah comes, that God's covenant will prevail over four successive world empires.

b. That is Daniel's theme all the way through his book. He is *not* aiming at the 2nd coming of Christ, but the *first* coming.

c. He is aiming at predicting the long centuries of testing and trying the saints of God (both Old Testament saints and New Testament saints) until the kingdom is given to them, and they become victorious over the fourth beast.

B. Triumph of the Saints

1. This cannot be the end of the world because the kingdom is given to the saints in conjunction with the judgment upon the fourth beast and that is Rome.

2. Furthermore, the kingdom was "given" to the saints at the *first* coming of Christ (cf. Lk. 12:32; 22:29; Rev. 1:9, etc.).

3. Why would it necessitate the fall of Rome before the kingdom could be "given" to the saints?

SO THE CHURCH COULD REALLY MOVE OUT OF ASIA MINOR AND GREECE TO THE UTTER MOST PARTS OF THE EARTH!

4. Domitian was assassinated by one of his wife's servants and his body was cremated by his nurse and the ashes deposited in the temple of the Flavian family.
   The Roman Senate denounced him, had his images and the votive shields engraved with his likeness brought smashing down, decreed that all inscriptions referring to him be effaced and all records of his reign obliterated. Domitian's dominion was "destroyed to the end."

5. Then, in 313 A.D. Constantine issued the edict of toleration which made Christianity legal and it was able to "conquer" the beast.

6. How was *dominion* given to the saints?
   IT DEPENDS ON WHAT ONE CONSIDERS DOMINION! WHAT IS THE MOST IMPORTANT "DOMINION"—IS IT TERRITORY? SEE POINTS TO PONDER AT END OF LESSON!

7. The kingdom of God, the church, has outlasted all other kingdoms—and the resurrection of Christ proves it will be eternal—not even death can wipe it out.

8. It is able to "bring every thought captive in obedience to Christ" in people from all tribes and nations and peoples and languages (Rev. 7). IT CONQUERS CULTURE, RACE, AND ALL OTHER BARRIERS!

IV. THE GOAT AND THE RAM, 8:1-8

A. The Ram is Medo-Persia (see 8:20)

1. Why is it important that God reveal the struggles between Persia and Greece?

2. Both empires will have tremendous effects on the messianic "remnant" of Jews. Persian confrontations for Jews would produce assimilation of Jews into far reaches of civilization. Freedom for Jews put them into high places, made synagogues available, preserved Jewish scriptures, etc. Persia's "magnification" of itself far and wide made all this preparation for the "kingdom of God" possible.

3. Two horns are two parts of Medo-Persian coalition. Taller horn came up last (Persia). Ram is symbolic of princely power (Ezek. 34:17). The ram likes to butt things, yet there is something of staid and sober character to it—not as flamboyant as he-goat.

Persian soldiers, such as this one, conquered the Babylonian Empire and Egypt. Until faced with the Greek armies, the Persians never lost a battle.

158

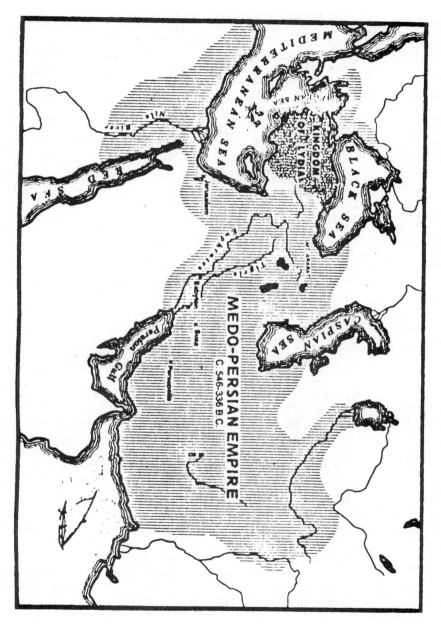

MEDITERRANEAN SEA

RED SEA

Nile River

KINGDOM OF LYDIA

BLACK SEA

CASPIAN SEA

MEDO-PERSIAN EMPIRE
C. 546-336 B.C.

Persian Gulf

4. Persia conquered a very large territory to the west, south and north of its own location and did not conquer east because it already controlled as far east as India.
5. Persian empire lasted 200 years.
   a. gave the world the longest peace in history until Rome
   b. gave opportunity for great commercial exchange
   c. gave the world an "international" language in Aramaic
   d. gave rapid communications and good roads; international coinage
   e. gave great human freedoms to many different religions and cultures under its domain.
6. Persian respect for truth and honor, and their humane and chivalrous character, was the secret of their nation's successes. Later "playboys" such as Xerxes (Ahasureaus) frittered many of these successes away by not protecting the human rights their royal predecessors had cherished.

   The Persians were the founders of religious freedom on a world basis. The Jews speak well *only* of the Persian empire.

   That is interesting in the light of the hatred today between Jews and Iranians!

   Rome tried to adapt many of the Persian practices, but Rome was unable to develop religious freedom because of her pride in insisting on making emperors become gods.
7. Under Darius Hystaspes the Persian government even helped bear the expense of erecting Israel's new commonwealth and temple.
8. Isaiah 44 and 45 predict Cyrus, the Persian, will become God's "anointed" to return a "remnant" to Palestine and start the messianic program moving again. Isaiah predicts Cyrus would bring about the peace to the world necessary to accomplish this.
9. The magnanimity of the Persians was a real test for the Jews— the majority of them decided to stay in Persia—only 50,000 returned to Palestine.

B. The He-Goat is Greece

1. A fitting symbol for its ruggedness and power, sure-footedness and quickness.
2. Alexander the Great swept across the world stage literally "flying" from west to east, hardly stopping, and conquered the world in less than 10 years. Reaching India, he wept because there were no more worlds to conquer.

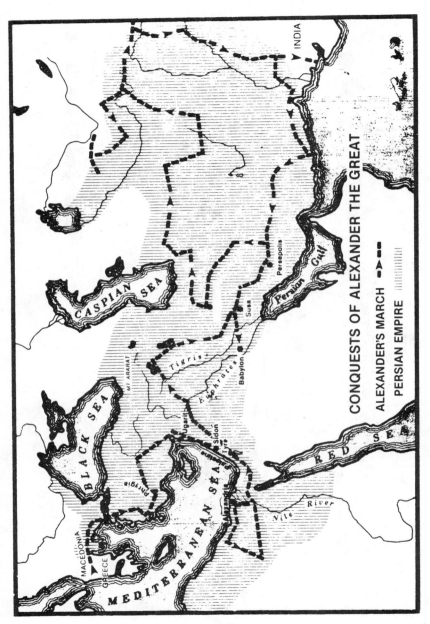

CONQUESTS OF ALEXANDER THE GREAT

ALEXANDER'S MARCH

PERSIAN EMPIRE

INDIA

CASPIAN SEA

Persian Gulf

Persepolis

Susa

Tigris

Euphrates

Babylon

MT ARARAT

BLACK SEA

Ugarit

Sidon

Tyre

Phrygia

MACEDONIA

GREECE

MEDITERRANEAN SEA

RED SEA

Nile River

3. The "conspicuous" horn was Alexander. He had such impact on civilization that cities are named after him, even gods of the Buddhists bear his image.

4. Greek conquests introduced the world to Aristotleian logic, Greek architecture, Koine Greek language (New Testament Greek). Western culture coming with Greek conquests prepared the world for a spread of Old Testament scriptures even more widely into the West (and later for New Testament faith).

5. Great anger points to Alexander's motive for attacking Persian empire because Persians had so often attacked Greek city states and burned them under Xerxes, et al.

6. Alexander won an empire covering more than 1.5 million square miles.

Alexander the Great, king of Macedonia, has been called a military genius. His empire was the largest the world ever had known.

7. Four horns coming up in place of the great horn are parallel to the four heads of the leopard of ch. 7 and represent the four-way division of Alexander's empire at his death when he was 32 years old.

8. Daniel will focus on only *one* of those four in this chapter, because it will have much to do with the future of the messianic remnant.

V. THE LITTLE-GREAT HORN AND THE PRINCE OF THE HOST, 8:9-17

A. Antiochus IV is the "little horn" here.

1. He comes out of the Greek empire (actually from the Seleucids).

2. All the Seleucid rulers before this "little horn" are not mentioned until Dan. ch. 11—the one which has most to do with tribulations for the Jews in Antiochus IV.

3. This "little horn" is *not* the same as the one in ch. 7.

4. The "glorious land" is Palestine, Canaan, land of "promise."

5. "Host of heaven" are God's covenant people (cf. Ex. 7:4; 12:41;

Little Horn grows great toward the glorious land.

Jer. 33:22; Dan. 12:3) they are also referred to as "stars."

6. Antiochus IV would bring some of God's covenant people down by seducing them to violate their holy covenant relationship to God (cf. Dan. 11:32).

7. He will grow exceedingly great toward the Jews and subject them to many indignities and persecutions.

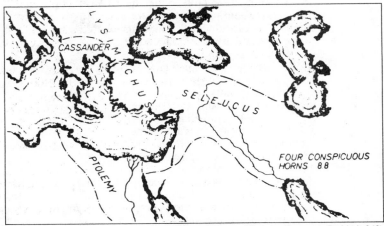

Four-way division of Greek empire at Alexander's death—only Egypt and Syria are of concern to Daniel (ch. 8-12).

B. Antiochus IV magnifies himself

1. Even to the Prince of the host. He arrogated to himself prerogatives that only the Messiah or God Himself would assume. He considered himself equal to God and ordered a likeness of himself to be placed in the temple of the Jews and worshiped as God (I Macc. 1:21-25).

2. He forbade the Jews to offer their regular sacrifices (I Macc. 1:44-47)—"took away the continual burnt offering."

3. He robbed the Jewish temple, offered a sow (pig) upon the altar, and ordered the Jews to stop circumcising their children and to offer swine's flesh in the temple also (Josephus, *Antiquities*, XII; V; 4).

4. Great numbers of the Jews made "covenant" with Antiochus (I Macc. 1:12-16).

5. He burned Hebrew copies of the Old Testament and killed those who were found possessing them (I Macc. 1:57-62) (Josephus, *ibid*) "truth was cast down to the ground."

6. The length of Antiochus' devastation upon the Jews:

164

a. The statement is revealed from heaven
b. It is 2300 evenings and mornings—this would be understood by a Jew as 2300 days (Genesis, ch. 1 an evening and a morning is a day).
c. It is probably to be understood as a "round number" and not exact.
d. However, Antiochus began all this sometime in 171 B.C. (persecuting the Jews) and terminated it at his death sometime in early Spring, 164 B.C.—6 years, 3 months, and 20 days would be about 2300 days (365 days per year, 30 days per month).
e. The phrase "then shall the sanctuary be cleansed" makes it very plain that what is really marked by the 2300 days is the period of the desecration of the Jewish temple. IT HAS NOTHING TO DO WITH THE END OF THE WORLD!

C. Antiochus will "prosper" until the "time of the end"

1. This vision was meant to be understood even by Daniel! It is not a secret.
2. Now what "time of the end" would Daniel be looking for? The end of the Jewish age and the beginning of the Messianic age, of course.
   THAT IS WHAT IS TOLD TO HIM IN EXACT YEARS IN THE NEXT CHAPTER (CH. 9)!
3. This has nothing to do with the 2nd coming of Christ because Jesus said plainly no one would know that time!
4. The time of the end and the 2300 evenings and mornings has to do with the "latter end of the indignation" (8:19) and the end of Antiochus IV (8:25-26) which will come close to the end of the Jewish age.

VI. GRIEVOUS TIMES AND RETRIBUTION, 8:18-27

A. God's "indignation" will end.

1. All that Daniel is seeing pertains to the latter end of the indignation, 8:19.
2. The term indignation refers to God's wrath upon sin (Isa. 10:5, 25; 26:2).
3. God's indignation on sin did not end until the Messiah came and atoned (cf. Dan. 9:24-27). The return from the captivities was *not* the end of God's indignation.
4. The terrible times of Antiochus IV will come *near* the end of the indignation and near the time when the Messiah comes to deliver the whole world from God's wrath.

The important thing to remember is the *kind* of indignation from which the Messiah delivers—the Jews (and many since) have interpreted the messianic deliverance as something political, earthly, physical.

BUT THAT IT IS *NOT* PHYSICAL IS PLAIN FROM THE NEW TESTAMENT. His kingdom is not of this world.

B. Indignation will end at a specified time in connection with the last days of Persian and Greek empires.

1. Daniel is not to be mistaken about when God will bring all this terrible testing of the messianic remnant to an end.

2. An even more exact and terrible picture of Antiochus IV is painted.

(This is even more detailed in ch. 11)! God does not want the Jews to give up when Antiochus comes. "A word to the wise is sufficient!" "Forewarned is forearmed!"

3. When the persecution of Antiochus and the Maccabean revolt came, centuries after Daniel's prophecy, it produced the effect God wanted—it produced a great messianic longing in the hearts of the faithful Jews.

4. There would be a "fourth beast" after the Ram and He-goat and the Seleucid "little horn."

During the time of this "fourth beast" (Rome) the Messiah would come. But Daniel leaves his wickedness to be detailed by John in the book of Revelation. He will put the Old Testament dispensation to destruction (Dan. 9:24-27) and test the saints of the New Testament.

C. This "contemptible one" (see Dan. 11:21) will be brought to an end himself.

1. His end will be "by no human hand"; i.e., it will appear to be by the direct intervention of Providence that this one shall fall. God will have a hand in his end. We will comment more precisely on this in chapter 11.

2. Daniel is to "seal" this prophecy. Not hide it or make it unknown, but *confirm* it, *preserve* it from being tampered with, *authenticate* it as true.

3. God *did* want the Jews to know *when* the Messiah would arrive. Jesus called two Emmaus disciples "foolish men and slow of heart to believe all that the prophets" said about the Messiah when they did not recognize Him (Lk. 24).

He even expected the Jews to recognize what *kind* of kingdom the Messiah would initiate!

THEY WERE TO UNDERSTAND THE PROPHECIES OF DANIEL!

166

APPREHENSION:

1. Why does the Bible symbolize great world governments as "beasts"? (See Dan. 7; Isa. 27:1; 51:9; Ezek. 29:3; 32:2; Rev. 13, etc.)
2. Does God really permit great empires to "devour much flesh" and does he give them dominion? (Dan. 7:5-6) Did God give Russia its dominion?
3. How did the dominion of the "rest of the beasts" get prolonged in the "little horn" of the fourth beast? (See Rev. 13:1-2.)
4. How does the time for the saints to receive the kingdom fit into the judgment of the "little horn" of the fourth beast? (Dan. 7:15-28)
5. Who is the "ram"? Who is the "he-goat"? Who is the "little horn" of 8:9?
6. What are the 2300 days? (8:14) What "time of the end" do they signal?
7. Who is the king of bold countenance"? (8:23-25)
8. What does God promise in spite of all the beastliness of ch. 7-8?

APPLICATION:

1. All human governments are, to varying degrees, *beastly.* That is they all emphasize the earthly, animalistic part of man and de-emphasize the spiritual. They all survive, like beasts, by force and by preying upon man's rights and freedoms.

    Some are more beastly than others. Some human governments are humane but only when they acknowledge the sovereignty of God Almighty (like Nebuchadnezzar did). The only way to keep human government from becoming like raging, cruel, blood-thirsty animals is to keep them acknowledging the Lord God's sovereignty over man.
2. If that is the case, why do we have to have human government at all? Because men not born again into the kingdom of God will not do what is right in this world without the application of *force* (see I Tim. 1:8-9; Rom. 13:1-7; I Pet. 2:13-14).

    Human laws that are not enforced, are not laws. Society cannot survive without law and enforcement of that law in this wicked world. Satan is behind all anarchy (attempts to overthrow government by law). The Christian must be the kind of person who does not have to have force brought to bear on him to get him to keep good and true law. He obeys what is right because that is his nature to do so, because he *loves* truth and goodness.

    But sinners do not love truth and goodness—they hate it. Therefore, they have to be forced to be good!
3. Human governments derive their *dominions* from God. Daniel makes that very plain in his predictions. And all these human dominions are allowed by God for the *ultimate purpose* of preparing for and spreading

forth of His kingdom, the church! That was true of the Old Testament empires and Rome, and it is true of human dominions today! Thank God, the early Americans believed this:

"Let us beware that we do not impute these signal divine appearances in our favor to any peculiar excellence in our national character. Alas, the moral face of our country effectually confutes such a vainglorious statement. Crimes of the blackest hue, countless multitudes of abominations, mark the visible character of this great, this highly favored community, and still provoke the great displeasure of heaven. . . . Let us remember that for His own sake, He hath done these great things, not for any righteousness in us. . . . But that His own name might be exalted, that His own great designs . . . extending the kingdom of His Son, may be carried into effect."
— Sermon by David Tappan, Newbury, Mass., 1777

So spoke many great preachers and statesmen in those days! God shed His grace on America in order to further His kingdom in the world! MAY IT CONTINUE TO BE SO!

4. God gave Daniel a vision of the majestic, sovereign throne of God and the Son in order to give the *divine perspective to history*. The human, finite, limited perspective of history is what makes men pessimistic existentialists who say, "Life is never more absurd than at the grave," or, "There is meaning only in meaninglessness."

The terrible tragedies, the instabilities, the aimless recycling of human nature one generation after another, would turn any thinking man into despondency and despair if he views history only from the past and the present.

Once he knows there is a God, outside of history, exercising supernaturally wise, good and truthful control over it as he brings it to a conquest of the holy, good, true and just purpose he has decreed, man becomes a faithful optimist conforming himself to the nature of this Sovereign.

5. God's kingdom obtains its sovereignty through the *incarnation* of the Son. The Son became flesh and conquered sin in the flesh and provides the impetus of grace and faith. He does not have His dominion by force but by love, and by faith.

Of course, God has the power to banish from His presence forever those who do not wish to willingly surrender to His rule. But to dwell in His presence will not be by force. If you do not want God, do not fret, He will not force Himself upon you.

6. The saints are given *dominion*. But that is *not* territorial dominion. It is not the land of Palestine, or the European Common Market, or America, God gives his saints. Their dominion is much *greater* than all this. It is dominion over sin (Rom. 6:1-23). It is conquest—yea, more

than conquerors,—of all that can keep us from the love of God (Rom. 8:1-39). It is dominion over the power of the devil (Heb. 2:5-16). It is dominion over our circumstances for we can be content no matter what they are (Phil. 4:4-12).

Sin, rebellion against truth, is the ultimate trap, the eternal enslavement. The truth makes free, even when the body is imprisoned.

7. The court of *heaven* has authority to judge all human endeavors. And it does, indeed, pass judgment and dispose and impose upon mankind any circumstance of history it deems advisable.

The Roman empire called itself "eternal" but it lasted only 400 years in its western form. Today it exists only as ancient history! The court of heaven sits reviewing America's case today. Her judgment is inevitable. The *time* for her banishment is uncertain as far as man is concerned, but the fact of it is inevitable.

All human philosophies and systems have been weighed in the balances and found wanting. Every man seems to have his own idea about what God will do with individuals and masses. Most men expect God to make His judgments according to their ideas. BUT GOD'S JUDICIAL SYSTEM HAS ALREADY BEEN DECIDED, WRITTEN DOWN AND CONFIRMED. "Whoever does not obey the Son is condemned already" Jn. 3:36.

8. God sifts and tests men to prepare them for his kingdom. He will have no untried, untested, unproven people in his heaven!

God told the Jews that the wilderness wanderings were to "test" them (Heb. 3:8).

He told them the Babylon captivities were to "sift" them (Amos 9:9). Jesus told Peter that he was going to allow Satan to "sift" him (Lk. 22:31). Daniel predicted the days of Antiochus were to "test" the Jews (Dan. 11:35). Peter said Christians were to be tried by persecutions (I Pet. 4:12). The book of Revelation represents the great tribulations of the Roman empire were to "test" the saints (Rev. 3:10).

Jesus was tested—met the test by faith—and anointed God's Son by meeting the test.

God tests your faith in order to produce steadfastness in yor commitments (James 1:3). If He didn't test it, you would lose your ability to endure and thus lose your inheritance!

9. God knows the future. Names change, territories change, but the principles remain the same. Great nations struggle, lock horns, attack God's redemptive program, but out of all the agony, destruction, apostasy, human arrogance, God's immutable purposes roll on, inevitably, inexorably, and men are given the opportunities to make moral and mental choices which will determine their eternal destinies as they fit into His immutable program. Men and their pronouncements come and go; human "stars" rise and fall; BUT GOD'S BOOK HAS PROVEN ONCE FOR ALL

THIRTEEN LESSONS ON REVELATION

THAT GOD KNOWS, SEES, OVERRULES AND USES HISTORY TO HIS OWN GLORY FOR THOSE WHO BELONG TO HIM BY CHOICE! All men have their day before the court of heaven—what they do about heaven's decrees determines their eternal existence.

A British soldier one night was caught creeping back to his quarters from the nearby woods. Taken before his C.O., he was charged with holding communications with the enemy. The man pleaded he had gone into the woods to pray by himself. That was his only defense. "Down on your knees and pray now!" roared the officer, "You never needed it so much!" Expecting immediate death, the soldier knelt and poured out his soul in eloquent prayer. "You may go," said the officer simply, when he had finished, "I believe your story. If you hadn't drilled so often, you could not do so well at review."

No wonder Daniel is called a man of "excellent spirit." To read his prayer in this ninth chapter is to be shamed with the thought of one's own lack of humility and fervency in prayer. Daniel drilled so often he was able to do excellently at review time.

While reams of paper and hours of speech have been expended on discussing Daniel's prophecy of the "70 weeks," far too often his magnificent prayer bas been neglected. It is one of the most beautiful prayers of all the Bible. It should rank alongside the 23rd Psalm. If you have ever felt like Jesus' disciples when they begged, "Lord, teach us to pray," you may find most of your answer when you analyze Daniel's prayer in 9:1-19. Incidentally, his prayer is crucial to understanding his prophecy.

We will be studying the great prophecy of the Messiah in 9:24-27. It will help you with answers to so much false teaching in the religious world today. But most important, read Daniel's prayer about 7 times this week.

SEVENTY SEVENS

THE PRAYER, THE PRINCE AND POSTERITY

by Paul T. Butler

Daniel 9:1—10:21

Introduction

I. THIS IS THE HEART OF DANIEL'S PROPHETIC MINISTRY

    A. Daniel 9:24-27 is the very focal point of Daniel's prophecies and all Old Testament prophecy!

        1. Sir Isaac Newton, one of the greatest scientists the world has ever known, wrote a commentary on the Prophecies of Daniel and the Revelation.

2. He described Daniel 9:24-27 as "the foundation stone of the Christian religion," because centuries in advance it gave the exact time of the appearance of the Messiah and the date of His death, as well as a comprehensive description of His saving work in heaven and earth. The prophecy likewise tells what would be the fate of the Jews upon their rejection of the One whose coming they had long anticipated. The destruction of Jerusalem in A.D. 70 was history's testimony that the offerings and services of the sanctuary had met their fulfillment in the coming of the promised Anointed One (Messiah).

B. Everything else Daniel predicts is secondary and preparatory for what he predicts in this chapter.

II. THE TIME OF THIS PROPHECY

A. In the first year of Darius (Gubaru), about 536 B.C. (3rd year of Cyrus)
   1. Daniel is 80 or 90 years old.
   2. The release of the Jews from captivity to return to Palestine has just occurred. Reports of troubles are coming back to Daniel.

B. Many so-called great events of history are happening about this time.
   1. Many of the alleged great "world-religions" were being formed about this time; Bhuddism, Taoism, Janism, etc.
   2. Greek democracy was beginning to reach its peak as well as Greek science and philosophy.
   3. But the most important event was that some 50,000 former Jewish prisoners-of-war had been released to return and begin the process of fulfilling Daniel's prophecy of 9:24-27.
   4. Much testing and tribulating (pressurizing) of this "messianic" people would come before the fulfillment.
      To be exact, there would be 490 years of "trouble," but the details of that are to be explained in ch. 10-12.

III. CHRISTIANS STUDY THIS PROPHECY THOROUGHLY AND RE-PEATEDLY.

A. Jewish rabbis forbade the teaching of Daniel 9:24-27 because it meant Jesus Christ was the Messiah.

B. Daniel 9:24-27 is incontrovertible evidence that Jesus Christ was the Messiah. There is no better evidence in all the Old Testament.

C. Josephus writes of Daniel: "The several books that he (Daniel) wrote and left behind him, are still read by us till this time, and from them we believe that Daniel conversed with God, for he did not only prophesy of future events as did the other prophets, but he also determined the time of their accomplishment." *Antiq.* X:11:7

D. This is why unbelieving critics want to date the book of Daniel at the time of the Maccabeans, to get away from fulfilled prophecy.

Discussion

I. REPENTANCE, 9:1-14

A. Rebellion confessed, 3-6

1. Daniel confesses that the captivity of God's people is due to their stubborn rebellion (see Isa. 30:9-10; Jer. 6:16-19; Ezek. 2:1—3:11, etc.).
It is exactly what Moses warned against, Deut. 28.

2. Daniel admits his sin and that of his people and that they deserve nothing but God's wrath.

3. Daniel observes that God promised to end the captivity after 70 years and apparently assumes that will be the end of God's wrath—or perhaps he is confused from the earlier revelation in ch. 7-8 about "troubled" times to come upon the Jews in the far distant future.

4. Daniel's main concern in this prayer is to implore God to keep His name clear of any taint of unfaithfulness by going back on His promise to provide forgiveness for the Jews.

5. DANIEL IS PRAYING FOR BETTER EARTHLY CIRCUM—STANCES FOR HIS PEOPLE . . . HIS PRAYER IS ALSO FOR SPIRITUAL DELIVERANCE, BUT HE HEARS OF THEIR TROUBLES BACK IN JERUSALEM AND HAS DOUBTS AS TO WHETHER GOD HAS FORGIVEN THEIR SINS OF IDOLATRY OR NOT! God needs to clear this up for Daniel.

6. Understanding this is important in understanding the angel's answer to Daniel's prayer in 9:24-27!
The answer is: Complete withdrawal of the "indignation" of God is *NOT* at the restoration of the Jewish commonwealth *but is centuries away,* at which time Judaism will be abrogated and destroyed!

172

THE PRAYER, THE PRINCE AND POSTERITY

B. Rejection agreed with, 7-11

1. Apparently Daniel thought the captivity or "indignation" was about to be prolonged on account of the sins of the people, so he prayed for the mercy of God.

   And, he was right. God still needed to purge the Jewish nation down to a "holy stump" and even down to a "holy seed"—remember Isaiah, ch. 6?

   The next 500 years of tribulations, after Daniel, would accomplish that.

   God needed a small remnant which would be eager for a *spiritual* deliverance (like Mary, Joseph, the aged Simeon, John the Baptist, Joseph of Arimathea, and others).

2. Daniel made confession. The word in Hebrew *todah* means to *acknowledge* (Gr. *homolego,* means "to say the same as"). In other words, Daniel acknowledged and said the same as God said about Judah's sinfulness. They had sinned openly, willingly, deliberately and shamefully. The Hebrew word *bosheth,* "confusion" means *shame.* They were guilty—no one else, certainly not God, for their shame.

C. Refusal, 12-14

1. Daniel's prayer is one of *complete* humility. He expresses the attitude that even after almost 70 years of captivity the Jewish people are still sinners. They have not gotten so holy they now deserve anything from God but his wrath, (13). NO ONE EVER ATTAINS!

2. Daniel acknowledged or confessed God's justice in their punishment. God as the only absolutely holy, just, fair, faithful Being is imperative. It is not optional! God must keep his name absolute. He must be *trusted* to be righteous in everything he does! Man is not given the prerogative of disagreeing with God's ways!

3. God confirmed his word as absolutely inviolable when he took the Jews captive. What God promises and warns, he surely fulfills!

4. Ultimately, every human being will surrender in obedience to the word of God. They may go to heaven, or they may go to hell, but obey Him they will surely do.

II. REQUEST, 9:15-19

A. Release, 15-16

1. Daniel makes his appeal on the basis of God's faithful nature. And God is not only faithful to judge his enemies, he is also faithful to deliver those who trust in his promises. So Daniel appeals to God to deliver his people on the basis of God's

173

actions in the past (Egyptian exodus). In delivering those who trusted him then, God made a name for himself. Daniel appeals to God to keep his name sacred and keep his promise to rebuild Jerusalem. But Daniel thinks of this as God's forgiveness.

2. The Jews had become a "byword" (as Moses predicted) because they had so completely heathenized themselves and turned away from their "roots" and their God.

If the Jews were a byword, so was their God. His name was not respected because of them.

Daniel is concerned about the reputation of God. God's reputation must be vindicated, established, once and for all.

B. Restore, 17

1. So, Daniel prays first and foremost, that everything God shall do is for *his* namesake!

2. He begs God to restore the Temple and Jerusalem so that the world will know the power and majesty and faithfulness of Jehovah.

3. So long as the Temple and Jerusalem are in ruins, the heathen world will pass by and mock and ridicule Jehovah. That must not be! Not if the world is going to have anything certain by which to be saved.

GOD MUST CARRY OUT HIS MESSIANIC PROGRAM OF REDEMPTION AND HE PROMISED TO DO IT IN JERUSALEM, THROUGH THE JEWISH REMNANT. BUT JERUSALEM IS DESTROYED AND THE JEWS ARE NOT A NATION! ENEMIES ARE OPPOSING THEM!

4. Daniel is not interested in restoration of the Temple and city for Jewish pride; he is not interested in change of circumstances just for ease and comfort (in fact most Jews were more comfortable in Persia—return to Palestine meant more suffering as Daniel already had predicted).

C. Rebound, 18-19

1. There is an emphatic repetition throughout this prayer insisting that God's glory be vindicated in everything.

Sinning man deserves only judgment. If the Jews are delivered at all it will be entirely due to the very nature of God—mercifulness. This is the whole point of any prayer—God seeks contrition and penitence in prayer in order that He may do for man just what He has made up His mind he wants to do for man all along!

2. Prayer is not to get things from God—it is to *get you for God!* Prayer is to get the believer in the right nature or character to receive what God has decided before the prayer to give if the believer will just receive.

THE PRAYER, THE PRINCE AND POSTERITY

Prayer does not change God—it changes believers!
If prayer changes God, why didn't he remove Paul's thorn
in the flesh?

3. God cannot and will not act to bless any man if that man does
not pray believing that whatever he receives is a blessing!
Man changes—God acts. Prayer does not change things—
prayer changes man.

4. Daniel's prayer that God will act in the interest of His Own
perfect will is what God wants from Daniel. That way, whatever God does with the Jewish people will be received as a
blessing (believing Jews, that is).

God only wants us to be better than we are. But he knows
that this can only come about as a result of man's seeking to
glorify his Creator and Redeemer. God acts to glorify his name,
not out of selfish egotism, but in order to bless his creation
(cf. Ezek. 20:9, 14, 22, 44; Isa. 48:9-11).

The inevitable result of God acting to glorify his own name
is that the man who accepts and acts in accordance with this
is thereby made a partaker of God's glory (cf. II Pet. 1:3-11).

5. When Jesus taught his disciples to pray, he said pray *first*,
"Hallowed be *thy* name, *thy* kingdom come, *thy* will be done,
on earth as it is in heaven. . . ."

6. The reason God could give Daniel the revelation of such terrible
testing of the Jewish nation is because Daniel was a man of
total surrender in prayer. Daniel did not go to God with a long
list of get-wells, give-food-tos, save-from-persecutions. Of course,
God wanted Daniel to depend on him for everything, but not
simply to be relieved of difficult circumstances.

III. REVELATION, 9:20-27

A. Seraphim, 20-23

1. Right in the middle of his praying, Daniel is approached by the
angel, Gabriel, in human form, to deliver God's answer to his
prayer.

2. Yes, God is going to deliver his messianic redemption through
a small remnant of believing Jews—BUT IT IS GOING TO BE
490 YEARS LATER, AFTER MUCH SIFTING AND TESTING
AND PURIFYING.

3. God knows what his beloved need before they even ask and is
able to answer before they get through praying.

4. God also knows that our greatest need is to seek His glory.

5. As long as man is self-confident and self-dependent he is in no
position morally, intellectually or spiritually to receive what

175

God has for him (building his character into the image of Christ). Man resisting the will of God demands and spends whatever comes his way only to confirm his own egotism.

6. Be assured that the "things" you pray for are no problem to God. He can give you exceeding abundantly above all you can possibly imagine or ask for, if you utterly, totally, unreservedly trust Him! The problem is not what you need—the problem is you!

B. Scope of the Seventy Sevens, 24

1. The Hebrew text is lit. "sevens, seventy of them." This has been understood by conservative exegetes (even Jews) to mean "seventy weeks of years" or 490 years. The 7-day week = 7 years theory or "day-year" theory of interpretation is confirmed by the Bible (cf. Num. 14:34; Lev. 25:8; Ezek. 4:6).

It would be difficult to exaggerate the signifigance of this passage (v. 24-27) in the teachings of dispensationalists and pre-millennialists. It is appealed to by them as definite proof that the entire "Church age" is supposed to occur during the events listed in v. 24-26; and the 27th verse of this chapter concerns the "7 years of tribulations" just before the "millennium."

2. These 490 years are *determined* (Heb. *chatak,* apportioned, divided) for Daniel's "people"—the Jews. God will use the Jews only 490 years more after Daniel. After that, their time is up! They will resist, of course, and God will have to destroy their temple and their nation.

The only time God had left for the Jews was this 490 years. He has nothing left for them now or ever, as Jews.

The only thing left for the Jew is New Israel, the church (cf. Gal. 6:15-16). When the times of the Gentiles are completed (at the end of the world), then all New Israel will be saved (Rom. 11).

Everything said by Daniel in this passage is fulfilled in Christ and the destructruction of Judaism. The "promises" made to the sons of Abraham are fulfilled in

THE PRAYER, THE PRINCE AND POSTERITY

"Seed" (singular) not in "seeds" (plural). And all who are in Christ are sons of Abraham (cf. 3:15-29).

NOW LOOK WHAT WAS LEFT FOR THE "REMNANT" OF DANIEL'S PEOPLE TO ACCOMPLISH!

3. *Finish* the transgression. The Hebrew word is *chalah,* bring to completion, fill-up-full, finish a thing or a task. This is clearly talking about the filling-up-full the cup of Jewish iniquity. *They would reject the Messiah, they would kill the Son of God!* They had sinned terribly in their idolatry and killing of the Old Testament prophets, but the full height and depth of their evil was yet to be shown when they would "kill the heir" (Mt. 21:33-45; Mt. 23:32-39). As as result God's wrath came upon them to the end (Gr. *telos*), to completeness, finally, by destroying their nation (I Thess. 2:16). God's wrath is still upon them if they are outside of Christ.

Because they "cut off" the "Anointed One" (Messiah) God's *end* came upon them as a flood (Dan. 9:26).

4. *Put an end* to sin. In the death of the Messiah God will triumph over man's rebellion and declare sin atoned for and give man the power, by faith, to overcome sin. By sovereign decree of grace God punished all sin in His Son (II Cor. 5:17ff.). All sin, even that done from Eden onward was done away with in the death of Christ (Rom. 3:21-26; Heb. 9:15-28). Sin no longer has dominion over those who trust in Christ's blood.

5. *Atone* for iniquity. Christ's death not only ends sin, it atones and reconciles God to man, man to God. God had to be appeased before He could be reconciled to avowed enemies of His (Rom. 5; II Cor. 5).

6. Bring in *everlasting righteousness.* This is one of the things the Holy Spirit, through the preaching of the apostles, was to do in the world—convince men of sin, of righteousness, and of judgment to come. God imputes righteousness to us, unearned, through faith in His Son; we practice righteousness relatively by the prompting of His love for us and our trust in His word.

7. *Seal both vision and prophet.* With the accomplishment of the work of the Messiah in fulfilling God's prophesied plan of redemption and the end of the Jewish dispensation, Old Testament prophecy was confirmed, fulfilled, validated and thus sealed—done! Paid in full! (cf. Acts 3:24; I Pet. 1:10-11; II Pet. 1:16-21; Rev. 19:11).

8. *Anoint a most holy.* Actually, the Hebrew text reads, "anoint (messiah) holy, holies." It is arguable as to whether this applies to the anointing of *Jesus,* by His resurrection from the dead,

177

as the Holy One of Israel, the Messiah ("today have I begotten you, today thou art my Son)," or whether it applies to the "holiest of holies," the *church*. (See Acts 10:38-43.)

Some dispensationalists insist that all these things have not yet been accomplished. They insist all this is to come after the tribulation and during the millennium. They say, for example, "to make an end of sins" means to eliminate moral evil completely from this world.

They contend that because the 70th week is still future, the first 69 weeks must be also or else we have a gap of over 2000 years between 69th and 70th week. That is, if the things listed above were completed with Jesus at his first coming, the first 69 weeks are past. Since the 70th week must be future to our day, then we must be living in a huge gap of 2000 years. How do you count 2000 years into the 490 scheme of things?

THAT PROBLEM DOES NOT BOTHER SOME PRE-MILLENNIALISTS, AS YOU SHALL SEE IN THE CHARTS THAT FOLLOW!

We believe that to insist all the above is yet future is absurd in the light of plain New Testament teaching!

C. Sequence of the Seventy-Sevens, 25-26

1. The fact (based on New Testament teaching) that the 6 items of v. 24 are Messianic settles the question of where the *70 weeks are to end*. They are to end in connection with Messiah's first coming. When Christ ascended to heaven and the Holy Spirit descended (Acts 2) there remained not one of the 6 items of v. 24 that was not accomplished.

2. In verse 25 we are told where the *70 weeks are to begin;* "the going forth of the word to restore and build Jerusalem." There are only 4 events to which this phrase may refer:

   a. The decree of Cyrus, 536 B.C. (Ezra 1:2-4)
   b. The decree of Darius, 518 B.C. (Ezra 6:1-5)
   c. The decree of Artaxerxes, 457 B.C. (Ezra 7:12-26)
   d. The decree of Nehemiah, 444 B.C. (Neh. 2).

3. The decree of Cyrus did not permit them to fortify their city as foretold in Gabriel's message.

   The decree of Darius allowed them to continue the work of Cyrus' decree—but not granted freedom from taxation or allowed to appoint magistrates, self-rule, establish a commonwealth. *Clearly, the decree of Artaxerxes, 457 B.C., is the one the 490 years are to be counted from.*

4. Another terminating point of time is given—"to the coming of Messiah." The Hebrew text reads, *'ad—mashicha nagid,* and the article is missing altogether. "An anointed one" is not an accurate translation.

178

This is the only text in all the Old Testament where the word *Messiah* is used specifically.

Taking Daniel's passage, and all the other passages describing the Messiah's coming and nature, there should have been no excuse for the Jews mistaking Jesus as the Messiah.

5. There should be no period (.) after "seven weeks" in v. 25. It should read, ". . . to the coming of Messiah, prince, there shall be seven weeks, then for sixty-two weeks it shall be built again." The 7 plus 62 go together as one unit of time making 69 weeks. During this 69 weeks, Jerusalem will be rebuilt but during *troubled times.*

   That is exactly what Daniel shall predict in ch. 10-12, the troubled times of Jerusalem.

   Ezra 4:7-16 (which chronologically should be between Ezra 10 and Nehemiah 1) tells of some troubled times, also.

6. In the 70th week (after the 62 plus 7) the Messiah shall be "cut off" and have nothing. Compare this with Isaiah 53:7-9! We learn from v. 27 that his "cutting off" will be in the middle of the last week (or middle of the last 7 years) for that is when the Messiah shall cause sacrifice and offering to cease. Jesus was born 4 B.C.; began his ministry at age 30 in 26 A.D.; crucified mid-30 A.D.; gospel mainly to Jews for next 3-1/2 years—then turned to Gentiles mid-34 A.D. THAT WAS FINISH OF 490 YEARS FOR JEWS. God, in grace, allowed the nation to continue another 35 years, then destroyed it, (66-70 A.D.).

7. "People of the prince who is to come shall destroy the city and the sanctuary . . . " etc.

   Some say this refers to the Romans since they are referred to as God's "army" in the parable of the Marriage of the King's Son (Mt. 22:7).

   Others say this refers to the Jews themselves who wrought such destruction of the city of Jerusalem before the Romans ever started their assault. WE PREFER THE LATTER INTERPRETATION HERE.

8. The destruction of Jerusalem and the nation mentioned here is not to be included in the 490 years. As far as God was concerned Jewish time ended when the gospel had been preached thoroughly among the Jews by 34 A.D.

   As far as God was concerned sacrifice and offering ceased when the Messiah was crucified and arose. He was through with the Jews, as such, in the program of redemption at the cross.

D. Subsequent to the Seventy-Sevens, 27

179

THIRTEEN LESSONS ON REVELATION

1. During the last 70th the Messiah will make firm a covenant with many.
   The 3-1/2 years of Jesus' public ministry he was in favor with the multitudes—they heard him gladly. The rulers had him crucified. Then for 3-1/2 years more the covenant was confirmed among many Jews as thousands became obedient to the faith. After his crucifixion, for the latter of the 70th, because he atoned, sacrifice and offering was no longer efficacious. Of course, sacrifice and offering were forever abrogated at the cross, but in this passage we are dealing only with 490 years —and nothing beyond that except the destruction of Jerusalem.

2. Upon the "wing" of abominations shall come one who makes desolate, until the decreed end is poured out on the desolator. Some say this is the Jewish people destroying their own city. Some say it is the Romans. WE BELIEVE THIS REFERS TO THE ROMANS.
   The Romans built up siege walls around the city and let the Jews do most of the destruction themselves for about 3 years. When the Jews were dying of starvation and had killed thousands of their own, the Romans attacked, tore down the walls, the temple, killed thousands more Jews and took thousands more captive to be sold as slaves.
   Jerusalem lay in ruins for years, until the Romans built a heathen temple on its grounds and worshiped Jupiter there. Finally, the end came upon the "desolator" (Rome) himself— John predicts that in Revelation. Of course, Daniel has predicted the end of Rome himself, ch. 2 and ch. 7.

Thus ends one of the most amazing and significant prophecies in all the Bible! The Old Testament predicts its own abrogation, its end. God's finish with the Jews was no accident. He planned it ages and ages ago. When the stubborn and unbelieving Jews would not acknowledge it, God had to use drastic measures to impress His plan on the world. But, amazing, there are some Christians who will not acknowledge this today.

The following charts show two views of the seven-seventies (or 490 years). Please note that on the pre-millennial view there is a "gap" or "time out" between the 69th week and the 70th week of 2000 years. That is between the first coming of Christ and the so-called "rapture" and "tribulation." These people say God does not count time in this 490 year prophecy so long as the Jews are not occupying Palestine. When all the Jews get back to Palestine, the rapture will occur and the 70th week will begin, and those left on earth will endure 7 years of tribulation during the 70th week. After that the millennium (1000 years) will begin. After that, Christ will come back at the Second Coming.

The second chart did not originate by Butler—it is the generally accepted view of non pre-millennialists.

A Premillennial View

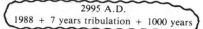
2995 A.D.
1988 + 7 years tribulation + 1000 years

DANIEL'S SEVENTY WEEKS

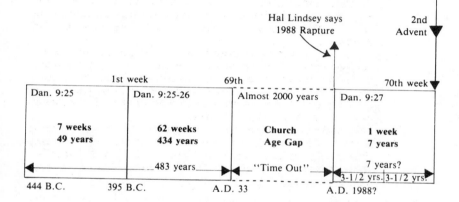

Hal Lindsey says
1988 Rapture

2nd
Advent

1st week		69th		70th week
Dan. 9:25	Dan. 9:25-26	Almost 2000 years	Dan. 9:27	
7 weeks 49 years	62 weeks 434 years	Church Age Gap	1 week 7 years	
	483 years	"Time Out"	7 years?	
			3-1/2 yrs.	3-1/2 yrs.

444 B.C.   395 B.C.   A.D. 33   A.D. 1988?

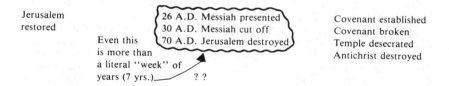

Jerusalem
restored

Even this
is more than
a literal "week" of
years (7 yrs.)   ? ?

26 A.D. Messiah presented
30 A.D. Messiah cut off
70 A.D. Jerusalem destroyed

Covenant established
Covenant broken
Temple desecrated
Antichrist destroyed

181

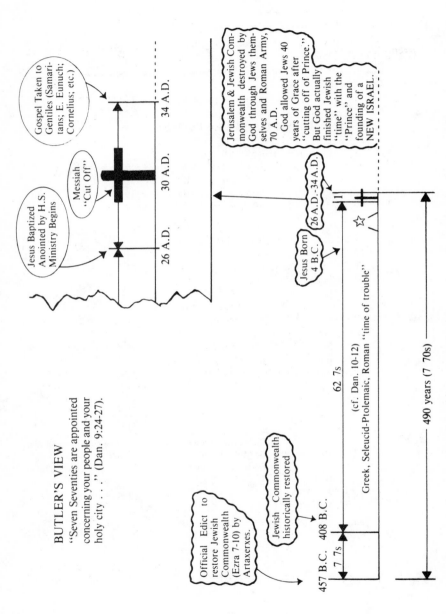

BUTLER'S VIEW

"Seven Seventies are appointed concerning your people and your holy city . . ." (Dan. 9:24-27).

Gospel Taken to Gentiles (Samaritans; E. Eunuch; Cornelius; etc.)

34 A.D.

Messiah "Cut Off"

30 A.D.

Jesus Baptized Anointed by H.S. Ministry Begins

26 A.D.

Jerusalem & Jewish Commonwealth destroyed by God through Jews themselves and Roman Army, 70 A.D.
God allowed Jews 40 years of Grace after "cutting off of Prince." But God actually finished Jewish "time" with the "Prince" and founding of a NEW ISRAEL.

26 A.D.-34 A.D.

Jesus Born 4 B.C.

62 7s

(cf. Dan. 10-12)
Greek, Seleucid-Ptolemaic, Roman "time of trouble"

Official Edict to restore Jewish Commonwealth (Ezra 7-10) by Artaxerxes.

Jewish Commonwealth historically restored

408 B.C.

457 B.C.

7 7s

490 years (7 70s)

182

THE PRAYER, THE PRINCE AND POSTERITY

IV. ANGELIC APPEARANCE, 10:1-9

    A. Apparently 3 years after the revelation in ch. 9 Daniel receives another revelation which helped him understand ch. 9.

        1. This message came to Daniel through an angel of God—a messenger.

        2. The angel appeared in human form —but

        3. The angel was so majestic in appearance everyone close was terrified. Some with Daniel did not see the angel or hear the message but the approach of the angel terrified them.

    B. Daniel fainted at the sound of his words.

        1. What did he hear that caused this —was it the loudness?

        2. I believe it was the content of the message that made Daniel faint.

Daniel and the Ministering Spirit

        3. He is told things about the realm of the next world that men do not know.

        4. What he is told is not guesswork nor fantasy. It is the brilliant, staggering TRUTH!

        5. It involved future centuries of warfare and struggle against the forces of hell for Daniel's people.

        6. What the angel told Daniel is detailed in chapters 11 and 12. What Daniel was to hear were all the gory details of a Jewish holocaust as terrible as that of Adolph Hitler's holocaust 2500 years later.

V. ANGELIC ANNOUNCEMENT, 10:10-14

    A. Daniel is told he is "greatly beloved."

        1. Daniel was a great man of God. One of the greatest of all in the Old Testament.

        2. Because he was "greatly beloved" God answered his prayer for revelation about the future of the Messianic people.

        3. God knew Daniel wanted to know this not simply out of curiosity, but in order to serve God's people—that he might be a vessel to strengthen them about their messianic destiny and the trials to come.

    B. The angel announces he has been struggling with "the prince of the kingdom of Persia."

1. Who is this "prince"? If he is able to "withstand" an angel of God, he must be a supernatural being himself. Apparently then, he is a demon from hell, an evil spirit, who was influencing the affairs in Persia (and in Greece 10:20).
2. The demonic, evil spirits were influencing Persians like Haman (in the days of Esther) to kill Jews.

   But God, through his providential care (apparently through angels like Gabriel and Michael) delivered them.
3. The vision the angel comes to deliver is for the "latter days" and that is proscribed as the period of history covered by the empires of Persia and Greece (10:20-21).

   This fits with what has been said in Dan. ch. 8, 9, 11, 12.

VI. ANGELIC ACTIVITY, 10:15-21

A. Daniel is dumbfounded. It is more than he can stand, mentally and emotionally. How can all this be—will my poor people be able to endure all this struggle against supernatural powers out of hell.

B. The angel gives Daniel strength. Must have been some kind of supernatural power.

C. The angel's question is rhetorical—"You do know why I came to you do you not?"
   1. To inform Daniel that great tribulations were coming on the Jews
   2. To inform Daniel that God would be with them and help them with power from heaven (in the person of ministering angels) (cf. Heb. 1:14, etc.)

D. God will be with them with power from heaven all through the "latter days."
   1. These princes of the kingdoms of Persia and Greece are not simply mortal kings—no mortal could have so successfully opposed an angel of God for a period of 21 days if one angel could smite 185,000 soldiers in one night (Isa. 37:36).
   2. They are evil spirits straight from hell allowed by these heathen rulers to influence their thinking and acting in opposing God's redemptive program in the earth.
   3. In the downward plunge away from truth and righteousness, the Gentile nations chose to worship and seek the fellowship of demons (Rom. 1:18ff.; I Cor. 10:20ff.) and so came under hell's direct influence.
   4. It would not necessarily mean bodily demon-possession such as the phenomena in the gospels where demons actually lived in the bodies of human beings. It could very well be evil spirits

184

influencing the minds of pagan rulers through false teachings. That activity continued on into the Roman empire. After Rome was defeated, the devil's activity in such wide-spread pervasiveness was restricted ("Satan was bound for a 1000 years"). The TRUTH went out to the far reaches of the world after Rome fell and had tremendous influence on culture, government, etc.

5. Of course, the devil and his "princes" are still at work, but they cannot deceive as many as before—THE LIGHT OF THE WORLD CAME AND DISPELLED THE DARKNESS!

6. If you do not think this is near to being right, you would change your mind if you had to live back in the days of Antiochus IV or the Caesars of Rome!

Life in Russia and China is even better today than it was before Christ came into the world!

APPREHENSION:

1. Why was Daniel concerned about the number of years of captivity? Was it some selfish concern? or was he concerned about God's integrity?

2. Why did Daniel spend so much time confessing sin? Is that such guilt good for people? Should we be this desperate in our prayers?

3. Why did Daniel pray everything for the Lord's sake? Shouldn't believers ask the Lord for anything for their own sake?

4. What are "seventy weeks"? When do they start? When do they end?

5. To whom is the period of 490 given? What 6 things are to be accomplished by the time this 490 is over?

6. Who is the "prince"? Who is the anointed one? How is he to be "cut off"? (See Isa. 53:8.)

7. What "city" is to be destroyed? Who will destroy it? Why?

8. What is the "abomination that makes desolate"? (See Mt. 24:15; Lk. 21:20.)

9. What is going to befall Daniel's people in the "latter days"? What does it have to do with the "prince of Persia" and "prince of Greece"?

10. Does God send his angels to "fight" for his people? today? (cf. Revelation).

APPLICATION:

1. Daniel was a man of the Word! He knew God's Book. Here is this man who had been receiving direct revelations from God and angels, but he is studying the writings of a former prophet, Jeremiah. His revelations did not make him an egomaniac. He did not think what the Lord told

him was all the Lord said. In fact, he was probably reading Jeremiah to see if what he had received squared with God's Book! Personal experiences, no matter how mystical or spiritual they may seem, must be tested by God's Book—not the other way around.

2. Prayer should be *first* and foremost a confession of sins! Any man who says he has no sin is a liar and the truth is not in him at all! Daniel's first concern in approaching the Lord was to confess sin. *Confess* means, "to say the same as" God says about sin. God says we are morally, deliberately, by choice, responsible for sin. He is not responsible for our sins. We are! God says we deserve absolute, final, complete banishment from his presence for sin. We must admit that. God says he will forgive our sin if we love him and keep his commandments—we must confess ("agree with") that.

3. Until men are willing to admit they deserve God's wrath, they are not in a position to be delivered from it. Until men are willing to admit they deserve God's wrath, they are not willing to accept His forgiveness by the free gift of grace through Christ's atonement in their place. Daniel was willing to admit this and thus was willing to admit that all mercy and forgiveness belonged to God.

4. God extends His mercy through the word of His prophets and messengers. Daniel confessed that he and his people were being punished because they did *not* listen to God's message. God's message is in His commandments—not in our subjective fancies.

5. Daniel prayed confessing that God's people (and thus God's name) had become a *byword* because of their sinfulness. In a very real way, *God's reputation* depends on the actions of those who claim Him as their God (cf. Rom. 2:24). In another sense, God will be God and be true even if every man is a liar and a hypocrite (cf. Rom. 3:4). God will always be God, but how most men first conceive of Him depends to a large degree on the actions of Christians.

6. Prayer is to change men—not God. God had already decided to return the Jews to Palestine before Daniel prayed. He had even revealed that to Daniel. But Daniel needed to pray to prepare himself for service by believing what he had been told and *humbly surrendering* to it. You see, their return would involve centuries of trial and testing. A man has to be brought to his "knees" in complete surrender to accept what God has already decided He wants to give him. God doesn't have to have our prayers any more than he has to have our money. WE NEED TO GIVE UP, GIVE IN, AND GIVE OVER.

   Daniel prayed—"For thy sake—for thy name's sake." THY WILL BE DONE!

7. Did you know the Gospel was in the law and the prophets? Rom. 3:21 says it was. You can find it in *Dan. 9:24* (among other places in the

186

prophets). Where else is it? How about Isa. 53:1-12. What excuse then did the Jew have for rejecting the idea of salvation by grace through faith—justification by faith and not by works of the law?

8. The time of Messiah's coming was *precisely* predicted. So was the destruction of the city of Jerusalem and the Temple. Why did so many seem confused or ignorant of Jesus' messianic claims? Were there some who were looking for the Messiah at about the right time? How about Simeon (Lk. 2)—Joseph of Arimathea (Lk. 23:51). Why was John the Baptist, who even had direct revelation confused?

   If Daniel 9:24-27 is so precise, why are Jews so ignorant of all this today? Why are non-Jews so difficult to persuade that Jesus is the Messiah of God? Did Jesus expect people of His day to know from the prophets that He was the Messiah (cf. Lk. 24:25ff.)? Did Jesus expect His disciples to know from the book of Daniel when Jerusalem was going to be destroyed? (Mt. 24:15; Mk. 13:14).

9. Did the death of the Messiah *really* bring an end to Old Testament sacrifices and offerings? (See esp. Heb. 10:1-18.) What would God think of anyone trying to find atonement for sin today through animal sacrifices when His Son has been offered for atonement? Would He excuse it? Would He accept it? Or would it be blasphemous?

   Why are there Christian people talking about the rebuilding of the Jewish Temple and reinstitution of Mosaic sacrifices and priesthood as if it were the will of God?

   Did God know in Daniel's time the Jews would have to be destroyed as a nation to give His redemptive program opportunity to go into all the world?

10. Chapter 10 of Daniel clearly teaches that what we see on earth in the struggles between Christianity and unbelief is simply a carnal manifestation of a much greater spiritual struggle going on in the *unseen* world! The fight for justice, truth, love, is not confined to man's limited sphere—it is cosmic—off out, millions of light years away, in eternity. What the Christian involves himself in when he becomes a follower of the Lord Jesus has to do with powers and realities beyond this transitory world (cf. Eph. 6:10ff.; II Cor. 10:3-5).

    Does that excite you? Does it frighten you? Does it convince you to get serious about your involvement in God's redemptive plan?

    What God revealed to Daniel—and to us in even more certainty in Christ and the New Testament—is that the forces of righteousness are more powerful than the forces of evil.

    God, the Invisible, supplies invisible, supernatural assistance from heaven for His redemptive people. But all who are not His not only have invisible supernatural enemies, but by choice become accomplices of that invisible wickedness.

THIRTEEN LESSONS ON REVELATION

What if God were to roll back a big opening so you could see into the spiritual world—the invisible world—and take a look at the power, deceptiveness, utter ugliness and wickedness of all that disagrees with God's Book, the Bible? WOULD YOU GET SERIOUS ABOUT LOVING WHAT THAT BOOK SAYS IS GOOD AND PURE AND LOVELY? HE HAS LET YOU SEE! THROUGH DANIEL'S EYES . . . THROUGH JOHN'S EYES (REVELATION).

Hang over these last two chapters of Daniel these words, ". . . through many tribulations we must enter the kingdom of God" (Acts 14:22). God will not have anyone who has not been tested. His purpose in the captivity and tribulation of the Jews was to "sift" them and purge them—to direct their minds and aspirations away from this world to the *spiritual* realities the Messiah would accomplish.

Harry Truman once said: "If you can't stand the heat, get out of the kitchen." Essentially that is what God said to the Jews through the persecutions and tribulations of Antiochus IV (Dan. 11-12). Do you realize Jesus spoke more about trouble and crosses and persecution than He did about human happiness? Check it out for yourself in the four Gospels! You may as well mark it down in your little black book—whoever will live godly in this world *will* suffer persecution, (II Tim. 3:12).

Jesus said to his disciples, ". . . the world hates you . . . Remember . . . A servant is not greater than his master . . . If they persecuted me, they will persecute you," (Jn. 15:18-20). God uses all this persecution by wicked men to put his children to the test. If you're not being tested, you're not his child (Heb. 12:1-17; I Pet. 4:12-14)!

The word *tribulation* in the New Testament means "pressure" or "tension." Tribulation does not always come in the form of persecution. It may be in the trauma of giving up worldliness. Every Christian trying to be true to Christ certainly suffers constant *tension* between self and surrender to God's Word. That is what God was doing with the Jews in the days of Antiochus IV—that is what he wants to do with our lives every day. We must decide if we are willing to "count the cost." Jesus said, "If you are not willing to pay the price, don't sign up" (Lk. 14:25-33)!

SEVENTY SEVENS

TRIBULATIONS AND TESTING

by Paul T. Butler

Daniel 11:1—12:13

Introduction

I. *WHAT* IS GOING TO HAPPEN TO THE JEWS FOR "SEVENTY SEVENS"? (490 YRS.)

    A. The *outlined* answer to that question was given Daniel in 9:24-27 (as well as in ch. 7-8).

TRIBULATIONS AND TESTINGS

1. Daniel had prayed for an answer to what seemed to him as a problem concerning God's reputation.
   a. Daniel understood and agreed with the captivity as punishment for the sins of the Jews in their idolatries, etc.
   b. Daniel did not approach God arrogantly, but in deep humility asking not on the basis of any righteous merit of his or the Jews, but jealous for God's holiness.
2. But now (536 B.C.) that God had delivered the "remnant" back to Judea, they were still having "trouble."
   a. Daniel apparently thought that deliverance from captivity should signal God's forgiveness of his people.
   b. If they had been forgiven, why should they be facing trouble back in Judea?
   This is the same problem a lot of Christians have about their lives not being all "roses" after they have been baptized.
3. God answered Daniel's prayer about the "end of the desolations of Jerusalem" (9:2) in the brief resume of 9:24-27. But it was *very* brief, leaving a number of details out.

B. The *detailed* answer to the above question is given in Dan. 11:1—12:13.

1. God knows *every* detail of this world and its inhabitants *before* these details come to pass in the time-frame. God knows everything! Everything that happens is *NOW* in relationship to God. There is no beginning and end with God.
2. He is not a provincial God. Not just the God of the Hebrews, but of all creation, of all time.
3. He is not a God of generalizations (like false gods). He does not give man every minute detail of every day of history, but what man needs, God *will* give.
4. That the Jews could never have reason to doubt God's sovereignty, God's redemptive *purpose,* or God's faithfulness, He gave detailed explanation of their future 490 years.

II. WHY IS THIS GOING TO HAPPEN FOR 490 YEARS TO THE JEWS?

A. Daniel had prayed that God act, for God's sake—to keep God's name (or reputation) invulnerable and invincible.

1. God had already promised that everything He would do with the Jews would be for the sake of His name.
   a. God would "try them in the furnace of affliction" for His sake (Isa. 48:9-11).
   b. He delivered them and punished them for His sake (Ezek. 20:9, 14, 22, 44, etc.).

189

B. God acted to keep His name's sake invincible, impartial and faithful so those who were willing might *know* that He was the Lord.
  1. God's fulfillment of His plan to redeem a people for Himself and redeem creation depends on men knowing Him and *trusting* Him.
  2. Man's enjoyment of that redemption depends on God's name.

Discussion

I. WARFARE, 11:1-20
  A. Persian-Alexandrian years, 11:1-4
    1. Verse 1 belongs to chapter 10.
    2. After the Cyrus-Darius (Gubaru) rule over Persia and Babylon there will be four more kings of Persia who will have effect on testing the Jewish people.
       Cambyses, Smerdis, Darius-Hystaspis, Xerxes (Ahasuerus)
    3. While some of the Persian kings were benefactors to the Jews, others were not.
       Of course, while Persian kings tried to conquer the world, the Jews, as well as the rest of the world, suffered.
    4. The Jews who had returned to Palestine in the third year of Cyrus met continual trouble from the Samaritans and others which Persian kings helped with occasionally (but not always).
    5. Then there was the attempted genocide of all the Jews by Haman in the days of Esther.
       The student may read of the Persian-Alexandrian years in the Bible (Esther, Ezra and Nehemiah; Haggai and Zechariah), and in Josephus' *Wars* and *Antiquities*.
    6. When Alexander the Great conquered the world, his intention to Hellenize all cultures presented great problems to the Jews. Many Jews gave in to the pagan culture of the Greeks; the Jewish high priesthood became corrupted.
    7. The release from the captivity would *not* bring the *messianic age* as some of the Jews might anticipate—that would be 490 years later. So God started telling Daniel all the details of the "troubled times" which would come while the Jews *waited* for the Messiah. From 536 B.C. to 323 B.C. 213 years.
  B. Seleucid-Ptolemaic years, 11:5-20
    1. The map on the following page shows the struggles between the Ptolemies and the Seleucids for control of Palestine as Daniel predicts it 200 years before it ever begins.
    2. The Ptolemies were Greeks (descendants of one of Alexander the Great's generals, Ptolemy) who ruled Egypt for approximately 200 years (from Alexander the Great to Julius Caesar).

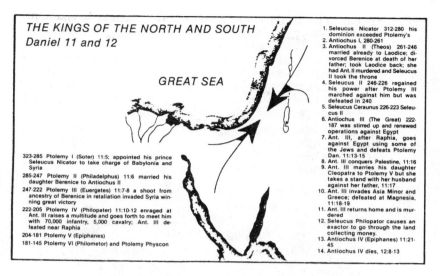

THE KINGS OF THE NORTH AND SOUTH
Daniel 11 and 12

GREAT SEA

323-285 Ptolemy I (Soter) 11:5; appointed his prince Seleucus Nicator to take charge of Babylonia and Syria

285-247 Ptolemy II (Philadelphus) 11:6 married his daughter Berenice to Antiochus II

247-222 Ptolemy III (Euergetes) 11:7-8 a shoot from ancestry of Berenice in retaliation invaded Syria winning great victory

222-205 Ptolemy IV (Philopater) 11:10-12 enraged at Ant. III raises a multitude and goes forth to meet him with 70,000 infantry, 5,000 cavalry; Ant. III defeated near Raphia

204-181 Ptolemy V (Epiphanes)

181-145 Ptolemy VI (Philometor) and Ptolemy Physcon

1. Seleucus Nicator 312-280 his dominion exceeded Ptolemy's
2. Antiochus I, 280-261
3. Antiochus II (Theos) 261-246 married already to Laodice; divorced Berenice at death of her father; took Laodice back; she had Ant. II murdered and Seleucus II took the throne
4. Seleucus II 246-226 regained his power after Ptolemy III marched against him but was defeated in 240
5. Seleucus Ceraunus 226-223 Seleucus II
6. Antiochus III (The Great) 222-187 was stirred up and renewed operations against Egypt
7. Ant. III, after Raphia, goes against Egypt using some of the Jews and defeats Ptolemy Dan. 11:13-15
8. Ant. III conquers Palestine, 11:16
9. Ant. III marries his daughter Cleopatra to Ptolemy V but she takes a stand with her husband against her father, 11:17
10. Ant. III invades Asia Minor and Greece; defeated at Magnesia, 11:18-19
11. Ant. III returns home and is murdered
12. Seleucus Philopator causes an exactor to go through the land collecting money.
13. Antiochus IV (Epiphanes) 11:21-45
14. Antiochus IV dies, 12:8-13

Greek cultural influence on Egypt was so strong it may even be seen in modern Egypt.

3. The Seleucids were Greeks (descendants of one of Alexander's generals) who ruled Asia Minor (Turkey), Mesopotamia (Iraq) and Syria for the same 200 years as above. Again, the Greek cultural influence on these areas is still strong today. Greek cultural impact was so strong on this part of the world it outlasted all other influences, including Roman.

4. The tremendous power of these two empires, with Palestinian Jews in between them, maintained constant pressure on the Jews to be assimilated into Greek culture.

A minority of Jews maintained their holiness and their messianic identity under this great pressure only at the cost of great personal faith and sacrifice.

C. Palestine a constant battlefield—a "no-man's land"

1. There was constant devastation of the land of Palestine as these two empires (Ptolemies and Seleucids) fought one another. Crops were ruined, cities and villages destroyed and plundered.

2. The empire which controlled Palestine levied heavy taxes upon the Jews to pay for their wars and build their own homelands.

3. Some of the Jews (violent men, 11:14) joined in with the Seleucids in their wars upon the Ptolemies. There were also Jews who favored the Ptolemies. So the Jews were divided in their loyalties

to these two empires which continually caused the Jews trouble.
4. These two empires and their kings continually robbed the Jewish temple of its treasures to finance their wars.
5. It was during these times when it appeared the majority of the Jews were willing to lose their exclusive identity as a "people set apart to Jehovah" that a small minority of Jewish people formed what was called, the *"hasidim"* (or holy ones) which probably gave rise to the later group called *Pharisees.*

D. Again, therefore, the Jews are given *detailed* information about a long period of time of "trouble" for them before they could expect the Messiah (Anointed One) to appear.
From 323 to 171 B.C.—152 years.

II. WICKEDNESS, 11:21-45

A. Seductive, 11:20-28
1. The worst was yet to come. Antiochus IV became ruler of Syria. He called himself Antiochus Epiphanes (meaning, "Illustrious One"). The Jews called him Epimanes (meaning, "Mad One").
2. He gained the throne of Syria through deceit, murder and intrigue. He was not the rightful successor ("royal majesty has not been given").
3. He is called by *God* the "contemptible one."
4. He took the rightful high priest of the Jews off his throne and put his brother, Jason (Greek name for Joshua) in office because Jason loved Greek culture and promoted it for the Jews.
5. Then to solidify his control over the Jews, he deposed Jason and put Menelaus (of the tribe of Benjamin—not supposed to be high priest at all) in the office of high priest. Menelaus paid a big bribe to Antiochus to get the office.
6. Antiochus stationed a garrison of heathen, Syrian soldiers right in the temple precincts of Jerusalem. This enraged the holy Jews.
7. Antiochus IV attacked Egypt three times during this early part of his reign.
8. Fighting Egypt, Antiochus IV found himself fighting against some of his nephews (due to all the intermarrying of Seleucids and Ptolemies—which Daniel also predicted 200 years before they took place, i.e. 11:5-7; 11:17).

In all this Antiochus IV and some of his relatives in Egypt were trying to unite these two empires so there would be no more warring between them. But it did not come to pass because it was not yet time in the schedule of God for these struggles to cease—just as Daniel prophesied, "for the end is yet to be at the time appointed" by God, 11:27.

9. While Antiochus IV was trying to subdue Egypt (the Ptolemies), the Jews who followed Jason tried to attack Jerusalem and depose Menelaus from the high priesthood. But Jason was defeated and Menelaus turned all the temple treasury over to Antiochus IV, to keep his support.

10. Antiochus IV returned to Syria to take care of some pressing political affairs. But he knew that Judea was a boiling pot of revolt—so he had his heart set on grinding the Jews into submission. He hated them with malice because they (the minority of hasidim) would keep agitating their fellow Jews to throw off the heathenism he tried to impose.

B. Spiteful, 11:29-35

1. Again Antiochus IV tried to subdue Egypt. This time a Roman legate met him at Alexandria and ordered him to return to Syria and leave Egypt alone. Rome was powerful enough at this point in time (168 B.C.) to have subdued most of the Mediterranean world (incl. Greece). Rome had made an alliance with Egypt to protect her against enemies.

2. The Roman representative, Popillius Laenas, drew a circle in the sand around Antiochus IV and told him he must make up his mind before stepping out of the circle whether he would withdraw from Egypt or fight Rome! Antiochus IV decided discretion was the better part of valor, and withdrew. ("ships of Kittim" refers to western regions of the Mediterranean—or Rome). Antiochus IV had lived in Rome as a young man when he was taken there as a hostage and knew the Roman power.

3. Enraged (11:30) Antiochus IV turned back toward Syria. But he took out his rage on the Jews ("the holy covenant"). Thus began one of the darkest nights of Jewish history.

   Some of the Jews (the majority) forsook their Jewishness and did as Antiochus IV demanded.

4. Antiochus IV decreed that all Jews must worship Greek idols.

   a. He had a statue of Jupiter made (in his own image) and set up on the very altar of the Temple in Jerusalem.

   b. He robbed the Temple of its holy vessels and broke them and melted them down.

   c. The Syrians put up idolatrous altars all over the Temple and land, and practiced fornication with their priestess prostitutes right in the Temple courts.

   d. Pigs were sacrificed in Temple altars and all over Palestine to heathen gods. Swine were "unclean" animals to Jews.

e. The worship of Bacchus (god of wine) was decreed—compulsory—accompanied by drunken orgies.

f. Jews were forbidden by threat of death to circumcise their male children. Some did and were hacked to pieces with their children.

g. All copies of the Hebrew scriptures which could be found were burned and those who tried to protect them were killed, burned alive with the books.

h. Syrians forbade the keeping of the Sabbath. Those who tried were caught, their children tied about their neck and they were flung off the highest pinnacle of the wall of Jerusalem.

i. More Syrian soldiers made the Temple their barracks.

5. One very heart-rending incident bears noting: II Macc. 7:1ff. Seven brothers, with their mother, were ordered to eat swine's flesh. When they first refused, they were tortured with whips and scourges.

When they persisted in refusal the first (oldest son) was scalped, his tongue cut out, his feet and hands cut off, and all this along with the rest of the boy was fried to death in a huge, bronze frying pan.

One son after another, seven in all, were done this way while the mother was forced to watch.

This mother never gave in to the Syrians, but exhorted each son that God would raise him from the dead, because they held the law of God dearer than their physical life! (See Heb. 11:35-38). THE WORLD WAS NOT WORTHY OF SUCH HEROES OF THE FAITH!

6. Many of Israel consented to this and sacrificed to idols, and profaned the Sabbath (I Macc. 1:45, 55) and turned upon their own people with the Syrians and drove the faithful Jews into caves, deserts and hills.

7. Antiochus IV determined to stamp out the Jewish religion completely. He took away the continual burnt offering (11:31).

8. Thousands and thousands of Jews were slain (11:32-33).

9. Jews who were wise (probably who had read Daniel's prophecies and believed them) understood what this was all about.

"Now I beseech those that shall read this book (II Maccabees) that they be not shocked at these calamities, but that they consider the things that happened, not as being for the destruction, but for the correction of our nation" (II Macc. 6:12ff.).

10. The Hasidim raised up a band of Jewish "freedom fighters" and helped protect their brother Jews who wanted to resist

paganism—they killed even those of their own countrymen who practiced paganism (I Macc. 2:42ff.) (11:34).

11. This is when the house of Mattathias (of the family of Hasmonean) organized the great "Maccabean" revolt. Judas was the first nicknamed Maccabeaus (which means Judas the "Hammerer").

12. The Jews were to be "refined, cleansed and made white until the time of the end" which was yet to come after the Syrian holocaust. The "time of the end" as has already been thoroughly established by Daniel, is the end of the Jewish dispensation and the coming of the Messiah during the Roman empire (Dan. 9:24-27). The "time of the end" will be more explicitly established in ch. 12, as the end of the Jewish dispensation (12:7).

C. Supercilious (arrogant), 11:36-39

1. Antiochus believed in no gods at all! He believed only in himself. There was no one greater than he! Not even the gods of his own people.

2. Antiochus was contemptuous of the God of the Hebrews. He had no respect for the Jewish religion or any other religion.

3. His power to demonstrate contempt for everything and everyone but himself would "prosper" until the indignation is "accomplished." We have already learned that the *indignation* would *not* be *ended* until time for the Messiah to come and do the 6 things of 9:24-27. More specifically, the vision of the "little horn" out of Greece—Antiochus IV—was for the "latter end of the indignation" (see Dan. 8:9-26).

4. Antiochus IV believed in war! His Greek forefathers, like Alexander the Great used war, but believed in intellectualism, the mind, logic, philosophy—culture. Alexander was going to create Utopia by infusing the world with Greek wisdom. But Antiochus IV believed in war (like Nietzsche and Hitler and Lenin—the Communists believe in war, don't think they don't!)

5. Antiochus IV preferred the Roman gods of war. He considered the temples of all other religions as opportunities for robbery and financing his wars.

D. Stopped, 11:40-45

1. Antiochus was strong and terrible. He eventually controlled the largest of the 4-sections of Alexander's Greek world.

2. His control was based wholly on force, war, terror, ungodliness. That has the seeds of destruction already sown in itself. "Those who live by the sword shall perish by the sword."

Human beings who have any faith in God cannot be or will not be enslaved forever.

The truth, known and trusted, will always drive those who trust it toward freedom!

3. Antiochus' ungodly contempt for truth, justice, and goodness soon precipitated the Hasmonean revolt under the Maccabean brothers. Those Jews who committed themselves to God's Word and were willing to sacrifice their lives, freed the Jewish people from the Syrian enslavement.

4. In 165 B.C. Antiochus IV received alarming news from Parthia (Iran) and Armenia about a revolt in his empire. He withdrew the largest part of his troops from Judea to take to Parthia. Judas Maccabeaus inflicted such a defeat on the remaining Syrian troops they fled from Judea.

On Chislev (December) 25th, the Maccabeans cleared the Temple in Jerusalem of all pagan idols, etc., and reinstituted Jewish holy services there.

This date is observed by all Jews from that time forward to now as Hanukkah (Feast of Dedication, or Feast of Lights).

5. Antiochus IV, having suffered some defeats in war, retreated to Babylon, moved from there to Tabae in Persia, where he died "by no human hand" (8:25) of a sickness the book of Maccabees calls "worms" and others think was "consumption." Whatever, his death was exactly as God predicted it and not, considering his being hated by so many, by assassination or slain in battle.

6. The heroic Maccabean struggle lasted another 30 years. Many Jews sacrificed much to gain their freedom from Syria. In 134 B.C. they were free. But about 70 years later (64 B.C.) Pompey, Roman general, invaded Palestine and placed the Jews under Roman rule. 60 years after that (4 B.C.) the King of the Jews was born—Messiah. 70 years after that (66 A.D.) the destruction of Jerusalem began. Antiochus IV lasted from 171 to 164 B.C.

III. WISDOM, 12:1-13

A. God will not let His redemptive program become extinct.

1. He will fight for his people through his servants such as Michael.

2. It may appear to men that all of the messianic future is lost. There will be a time of trouble such as never has been since there was a nation till that time.

3. Antiochus IV's threat to the messianic destiny was more severe than the Egyptian bondage, than the time of the Judges, than the divided kingdom, than the captivities in Babylon.

4. But God will bring that also to an end. This too shall pass!

B. When Antiochus IV comes to this end, God will deliver all his people written in the book of life. *The Messianic deliverance!*
1. This deliverance is *spiritual* and not political. God revealed to Daniel it would be spiritual in Dan. 9:24-27 (and other places like Dan. 7, etc.). This deliverance is interpreted as spiritual and through the Messiah in the New Testament (see Luke 1:32-33; 1:47-55; 1:68-79 and all the rest of the New Testament).
2. It delivers from sin all the faithful saints of God from Abel, Enoch to this day (cf. Heb. 9:15; Rom. 3:25).
3. Many saints of God who had already died (Moses, Abraham, David, etc.) would be resurrected to life through the deliverance to come in the Messiah.

C. The troubled times, used wisely, would turn many to righteousness.
1. The whole point of the terrible times of Antiochus IV, as God was using them, was to "refine, cleanse, and make white, until the time appointed for the end" (11:35).
2. Many would, if they were wise, purify themselves and make themselves white and be refined (12:10).
3. "It is a sign of great goodness when sinners are not allowed to go on in their ways, but are punished . . . therefore God never withdraws his mercy from us (Jews) but he chastizes his people with adversity and does not forsake them" (II Macc. 6:13-16).

D. The troubled times would confirm God's Word as trustworthy and would cause many to "run to and fro" and increase their knowledge of it.
1. This is what is meant in 12:4.
2. "Seal the book" means *not* hide it, but let it be confirmed that what you have predicted is true.
3. This would be definitely confirmed when the predictions came to pass in the days of Antiochus IV.
4. Josephus depicts many Jews turning to the writing of Daniel when the days of Antiochus IV came to see what God's Word had to say about those times.

E. Troubled times would presage the end of the Jewish dispensation.
1. "When the shattering of the power of the holy people comes to an end all these things would be accomplished" 12:7b.
2. Daniel has already predicted this in 9:26-27.
3. Jesus expected people of his day to understand the Jewish dispensation was to end with the Messiah's coming (Mt. 24; Lk. 21; Mk. 13).
4. The writer to the Hebrews expected the Jewish Christians to

have understood that and thus not be pressured to return to Judaism. ". . . when you see the Day approaching" Heb. 10:25 is end of Jerusalem!
5. The end of the Mosaic dispensation would accomplish all Daniel wrote about!
THERE IS NOTHING LEFT IN DANIEL'S PROPHECIES TO BE FULFILLED.
Those who use and abuse Daniel's prophecies to make them yet future to the 20th century are not as careful as they should be in the application of accepted hermeneutical principles.
The proper way to look at Daniel is to consider chapters 7-12 as one unit. These chapters are inseparably connected.'
Jesus confirmed that Daniel's prophecies "of the end time" were connected directly to the destruction of Jerusalem and Judaism (Mt. 24; Mk. 13; Lk. 21).
F. "How long shall it be till the end of these wonders"? 12:6 Answer: (12:11) 1290 days plus 45 days = 1335 days

Premillennial view of Dan. 12:4-13
a. There will be 1260 days plus 30 (1290) from the middle of the "Tribulation" (they refer to Dan. 9:27 as the "tribulation") to an "undefined" termination (or 3-1/2 years plus 30 days).
b. The purpose of the "plus-30-days" beyond the alleged time of Christ's return is an extra month for the judgment of Gentiles and Jews to determine who will be worthy to enter the kingdom.
c. An additional 45 days to the 1290 (making a total of 1335) will be "necessary for setting up the government machinery for carrying on the rule of Christ . . . the true border of Israel will have to be established and appointments made of those aiding in the government." GOD HAS TO HAVE 45 MORE DAYS FOR THIS?!

APPREHENSION:

1. Who is the fourth king after Cyrus? (see the book of Esther). What did he have to do with troubles coming upon the Jews?
2. Who is the "mighty king" of 11:3; why didn't his dominion go to his posterity; how did Daniel know this?
3. The kings of the south (Ptolemies—Egypt) and of the north (Seleucids—Syra) were constantly at war—what did that do to Jews in Palestine? (see 11:10, 14, 22, 24, 28).
4. Did all the Jews remain faithful to God's word during the Syrian troubles? (see 11:14, 30, 32, 34).

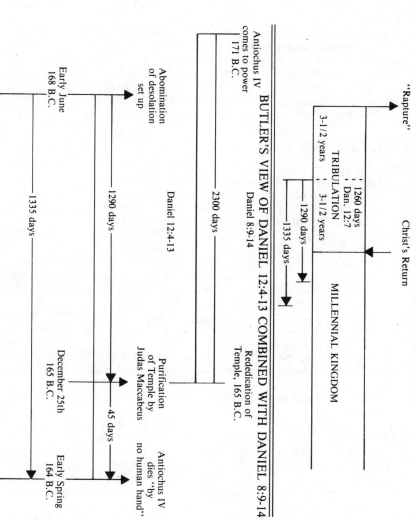

PRE-MILLENNIAL VIEW OF DANIEL 12:4-13

"Rapture"
Christ's Return

1260 days
Dan. 12:7

TRIBULATION
3-1/2 years   3-1/2 years

1290 days

1335 days

MILLENNIAL KINGDOM

BUTLER'S VIEW OF DANIEL 12:4-13 COMBINED WITH DANIEL 8:9-14

Daniel 8:9-14

Antiochus IV
comes to power
171 B.C.

2300 days

Rededication of
Temple, 165 B.C.

Abomination
of desolation
set up

Daniel 12:4-13

1290 days

45 days

Purification
of Temple by
Judas Maccabeus

Antiochus IV
dies "by
no human hand"

Early June
168 B.C.

December 25th
165 B.C.

Early Spring
164 B.C.

1335 days

199

5. What results accrued to those who believed in God from these troubles? (see 11:32b, 35; 12:1-3; 12:10, 12). What would they "understand"? (11:33; 12:10)
6. What "time of the end" is predicted by Daniel? (11:35, 45; 12:4, 7, 9, 11, 12, 13). What does "shattering . . . the holy people" have to do with it (cf. 9:24-27)?
7. The parents of Anna the prophetess (see Lk. 2:36-38) probably lived in the days of Antiochus IV. They must have taught her to look for the Messiah. Read Luke, ch. 1-2 in connection with Daniel 11-12. (also, Heb. 11:32-40).

APPLICATION:

1. What if you were told the precise details of history for your children and grandchildren and great grandchildren? What if it was as *troubled* as those of the Jewish generations were going to be? WOULD YOU MAKE EVERY EFFORT TO EMPHASIZE SPIRITUAL PRIORITIES? Would you be as concerned with the superficial as you are now?
2. Palestine was to be torn by war for over 300 years by Ptolemies and Seleucids. Some of the Jews were brutalized and joined with the Seleucids in warring against their own people. Some Jews were driven to God and had their faith strengthened. What if the U.S. became a constant battlefield between Canada and Mexico—how would you survive? Why does war brutalize some and soften others?
3. The Ptolemies and Seleucids compromised practically every accepted moral of humankind to control the eastern Mediterranean (Palestine). They robbed, killed, lied, flattered, used their women as pawns. How far will men go in the political arena to reach their goals? Does the end justify the means? In politics? In evangelism? In fund raising? In personal, daily living?

   What is a church or religious institution profited if it gain funds and forfeits its soul?
4. Is God contemptuous of some human beings? Why would God call Antiochus IV "The Contemptible One"? What makes a person contemptible with God? Do you remember what Paul said of Elymas (Acts 13:10)—"Son of the devil, enemy of all righteousness, full of all deceit and villainy . . ." All Elymas did was, oppose Paul, withstand the gospel and try to turn away the Proconsul Sergius Paulus from the Christian faith!

   Will God really show His contempt of all who do not know Him and do not obey the gospel of Jesus Christ? (II Thess. 1:8-9)
5. If you had to endure a holocaust like that of Antiochus IV, would your faith survive? What if they burned all your Bibles—would you know

enough of the Word to sustain you? What if they dismembered your children and burned them alive? Would you encourage them to hope in the resurrection? *Do some blame such holocausts on chance or men in order to sidestep the issue of trusting a God who permits it for the purpose of sanctification?* One Jewish writer (Rubenstein) said, "After Auschwitz (Hitler's holocaust) to trust in providence in the traditional (Biblical) sense is immoral as well as impossible, since it turns God into an accomplice of Hitler, deliberately willing the slaughter of the chosen for no other reason than the crime of being chosen."

6. Many Jews in the days of Antiochus IV joined themselves to paganism rather than suffer. Many Christians in the days of Roman persecution renounced the faith, betrayed fellow Christians, and worshiped the emperor rather than suffer. How committed are you to Christ? What would you be willing to endure for Him? Do you have a point beyond which you would not go in professing your faith and living it?

7. Antiochus IV worshiped power, war. Why do some think war is the way? Why do some think the U.N. will bring an end to war? Will it? Are Christians right to proclaim that the kingdom of God will produce peace among men? Should the new birth bring an end to all human hostility? Have all those born again ceased to be hostile with one another?

8. God brought an end to Antiochus IV. But look how long it took! Look how much suffering the Jews had to endure before it ended. What is your time-quotient with God's promises to you? Can you wait upon the Lord? What if it doesn't come in your lifetime? (see Heb. 11:32-40).

9. What kind of deliverance do you expect from God? Do you feel like you have spiritual deliverance? Is this your first priority in life? Could you feel like you had spiritual deliverance if you had to live in a time like Antiochus IV?

10. Are you wise? How many have you turned to righteousness? What's wisdom about God's Word for if it isn't for using to turn some to righteousness? Is it to keep for yourself? Did Christ keep his godly wisdom to Himself? Did Paul?

The wisest man in the world is not the sharp money investor, or the Nobel Prize winning scientist, but the Christian who converts others! How beautiful upon the mountains are the feet of him who brings good tidings . . . Isa. 52:7.

11. If the Jews were expected by God to be wise and understand the symbolic, shadowy, prophetic writings of Daniel and from them turn people to righteousness and from them purify themselves, WHERE SHOULD YOU AND I BE IN WISDOM, UNDERSTANDING AND PURIFICATION FROM THE FULFILLMENT OF ALL THE OLD TESTAMENT IN CHRIST AND THE NEW TESTAMENT???

Will the Maccabeans stand up in the judgment and condemn us for in Christ a greater than Daniel is revealed to us?

THIRTEEN LESSONS ON REVELATION

12. If Daniel was to conceal ("shut up and seal") what was in his book until *the* end of time, how come so many prophecy experts know what he is saying, now, before *the* end? The Hebrew phrase would read literally, "until time of *an* end . . ." There is no definite article with "end" in Dan. 12, indicating an indefinite end. Daniel's prophecies are for *Antiochus' end* and *Judaism's end*.

13. God told Daniel to go about his task until his end and then he would "stand in his allotted place." Do you think God has an "allotted place" for you, individually, personally, at the end of your task on earth? If God is in charge of our "allotted place" at the end, is there any reason for us to compete with one another for a place? Do you think of heaven as a place where everyone is recognized or "placed"—or do you think of it as place of mass confusion and where there are no longer any responsibilities or work? What will it be like?

Lesson Twelve
(Matt. Ch. 24-25)

As with Daniel, so with Matthew 24. Many writers and teachers of Bible prophecies have commingled the predictions of Jesus in Matthew 24 with Revelation and Daniel to form their bizzare, unrealistic and hypothetical pictures of the "rapture, tribulation, and millennium." The application of accepted hermeneutical principles will clearly show that the first half of Matthew 24 applies only to the destruction of Judaism.

A U.P. survey says the typical American is 27; does not read one book a year; is materialistic; satisfied with small pleasures; bored with theological disputations. Although he may attend church 27 times a year, he is not interested in the supernatural . . . concerned with neither heaven or hell . . . has no interest whatever in immortality. His principal interests are football, hunting, fishing and car-tinkering.

Everywhere we look, young people are being taught that the present moment, however exciting or ridiculous, is the thing that matters and that *deliberate rejection of the past or future* is the only alternative left to life today! Some are saying that Henry Ford was right when he said, "History is bunk," and that even a study of history will be of no use to coming generations.

In Matthew 24 and 25, Jesus says just the opposite! History has a meaning —a divine meaning. Some sage once said, "The past is prologue." Jesus is telling His apostles, and all the world, that history is headed for a goal. History is not a record of unintelligible accidents. Indeed, the Bible is God's editorial column analyzing the daily news. In the Bible we see history's meaning from a God-perspective.

History, looked at from the divine record, is a series of judgments and redemptions. God's Book teaches it—history confirms it. God judged the world through the Flood, but He redeemed it there also. God judged Egypt but redeemed His covenant people. God judged the Israelites in the captivities, but He also redeemed them from the dispersion. Jesus' Olivet Discourse (Matt. 24) is a prediction of a final judgment of Judaism for rejecting the Messiah. But out of this great judgment will come the victory of the Messiah's new Israel (the church) and redemption for all who will answer the invitation.

Matthew 24 (esp. 24:1-35) has been mishandled, misinterpreted and misapplied by many religious factions. It is being severely abused by so-called "prophecy preachers" today who are confusing thousands of believers.

THE MESSIAH HAS COME

AUTHORITY IN HISTORY'S TIMES

by Paul T. Butler

Matthew 24:1-35

Introduction

I. HARROWING TALK

A. Complexity of this text makes it essential that the student avail himself of a harmony of the gospel accounts as an aid to understanding it.

The two other Snoptic gospels, Mark and Luke, have the same discourse but with some additions.

See, Mark 13:1-31 and Luke 21:5-33.

B. Second, it is *imperative* that the student know that immediately preceding this discourse on the destruction of Jerusalem and Judaism, Jesus uttered the following two eschatologically *startling* statements:

1. He condemned the Pharisees, denouncing them as "sons of hell" (Mt. 23:15) and pronounced upon them "all the blood" of the righteous shed upon the earth (Mt. 23:31-35). Most Jews would consider the fall of the Pharisees the end of the Jewish "world." The Pharisees were the "keepers" of the Jewish culture and system.

204

2. He declared the "house" of Judaism *"desolate and forsaken"* (Mt. 23:36-39). This is terminology Jeremiah and Ezekiel used to warn their contemporaries of the Babylonian captivity and destruction of the city and Temple by Nebuchadnezzar (Jer. 19:8; Lam. 1:4; Ezek. ch. 8-11).

C. Third, it is *imperative* that the student know that *right after* the discussion of the widow's mite offering into the Temple treasury (Lk. 21:1-4 and Mk. 12:41-44), Jesus preached the alarming sermon on Death and Life, (Jn. 12:20-50). This also, just before the prophecy of the destruction of Jerusalem, contained startling statements!

1. Jesus said, "Now is the judgment (Gr. *crisis*) of this world (Gr. *cosmos*) now is the ruler of this world thrown out (Gr. *ekblethesetai exo*)."
2. The word *"cosmos"* means, "order, system, establishment."
3. Thus, the statements "Now is the crisis of this cosmos" in itself was enough to precipitate the questions of the apostles about the destruction of Judaism and Jerusalem.
4. It was very plain to the apostles Jesus was predicting the destruction of the present Jewish order, involving the desolation and forsakenness of the Temple and the nation—in that generation!

II. HEBREW TRADITIONS

A. Jewish scribes had divided their eschatology into three eras

1. *Olam hazzeh:* the order then existing
2. *Athid labho:* the age to come after that existing order
3. *Olam habba:* the world to come
4. In some rabbinic tradition, the age to come and the world to come blended into one.
5. The existing order was to be succeeded by the "days of the Messiah" which would stretch into the coming age and end with the world to come.
6. According to the rabbis, the birth of the Messiah would be unknown by His contemporaries; he would appear, carry on his work, then disappear—probably for 45 days; reappear, destroy the hostile powers of the world (notably "Edom"—which symbolized Rome, the 4th and last world empire listed by the prophet Daniel). Israelites would be brought back to Palestine from all over the world through miraculous deliverances and, according to the Midrash, all circumcised Israelites would then be released from Gehenna, and the dead Jews raised

205

(according to some, by the Messiah). This resurrection would take place in Palestine so that those who had been buried elsewhere would have to roll underground—in great pain—until they reached the holy land of Palestine.

B. In the coming age, *athid labho,* the rabbis wrote that all resistance to God would be concentrated in the great war of Gog and Magog (cf. Ezek. ch. 38-39), and there would be an intensification and focusing of all wickedness upon Israel in her land.

   1. Israel's enemies would 3 times assault the Holy City to destroy it, but each time be repelled. The city would suffer ravage, but not complete destruction.

   2. When Israel's enemy was destroyed completely, the Holy City would be gloriously rebuilt and inhabited. The new city would be lifted nine miles high, and extend from Joppa to the gates of Damascus.

   3. The new Temple would contain everything which had been absent in Herod's temple (golden candelabra, the ark of the covenant, the heaven-lit fire on the altar, the Shekinah and the cherubim).

   4. The ancient ceremonies of the Mosaic Law, plus rabbinic traditions would be practiced.

C. The end of that age would blend right into the world to come, *olam habba,* a glorious period of holiness, forgiveness and peace.

   1. In this new age and circumstances, angels would cut gems 45 feet square and place them in the city's gates.

   2. The walls of the city would be of silver, gold and precious gems, and precious jewels would be scattered all over the land which every Israelite would be at liberty to take.

   3. Jerusalem would be as large as all Palestine and Palestine as large as all the world.

   4. Wheat would grow as high as the mountains and the wind would convert the grain into flour and blow it into the valleys of the land.

   5. Every woman was to bear a child, daily, so that ultimately every Israelite family would number as many as all Israel at the time of the Exodus.

   6. All sickness and disease would pass away; Israelites would not die; some Gentiles would live hundreds of years. The Messiah was to rule the world from Jerusalem which would be the capital of the world and take the place of Rome.

   7. The time of all this was among the seven things, according to the rabbis, unknown to man.

D. A war, a revival of that of Gog and Magog, would close the Messianic era.

1. The nations, which had to this point given tribute to the Messiah, would rebel against him, and he would destroy them by the breath of his mouth. Gentile rebellion would be 7 years in duration.
2. Israel would be left alone on the face of the earth.
3. Then the final judgment commences.
4. There is no resurrection for Gentiles at all, except to die again.
5. Gehenna, where all Jews but the perfectly righteous ones are kept in a sort of purgatory, gives up these dead Jews who are delivered to Abraham in heaven.
6. Final judgment is to be held in the valley of Jehoshaphat by God, leading the heavenly Sanhedrin, composed of the elders of Israel.
7. After judgment there would be a renewal of heaven and earth and the full implementation of *olam habba,* the world to come.

E. Now when Jesus spoke of the judgment of the Jewish hierarchy, the desolation of Jerusalem, and the "crisis of the cosmos," the apostles concluded that such catastrophic events would be signalling the end of the existing order, *olam hazzeh,* and the ushering in of *athid labho,* the coming age, and perhaps, *olam habba,* the world to come.

1. The disciples began to point, *incredulously,* at the huge stones of the Temple!

   Some of the great stones of Herod's Temple were, according to Josephus, 25 cubits long, 8 cubits high and 12 cubits wide. Using 18 inches to a cubit, one of these stones would be 38 ft. long, 12 ft. high and 18 ft. wide. Eight large sized American automobiles could be stacked into those dimensions.

2. The apostles asked three questions which indicates how influential the rabbinic interpretations had been on them, and how confused they were trying to reconcile that with Jesus' statements.

   a. Their first question was: "*When* will all ths destruction be?" (Mt. 24:3a; Mk. 13:4a; Lk. 21:7a).
   b. Their second question was: "*What* will be the *sign* that *You* are coming?" (Mt. 24:3b; Mk. 13:4b; Lk. 21:7b).
   c. Their third question was: "*What* will be the *sign* of the *consummation of the age* (Gr. *sunteleias tou aionos*)?" (Mt. 24:3c).

207

3. Recognizing the dangers inherent in their confusion, Jesus sets out immediately to reveal a number of future events and to specify that they are *not* signs of the rabbinic theories coming to pass, *nor* are they signs of the *consummation of the ages.* At the end of His discourse, He tells them that there will be *no signs* of the *consummation* of the ages. (We will deal with that subject in the next lesson).

4. But for the immediate future of these apostles and other believers of their generation, He gives some very practical instructions so they would not be led astray when the destruction of the Jewish system began!

   a. The destruction of Jerusalem and the Jewish commonwealth would not take place for more than 30 years after Jesus died and was raised from the tomb and ascended to heaven.

   b. It would begin in 66 A.D. and come to a climax in 70 A.D.

5. The apostles have not yet understood that Jesus must "go away." When He did return to His heavenly throne, they would long to have Him back (cf. Lk. 17:22). Great persecutions were to come upon them. They must live in daily expectation and faith in His promises. They would be vulnerable to false expectations of a coming messianic age as portrayed by the rabbis, because the circumstances preceding the destruction of Jerusalem were to be similar to rabbinic messianic eschatology. So Jesus spoke His warnings.

Discussion

I. PRELIMINARY SIGNS OF DESTRUCTION, Mt. 24:4-14 (Mk. 13:5-13; Lk. 21:5-19)

A. Pseudo Christs

   1. Jesus warned the apostles that their generation would experience the rise and fall of many who would come in His name, saying they were the Messiah (Anointed One), but the 1st century Christians were not to be led astray by these claims.

   1. In spite of all the excitement and troubles attending these pretenders, He was not then returning, nor was "the time at hand."

   2. Pseudo-Christs coming to proclaim the new age would precede the desolation of Jerusalem. Jesus predicted.

   3. There were many such imposters who deluded multitudes of the 1st century Jews into following them, claiming they would prove they were the Christ by exhibiting wonders and signs

208

by the power of God (cf. Josephus, *Antiquities,* XX, VIII, 5).
4. About 44 A.D. during the rule of Palestine by Fadus, Roman procurator, a man by the name of Theudas (*not* the one of Acts 5:36) gathered a large band of followers claiming he was a miracle working deliverer. About 54 A.D. (during the reign of Felix) an Egyptian claimed to be a deliverer with prophetic powers. Such pseudo-Messiahs were plentiful.
5. All these came to a climax 62 years *after* the destruction of Jerusalem in the great rebellion against Rome under the false Messiah, Bar Kokhba, 132-135 A.D.

B. Presaging Crises

1. Wars and rumors of wars

   a. The Greek word *polemous,* "war," is the word from which we get the English word, "polemics" and means "to fight."

   b. Rome was having increasing difficulty with civil war among Roman emperors and army generals.

   c. There was also an ever recurring necessity for Rome to defend the empire against foreign invaders.

   d. Jesus is probably predicting the increasing rebellious attitude of the Jews against Rome when He says this.

      Herod Agrippa, given his uncle Philip's territory by Caligula, set out to revenge his uncle Philip against Herod Antipas who had stolen Philip's wife (Herodias). Agrippa spread the *rumor* to Rome that Antipas was conspiring with the Parthians against Rome and would make war. He *rumored* that Antipas had in his arsenal at Tiberias enough armor to equip 70,000 men.

   e. Riots broke out in Alexandria, Egypt, between Egyptians and Jews of that city (37-38 A.D.).

   f. A riot broke out in Jamnia (western Judea) in 39 A.D. when some Gentiles erected an altar to the Roman emperor and the Jews tore it down.

   g. The Roman emperor sent two Roman legions (12,000 men) to Jerusalem to set up his statue in the Jewish Temple. Jews vowed to resist to the last Jewish death. Some Jewish Christians in Palestine thought this impending blood-bath was a fulfillment of Jesus' prophecy here. Caligula was assassinated, however, before this could be enforced.

   h. Claudius was forced to put down another riot in Alexandria with bloodshed (53 A.D.).

   i. After the death of Herod Agrippa I (in 44 A.D.), the Roman emperor again imposed a rule of procurators upon Judea which deeply agitated the Jews. And, in the days of the procurator Cumanus (48 A.D.), a Roman soldier from the garrison in Antonia exposed his genitals to the Passover crowds which infuriated them. The Jews rioted and Roman soldiers killed hundreds of Jews in supressing it (Josephus, *Antiquities,* XX, V, 3).

j. There were continuing frontier disputes between Jews and Samaritans—Jews and Gentiles rioted in Caesarea (cf. *Israel and The Nations,* F. F. Bruce, pg. 197-225).

k. Luke says, ". . . when you hear of wars and tumults . . ." The Greek word for tumults is *akatastasia,* "confusion, instability." All this was to precede the destruction of Jerusalem.

Luke says Jesus warned the apostles, "do not be terrified (Gr. *ptoeo,* "frightened, intimidated,") for this must first take place, but the end (of Jerusalem) will not be at once" Lk. 21:9. WHY THE EXHORTATION AGAINST BEING ALARMED?

Because Jesus is giving a very plain prediction of the holocaust coming upon Jerusalem and Judaism. But He has a work for these apostles to do in Jerusalem and Palestine which will take years to accomplish (Lk. 27:47; Acts 1:8). He does not want them to be terrified when wars and instability comes so that they will flee Jerusalem before the real holocaust comes.

2. Earthquakes and famines

a. Jesus warns them not to be terrified, even when these things happened or were rumored and headlined about the Roman empire.

b. Even such disasters as these were *not* signalling the immediate holocaust He was predicting.

c. One famine, recorded in the New Testament (Acts 11:29ff.) occurred about 45-46 A.D. and was very servere in Palestine. Luke tells how the church at Antioch sent relief to their Jewish brethren in Palestine. Josephus tells how Queen Helena, an Abiabene convert to Judaism (Abdiabene is east of the Tigris River) sent relief to the Jews for the same famine (Josephus, *Antiquities,* XX, II, 5).

d. Many destructive earthquakes have been recorded in the history of Syria which borders on Palestine. The Hauran beyond the Jordan is covered with signs of violent earth-shocks, and the cities on the coast of Palestine have suffered many quakes.

e. The New Testament documents a great earthquake in Palestine at the death of Christ (Mt. 27:51-54); one at Christ's resurrection (Mt. 28:2); one at Philippi in Macedonia (Acts 16: 26).

f. Josephus mentions an earthquake in the reign of Herod "such as had not happened at any other time, which was very destructive to men and cattle" (*Antiquities,* IV, V, 2).

g. Many such earthquakes could have happened and been recorded but the records destroyed when Jerusalem was burned and when Rome was burned.

h. Roman historians document numerous earthquakes in the 1st century in Rome 51 A.D.; Apamaea; Laodicea 60 A.D.; Amporia 62 A.D.; Tacitus and Seneca both mention earthquakes in Asia, Achaia, Syria, Macedonia, Cyprus, Paphus, Crete and Italy.

i. There is at least one pestilence mentioned by Josephus in Babylon 40 A.D. which killed some 30,000 people (*Antiquities,* XVII, IX, 8) and one in Italy 66 A.D. recorded by Tacitus. Many others may have been documented but the documents destroyed.

3. Great signs from Heavens (Lk. 21:11)

a. What Jesus probably meant by "great signs from heaven" were the catastrophies of "nature" such as volcanic eruptions, cyclones, meteors or other great storms from the heavens which often terrify men.

b. Josephus records the following signs which preceded the destruction of Jerusalem:

(1) a star resembling a sword stood over the city
(2) a comet that lasted a whole year
(3) at the Feast of Unleavened Bread, during the night, a bright light shone around the altar and the Temple so that it seemed broad daylight.
the eastern gate of the Temple, of solid brass, fastened with strong bolts and bars, requiring 20 men to shut, opened in the night of its own accord
(5) a great noise of a multitude was heard in the Temple saying, "Let us remove hence."
(6) chariots and troops of soldiers in their armor were seen running about among the clouds and surrounding the cities.

(7) 4 years before the war began, Jesus, son of Ananus, came to the feast of Tabernacles, when the city was in peace and prosperity, and began to cry aloud, "A voice from the east, a voice from the west, from the four winds, a voice against Jerusalem and the holy house. . . ." etc. Upon being scourged, he would cry with every stroke, "Woe, woe to Jerusalem!"

Some of these were probably imaginative—but the very fact that Josephus records them indicates they were being rumored around. AND THAT IS THE WHOLE POINT OF JESUS' WARNINGS HERE—TO KEEP HIS DISCIPLES FROM BEING TERRIFIED AT SUCH RUMORS SO THEY MIGHT FLEE.

C. Persecuting Countrymen

1. Afflictions

a. Severe persecutions to come upon His followers will *not* be signalling any imminent eschatological end.

b. Up to the time of Jesus' death, there were no severe persecutions of His followers. The authorities had determined to kill Jesus, but His followers were still free of such malice.

c. But immediately after His death, their tribulation would begin. Even this should not cause them to expect the imment destruction of the Jewish commonwealth.

Even this should not terrify them into fleeing Jerusalem and neglecting to fulfill their commission to preach the gospel there first.

d. As a matter of fact, being brought to trial in Jewish synagogues and prisons, and before Jewish rulers, would be an opportune "time for them to bear testimony" (Lk. 21:13).

2. Attitudes

a. They were not to "meditate beforehand" how to answer when hailed before persecutors. Luke uses the Greek words *me promeletan* which mean primarily "have no concern prior to."

b. The better way to translate the word is "be not anxious beforehand."

c. In other words, Jesus exhorts those who anticipate being called to questioning before tribunals need not distress themselves beforehand that they will not be able to endure the questioning or not have sufficient knowledge to give the testimony that they should. What Jesus wants them to say *will be given them between* His prophecy here and the coming persecutions.

212

d. This is not a promise of Jesus that they will need no preparation between these times. They will indeed be given many things to say from their own eyewitnessed experiences (Jesus' death and resurrection).

e. Jesus did not want the apostles to let His predictions of the coming persecutions fill them with anxiety ahead of time so that they might hastily decide to flee from Palestine immediately upon His death.

f. He desired to warn them here, at this moment, they would have a testimony of historical facts which none of their adversaries would be able to contradict. They need not be afraid they would have nothing to say.

3. Apostasy (False teaching, lawlessness and indifference)

a. All this would also characterize the Jewish society in which the apostles would live preceding the holocaust on the Jewish nation.

b. Persecution and apostasy is abundantly confirmed by pagan historians as well as by sacred history (New Testament) (cf. Gal. 1:7; 2:4; II Cor. 11:13-15; I Tim. 1:3-7; 1:19-20; II Tim. 3:8-9; Titus 1:10-11; Jude; II Pet. 2; Rev. 1:3; Acts 15:1, etc.)

c. The book of Acts thoroughly documents persecution of Christians and apostasy and lawlessness of the Jews before 70 A.D.

D. Preaching of Christian gospel throughout the world.

1. That is also documented as having happened before 70 A.D.

2. One must consider the Roman empire as the then civilized and traveled world.

3. Cf. Rom. 1:5, 8; 10:18; 16:26; Col. 1:6; 1:23.

4. It was the apostle Paul who made it abundantly clear in his epistle to the Hebrew Christians that Judaism was doomed and "near to passing away" (Heb. 8:13; 10:25; 12:25-29; 13:14).

And, so, very alarming words fell from the lips of Jesus. The apostles, combining with these words their undoubted knowledge of popular rabbinical traditions of the "coming age" were startled. Jesus wanted to allay their fears lest they be terrified into deserting their task. SO HE REVEALED TO THE APOSTLES THESE EVENTS OF HISTORY *BEFORE* THEY CAME TO PASS IN ORDER THAT THEY MIGHT TRUST HIM AND CARRY OUT THEIR JOB.

II. PRECISE SIGNS OF DESTRUCTION, 24:15-34 (Mk. 13:14-30; Lk. 21:20-32)

A. Pagan Profanation

THIRTEEN LESSONS ON REVELATION

1. This, and the signs following, Jesus predicts will be plainly observable to the generation then living. THEY ARE TO BE *IMMEDIATE* SIGNS THAT JUDAISM IS FORSAKEN AND DESOLATE AND THEY MEAN THAT THE *END IS IMMINENT* UPON JERUSALEM AND JUDAISM.
2. The desolating sacrilege, spoken of by the prophet Daniel, standing in the holy place, set up where it ought not to be (Mark), IS THE ROMAN ARMIES SURROUNDING THE CITY OF JERUSALEM, according to Luke 21:20.
3. This fulfills Jesus' parable of the Marriage Feast of the King for His Son, which was treated with contempt. The "King" sent *His armies* and burned their city and destroyed the people, (Mt. 22:7).
4. Daniel predicted the desecration of the Temple and the city by Roman armies as the consequence of the Jew's rejecting their "Anointed Prince" 490 years after the restoration of the Jewish commonwealth in 457 B.C. (see Dan. 9:24-27).
5. After a series of Jewish uprisings and riots, Jerusalem was first beseiged in November, 66 A.D. by the Roman legate of Syria, Cestius Gallus.

   a. He had marched to Judea at that time with the Twelfth Legion and surrounded the city on orders from Nero. Gallus occupied Bezetha, (northern edge of Jerusalem) but concluded his forces were too small to take the rest of the city so he withdrew.

   b. The Jews, assuming Divine providence had intervened to spare the city, took no advantage of the opportunity to flee. In fact, many Jews living in the immediate environs outside the city fled *into* the city for what they thought would be protection.

   c. On the way back to Syria Gallus and his forces were ambushed by Jewish insurgents at Beth-horon and the Romans suffered great losses.

6. When Christians saw Gallus' first seige, remembering Jesus' prophecy, they fled to Pella when he withdrew to Syria.

   Eusebius writes in his *History,* ". . . the people of the church in Jerusalem, being commanded to leave and dwell in a city of Perea, called Pella, in accordance with a certain oracle which was uttered before the war to the approved men there by way of revelation. . . ."
7. Nero sent his general, Vespasian, with 60,000 men (ten legions) to Judea in the Spring of 67 A.D. He conquered all of Judea and was about to beseige Jerusalem, when he was called back to

Rome after Nero's suicide. Vespasian became emperor and sent son, Titus Vespasian to Judea to put down the Jewish revolt.

a. Titus recaptured the Tower of Antonia July 24, 70 A.D.
b. August 5th, he caused the daily sacrifices of the Jewish priests to cease (see Dan. 9:27).
c. August 27th the Temple gates were burned.
d. August 29th (anniversary of Babylonian destruction of Solomon's Temple in 587 B.C.), the Sanctuary itself was set on fire.
e. While the sanctuary was burning, Roman soldiers brought their legionary standards (with the emperors image upon them) into the Temple area and offered sacrifices to the emperor there!
f. September 26, A.D. 70, the whole city was in Titus' hands. All during the seige and assaults on the city by the Romans, the Jews within had been reduced to such desperation there were atrocities the Jews perpetrated upon one another almost too horrible and gruesome to recount.

B. Terrible Tribulations and Deceiving Deliverers

1. Jesus specifically and categorically states of this terrible holocaust on Jerusalem, ". . . for *these are* days of vengeance, to fulfill all that is written" (Lk. 21:22).

a. Moses wrote that this would happen should the Jews reject the Prophet (cf. Deut. 18:15-18; 28:15-68).
b. Daniel prophesied these things would come to pass because the Jews would "cut off" their Anointed One (Dan. 9:24-27).
c. Jesus proclaimed they would "fill up the measure of their fathers . . . that upon them would come all the righteous blood shed on earth" (Mt. 23:31-36) because they were going to kill the Son of God.

2. Jesus said, "For great distress shall be upon the earth and wrath upon *this* people" (Lk. 21:23), "for then will be great tribulation *such as* has not been from the beginning of the creation which God created until now, and never will be," (Mt. 24:21; Mk. 13:19).

a. Some readers, confused, insist that such language cannot be referring to the destruction of Jerusalem, because there have been many tribulations since the destruction of Jerusalem much worse in statistics. Nazi Germany killed some 6,000,000 Jews in WWII. Then there is Hiroshima and Nagasaki—the prisons of Russian Siberia, etc.

b. There were worse disasters before Jerusalem—what about the Flood of Noah's day?

c. The term, *such as,* in the description of Jesus, really does not refer to the statistical magnitude of the tribulation—it refers rather to the *kind* of tribulation.

Jesus is anticipating the uniqueness of the cause and effect of the suffering and affliction—not the quantity or number suffering. Because of a. and b. above, we must explain what Jesus said, then, by quality or uniqueness. Note the below:

(1) This tribulation involved the final destruction of what once had been God's holy nation. This had never happened before. God rescued a remnant from captivity and restored their nationality. It will never happen again, since the church of Christ is now God's holy nation (I Pet. 2:9) and it will never be destroyed (Mt. 16:18) (Dan. 2:44).

(2) The circumstances of the Jews trapped in Jerusalem was unique in all of history. God had withdrawn His presence. They were abandoned to their own evil. The residents turned on one another in hatred and panic, and inflicted on themselves atrocities more horrible than even the Romans could invent!

(3) It was a tribulation suffered only by those Jews who had rejected Christ. Those who believed Jesus (esp. this prophecy) were saved from the disaster of 70 A.D.

(4) The Bible was written for all time—the "atomic age" as well as that of bows and arrows. For Jesus to try to compare the tribulation of Roman warfare with Hiroshima would mean nothing to the apostles. So, Jesus is simply saying, "In the frame-of-reference of what you apostles know and can visualize, Jerusalem's suffering is going to be the greatest." This is no contradiction of Jesus' omniscience. He is, in fact, condescending to the human limitations of the apostles. He did this at other times too. He told them a few hours later, "I have many things to say to you which you are not presently able to bear" Jn. 16:12ff.

(5) The holocaust of 70 A.D. was unique in the way Jews tortured murdered and despised Jews. Jerusalem was really self-destroyed. The Roman general, made every effort to spare the people, the city and the Temple, but the Jews were implaccable.

216

    (6) It may be that this great tribulation which began with the destruction of Judaism in 70 A.D., has continued with more or less intensity up to the present time! The Jews, since 70 A.D. have, in many lands and many centuries suffered great tribulation such as no *people* have ever known.

3. If those days had not been shortened. . . .

    a. Titus first thought to build a seige wall and starve the Jews *all* to death, or kill every last one of them.

    b. But then, with pressing business back in Rome, he stormed the city, killed and burned and took thousands of Jews captive.

    c. Thus many thousands of Jews were saved alive who would have otherwise perished (Josephus, *Wars,* I:12:1).

4. Jesus said "many will be led captive among the nations, and Jerusalem will be trodden down by the Gentiles, until the times of the Gentiles are fulfilled" (Lk. 21:24).

    a. Jerusalem will be desolate until God brings it to an end. But how long will that be?

    b. The passage in Romans 11:25-26 gives the clue. Until all Israel is saved. At that time the "full number of Gentiles will have come in."

    c. The question really focuses on the salvation of *all* Israel.

       (1) it is plain from the New Testament that *Israel is now* the church of Jesus Christ (both Jew and Gentile).

       (2) Rom. 9:8 ". . . it is not the children of the flesh who are the children of God, but the children of the promise. . . ."

       (3) Gal. 3:29 "and if you are Christ's, then you are Abraham's offspring, heirs according to promise."

    d. The "until" points to a time when God will have "grafted" into true spiritual Israel, all that through faith in Christ and obedience of that faith shall be saved. That is the end of time. Jerusalem will be trodden down by the Gentiles until the end of the world.

    e. The Jews had their time. They were allotted 490 years to fulfill their messianic destiny and bring the Messiah into the world and complete God's redemptive program (Dan. 9:24-27).

       They rejected their own Messiah and crucified Him. So the kingdom was taken from them and given to others (cf. Mt. 22:43).

       (1) In this new kingdom neither circumcision nor uncircumcision counts for anything, but a new creation.

(2) *All who walk by this rule are the Israel of God* (see Gal. 6:15-16).

(3) God has not absolutely rejected the Jews, neither have the Jews totally rejected Christ—a hardening has taken place only in part. There are still Jews coming to God through Christ today!

(4) But that is the only way God will accept anyone, forevermore! (cf. Jn. 5:23; 14:6; Heb. 10:10; 10:12-14, etc.). Genetic Jewishness counts nothing with God—never did, never shall (see Rom. 2:28-29; 4:9ff.; 9:22-26; Ga. 3:6-9, etc.).

(5) It has always been faith that made anyone a child of God.

(6) Paul initiated the taking of the gospel to the Gentiles (Acts 13:46).

(7) The time allotted for the Gentile ascendency over Jerusalem is until the end of all time when Christ delivers up the kingdom to God (I Cor. 15:23-28).

f. Until the end of time Jerusalem will be trodden down by Gentiles.

(1) Geographical Jerusalem and national Israel will be characterized as Gentile so long as the present world exists.

(2) So long as a Jew will not come to Jehovah by faith in Jesus Christ, he is a heathen, an unbeliever, one who crucifies Christ afresh, and for him there is no possibility of repentance before God (except through Jesus) (cf. Heb. 6:1-8; 10:1-31).

5. False Christ's and false prophets showing signs and wonders, attempting to lead many astray.

a. These pseudo-Christs would try to convince many to follow them into different places of alleged safety.

b. Jesus exhorts his apostles to "take heed, I have told you all things beforehand."

c. He says, ". . . as the lightning . . . so will be the coming of the Son of man." What Jesus is saying here is this: "Do not follow the pseudo-Christs; their signs will be obscure, deceitful and false. When the Son of man comes in His judgment upon this city, the signs will be unmistakable. The signs which I have told you will be as clearly visible as the lightning!"

(1) This interpretation of the Son of man's "coming" in 24:27 is in harmony with Jesus' next statement, "Wherever

the body is, there the eagles (Gr. *aetoi,* "vultures") will be gathered together" 24:28.

(2) Vultures easily ascertain where deadness is and hasten to devour it. The Romans pounced on the rotting carcass of Judaism. The Jews expected a Messiah to appear from out of nowhere and deliver them from the Romans.

(3) Those Jews within the beseiged walls of the city were especially vulnerable to false prophets and pseudo-Christs.

d. Jesus said this would be a sign that Jerusalem was about to be wiped away. The real Messiah did come in 70 A.D., with *His army* (Mt. 22:7), to destroy, not deliver Jerusalem.

6. These are some of the things Josephus says went on during the fall of Jerusalem (66-70 A.D.): *Wars, Books V and VI*

a. 3 different political parties of the Jews were within the city fighting one another for the 3 years of the seige.

b. They fought one another with such malice and abandon that 1000s of the innocent were slain in their "cross-fire"— even priests and worshipers in the Temple courts were slain in the very act of offering sacrifices.

c. These factions burned storehouses filled with food, polluted water reservoirs to keep others from having them, and thus caused the starvation of 100s of their countrymen.

d. Anyone who sought to escape the city, if caught by the Jews, was slain by having his throat cut.

e. Burial of dead bodies within the city was impossible, so they let the bodies rot, tramped over them, or threw them over the walls.

f. Some Jews tried to swallow their gold and escape the city, hoping to pass it after escape. Both their own countrymen and the Romans caught on to this. When such people were captured trying to escape, they were thrown to the ground and disemboweled alive and their gold taken from their intestines while they writhed in death.

g. Robbers plundered stores, homes, government buildings, torturing anyone found inside for food or other articles of value.

h. Children pulled the very morsels of food out of the mouths their aged parents, and parents did the same to their children.

i. Many Jews sold their homes, children, every possession for *one* handfull of wheat or barley.

j. One method of torture by Jews upon Jews was to drive wooden spikes up their private parts and this for no reason at all except to express anger.

k. Romans crucified Jews at the rate of 500 per day as they tried to escape. They ran out of wood for crosses so many were crucified.

l. Tens of thousands died of rampant disease and pestilence.

m. Some Jews leaped from the tops of the walls of Jerusalem, broke bones, mangled bodies and died. If they did survive and escape, they ate food when they could find it, so much and so rapidly they died.

n. Dead bodies were stacked in great heaps as high as houses.

o. Blood ran down the gutters and narrow streets of Jerusalem ankle deep.

p. Some ate from public sewers, cattle and pigeon dung, wood, leather, shields, hay, clothing, and things even scavenger animals would not.

q. Book VI:III:4, documents the incident of a woman roasting her own infant son and eating his flesh to stay alive (cf. Deut. 28:53).

r. Many false prophets told people to take refuge in the Temple, as a result 10,000 were slain and burned when Titus burned the Temple.

s. After the woman (mentioned above) ate the flesh of her own child, "the whole city was full of this horrid action immediately" Josephus.

t. Romans, upon capturing the entire city, slew every living person they encountered, "they obstructed the very streets with their dead bodies, and made the whole city run down with blood, to such a degree that the fire of many houses was quenched with these men's blood."

u. Josephus records that 1,100,000 perished and 97,000 were taken captive at this destruction of Jerusalem. Some estimates go as high as a total of 2,000,000.

v. Josephus concludes, ". . . thus the city was thoroughly laid even with the ground. . . ." Only three towers and a little part of one wall was left by Titus to "memorialize" his victory over the Jews.

C. Potentates Plummeting

1. Matthew says, "*Immediately* after the tribulation of *those* days. . . . Mark says, "But *in those days, after* that tribulation. . . . Luke says, "And there will be signs in sun and moon and stars, and upon the earth, distress of nations in perplexity at the roaring of the sea and the waves, men fainting with fear and with foreboding of what is coming on the world; for the powers of the heavens will be shaken."

All the Synoptics say, "the powers of the heavens will be shaken. . . ."

2. The very strong indication that this text is a continuation of the prophecy of the destruction of Jerusalem and Judaism may be seen from the following:

a. "Immediately" does not usually make room for much of a time gap—certainly not a gap of over 2000 years!

b. "When these things begin to take place . . ." in Lk. 21:28 surely is not referring to the Second Coming for there will be no signs pointing to its nearness—it will be instantaneous!

c. The further statement, ". . . this generation will not pass away till all these things take place" (Mt. 24:34; Lk. 21:32; Mk. 13:30) undoubtedly includes the sun and moon being darkened, stars falling from heaven, perplexity and distress of nations and the powers of the heavens being shaken.

3. This section is difficult for the Occidental (Western) mind, but not for the Oriental (Eastern). The careful Bible student will find much help in understanding this apocalyptic language of Jesus by giving attention to context and comparable passages from the Old Testament and from Biblical word usage.

This section is plainly couched in what is called "apocalyptic" language, similar to that of the Old Testament prophets and Revelation when predicting the "coming" of God in judgment upon pagan nations (or the nation of Israel). Apocalyptic language is characterized by its figurativeness, symbolism and drama.

a. Sun, moon, and stars darkened or falling from heaven is often stated symbolically in the Old Testament to picture any inexpressible calamity such as an overturning of kingdoms or cities or kings or religious potentates thought otherwise to be invincible. It is clear that Isaiah 13:10; 14:12ff.; 24:23; 34:1-4; Jer. 4:23-28; 15:9; Joel 2:10; 2:30—3:21; Amos 8:9; Micah 3:6; Hab. 3:11, and others, refer to the fall of kingdoms and kings in such terms. This kind of imagery goes back at least as far as Joseph and his brothers (cf. Gen. 37:9ff.). They understood it then.

b. Luke says, "distress of nations . . . in perplexity at the roaring of the sea and waves. . . ." This is picturing the distress of the wicked as these calamities of the destruction of Jerusalem roll over them like waves of the sea. Isaiah 57:20-21 uses the same symbolism. It may also refer to the overwhelming flood of the Roman army come upon Jerusalem (see Jer. 6:23ff., describing the flood of Babylonians to come upon Jerusalem in 606 B.C.).

c. The "powers of the heavens being shaken . . ." is apparently a figurative way of predicting the "shaking down" of the system of Judaism and the obsolete priesthood (cf. Heb. 8:13; 12:25-29; 13:13-14 with Isa. 14:12ff.; 24:21-23).

d. Then will appear the "sign of the Son of man . . ." or as Luke puts it, "And then they will see the Son of man coming in a cloud" with power and great glory." Jesus plainly told His apostles some of them would not taste death before they see the kingdom of God come with power and before they see the Son of man coming in His kingdom (Mk. 9:1; Mt. 16:28). He is saying here that when the destruction of Jerusalem occurs it will be unmistakable evidence to His followers, at least, that the Son of man has "come" to keep His word about taking the kingdom from the Jews.

e. Luke says, "men will be fainting with fear and foreboding . . ." Matthew says, "Then will all the tribes of the earth mourn." Jews had been scattered all over the world ever since the Babylonian captivity. These would certainly mourn and faint with fear when they learned of Jerusalem's obliteration by the Romans because they would fear the same treatment. This probably refers also to the prediction of Zechariah (12:10). There the Jews are predicted as mourning over the crucifying of their Messiah. John refers to this prophecy at the crucifixion (Jn. 19:37). The destruction of Jerusalem was God's wrath upon the nation for crucifying ("cutting off") the Messiah (cf. Dan. 9:24-27).

f. The Son of man coming on clouds of heaven with great power is a messianic term used by Daniel (7:13-14) in connection with Christ's first coming (*not* His second coming). This is probably what Jesus meant when He said the same thing to the High Priest warning him of the consequence of crucifying the Messiah (cf. Mt. 26:64)—the destruction of Judaism.

g. And He will send out His angels with a loud trumpet call, and they will gather his elect from the four winds, from one end of heaven to the other. Luke says it this way, "When these thing begin to take place . . . your redemption *is drawing* near." Luke does not say, ". . . your redemption *is here*" *in the twinkling of an eye!*

(1) when the fall of Judaism is accomplished, the fruitless fig tree will have been withered, and a great obstacle standing in the way of the gospel unto the whole world will be removed (cf. Mt. 21:18-22; Mk. 11:12-14; Mk. 11:20-25).

(2) From that time onward God will signally build up His kingdom. It shall be fully and exclusively established and recognized when the Jewish system comes to an end. This note of Luke in 21:28, ". . . now when these things begin to take place . . ." is *parallel* to his note in 21:31, "So also, when you see these things taking place . . ." and both of them refer to the *visible* destruction of Jerusalem.

(3) Isaiah predicted that God would create a new "land" or "nation" with "one stroke . . . in one day" *before the old nation had passed away* (Isa. 66:7-9). But Isaiah also predicted that this new nation (the church) would "go forth and look on the dead bodies of the men that have rebelled against me . . ." (Isa. 66:24). These prophecies, we believe, refer to the establishment of the New Israel, the church, on the day of Pentecost—and the subsequent destruction of the old order, Judaism.

D. Readily Recognizable

1. Parable of the fig tree.

   a. Jesus was using an illustration His disciples, as outdoors men, could readily understand.

   b. Russell Boatman says, "A budding tree, whatever its specie, is a sign that 'spring has sprung' and 'summer is nigh.' Thus He was telling His disciples that when they should see the things He had enumerated, they should know the fall of Jerusalem was at hand."

   c. The signs of Jerusalem's destruction and God's judgment of the Jewish establishment (the rulers included) will be as easily recognizable as the signs that summer is drawing near!

   d. When they see the preliminary signs and the immediate signs they are to know that Jesus, the Son of man, is near, indeed, at the very gates of Jerusalem for judgment.

   e. They may also know that the kingdom of God is imminently to be established exclusively in the church of Christ (Lk. 21:31).

2. Paul wrote to the Hebrew Christians to encourage them not to go back to Judaism (in Hebrews), but to hold fast to Christianity, "and so much more as they were seeing the Day approaching" (Heb. 10:25).

   a. What day could Jewish Christians *see approaching?*

   b. The answer is, of course, the approaching destruction of Jerusalem and Judaism—certainly not the Second Coming of Christ.

    c. Their "redemption" would be the breaking of the strangle-hold of Judaism from the throat of the infant Church, allowing it to survive the Judaizers.

3. "This generation shall not pass away till all these things take place."

    a. The first thing the careful student will do is compare the same usage of the word *generation* in Mt. 16:28; Mk. 9:1; Lk. 9:27; Mt. 11:16; 12:41; 23:35-36.

    b. Generation does not mean "race" as some have thought. It plainly means a life-span of some 35-40 years.

    c. "All *these* things . . ." refers back to all the tribulations predicted from Mt. 24:4 through Mt. 24:34 (and parallels).

    d. Notice the significant and continued use of *"these"* (contemporary things) all the way through the aforementioned sections. But *after* Mt. 24:34 (and parallels), Jesus begins using *"that"* to refer to His Second Coming when heaven and earth *is* to pass away.

4. Summarizing, it is clear that all Jesus has said or predicted in His Olivet Discourse up to this point applies strictly to the destruction of Jerusalem and Judaism. Note the following points:

    a. "All these things . . ." indicates that *all* which He has said *prior* is said of the destruction of Jerusalem.

    b. Up to this point in the discourse, Jesus says everything that is to happen is to happen in those *days* (plural). Everything after this point is in that *day* (singular). The phrase, "that day" (singular) is a widely used phrase in the New Testament to speak of the end of the world and the Second Coming.

    c. The conjunction "But" in Mt. 24:36; Mk. 13:32; Lk. 21:34 is a definite word separating that which has been predicted earlier and able to be known, from that which follows the conjunction which cannot be known by signs.

E. Transitional Statement, Mt. 24:35; Mk. 13:31; Lk. 21:33

1. "Heaven and earth *will* pass away, but my words will not pass away. . . ."

2. The apostles were shocked. It was if the world was coming to an end!

3. Jesus says, "Indeed, the world *is* going to come to an end—however, the destruction of Jerusalem is *not* the end of the world."

4. Meanwhile the words He predicts of Jerusalem will not pass away—they will come to pass no matter how incredible they may be to Jews!

MATTHEW, CHAPTERS 24 THROUGH 25

APPREHENSION:

1. What motivated the disciples to "point out" to Jesus the buildings of the temple? Mt. 24:1
2. What is the "end" Jesus is saying "is not yet" in Mt. 24:6?
3. Could all the signs predicted by Jesus in Mt. 24:3-13 have occurred before 70 A.D.?
4. Could the gospel have been preached throughout the whole world before 70 A.D.? Mt. 24:14 (cf. Rom. 1:5, 8; 10:18; 16:26; Col. 1:6; 1:23).
5. What is the desolating sacrilege spoken of by the prophet Daniel? Mt. 24:15 (cf. Dan. 9:24-27; Lk. 21:20).
6. Could Mt. 24:29-31 possibly refer to the fall of Jerusalem—or must it refer to the end of the world? (cf. Isa. 13:10; 14:12; 24:23; Jer. 4:23-28; 15:9).
7. What is the lesson to be learned from the fig tree? Mt. 24:32-35
8. Why did Jesus pronounce such dreadful judgment upon Jerusalem? (cf. Mt. 21:33-43; 22:1-14; 23:29-39; Deut. 18:18-19; 28:15-68).

APPLICATION:

I. HISTORY IS HEADED FOR JUDGMENT

A. This universe in which we live is headed for a climactic holocaust.

1. All the great catastrophic, cataclysmic events such as the downfall of Assyria, Babylon, Persia, Rome and Jerusalem are not the end of history BUT THEY ARE PREDICTIONS, SIGNS OF THE INEVITABLE END OF HISTORY.
2. Every judgment and every redemption in history typifies God's moral principles of Divine government over history. The book of Daniel and the book of Revelation are both great moving-picture scenarios, as it were, of how history predicts and prefigures God's judgments and redemptions.
3. God has been trying to warn the world ever since the Flood that an end to history is coming.

B. Loren Eiseley, Professor of Anthropology at the University of Pennsylvania comments on *mankind's indifference* to the loud lessons of history: "A yearning for a life of 'noble savagery' without the accumulated burdens of history seem in danger of engulfing a whole generation, as it did the French philosophers and their 18th century followers. Those individuals who persist in pursuing the mind-destroying drug of constant action have not only confined themselves to an increasingly chaotic present— they also, by deliberate abandonment of their past, are destroying the conceptual tools and values that are the means of introducing the rational into the oncoming future."

1. Even today the judgments of the Almighty God march over a world that continues, for the most part, to ignore and disobey Him.
2. History, nature and the gospel revelation cry out, "Repent" but only a few choose to do so.

II. HISTORY IS HEADED FOR REDEMPTION

A. Bertrand Russell, 97 years old, completed his autobiography. He looked back over a life that held little meaning for him and looked ahead to the specter of ultimate obliteration (he hoped). After mentioning the wish to "see the people one is fond of," he asked, "What is there to make life tolerable? We stand on the shore of an ocean, crying to the night and the emptiness; sometimes a voice answers out of the darkness. But it is the voice of one drowning; and in a moment the silence returns. The world seems to me quite dreadful; the unhappiness of many people is very great, and I often wonder how they all endure it. To know people well is to know their tragedy; it is usually the central thing about which their lives are built. And I suppose if they did not live most of the time in the things of the moment, they would not be able to go on."

Betrand Russell is dead now. He is undoubtedly still standing on the shore of the great gulf separating Him from Christ, still crying out into the night, but hearing only the voices of those drowning.

B. There is One who died and is Alive Forevermore. He is the One Worthy to take the scroll of history and open its seals—(Rev. 5:1ff.). He is the Lamb, victorious over, sovereign over history.

By His death and resurrection He has redeemed (purchased) history. Those who believe in Him and trust their whole life to Him will share in His redemptive consummation—He has promised this, and He kept every promise He made, even the one concerning His conquest of death!

There are those who would insist today that "authentic existence" must be discovered only in the here-and-now, not in some sweet "by and by." But in a few ticks of the clock, the present will be the past and the past is closed to everyone but God. All man has open to him is the future.

Christians look back, rightly, to that once for all event that took place in Bethlehem. He was born to die—to seek and to save. But this same Son of Man has a still unfilled purpose, and it is toward this that we should now concentrate our hope. This One who came the first time in humiliation is coming again in glory!

The life hereafter is a subject of universal and timeless interest. This is as it should be. Man is created for eternity. God has put eternity into the mind of man (Eccl. 3:11). This present life, however significant, is only the beginning of a never-ending life of either blessedness or terror.

Life and time in this world are tentative. David, king of Israel, wrote, "Jehovah . . . let me know how frail I am . . . Surely every man is mere breath . . . He heaps up riches, and knows not who shall gather them" (Psa. 39). Statistics say that every 20 seconds a person dies in the U.S., and the death rate for the whole world is about 20 times that of the U.S. Throughout the world, a person dies every tick of the clock!

Our lesson is a series of parables from the Lord of life and time testifying to the consummation of history and final judgment. Jesus tells the world in these parables when to expect judgment, how to prepare for it, and what it will be like.

MATTHEW

THE MESSIAH HAS COME

AUTHORITY IN HEAVEN'S JUDGMENTS

by Paul T. Butler

Matthew 24:36—25:46

Introduction

I. APPROACH

A. Divest yourself of all presupposed theories about the Second Coming of Christ and simply let the Bible say what it's authors intended to say. There are four main rules of interpreting the Bible:

1. The true interpretation is *what the author intended to say*—not what the reader wants him to say.

2. God's word has *one intended meaning,* not many conflicting ones.

3. *God is able to say* what He wants to say, and He knows to whom He is speaking. He does not intend to confess or obscure, but to reveal.

4. The language of the Bible *is the language of man*—and is to be interpreted by the same methods and principles as are appropriate for all human language.

B. Expect to understand what Jesus says about His Second Coming—at least as much as He reveals.

1. Do not expect to be confused.
2. Remember that Matthew 24 and 25 are not the only information in the Bible about Christ's Second Coming.
3. Let me suggest that the Old Tesatment says *nothing* about His Second Coming. There was no point in the prophets trying to instruct the Jews on His Second Coming when they had all they could do to convince the Old Testament people of His *first* coming!
4. Other *major portions* of scripture dealing with Christ's 2nd Coming are: (in the New Testament)

   a. I Cor. 15:23-58 (dealing with the *fact* of the resurrection)
   b. I Thess. 4:13—5:11 (to prove that there will be no "secret rapture" of some saints before others at the 2nd Coming).
   c. II Thess. 2:1-12 (predicting the destruction of *the* man of sin and of *all* men of sin at Christ's 2nd Coming).
   d. II Pet. 3:1-13 (a warning against scoffing at the doctrine of the 2nd Coming).
   e. Revelation, chapters 20:7—22:21

   Of course His 2nd coming is mentioned numerous times in the New Testament but in more isolated portions.

II. APPLICATION

A. It should be evident as we study this lesson that what Jesus is most concerned that men believe about His 2nd Coming is the application of the fact to the way they live!

B. Application of life here is, indeed, the focus of all the New Testament says about the 2nd Coming.
   The focus is certainly *not* on time tables or battlefields or the destiny of the Jews or the land of Palestine.

C. "It is not for you to know times or seasons . . . you shall be my witnesses." (Acts 1:7)

D. ". . . he commands all men everywhere to repent, because he has fixed a day . . . and has given assurance to all men . . ." (Acts 17:30-31).

E. ". . . comfort one another with these words . . ." (I Thess. 4:18).

F. "Since all these things are thus to be dissolved, what sort of persons ought you to be in lives of holiness and godliness . . ." (II Pet. 3:11ff.).

MATTHEW, CHAPTERS 24 THROUGH 25

Discussion

I. WAIT, 24:36—25:46

A. It is futile, at best, and apparently *contrary* to the will of Christ to try to determine when the Lord is coming again for redemption and judgment.

1. No one knows when the *consummation* of the age is to arrive in time.

    a. Jesus Himself said: "But of *that* day and hour *no one knows,* not even the angels of heaven, nor the Son, but the Father only" 24:36.

    b. Jesus reiterates this emphatically throughout our lesson—note:

    Mt. 24:36 ". . . of that day and hour, no one knows . . ."
    Mt. 24:37-39 ". . . as in the days of Noah . . . they did not know . . ."
    Mt. 24:42 ". . . watch . . . for you do not know . . ."
    Mk. 13:35 ". . . watch . . . for you do not know . . ."
    Mt. 24:44 ". . . at an hour you do not expect . . ."
    Mt. 24:51 ". . . when not expected . . . when not known . . ."
    Mt. 25:13 ". . . you know neither the day nor the hour . . ."
    Mt. 25:19 ". . . after a long time . . ."
    Mt. 25:31 ". . . when(?) the son of man comes . . ."

    c. The rest of the New Testament emphatically teaches that no one will know when Christ returns.

    The New Testament emphasizes His return will be "like a thief in the night" I Thess 5:1-4; II Pet. 3:10 (see also II Thess. 2:1-2).

2. To explain Jesus' emphatic statements by saying that Jesus simply did not know the year, or the day of the month, or the exact minute when He would return, but that He *did* tell us certain signs to look for and then know that it is *near,* makes this whole context ridiculous!

3. Jesus did not even know any signs to reveal about His 2nd Coming—none are told!

4. If Jesus knew the time of His 2nd Coming but, as He did, declared He would not tell it (or could not), the temptation to read into His every statement some subtle prediction as to the time would consume the energies of all Christendom.

    That is why Jesus was so emphatic to say, *"No one knows! Not even I!"*

5. There is no excuse for anyone trying to predict the time of His

return when we understand that even Jesus Himself did not know!

B. The most important thing about eschatology is its emphasis on the certainty of the end of this world and judgment.

1. Jesus and the apostles always spoke of His return in terms, not of time, but of results—judgment and redemption.
2. He is coming back—the world can believe that. The world had better believe that! His return is as certain as His resurrection.
3. We do not need to know when or how—we do not even need to know what kind of body we shall have (I Cor. 15, etc.).
4. WHAT WE NEED IS TO TRUST HIM, WORK FOR HIM, WAIT FOR HIM AND WELCOME HIM.
5. It is the work of the devil to divert our attention from the real focus of His return by getting us to be curious about "times and seasons."

C. There will be no abnormal, extra-ordinary "signs" pointing to a definite time for His return, Mt. 24:37-42.

1. It (Christ's *parousia*) will be just like the coming of the Flood in Noah's day.
2. Life going on in its *normal* path; marrying, building, eating and drinking—business as usual—*SUDDENLY THE END.*
3. Those of Noah's day "did not know until the flood came" (24:39)—the *only warning they had was the faithful preaching of Noah.* THERE WERE NO PRELIMINARY SIGNS!
4. Two women will be grinding at the mill—one is taken, one is left.
   a. This has nothing to do with a "secret rapture"
   b. Its emphasis, in the context, is to focus on the unexpectedness of Christ's 2nd coming.
   c. Especially does it emphasize the need to be ready every moment, even when working in the field, or at the time of household duties, for no one knows when He is coming. He will come when people are going about their *daily business*—and most of the world will not be prepared, because they are not being alert at every moment!
5. Luke's parallel to this is in Lk. 21:34-36
   a. Jesus said there, men and women who believe Him need to guard against being weighed down with dissipation and drunkenness (Gr. *kraipale,* lit. "headache, hangover, stupor" is translated dissipation); (Gr. *methe,* from which we get methanol, methane, etc., is translated, drunkenness). When

230

Jesus returns, a large portion of the world will be in a stupor from revelry.

b. Believers also need to guard against being weighed down with the cares of this life.

(Gr. *merimnais,* lit. "divided mind" or "anxiety"—it is the same word as used in Mt. 6, "Be not anxious")

Many will be so divided in their loyalty, they will not be ready to leave this world behind when Jesus comes.

Remember Lot's wife! (Lk. 17:32)

c. The day of Christ's return will come *suddenly like a snare,* upon all who dwell upon the face of *the whole earth,* at the same time!

d. That day is going to "spring shut," suddenly, like a snare.

D. Christ will no more make a prior announcement about His return than a thief would who comes in the night to rob a house, Mt. 24:43-44.

1. The thief depends totally on the element of *surprise.*

2. Jesus is going to *surprise* the world (I Thess. 5:1-11).

3. There is absolutely no way to know ahead of time when the Lord is coming, if He says it is going to be a surprise! (II Pet. 3:10).

4. Jesus said this more than once (cf. Lk. 12:35-40). Jesus does not want the world to know *when* He is going to return.

5. He could not be any clearer than when He said, ". . . the Son of man is coming *at an hour you do not expect."*

And this is said even to those who are His disciples, to those who believe Him and study His Word and know it.

How then can people expect to find in His Word any indication of the *time* of His return?

E. After His "journey" from this earth back to heaven, the long passage of time before His return may make it appear He has "delayed" His return, but just when some may have thought that, He will return. Mt. 24:45-51.

1. In other words, the Lord has *purposely delayed* His return.

2. That does not mean, however, that it could not be at any moment.

3. He has delayed it in order to sift the true and faithful believers from those who are not.

The true and faithful will not be lulled into unfaithfulness by the delay. They will believe Him when He says, "expect Me *at every moment,"* don't think you can indulge yourselves for a while and then hope to anticipate My return by certain signs, ahead of time!

4. This is what the "wicked servant" hoped for—he expected a signal or a prior announcement from his Master that he was about to return. He would then leave off self-indulgence and get ready for the return.
5. The wicked servant fooled himself by speculating about the time of the Master's return when the Master had said nothing at all about the time of His return!
   Such speculation is debilitating to the church and dangerous (I and II Thess.)!

F. Five of the ten virgins thought they knew the Bridegroom's schedule for coming—they believed they could anticipate it, Mt. 25:1-13.

1. They were not ungodly or immoral or hypocritical . . . they just knew He would not come unexpectedly.
2. It never entered their minds that He might tarry.
3. In spite of the emphatic insistence of this parable: ". . . you know neither the day nor the hour . . ." (25:13), men still assume they can know, or men still assume He is not coming back at all.
4. Jesus calls these 5 virgins, *"morons"* (that is the Greek word used, *morai,* in 25:2).
5. It is *moronic* for anyone to think he can know the Bridegroom's day or hour of return!

G. The Lord will return at any moment—He is coming back when men will be going about the normal, everyday affairs of life, Mt. 25:14-46.

1. Some people will be putting their talents to work, others will not.
2. Some people will be feeding the hungry, welcoming strangers, visiting the sick and the imprisoned—others will not.
3. There is no indication that any great holocaust will be going on world-wide when He returns.
4. There is no indication that evil will be any worse than it is at any other time.
5. There is no indication that there will be some "one-world government" being led by some individual known as *the* "anti-christ." (John says there will always be *many* anti-christs—those who do not pay heed to the apostolic message are anti-christs)—see I Jn.
6. Mk. 13:31 uses Gr. word *kairos,* "time" generic—the time will be unknowable.

II. WORK, Mt. 24:36—25:46

   A. Watch

     1. Every parable in this lesson exhorts *watchfulness*

     2. In view of the certainty of the return of Christ for judgment and redemption—and in view of the certainty that no one knows when it will be—the proper preparation for it is to be constantly *working,* for the Lord.

     3. Working is equated with *watching.*

     4. The Greek word translated watch is *gregoreite* (it is the word from which the English name, *Gregory,* originates)
       It means, "be awake, be vigilant, be alert." It means *constant* vigilance.

     5. The only person a thief cannot surprise is the one who stays awake all the time—never goes to sleep.

   B. All must watch, not just some, Mk. 13:32-37.

     1. When the "man" went away on his journey and left his servants in charge, *he left each servant with his work.*

     2. It is not just a few in mankind who are to be alert, vigilant, expecting Him to return at every moment, it is everyone.

     3. God will hold *all men responsible* to be doing His "work" when He comes back.

   C. Do not let the "Householder's" "house" be broken into!, Mt. 24:43-44.

     1. The whole world is God's house, all creation belongs to Him.

     2. Men should stay alert and vigilant and not let Satan invade what belongs to God.

     3. At least Christians, who know that the Master can or should be expected at any moment, will be alert and watchful and faithful constantly. When He returns He will find His house (the church) not invaded by the thief.

   D. Serve faithfully, correctly and constantly in the Master's household, Mt. 24:45-51.

     1. The wise servant

       a. Does his job the best he knows to do it. Feeds the household.

       b. Does so at the proper time. He does not speculate about the time of the Master's return, but is faithful ONE DAY AT A TIME!

       c. When the Master finally comes back, the wise servant is found doing his job (*which is not to try to speculate* when the Master is going to return).

       d. Watching for the Master's return consists in faithful *service.*

2. The wicked servant
   a. Depends on his own judgment and speculates on the time of the Master's return when the Master has not even told the servant when He shall return!
   b. He is really unfaithful and disloyal in his heart and waits until he figures the Master isn't coming back to act upon his disloyal attitudes.
   c. He is a criminal at heart. He thinks of God as a policeman. He is "good" only when the Master is present.
   d. He is self-deluded through his own speculations, he scoffs at the need for faithfulness, and begins to exploit his fellow servants for his own selfish purposes.
   e. Speculating about *any* time of Christ's return is disobedient.
E. Gain wisdom, prepare, *fill your lamp!* Mt. 25:1-13
   1. Christians are "lamps" or lights to the world.
   2. Men cannot neglect to prepare, to fill their lamps, and be ready for the Bridegroom's return.
   3. How does one "fill his lamp"? Worship, study, read the Bible, pray, give, light the way for others.
   4. The key word is WATCH. This does not mean constant gazing into the sky (see II Thess. 2:1-2) or being deluded to the effect that the day of the Lord has come so that you leave off working for your living (see II Thess. 3:6-15), and withdraw into some commune or sect out in the wilderness.
   5. It *does* mean having some forethought for the future. It *does* mean to make spiritual preparation and continue to do so.
   6. One of the most inescapable lessons of life is the necessity of being prepared. Practically everything we do requires preparation. Hardly anything can be done at the last moment!

      The time of examination is not the time of preparation. No course of study can be mastered on the last night!

      No one can wait until the night before an extended journey and expect to make *adequate* preparations.

      Death and judgment are inevitable, yet millions go blithely on without preparing to face the Judge!
   7. We cannot borrow what must be purchased.
      a. Why didn't the wise give to the foolish (moronic)? Because there are some things which cannot be loaned or given to another.
      b. Character, obedience, preparation, desire, goals—these cannot be loaned or given to another.

    c. Character is something that must be developed by each individual—it cannot be loaned.

    d. We cannot borrow obedience, foresight, goals or character from someone else.

    "Save yourselves . . ." Acts 2:40; "Work out your own salvation . . ." Phil. 2:12.

8. We cannot recall lost opportunities.

    a. These maidens missed their one chance. They did not seize their one great opportunity!

    b. Every day brings us opportunities that we must not neglect— that may be the very day the Bridegroom returns!

    Today we have open doors. If we fail to go through those doors they will shut—shut us out from the joy of serving.

    c. The pathos of this parable is that the foolish girls failed. It wasn't that the groom didn't want them to enjoy his feast —they just failed to prepare themselves for it.

    d. Do that good deed today. There is always one there to be done—every day—you don't have to go to sleep and wait for one to come. PUT OIL IN YOUR LAMP TODAY!

9. If we are consumed with the question, "*When* will the Bridegroom return" we are consumed with the *wrong* question. The moment we dwell on when, we are in trouble.

    a. The real question is: "Does my lamp have oil in it—*now!* Is it lighting up *now!*

    b. If the door is shut to us to the Bridegroom's feast, it will be because of something *we* have left undone!

    c. The Bridegroom will be eagerly expecting, and ready for us—He is not willing that any have no oil in their lamps. The momentous question is: Are we ready?

    d. The foolish and unprepared when He comes cannot pin the blame on Him or on those who have prepared!

    The point of this parable is that the foolish are in no position to accept what the Bridegroom has to offer; they are completely unprepared, and when He comes it is too late.

    e. The groom does not wish to exclude them. They are simply unprepared to receive Him.

F. Put your talents to work, whatever they are, however many or few, trusting in *His* graciousness, Mt. 25:14-30.

1. All men are endowed differently in God's world.

2. God will not demand all men produce the same. Each man will be matched against his endowed abilities and opportunities.

3. Every servant must produce according to what he has—not according to what he does not have!
4. This parable clearly teaches that watchfulness does not mean idleness.
5. Each servant receives something. Not a single servant is passed over.
6. Each did not receive the same. Each was given an amount in keeping with what the Master deemed fitting.
7. In the parable, those who received the five and the two, went immediately to work. Their success did not come without effort on their part. They may have been tempted to waste or to keep safe, but they didn't—they gained because they labored.

    Do not forget, however, they could have gained nothing if the Master had not given them everything they had to start with!
8. The one who received only one failed.

    a. Perhaps he was ashamed that he only had one talent. Not wanting to do what appeared the least—he did nothing. Some are like that. If they can't do the largest, they won't do anything.
    b. Perhaps he did not have the courage to work. If a man is not willing to pay the price of hard labor in service to the Master, he will produce nothing.
    c. *Most important, he did not trust his Master.* He believed he would get a dishonest deal from his Master. Some people look upon God this way.

        Such a view of God is what satisfies the productivity of many servants. God does not simply "order and demand." He loves and pities and extends his grace and mercy. God is not only just, fair and honest, He is gracious. He gives the means, the motive and the power to do it—*and then rewards us for doing it!*
9. COULD IT BE THAT WE DON'T DO WHAT LITTLE WE CAN FOR THE LORD, BECAUSE WE DON'T TRUST THE LORD TO BE FAIR AND GRACIOUS IN HIS JUDGMENTS?

    COULD IT BE THAT WE THINK THE LORD EXPECTS SOMETHING "BIG" AND "SPECTACULAR" OUT OF EVERY-BODY, AND SINCE WE CAN'T DO THAT, WE WON'T DO ANYTHING?

    LOOK AT THE NEXT PARABLE!

G. *Give* what you have; help those in need (which is everyone in some area or another—either in physical or spiritual need)—for helping people is serving Christ, Mt. 25:31-46.

1. This parable pictures all of humanity facing a final, irreversible judgment. It is more than a parable, it is a realistic prophecy.
2. Jesus makes this prophecy the criterion or standard of judgment because such conduct is the final proof as to whether a person is really His disciple or not (see Jn. 13:35).
3. On the judgment day it will be a question of how well our deepest feelings and our mouthed professions have been expressed by our positive actions toward others (cf. James 1:22-27; 2:1-26; I Jn. 4:17-21).
4. Jesus puts the principle of "working for Him," or "giving" within the reach of *everyone* of His disciples.
   a. Things done or given here were simply things, helpful things, everyone can do.
   b. Too often we feel that what we can do is too little—so we do nothing at all.
   c. Yet what the "righteous servants" did in this account is what everyone of us could do.
   d. How important is *one* act of unexpected kindness—*one* word of comfort or "good news" to a man who does not have it? ONLY ETERNITY CAN TELL!
   e. Every cup of cold water in His name will be considered faithful service by the Master.
5. Note that those who had done these simple things of goodness and mercy were absolutely *unaware* of their importance.
   a. They had done these things without being coerced, without being solicited, and without expecting any reward.
   b. Their kindnesses were spontaneous.
   c. Most remarkable, they did not realize they had really been giving to Christ all along.
   d. They were startled to learn they had actually *ministered to Christ.*
   e. Every good deed from an unselfish motive is a ministry to God.
6. This prophecy poses a situation every person needs to contemplate:
   a. Suppose Christ were on earth today—what would be my attitude toward Him?
   b. Of course Christ is not here in flesh and blood—but His brothers are.
   c. Whatever we do for them, we do for Him. God is a father, all men are His children. Can we do good to God without doing good to His children? Love me, love my children. Love my children and you love me.

d. Although this parable by itself does not mean that benevolence alone is sufficient to save a person—yet lack of benevolence is sufficient to condemn a person as unworthy of Christ.

III. WELCOME, Mt. 24:36—25:46

A. Christians should look forward with eagerness to the return of Christ and judgment of the world.

1. Paul told the Thessalonians to "comfort" one another with the hope of His 2nd coming (I Thess. 4:18).
2. Peter said we will "rejoice and be glad when His glory is revealed" (I Pet. 4:13).
3. Peter said we should be "waiting for and earnestly desiring" the coming day of God (II Pet. 3:12).

B. Our lesson in these verses here tells us why the Christian should earnestly desire His return:

1. There will be the *separation* promised by God of all those who want Him and His righteousness, from all the wicked who have manifested by their evil that they do not want Him and His Way.

a. Men in the fields and women at the grindstones who have not been faithful to His Word and His Way, and have not "watched" will be left to destruction.
b. Those who have concentrated on getting and keeping what God has declared is doomed, carnality, will be doomed along with it.
c. Those who have faithfully served and kept God's house in order will not have to go on dwelling with those who have mocked God and exploited His servants.
d. Those who have faithfully, and at sacrifice of self-indulgence, kept their lamps filled, will not have to endure the carelessness and disrespect of others for the Groom any longer.
e. Those who trusted their Master and put their talents to use will no longer suffer the mockery of those who mistrusted the Master and were contemptuous of Him.
f. Those who want to be helpful and kind and loving will no longer have to live with those who hinder and hate helpfulness, kindness and love.

2. *Dominion* will be given to faithful servants, fellowship, sharing with God in reigning over His new heaven and new earth.

a. Because they have proved their faithfulness to have such dominion great and eternal things by being faithful over the little and temporal things.

238

b. He will set the faithful over all his possessions (Mt. 24:47).
c. He will set the faithful over much (Mt. 25:21, 23).
d. He will even give the faithful more than he deserves—the faithful will be given what would have been given to the unfaithful.
e. The faithful will inherit the kingdom which God Himself has prepared (Mt. 25:34).

3. *Festive joy* in the presence of the Bridegroom will be the reward of the faithful, (Mt. 25:10, 21).

a. A crown of glory will be given the faithful, II Tim. 4:8; I Pet. 5:4.
b. Whatever the judgment will be, there is no human experience with which to compare it.

God is preparing for those who love Him an eternal weight of glory *beyond all comparison!* (II Cor. 4:17).

c. Since He gave us His Son, He is also going to give us *all things* (Rom. 8:32)!
d. Whatever Christ inherited from the Father for His faithfulness, the Father will give us also, for we are fellow heirs with Him provided we suffer with Him (Rom. 8:15-17).

C. Paul's conclusion to his great dissertation on the certainty of the resurrection and judgment is the Christian's comfort:

"Therefore, my beloved brethren, be steadfast, immovable, always abounding in the work of the Lord, knowing that in the Lord your labor is not in vain" I Cor. 15:58.

APPREHENSION:

1. Why did Jesus not know when heaven and earth would pass away? Mt. 24:36
2. In what way is the Second Coming of Christ and the end of the world to be like the days of Noah? Mt. 24:37-42
3. Here, you should read, Mark 13:34-37: *What* is the "work" the "master" left for *each* of his servants? Are you doing yours? Mk. 13:34-37
4. What would be "an hour men do *not* expect" the Lord to return? Mt. 24:44 When does a thief break into a house? Would Jesus slip up on the world?
5. Who is the "faithful and wise" servant? Mt. 24:45-51
6. There were five wise virgins—how were the other five characterized? Mt. 25:1-13 Do you know any like the latter five? Have you spoken to them?

7. If the "virgins" parable teaches constant alertness, what does the "talents" parable teach? Mt. 25:14-30
8. What does the last parable, Mt. 25:31-46, tell you about preparing for judgment?

APPLICATION:

Police court annals tell the story of a young man who registered at one of the leading hotels in N.Y. shortly after the turn of the century. He wrote down one of the most famous names in the U.S. and the hotel clerk was very deferential to him. He had an air of being "to the manner born." When packages began to arrive from several large furnishing houses and jewelry stores, the hotel received them and paid the accounts. After a few days the time for settling came. The young man brushed them off with excuses, which aroused the suspicion of the local hotel management. They notified the police and a quiet investigation revealed the startling fact that the famous man whose name the young man had written on the register with "junior" after it, did not even have a son. The young man, confronted by the authorities, put on an air of bravado; be blustered that there was some mistake. Finally, it became necessary to take him down to Wall Street to the office of the well known millionaire. The man walked into the room and looked at the boy and said, "I never laid eyes on this young man before in all my life." That sealed the doom of the imposter.

Multitudes of people who claim that God is their Father are just as guilty as was this young man. In order to address the Creator as Father, an individual must have accepted the truth which makes this relationship possible.

On the great judgment day, there will be a separation, made by the omniscient Christ. Those who love Him, want Him and are willing to surrender to Him, will be permitted to do so without any hindrance—to their highest potentialities. Those who wish to be rid of every vestige of God's presence and dominion shall be granted their wish. Those who wish to be alone with themselves in their rebellion will be allowed to do so. Those who desire falsehood, dirtiness, perverseness shall be surrounded by it! That is how God treated Israel with their mania for idolatry—He sent them into heathen captivity! That is how John says God will treat men at the final reckoning—"let the filthy still be filthy" (Rev. 22:11).

WHAT YOU REALLY WANT HERE IS WHAT YOU WILL WANT THERE! WHAT YOU REALLY ARE HERE IS WHAT YOU WILL BE THERE! THAT IS THE WAY GOD HAS ORDERED IT TO BE!

Lesson Thirteen

QUESTIONS ABOUT WHETHER THE DEVIL CAN ACTUALLY PERFORM SUPERNATURAL DEEDS OR NOT

1. There is only one Creator. No one else ever creates anything.

   God is said to have given the devil permission to take away Job's property. Job said, "The Lord gives and the Lord takes away." The devil did not have that power of his own. He probably tried to get Job to think he did, but Job was not persuaded. Is Job right or wrong? Did God take away, or did the devil?

   Can Satan give an order that "fire should come down out of heaven" or make an image breathe (Rev. 13:11-17). Who is in charge of ordering things in heaven (or on earth)? Satan or God? While men were convinced the "beast" was invincible (Rev. 13:4), God revealed through John that the beast was human (Rev. 13:18), not supernatural, not divine, not to be worshiped!

2. Only God is Almighty. How does one distinguish what or who is almighty from that which is not?

   If the distinguishing criteria of almightiness appears in two persons or realms, can both be almighty? If only one can be real, what is the other?—partly real?

   It is a law or logic that two contradictory propositions cannot both be true!

3. If one says we distinguish what we are to believe as actual or real by whether the attending message or doctrine is true and good or not, how does one substantiate which message is good? If we say the message of God does not lie, how do we determine it does not lie? If the devil has supernatural power how are we to determine that his message is not substantiated as "good" and those who claim to speak for the Lord as "bad"?

The ethical value of what God says is good cannot be substantiated on the basis of pragmatism (it works) because that makes every person able to say what works for you doesn't work for me. The *absolute* ethical value of God's statement of "good" depends on authority. Authority depends on demonstration of faithfulness and sovereignty in the absolute degree. How could that allow for *real* supernaturalism to be arrogated to someone else?

4. Did the devil have the real power to produce what he promised in the Garden of Eden? II Cor. 11:3 says he deceived Eve by his cunning to lead her thoughts astray.

II Thess. 2:9-12 says the devil, through the "lawless one," is to do *pretended* (Gr. *pseudo, false, fake) signs and wonders, with all wicked deception* (Gr. *apate,* cheating, beguiling, false impressions, unscrupulous) for those who refuse to love the truth. God will send to them a *working* (Gr. *energeian*) of *error* (Gr. *planes,* astray, wandering, planet) to believe the *lie* (Gr. *pseudei*) for those having not believed the truth, but are having pleasure in unrighteousness.

Does that sound like actual miracles are going to be given to lead people astray?

5. The supernatural things done by God (and his representatives) are said to be moral *facts* in themselves which in turn delinate in man's experience the existence and nature of God (cf. Rom. 1:18ff.; Acts 14:15-18; Acts 17:22-31, et al). If there are other supernatural facts being done which are capable of competing on the same level, in the realm of the factual, what do they delineate—that there are two Gods? If these two supernatural facts are both facts, how are we to decide to which ones to surrender? the one who seems to have the most workable doctrine?

6. Is Satan's power to deceive in the reality of a supernatural event actually done or is it in the interpretation he wishes us to make of the event which *appears* to be a supernatural event? If it really is a supernatural event accomplished by the devil (or a human being today), what interpretation are we to make?

7. Paul writes that we should not let the devil *defraud* us (Gr. *pleonektethomen*) by being agnostic about his *devices* (Gr. *noemata,* mentality— not miracles) II Cor. 2:11.

QUESTIONS - CAN DEVIL PERFORM SUPERNATURAL DEEDS?

The mind is powerful. Ideas and thoughts have tremendous capabilities. Mental, psychological trauma has caused amazing effects over personalities and even over physical functions.

8. Jesus stated that it was a logical impossibility that Satan would cast out demons for Satan would be defeating himself. Therefore, when demons are really, actually cast out, only the Lord could be doing it. If alleged modern exorcisms are actual, then Jesus is working through Catholicism, through witch-doctors, etc. The Jews of Jesus time did not really cast out demons or they would have had the evidence to really accuse Jesus of blasphemy.

9. Two passages in Deuteronomy appear to conflict. Deut. 13:1-5; 18:20-22.

Perhaps Deut. 13:1-5 means, If what a prophet gives as a sign or wonder *appears* to come to pass, and if he says, Let us go after other gods . . . do not follow him . . . his signs are really false.

One should not go after other gods because one knows what has appeared to come to pass has only appeared to do so. Only true prophet's signs and predictions factually come to pass.

10. Those who did not repent of their sorceries, Rev. 9:21, repented not of *pharmakeion*—the Greek word for "sorceries" is the word from which we get English, pharmacy. Is it possible that the "sorcerers" worked their alleged signs and wonders by chemicals and pharmaceutical properties.

The word translated *magic* (RSV) in Acts 19:19 is Gr. *periergos* and means *curiosity, inquisitive,* or, literally, "Things that are appearing to work—*superfluous.*" Things not reality, but things in the realm of question or doubtful.

Elijah's challenge to the prophets of Baal is instructive. Elijah said, "How long will you go limping with two different opinions? If the Lord is God, follow him; but if Baal, then follow him." And during the contest the prophets of Baal could *not* call down fire from heaven! even though they cried aloud, and cut themselves after their custom with swords and lances until the blood gushed out of them. Here is the time for the devil to do a miracle, if he can!

11. Let us consider again the text in Job.

a. God said to Satan, "Behold all that he has is in your power. . . ." The Hebrew word is *yadeka* from *yod,* literally, "Hand." This word is used metonymically for "power" in Deut. 32:36; II Kings 19:26; Job 5:20; Psa. 22:20; 49:15; Isa. 37:27; 47:14; Dan. 6:27; Hosea 13:14; and Micah 2:1, but never of any supernatural power.

b. Job's first disaster was perpetrated by the Sabeans falling upon his servants and slaying animals and servants. The devil could have put it into the minds of *men* by the vehicle of falsehood (communicated in language) to do this.

243

Job's second disaster is said specifically to be the fire *of God* falling from heaven.

Job's third disaster was the Chaldeans raiding and slaying with the sword—nothing supernatural here.

Job's fourth disaster is the death of his children *while they were drinking wine,* during a windstorm. Perhaps they were deceived by Satan into getting drunk and could have escaped the windstorm had they not been drunk. Does not necessarily have to be a supernatural, occult, windstorm which the devil worked—it could be God's windstorm.

c. Job, chapter 2:

God says to the devil, ". . . you moved *me* against him" (2:3) "to destroy him. . . ." The devil moved *God* to destroy Job!

The devil says to God, ". . . put forth thy hand now, and touch his bone and his flesh, and he will curse thee to thy face . . ." (2:5). The devil knows that only God has the supernatural power to touch Job's flesh.

In 2:7 the Hebrew text literally reads, "So went out Satan from the face of Jehovah. And *he struck Job with burning ulcers, bad, from the sole of his foot to the top of his head."*

Who is the antecedent of "he"—God or Satan? The nearest is God.

d. If it is God really exercising *His* supernatural power in all this what does God give into the "hand" of Satan?

I think it is simply the permission for Satan to try to *deceive* Job (and the world) into *thinking* he (Satan) is exercising this power. Satan has permission from God to *pretend* this or these powers belong to him.

How does Satan pull off this pretense? By lying to men and letting men use all human craftiness at their disposal to make it appear what is being done is supernatural.

The devil, by lying, tempted Job (through his friends) to think what had befallen him was evil. It really was chastening. All that we think about physical discomfort or loss is that there is some supernatural evil doing evil to us. Actually it is all chastening. What is evil about it is the lie that it is not in the sovereign control and will of God. It is the *power of fear* (of death) by which Satan enslaves men (Heb. 2:14-15). Satan has no power to supernaturally kill (or even naturally), or make alive. He has the "power" only to lie to people that he has such power.

12. Judas had power to do miracles (Mt. 10:1ff.). He also allowed the devil to come into him. Who gave him power to do miracles?

244

SICK SOCIETY SIGNS OWN DEATH CERTIFICATE

Simon the Sorcerer wanted to buy Holy Spirit power to do miracles but Peter said, "you have neither part nor lot in this matter" (Acts 8:18-24).

It is possible, therefore, that those who would prophesy and exorcise demons in Mt. 7:21 did so through power given by God and then later became those "working lawlessness" (Gr. *ergazomenoi ten anomian*) (Mt. 7:23), just like Judas.

13. Or, do we propose that everything which *appears* to be miracle *is*—but that only *some* are from God and *some* are from the devil?

How do we decide which are which? Do we have to decide? We are told we should not permit ourselves to be deceived—if we do not decide which are from God, we are in danger of being deceived.

If it is to be decided on the basis of which doctrine or works are good or evil—how do we decide that? From the Bible? How do we decide the Bible is speaking the truth? And does the Bible really say the devil has authority and power to do a real miracle?

How was it decided at the very first (in the garden of Eden)? How did God expect Eve to be able to decide whether the devil could produce what he promised so she could make the decision of faith?

OR IS FAITH A "LEAP IN THE DARK" AFTER ALL?

This is not an attempt to deny the Scriptures—it is an attempt to understand them.

A SICK SOCIETY SIGNS ITS OWN DEATH CERTIFICATE

Introduction

I. SOCIETY IS MUCH LIKE THE HUMAN BODY

A. It is structurally and functionally sound only when it maintains integration or wholeness by adherence to specific logical and moral principles.

B. The Creator has made the whole universe to be sustained by logical and moral principles. Individuals, families and nations

1. Even that which man has called "natural law" is sustained, reason dictates, by a Divine power which is just, logical, good and purposeful.

2. If the power behind what man sees in "natural" phenomena, and there must be a power behind it, were capricious, evil and without purpose, life as we know it could not exist.

C. When the logical and moral principles are disobeyed, disintegration, dissipation and death follow—whether personally, or socially. When disintegration of the social structures begin to occur, one may logically conclude the society is sick.

II. EXAMPLES OF SICK SOCIETIES WHICH BROUGHT ABOUT THEIR OWN DEATHS BY DISOBEYING THESE PRINCIPLES.
  A. Many ancient cultures exemplify our proposition
    1. Egypt
    2. Babylon
    3. Persia
    4. Greece
    5. Each began in austerity, self-discipline and adherence to certain standards of justice and decency.
    6. Each eventually turned to emphasizing materialism, fleshly indulgence, exploitation of human rights.
  B. Two societies exemplifying this which fall within biblical history
    1. Jews of the divided kingdoms (recorded by the Old Testament prophets)
    2. Roman Empire after the 1st century (as predicted by Revelation)

III. IS OUR SOCIETY SICK?
  A. Item in Joplin Globe, 12-14-75, entitled, *Shoplifting: Rapidly Growing Crime,* A Boston police detective analyzed his experience as: "A dire picture of a very sick society."
  B. T. V. commentators; Talk-show hosts; Newspaper editorialists; Government officials; Sociologists; Educators; and the common working public are all pronouncing the sickness of our society.
  C. Aleksandr Solzhenitsyn (Nobel prize winner, exiled from Russia, having spent many years in Russian political concentration camps) speaks and writes (Dec. 1975 Reader's Digest) with fervor and alarm about the sickness of Western civilization.
  D. U.S. is not the only sick society.
    1. Joplin Globe, 9-21-75: Denmark: 25% emigration of total population out of the country; middle class pays about 60% in taxes; 55% of people say Danish society is moving toward undisciplined, alienated and stress-burdened generation.
    2. Reader's Digest, Jan. 1966, article on sickness of Great Britain.

I. SYMPTOMS OF A SICK SOCIETY
  A. Social Anarchy
    1. Fractured families
      a. Jews - Adultery, rebellion against parents, divorce was rampant

246

during divided kingdom: Jer. 5:7-8; Hosea 4:1-2; 7:4; Amos 2:7; Micah 7:5-6; Mal. 2:10, 15.

b. Rome - Caligula lived in habitual incest with his sisters; Nero married a homosexual boy in public ceremony; Messalina, wife of Claudius went at night to serve in a common city brothel; Seneca writes, certain noble ladies reckon their years by the number of husbands . . . leave home in order to marry and marry in order to divorce. In such a society children were a misfortune . . . drowned by mothers, left to die of cold and to be eaten by dogs . . . a Roman father entering a brothel might well be served by his own abandoned child.

c. America - Every 90 seconds another American marriage is dissolved; homosexual marriages are permitted; homosexual churches; pornographic movies are being made where people are actually tortured and slain; high public officials (Presidents) entertain prostitutes in the White House; FBI reports 29% of all murders are within families—mates killing mates, parents killing children, children killing parents.

2. Commercial chaos

a. Jews - Materialism was god, cheating, robbery, extortion, waste, exorbitant taxation was all-pervasive: Isa. 5:8; 9:19-20; Hosea 12:8; 13:6; Amos 3:15; 5:11; Micah 2:2; 3:5; Mal. 3:8-9; Isa. 28:14-15; Jer. 8:5-11; 9:4-5; Hos. 10:4; 12:1, 7; Amos 8:5; Micah 6:10-12; 7:5-6; Hosea 4:1-2; 7:1.

b. Rome - Tacitus began his history: "I am entering on the history of a period rich in disasters, frightful in wars, torn by civil strife, and even in peace full of horrors." Exorbitant taxation to support rich men's indulgences; slave labor; millions on government dole; costly wars; rebellion of working class; private enterprise controlled by the State unparalleled in history; breakdown of discipline in the armed forces; cheating and robbery.

c. America - There are nearly 300,000 robberies each year in U.S. Over 2,000,000 burglaries each year with loss of 600 million to property owners. 140 million shoplifters per year costing $5 billion to store owners which buying public eventually pays for; woman in Florida in maxi-dress walked out of store with 19-inch color TV between her legs! Crime in America, statistics prove, not primarily committed by poverty class but by middle-to-high income people! doctors, lawyers, teachers, nuns, priests, ministers, rabbis; one doctor making

247

$300,000 per year just on medicaid patients plus $250,000 per year on other practice and some medicaid patients using other people's cards; welfare programs of New York City bankrupt it! Read, *The Permissive Society* by Boris Sokoloff, pub. Arlington House, and *Poverty Is Where The Money Is,* by Shirley Scheibla, pub. Arlington House. Social Security funds depleted and in deficit; food-stamp rip-offs. COMMERCIAL, FINANCIAL CHAOS!

3. Lawless legions

   a. Jews - rebellion and rejection of discipline, murder, drunkenness, complacency; injustice; Isa. 1:2; Jer. 44:15ff.; Ezek. 3:6-7; 5:5-6; Hos. 10:3; Isa. 5:7, 23; 10:1-3; 33:8; Jer. 5:26-28; Hos. 10:13; Amos 2:7; 4:1; 5:10-12; 6:12; 8:4; Micah 2:2; 2:8-10; Isa. 5:22; 28:1-13; Hos. 4:11, 18; Amos 2:12; 4:1; 6:6; Zeph. 1:12; Ezek. 13:10; Amos 6:6; Hosea 4:1-2; Micah 7:1-2.

   b. Rome - men in high offices, slaves, informers, workers robbed and ruined in every direction amid universal hatred and terror according to Tacitus. Juvenal says: honesty is mouthed and disregarded, and it is to their crimes that men owe their riches . . . vice, gambling was rampant and at its acme. Seneca looked at the Roman Forum and said there were as many vices gathered there as men . . . every place is full of crime and violence . . . innocence is not rare—it is nonexistent.

   c. America - In Ellensburg, Washington, authorities were faced with a pistol-packing gang of juneviles from junior high school who threatened to shoot up the Juvenile Court to free one of their leaders (Joplin Globe, 1-1-76); School teachers defying a court injunction; In Washington a college student resisted a holdup and was shot dead. The armed robber-killer pleaded guilty. But the judge said, "I don't think it would be to his advantage or to society's to send him to prison." (Paul Harvey); In Chicago last year there were 1000 crimes per day—only 7% were indicted and only 3 out of 100 indicted ever went to jail. Women are raped in Washington D.C. on parking lots in broad daylight; old people are attacked and robbed on the Joplin Mall in broad daylight; politicians consider themselves above the law; citizens take the law into their own hands; In Atlantic City, a motel owner saw 4 boys breaking in. At gunpoint he held them for police. Two had done time. But the N.J. judge released

SICK SOCIETY SIGNS OWN DEATH CERTIFICATE

the 4 burglars, and a grand jury indicted the motel owner for carrying an unlicensed gun. SOCIETIES CANNOT EXIST WITHOUT LAWS. LAWS THAT ARE NOT ENFORCED ARE USELESS! WITHOUT PENALTY THERE IS NO LAW!

B. Political Disintegration

1. Personal lives

   a. Jews - their kings and princes were adulterers, deceitful, drunkards, idolaters, arrogant: Isa. 1:23; 3:1-12; 32:5-6; Hosea 7:5-7; 8:4; 9:15; Micah 3:9-11; 7:3; Zeph. 3:3 (see other references in Social Anarchy which apply).

   b. Rome - Julius Caesar consorted with homosexuals; Caligula wanted to appoint his horse to the Roman Senate; Nero was a 17-year-old profligate when he became emperor; Nero poisoned his cousin and ordered his mother killed; Domitian ruled like Hitler and Stalin purging his own political system by murder, etc.; political jealousy between leaders led to eventual break up of the empire.

   c. America - Presidents (FDR, IKE, JFK) have had their paramours. Teddy Kennedy's exploits and coverup of the judicial facts; Truman, Johnson, Nixon, Agnew and their financial subterfuge; Congressmen and their porkbarrelling; rake-offs; junkets. Many political officer-holders and their affiliations with criminal characters.

2. Philosophies of government

   a. Jews - trust in military establishment; trust in foreign alliances; socialistic; materialistic; idolatrous; despising God; deceit; pride in human nature: Isa. 2:7; 30:1-2; 31:1; Hosea 5:13; 8:9-10; 10:13; *socialism* Micah 3:5; *partiality* Isa. 3:9; Mal. 2:9.

   b. Rome - advocated imperialism world-wide in order to provide revenue for their luxuries; advocated aristocracy and slavery; forced middle-class to pay very high taxes to pay for "dole" for slaves and poverty-class as well as for public works and indulgences of the rich.

   c. America - socialistic! guaranteed wage; welfare; socialized transportation; socialized medicine; socialized education; socialized industry. Socialism is killing Denmark, Sweden, Great Britain.

YES, WE HAVE ALL THE SYMPTOMS OF A SICK SOCIETY. WHAT HAS BEEN WRITTEN HERE CAN BE MULTIPLIED BY AS MANY COMMUNITIES AS THERE ARE IN THE U.S. NO COMMUNITY IS IMMUNE!

C. Cultural Degradation (Music, Art, Literature, Theater)

1. Jews - music became vain (empty, meaningless) and profane; art took on the grotesque, obscene form of the pagan idols; they "kissed calves" and practiced all the "artistic" rituals of idolatry: Amos 5:23; 6:5; Ezek. 8:10, 14; Hosea 13:2; "they consecrated themselves to Baal and became detestable like the thing they loved" Hosea 9:10.

2. Rome - Romans were great builders but their materialism and paganism tended to make most of them contemptuous of art and culture (the Greeks were idealists); the Roman theater was debased; they were more interested in the slaughter and blood of the games in the arena (179 days of each year devoted to games at one time—11,000 men and 15,000 beasts fought that year to the death); gluttony and spending was their main pastime, they built vomitoriums in their homes where people might go and gag themselves and vomit so they might return to the banquet table and eat more; Nero played dice for $90,000 per point. Seneca says this was all due to their boredom . . . they are restless because they are left with nothing to do, and they do not know how to dispose of their leisure. Their songs were praise to wine, fertility, the emperor and gladiators.

3. America - loud, obscene, cynical, anarchistic, rebellious MUSIC; senseless, formless, obscene, pessimistic, anarchistic, destructive ART; obscene, politically anarchistic, religiously blasphemous, sadistic, THEATER.

II. DIAGNOSIS OF SICKNESS (Why?)

A. Falsehood, irrationality, lying doctrines about God and men

1. Jews - idolatry, despising God, lack of knowledge of God and His Word, listening to diviners and soothsayers, false religious teaching Isa. 2:8; 40:18-20; 41:21-24; 44:9-20; Jer. 10:1-5; Ezek. 8:9-10; Hosea 4:12-13; 13:2; Isa. 1:4; 30:9-11; 5:24; Jer. 6:10-19; 36:20ff.; Micah 2:6-11; Mal. 3:14; Isa. 2:6; 8:19; Zeph. 1:5; Isa. 1:3; 5:12-13; Jer. 6:16; Hosea 4:6 *stupidity* Jer. 1:5; 2:27; Hosea 7:11 *false teaching* Jer. 5:12; Ezek. 13:6; Hosea 9:10; Zeph. 3:4; Mal. 2:7-9.

2. Rome - The Romans were cynical and skeptical of their idol-gods Diodorus Siculus writes, the myths that are told of the affairs in Hades . . . are pure invention. Philosophers considered all religions false. To the Cynics the Olympian gods were both man-made and man-like creations. There was nothing true for man to refer to for moral, social or personal decisions. Romans all practiced astrology. Romans 1:21ff. ". . . they became

250

futile in their thinking and their senseless minds were darkened. Claiming to be wise, they became fools, and exchanged the glory of the immortal God for images resembling mortal man or birds or animals or reptiles.''

3. America - In an article in Time Magazine, 3-13-72, entitled, "The New Cult of Madness: Thinking as a Bad Habit'' the writer says: "Many intellectuals have even given up thinking— or tried to—as if it were a bad habit. Scrambled across their work as guidance for the public is the new and purgative graffito: 'Nothing makes sense.' . . . Reason and logic have . . . become dirty words—death words. They have been replaced by the life words 'feeling' and 'impulse.' Consciousness—the rational—is presumed to be shallow and unconsciousness—the irrational—to be always interesting, often profound and usually true.''

   a. Nietzsche, German philosopher, prophesied, "All that is now called culture, education, civilization will one day have to appear before the incorruptible judge, Dionysus, the Greek god of ecstasy, intoxication and madness.'' IN LARGE SEGMENTS OF OUR SOCIETY THE ANTI-MIND ATTITUDE PREVAILS (EVEN IN CHURCHES)!

   b. Charles Darwin (evolution) and Sigmund Freud (psychoanalysis) are the two men most responsible for the derogation of reason and belief in America.

   c. Boris Sokoloff, says in *The Permissive Society*: "Freud's doctrines, and particularly his ethics, are the product of his concept of the human race. There is no purpose in man's existence. There is no goal in mankind's presence on the earth. There is no God or Supreme Power. And if this is so, 'all is permitted,' as Russian nihilists of a century ago declared. Thus the ground for *extreme permissiveness* is firmly planted by Freud. Man is born only to die. He must profit while he lives. His life is dominated by a pleasure-sexual instinct. Man wants only pleasure; he avoids pain. He does not like to work, because it is society or a nation which represses his instinctual driving and by doing so makes him miserable and unhappy, inducing neurosis. All men are neurotic. The human race is neurotic. The fault is that of society, or what we might call 'The Establishment.' . . . culture and civilization bring about an ever-increasing and overpowering neurosis . . . the individual has no obligation toward society. It is society which must take care of the individual, for he is the victim of The Establishment.''

    d. Psychoanalysis demands that patients talk and think about themselves, specifically of their sexual feelings. The analyst incites the swollen ego to grow even more with the result that patients become self-centered, conceited, and selfish. Psycho-analysts' efforts are directed to prove to patients that they are right, that there is no reason to blame themselves for anything they have done.

    e. Many politicians and intellectuals of the 1920s and 30s adopted Freudian doctrines. Especially is this true of the so-called "social-prophets" of that era—writers, playwrights, and sociologists (Hemingway, Theodore Dreiser, F. Scott Fitzgerald, Tennessee Williams, Eugene O'Neill, etc.).

B. Reversal of Values; Perversion; Exploitation of man

  1. Jews

    a. Reversal of values: Isa. 5:20; 29:16; Micah 3:1-2; Amos 5:14-15; Mal. 3:15

    b. Exploitation: Hosea 4:8-9; Amos 6:6; 8:6; Micah 3:11; Jer. 23:1-4; Ezek. 34:1-24

    c. Depravation of Women: Isa. 3:16ff.; Ezek. 13:18

    d. Permissive attitude: Hosea 5:4

  2. Rome

    a. Evil was called good; Nero sexually attacked his own mother; homosexuality was chic among the upper classes of Romans.

    b. Religion was used to keep the masses afraid of the State.

    c. Working class was exploited for taxes.

    d. Only in the blood and death of the arena could jaded emotions find any thrill.

    e. Seneca writes: "Man, an object of reverence in the eyes of man, is now slaughtered for a jest and a sport." Life became a mere drug on the market. The expenditure of money and life is almost beyond belief.

  3. America -

    a. Playboy sexism calls promiscuity good and biblical sex evil.

    b. Leftwing politics calls anarchy and nihilism good and governmental structure and restraint evil.

    c. Liberal judiciaries coddle criminals and scorn citizenship and patriotism.

    d. Sports, Movies, Drug-addicted Singers, make millions of dollars and are idolized while educators, ministers, and soldiers are ridiculed and paid hardly enough to live.

    e. Twelve of *People* magazine's "Most Intriguing People of

SICK SOCIETY SIGNS OWN DEATH CERTIFICATE

1975" Richard Zanuck, producer of the gory "Jaws"; Frank Fitzsimmons, Labor racketeer; Charles Manson, demonic murderer; Cher, sex symbol singer; Teng Hsiao-ping, Communist leader; Patricia Hearst, revolutionary; Christina Onassis, multi-millionaire heiress; Leonard Matlovich, homosexual in Air Force; Rosemary Rogers, authoress of sex novels; Werner Erhard, guru of "est," new groupie therapy; Woody Allen, vulgar comedian; Don King, promoter of Muhammed Ali. NO WONDER OUR SOCIETY IS SICK IF THESE ARE OUR HEROES!

   f. Exploitation: *The Hidden Persauders,* by Vance Packard

     (1) ". . . many of us are being influenced and manipulated, far more than we realize in the patterns of our everyday lives."

     (2) *"Public-relations experts are advising churchmen how they can become more effective manipulators of their congregations."*

     (3) "One of the main jobs of the advertiser . . . is not so much to sell the product as to give moral permission to have fun without guilt."

     (4) "They (social scientists) now study irrationality . . . to gather data that may be used by salesmen to manipulate consumers."

C. Disillusionment, pessimism, despair, complacency

   1. Jews: Isa. 57:1-5; Jer. 9:1-6; Ezek. 13:10; Amos 6:1, 6

   2. Rome: We have already documented the disillusionment, pessimism and despair of many of the Roman philosophers and historians.

   3. America

     a. Music - "Alone Again, Naturally." "Is That All There Is?"

     b. Lit. - Camus says in, *The Myth of Sisyphus,* the only truly significant philosophical question is suicide. Why should I not snuff out my life? Why should I make the effort to go on living.

     c. Existentialism says meaning is found in meaninglessness— life is a meaningless series of disconnected events.

     d. Joplin Globe, 11-24-74, art. entitled "Panelists See Modern Man Losing Historical Direction," "Frizzy-haired geneticist James Watson shocked his distinguished audience when he said, 'God is a cop-out.' The message of the past 30 years, he said, is that 'nothing is going to get better.' He also said, 'It would be nice to believe that there is something distantly wonderful that keeps everything in line, but there is no reason for it.' "

e. B.F. Skinner, psychologist, says, "Society can no longer afford freedom—control over man's conduct and culture is essential."

f. Schlesinger's *Catcher In The Rye,* required reading in many U.S. high schools, is not only vulgar but filled with despair-philosophy.

g. Camus, Sartre, Hemingway and other existentialists are popular literary idols of U.S. educational institutions.

D. OUR SOCIETY IS SICK. IT HAS ALL THE SYMPTOMS. IT IS NOT DIFFICULT TO DIAGNOSE THE CAUSES. CAN ANYTHING BE DONE?

III. PRESCRIPTION

A. Teach (cf. my OBC convention sermon, 2-19-75, *Isaiah, Vol. II)*

1. We must cease trying to entertain and manipulate people; society cannot be made well by entertainment. Even the church sometimes tries to cure the ills of society by copying the entertainment world.

2. Paul wrote in I Cor. 15:33 that "evil *homilia* (Greek for, teaching) corrupts good morals." *Good* teaching will build good morals.

3. John Stott in his book, *Your Mind Matters,* says, "The battle is always won in the mind. It is by the renewal of our mind that our character and behavior become transformed."

4. The Old Testament prophets stressed *teaching, learning* the Word of God above everything, in order to cure their sick society.

5. Above all else we must teach the world that the deity of Christ, the supernatural revelation of the Scriptures, and the divine origin of the church can be established on reasonable, historical, scientific grounds. That Christianity is a matter of the intellect primarily, not moods and feeling primarily, and not of human origin, MUST BE THE CHURCH'S BASIC PROGRAM OR THRUST!

6. Then we must convince the world of the reality of sin; of the possibility of righteousness and justification by faith; and of the judgment to come.

B. Love

1. Not just human love. *Agape,* love that is a matter of the mind, direction of the will. Not just feeling.

2. This kind of love involves discipline, divine guideline of conduct.
3. It involves facing reality and accepting responsibility.

    a. This is the kind of love the prophets had for their sick society. IT IS THE KIND OF LOVE JESUS AND HIS APOSTLES HAD!

    b. (See my sermon, "Love Is A Many Splendored Thing.") See also the book *Reality Therapy*, by William Glasser, pub. Harper & Row.

4. It involves making oneself vulnerable to being hurt and rejected and caring for those who hurt and reject and acting always in their best interests.

Conclusion

I. THESE PARALLELS NEED QUALIFYING

  A. Jews were specially chosen by God's sovereign choice (not because *they* were special) (see Romans 9-11) as a people through whom He might bring the Messiah to the whole world. They were a theocracy, at first, and their political, social and national structure was directly united to their religious constitution. Later it was a monarchy.

  B. The Roman empire was world-wide. It was an imperialistic political system, that is, it conquered and governed the known world of Western civilization and much of Eastern civilization. It was a republic at first, governed by a Senate and administered by an appointed chief executive. Julius Caesar became sole monarch or dictator (emperor) and Rome was ruled by emperors ever after that. It had a state religion.

  C. The U.S. is a republican-democracy. Its legislators are (theoretically) elected by its populace and its chief executives, also elected by the people, appoint other administrators. It is not imperialistic. One of its chief tenets is separation of religion and state.

II. YET THERE ARE FUNDAMENTAL PRINCIPLES OF GOVERNMENTS AND SOCIETIES WHICH MUST BE FOLLOWED BY ALL (AND TO WHICH ALMIGHTY GOD HOLDS ALL RESPONSIBLE) OR THEY DESTROY THEMSELVES.

  A. All governments are ordained by God (Rom. 13:1-7; I Pet. 2:13-17)

  B. All government is originated for God's purposes of terror to bad conduct and reward to good conduct (Rom. 13:1-7; I Tim. 2:1-4)

  C. Government is ordained to protect its citizens and to insure their fundamental human rights—but *not to provide* its citizens what they can earn for themselves.

D. Governments are to protect the sacredness of life; provide justice for litigations; protect the citizen's right to own private property; and to honor its treaties with other countries (cf. Obadiah 10-14; Amos 1:9).

III. GOVERNMENTS FORFEIT THEIR RIGHT TO EXIST WHEN THEY:

A. Reject the revealed truth (in the Bible) as to their origin and purpose and let falsehood, irrationality, reversal of values and disillusionment to permeate their society . . . because this brings

B. Social anarchy, commercial chaos, lawless legions of citizenry

C. THE LIFE-BLOOD OF ANY SOCIETY IS TO KNOW THE TRUTH, LOVE THE TRUTH AND DO THE TRUTH.

A LIMITED BIBLIOGRAPHY HELPFUL IN THE AREA OF AMERICA'S SICKNESS

1. *The Permissive Society,* by Boris Sokoloff, M.D., pub. Arlington House
2. *Poverty Is Where The Money Is,* by Shirley Scheibla, pub. Arlington House
3. *The Dust of Death,* by Os Guinness, pub. Intervarsity Press
4. *Hang Tough,* by John Bonner, pub. Bethany Fellowship
5. *Despair, A Moment or A Way of Life,* by C. S. Evans, pub. IVP
6. *The Drug Users,* by A.E. Wilder Smith, pub. Shaw
7. *The Untapped Generation,* by David Wilkerson, Zondervan
8. *The World Under God's Law,* by T. R. Ingram, pub. St. Thomas Press
9. *Relativism in Contemporary Christian Ethics,* by Erickson, pub. Baker
10. *Reality Therapy,* by Wm. Glasser, pub. Harper and Row
11. *Teddy Bare,* (an expose of Senator Edward Kennedy's affair at Chappaquiddick) by Zad Rust, pub. Western Islands
12. *Education In America,* by G.C. Roche, III, pub. FEE
13. *Darwin, Before and After,* by Robert E.D. Clark, pub. Moody Press
14. *Christian Counter-Attack,* by A. Lunn and G. Lean, pub. Arlington House
15. *Classroom Countdown,* by Max Rafferty, pub. Hawthorne
16. *The Hidden Persauders,* by Vance Packard, pub. Pocket Books

ESCHATOLOGY

Non-Biblical and Biblical—A Brief

Introduction

I. DEFINITIONS

A. Eschatology is from Greek, *eschatos,* last, *logia,* knowledge or

ESCHATOLOGY

study. New Testament eschatology is generally: a study of last things, i.e., studying what the Bible says about the end of this world and the 2nd Advent of Christ, judgment, etc.

B. There are many differing eschatological theories in the religious world today. Postmillennialism; Premillennialism; Dispensationalism; Amillennialism; each one of these having different theories.

C. We are going to deal with the general subject rather than with any specific theory.

II. IMPORTANCE OF THE SUBJECT

A. A man's eschatology inevitably affects his:

1. Hermeneutics
2. Politics
3. Evangelism
4. Fellowship (Unity)
5. And, as a result of the above, his Ethics
6. We shall amplify this later in the study

B. The Bible says a great deal about eschatology

1. The eschatology of the Old Testament ("last things") refers mainly to the last of the Old Testament dispensation and the coming of Christ and the church.
2. The eschatology of the New Testament refers mainly to the Second Coming of Christ.
3. Most New Testament books have references to His Second Coming / Judgment

Discussion

I. ERRONEOUS ESCHATOLOGY

A. The Late Great Planet Earth

1. "The nation of Israel cannot be ignored; we see the Jews as a miracle of history . . . have survived as a distinct race . . . can trace their continuous unity back nearly 4000 years" pg. 45, etc. Answer: Who is a Jew? (Rom. 2:28-29) Who is Israel? (Gal. 6:15-16). Jacob Gartenhaus, president of International Board of Jewish Missions, born in Austria and educated in rabbinical schools there, says: "No Jew today can trace his ancestry back beyond two or three hundred years." *Christianity Today,* 3-13-70.

There are only 3 million people in Israel today and 12% of

those are Arabs; 3% are Christians. There are more Jews in New York City than in Israel.

The government of Israel today cannot even decide who a legal Jew is. Is Sammy Davis, Jr. a Jew? Will Jerry Lewis take up residence in Israel? Unlikely they will do so willingly!

2. Hal Lindsey predicts the return of the Messiah in 1988. ". . . within forty years or so of 1948, all these things could take place . . ." pg. 54. He says in his booklet, *Homo Sapiens, Extinction or Evacuation,* pg. 20, "You are the generation seeing these things; you are in the generation which is not going to see physical death. I expect one day in my life to be physically called to see the Lord in the air, without seeing death."

Answer: I would like to have that assurance but I hesitate to jeopardize my credibility with such absolute predictions in view of so many other absolute predictions missed.

3. By 1988 the Jewish Temple and reinstitution of Jewish system of sacrifices will have to be accomplished (pgs. 54-57).

Answer: This contradicts the teachings of Romans, Galatians and Hebrews as to the abrogation of the Jewish system of sacrifices and the finality of the Christian system.

4. In his attempt to make Russia and Egypt the object of Daniel 11 (kings of north and kings of south) he says Cush means "black man" in Hebrew (pg. 13-14 of *Homo Sapiens*). One Hebrew lexicon (Youngs) out of scores of others gives "black" as a meaning of the Hebrew word Cush. All other lexicons give another Hebrew word as the word used for "black."

Answer: Daniel 11 very evidently refers to the history of the Seleucids to the First Coming of the Messiah.

5. On page 112 Lindsey talks of the False Prophet he says is predicted in Rev. 13:11-18 and thinks the False Prophet will be from the tribe of Dan.

Answer: The 12 tribes of Jews in Revelation 7 which so many think apply to the restored Jews in Israel do not even include the tribe of Dan!

6. On page 139 Lindsey says I Cor. 15:50 teaches that Christians cannot inherit the Kingdom of God in the type of bodies we now have—flesh and blood. However, he says, the gospels and the Old Testament teach there will be certain people who *will* inherit for a time the Kingdom of God in bodies of flesh and blood. And this is going to be the millennial kingdom ruled over by Christ here on earth!

Answer: Does God contradict Himself? Is His Spirit the author of a confusing revelation?

258

ESCHATOLOGY

7. There are *many* more exegetical and hermeneutical errors in this book and his other books. We cannot deal with them all in this study.

B. Seventh Day Adventists ("Signs Of The Times")

1. Following Ussher's chronology William Miller interpreted the 2300 days of Daniel as 2300 years and predicted Christ would return to earth in 1843. That didn't happen so they set Oct. 22, 1844. That didn't happen, so they said Christ passed from one section of heaven to another in 1844 to perform a work known as the "investigative judgment."

2. Their view of the 1000 years of Rev. 20: "During the one thousand years the earth lies desolate; Satan and his angels are confined here; and the saints, with Christ, sit in judgment on the wicked preparatory to their final punishment."

C. Jehovah's Witnesses ("Watchtower")

1. "There is another way that helps confirm the fact that we are living in the final few years of his "time of the end" (Dan. 12:9). The Bible shows that we are nearing the end of a full 6000 years of human history. . . . According to reliable Bible chronology, Adam and Eve were created in 4026 B.C.E.

4026 B.C.E. to 1 B.C.E.	4025 years
1 B.C.E. to 1 C.E.	1 year
1 C.E. to 1968 C.E.	1967 years
Total to autumn 1968	5993 years

2. "This would leave only seven more years from the autumn of 1968 to complete 6000 full years of human history. That seven-year period will evidently finish in the autumn of the year 1975." Quoted from "Awake" dated Oct. 1968.

3. They predicted Christ came to earth in 1914, *invisibly!*

C. Oswald J. Smith, in his book, *Is the Antichrist at Hand?*, said:

1. "I have been studying with interest . . . the prophetic writings of . . . diligent students of the Bible. . . . Of all . . . those who have undertaken to work out the chronological forecast, there is not one who sets any date beyond 1934. The earliest suggested by these writers is 1928."

2. "If our chronology is correct, it means that all these things, including the Great Tribulation, the revival of the Roman Empire, the reign of the Antichrist and the Battle of Armageddon, must take place before the year 1933."

259

THIRTEEN LESSONS ON REVELATION

D. Some Other Date setters:

1. Augustine calculated the end of human history would be about 650 A.D.
2. Then eschatology buffs focused on the year 1000 A.D.
3. Then the Second Coming was predicted for 1044, 1065, and other dates.
4. I.M. Holdeman, pastor First Baptist Church of New York, said in 1911, ". . . the hour is ripe for the moment when the Lord shall descend and gather His Church to Himself."
5. W.E. Blackstone, in his book, *Jesus Is Coming,* printed in 1898, said, ". . . His coming, the rapture, is near."
6. In January, 1963, a well-known Bible teacher in So. California entitled an article "Jesus Will Come in 1968!"
7. On April 17, 1971, the Minneapolis Star carried a Review of a book, *God, History and the End of the World,* in which Kenneth Aune, the author, claims that in March, 1990, will come the battle of Jerusalem, the return of Jesus Christ, and the battle of Armageddon.
8. May 10, 1974—an Israeli tour guide (see *Christian Standard,* Ed. 8-18-1974.

II. EFFECT OF ERRONEOUS ESCHATOLOGY

A.   Confusion and Ridicule

1. The non-Christian world looks at the multitude of different predictions

   a. It scorns and ridicules Christianity and the Bible and the Church because every date set in the past (set by apparently sincerely convinced prophecy scholars) has been wrong!
   b. It asks, Is there any truth to the Bible at all; if so, which religious group has the truth—they all differ on one of the most important doctrines of the Bible, the end of time.

2. Even Christians are prompted to become disillusioned and suspicious of their Bible teachers when faced with the errors and confusion.

B. Erroneous Hermeneutics and Wresting the Scriptures

1. The theory of Premillennialism and Dispensationalism asserts that Christ came to earth for the purpose of setting up His kingdom. Quite by surprise, He was rejected by the Jews, however, and established the church instead. When He returns, He will allegedly raise only the righteous dead, after which He will restore national Israel, sit upon David's literal throne in Jerusalem and subsequently reign for 1000 years. After this, the

resurrection of the wicked dead and the final judgment are supposed to occur.

2. This violates proper hermeneutics because:

a. It reflects upon the integrity of Bible prophecy by implying that the Jewish rejection of Christ was a miscarriage in God's plan. However, the Old Testment clearly foretold that rejection (Isa. 53:1ff.; Jn. 12:37-38; Psa. 118:22-23; Mt. 21:46, etc.).

b. It denies plain Bible teaching concerning the establishment of the kingdom in the first century (Dan. 2:44; Isa. 2:2-4; Acts 2:16-17; Col. 1:13; Rev. 1:4, 6, 9).

c. It suggests that the church was not a part of God's eternal purpose, but only an interim (parenthesis) emergency measure (Eph. 3:10; Rev. 13:8; Acts 20:28).

d. It denies that Christ is now seated on David's throne (Zech. 6:12-13; Heb. 8:1; Lk. 1:32-33; Acts 2:30; Rev. 3:21; I Cor. 10:11).

e. It denies that we are in the last days (Acts 2:16-17), and that Christ's next coming will end this world . . . (I Cor. 15:24; Lk. 17:26-30).

f. It teaches, contrary to the Bible, that Christ will come again to deal with sin through a Jewish economy (Heb. 9:28).

g. It affirms, contrary to Scripture, that there will be two literal resurrections from the dead, 1000 years apart (Jn. 5:28-29; Acts 24:15).

h. It denies the *expressed* symbolic nature of the book of Revelation by literalizing its figures (Rev. 1:1; 20:1-6).

i. It denies that through the redemptive work of the First Coming of Christ *only,* must Jew and Gentile become "one" (Gal. 3:1ff.; Eph. 2:11-22, etc.).

j. It denies that "Zion" of the Old Testament Prophets has its fulfillment in the New Testament church (cf. Heb. 12:22).

C. Unjust Politics

1. Oswald T. Allis in an article in *Christianity Today,* entitled, Israel's Transgression in Palestine, Dec. 24, 1956, made an ethical evaluation of the Zionist/U.N. partioning of Palestine.

2. The Zionists appeal to Gen. 18:18 to prove the Jews should claim sovereignty of Palestine. BUT DOES THIS SCRIPTURE GIVE THE ISRAELIS A CLEAR TITLE TO PALESTINE? NO!

a. This promise was conditioned upon obedience. The Jews have disobeyed God from the days of Moses even to the rejection of the Messiah.

261

b. Any restoration of the Jews was conditioned upon repentance (Deut. 30:1-10).

Any return to a Jewish system to seek the Lord would place them in a position "impossible to repent" (cf. Heb. 6 & 10).

c. The dispersion of the Jews and the taking of their place from them was a punishment from God (Mt. 21:43; 25:2; Lk. 21:24).

d. Jesus and His apostles predicted the end of the Jewish economy and nationalism (Jn. 4:23; Lk. 4:23-29; Eph. 3:1-13, I Thess. 2:14-16).

e. There is little spiritual difference between the Jews of America and the Jews of Palestine. A believing Jew is today as near heaven in the U.S., where 5 million of his fellow Israelites now live and apparently expect to continue to live, as if he were in Jerusalem. An unbelieving Jew is just as far from heaven in Jerusalem as he would be in New York or London.

e. The attempt to restore the Jews to Palestine has proved to be unjust in itself and highly dangerous to the peace of the world. Palestine did not belong to the British. It did not and does not belong to the U.N. The persecution of the Jews by the Nazis and now by the Russians is unjust. But allowing the Jews to take possession of a large part of Palestine and to force hundreds of thousands of Arabs out of it is an equally grievous wrong.

D. Division and Schism

1. Christians may have widely divergent views in regard to the Second Coming of Christ.

2. All views must be submitted to the crucible of proper hermeneutics.

3. But division comes when the particular view is overemphasized to such an extent that it becomes a "test of fellowship."

4. And this continues to be made such a test of fellowship by churches, colleges, and individuals.

5. It also becomes a heresy when it draws people away from the church (Armstrongism, J.W.s, etc.).

E. Evangelism

1. It tends to stifle evangelism because it majors in prophecy dates, charts, signs, etc., and minors in the plan of salvation given in the New Testament.

2. It tends to unethical, scare-tactic, pressure evangelism.

3. Many use the "signs of the times" (the phrase is used only once in the Bible, Mt. 16:3, and referred to His *first* coming, not

262

His 2nd) *to bring believers into line, and convert hard-case unbelievers.*

4. This approach seems to say that what is really important is to be in good shape at that particular point in time when Christ appears about to return. It's the old I-don't-want-to-be-caught-in-there-when-Jesus-returns syndrome. It suggests in a veiled way that the mark we get on our ethical report card is the mark we happen to receive on the pop quiz given at the Parousia rather than the cumulative grade for the entire course.

Jesus said, ". . . occupy till I come" Lk. 19:13. He did not say, "Only be found occupying when I come."

F. Some very extreme views connected with eschatology:

1. "Russia with all of her current sattelites and all she might acquire in the future, will not be able to successfully invade Israel. ISRAEL IS INVINCIBLE UNLESS GOD IS VULNERABLE," Maranatha Trumpet.

2. "Christ will not come back to the earth until the Jewish people ask Him to come back. . . . This is the basis of the Second Coming of Christ. . . . Satan knows that once Christ returns his career will be finished . . . He also understands that Christ will not come back until the Jews ask Him to come back. If Satan can succeed in destroying all the Jews before they have a chance to ask Christ to come back, Christ will not come back and Satan will be safe. That is why Satan is in an all-out campaign to destroy the Jews. . . . The power of the Second Coming of Christ is very much in the hands of Israel," *The Chosen People*, May 1975.

3. "This false Messiah will fool the Jews by doing miracles through the devil who will have entered his body in the middle of the 7 years. At this point in time, the Jews will look in the Bible to see if this man comes out of the predicted blood line of David. The Jews will find that this line or family tree ends with Christ (since he was killed and had no children). The Jews will also discover that the prophecies about the true Messiah fit only Christ. When the Jews have finally repented of their misconception about Christ, the world will see the appearance of Jesus Christ in person who will come in power and force to establish a Kingdom of Peace to last 1000 years on this present earth. The Jews will finally have their promised kingdom which in the final analysis, fulfills Old Testament promises to the Jews." An unsigned paper in the author's files.

III. ESSENTIAL ESCHATOLOGY

A. Certainty of His Coming

THIRTEEN LESSONS ON REVELATION

1. The most important thing about biblical eschatology is its emphasis on the certainty of the end of this world order, the Coming of Christ, and judgment.
2. *The Coming Judge,* by Seth Wilson, pub. *Christian Standard,* 4-12-58: "He (Jesus) is far more than a prophet in the past. He is a power in the present. And He is the most certain and significant of all the prospects for the future!"
3. There is only one way to be certain Jesus is Coming Again— that is to take His word for it. He promised it and His promises are *authenticated* by His resurrection from the dead.

   "The times of ignorance God overlooked, but now he commands all men everywhere to repent, because he has fixed a day on which he will judge the world in righteousness by a man whom he has appointed, and of this he has given *assurance* to all men by raising him from the dead" (Acts 17:30-31).

   THE ONLY SIGN FOR ASSURANCE WE NEED THAT HE IS COMING AGAIN IS HIS RESURRECTION. THAT ASSURANCE WILL CALL MEN TO REPENTANCE.

   The eyewitnessed, empirically verified, historically authenticated resurrection is *all-sufficient* testimony to His Second Coming. Human predictions about "signs of the times" are subject to all the enigma and vagary of speculation.
4. Jesus promised His return: Matt. 16:27; 24:30b; 24:37-42; 24:43-51; 25:1-13; 25:14-31; 26:64; Lk. 17:26-30; 19:11-27.
5. The angels promised His Return: Acts 1:11.
6. The apostles promised His Return: I Thess. 4:16; Acts 3:20-21; I Pet. 1:7; 5:4; II Pet. 3:3-4; James 5:7; Heb. 9:28; I Jn. 2:28; Rev. 1:7; I Cor. 1:7; 4:5; 11:26; 15:23; Phil. 3:20-21; Col. 3:4; I Thess. 1:10; 2:19; 3:13; 4:16-18; 5:1-4, 23; II Thess. 1:7-10; 2:1-8; I Tim. 6:14-15; II Tim. 4:1-8; Titus 2:13.

B. The Time of His Coming

1. "But of that day and hour *no man knows,* not even the angels of heaven, nor the Son, but the Father only" (Mt. 24:36; Mk. 10:32-33). THE TRUTH OF THAT STATEMENT HAS ALREADY BEEN VERIFIED BY THE SPECULATORS OF THE PAST WHO WERE SURE THEY KNEW FROM THE "SIGNS OF THEIR TIMES."
2. He will Come "as a thief in the night" (I Thess. 5:2-3; Mt. 24:27-51; 25:1-13; II Pet. 3:6-10). There will be no preliminary announcements ahead of His coming! He will come unexpectedly—suddenly!
3. *No one will miss knowing* when He comes—there will be *no secret* coming or rapture. The next time Jesus comes it will be with a shout and trumpet blast to be heard by all the living and the dead

264

ESCHATOLOGY

—*every eye* shall see Him (cf. Mt. 24:26-31; I Cor. 15:52; I Thess. 4:16).

4. THE EMPHASIS OF THE NEW TESTAMENT IS THE NEED TO *BE READY AT ALL TIMES!* Setting dates; making lists of "signs of the end"; speculative and divisive dogmas devitalize and weaken this readiness!

5. He is Coming when people will be doing the normal things of life, "eating and drinking, marrying and giving in marriage" (Mt. 24:37-38).

6. There will be no abnormal, extra-ordinary "signs" pointing to His "soon" coming. "The Son of man is coming at an hour you do not expect" (Mt. 24:44).

C. Particulars Concerning His Coming

1. Seth Wilson, ibid: "The Lord has revealed only a few particulars . . . of the great events which will take place when He comes. No doubt there are many things in store for us that we have not been told because we could not grasp and appreciate them now. Very likely some of the things predicted will not happen as we imagine them."

2. The dead will be raised (I Thess. 4:16; Jn. 5:28-29).

3. Those alive will be changed into bodies fitting them for their eternal destiny (Phil. 3:21; I Cor. 15:52-54; Rom. 8:23-25).

4. The redeemed will (the resurrected and changed—all together) be with the Lord (I Thess. 4:17).

5. The world and its carnal works will be burned up, melted, (II Pet. 3:11-13).

6. A crown of glory will be given to the faithful (II Tim. 4:8; I Pet. 5:4).

7. Christ, with His angels, will execute judgment upon all men (II Tim. 4:1; Jude 14-15; Acts 10:42; 17:31; Jn. 5:22-29; II Cor. 5:10, etc.).

8. Many will be rejected who thought they were saved (Mt. 7:21-23; 22:13-14; Lk. 13:25-27, etc.).

9. The opportunity for salvation will be forever closed (Lk. 13:25-28).

10. There will be grief and terror in the hearts of many because they are unprepared to meet Him (Mt. 24:30, 50, 51; 25:30, etc.).

IV. EFFECT OF ESSENTIAL ESCHATOLOGY

A. Purity of Living

1. "Since all these things are thus to be dissolved, what sort of persons ought you to be in lives of holiness and godliness,

265

waiting . . . for the coming of the day of God . . ." II Pet. 3:11-12.

2. ". . . we know that when he appears we shall be like him, . . . and every one who thus hopes in him purifies himself as he is pure" (I Jn. 3:2-3).

3. MORE EMPHASIS ON THE CERTAINTY OF HIS COMING AND ON THE IMMINENT URGENCY OF IT (DAILY, HOURLY URGENCY) WOULD PROMOTE MORE GODLINESS THAN ALL THE PROMOTIONAL GIMMICKS AND ENTERTAINMENT SESSIONS OF ALL THE CHURCHES PUT TOGETHER!

4. *More* sermons are needed on Judgment, The End of the World, The Second Coming.

B. Encouragement For Endurance of Trials and Tests

1. ". . . we who are alive . . . shall be caught up together . . . to meet the Lord in the air; and so we shall always be with the Lord. . . . Therefore comfort one another with these words" (I Thess. 4:17-18).

2. "But rejoice in so far as you share Christ's sufferings, that you may also rejoice and be glad when his glory is revealed" (I Pet. 4:13).

3. CHRISTIANS WHO TRUST THAT CHRIST IS COMING AGAIN TO RIGHT ALL WRONGS, TO VINDICATE ALL COMMITMENTS, TO JUDGE ALL SECRETS. . . . TAKE COURAGE AND ENDURE, CONFIDENT THAT CHRIST WILL VINDICATE THEM *PERFECTLY!*

C. Evangelism

1. "For we must all appear before the judgment seat of Christ, so that each one may receive good or evil, according to what he has done in the body. Therefore knowing the fear of the Lord, we persuade men . . ." II Cor. 5:10-11.

   THE REMAINDER OF THAT CHAPTER SPEAKS OF BEING AMBASSADORS FOR CHRIST.

2. "He has commanded all men everywhere to repent, in that he has appointed a day in which he will judge the world. . . ." Acts 17:31.

3. JESUS MAY COME TODAY! WE MUST PREACH THE WORD WITH ALL URGENCY IN SEASON AND OUT OF SEASON. EVERY MAN AND WOMAN MUST AT LEAST HEAR AND BE GIVEN OPPORTUNITY TO RESPOND!

4. "It is like a man going on a journey, when he leaves home and puts his servants in charge, *each with his work. . . .*" Mk. 13:34. "Who then is the faithful and wise servant, whom his master has set over his household, to give them their food at the proper time?

ESCHATOLOGY

Blessed is that servant whom his master *when he comes shall find so doing"* Mt. 24:45-46.

D. Contemporaneity

1. Michael Green in an article in *Christianity Today,* 1-1-65 says: "I believe that in this biblical doctrine of the Christian hope (the Second Coming) we have an intelligible answer to the modern quest for purpose in the world."
2. Quest for Personal Identity: Man is in quest of personal identity. What is he worth? What does he matter? What is his destiny? That God is Coming Again in His Son to consummate His great redemptive work for *man* (the end of God's whole cosmic scheme) in a *personal* appearance is a message that is relevant in our depersonalized age!
3. Quest for Realism: Man is skeptical in our age of any theory of regeneration or redemption of society or the cosmos which is unsupported by hard facts.

   Is the Christian doctrine of a returning, redeeming Christ realistic in the 20th century? . . . Is the Christian optimism that "all will be well in the end" justifiable? Or is it a fantasy, a fairy tale like all the schemes of men?
4. The Christ who came and who will come, just because of this, IS COMING TO US DAY BY DAY, CHALLENGING US CONSTANTLY FOR AN ENTRANCE INTO OUR LIVES . . . SEEKING OUR FELLOWSHIP!
5. God's purpose is to demonstrate NOW, in this world, this transitory world, the beauty, power, holiness, and permanence of the age to come. He who has called us out of this world is Holy. He who will come for us is Holy. In the meantime, He has given us His Holy Spirit to work out in our lives something of the character of the age to come.

Conclusion

I. ERRONEOUS ESCHATOLOGY BRINGS REPROACH UPON GOD'S WORD AND HIS CHURCH: IT CREATES DIVISION: IT DISCOURAGES: IT HINDERS PRODUCTIVE BIBLE STUDY.

II. ESSENTIAL ESCHATOLOGY DOES NOT CREATE DIVISION: PROMOTES PURITY OF LIVING: GIVES ENCOURAGEMENT: URGES EVANGELISM: FILLS THE NEEDS OF CONTEMPORARY MAN.

III. THE LORD DOES WANT US TO KNOW SOME THINGS ABOUT THE FUTURE. He wants us to know that Christ is coming personally to this world of time and space again just as certainly as He came forth from the dead in a time-space event.

THIRTEEN LESSONS ON REVELATION

He wants us to know there is a "far more exceeding and eternal weight of glory beyond this world which will be destroyed completely. Therefore let us be steadfast, immovable, always abounding in the work of the Lord . . . for we know our labor is not in vain in the Lord.

A LIMITED BIBLIOGRAPHY OF BOOKS AND ARTICLES HELPFUL IN THE AREA OF ESCHATOLOGY

Books

1. *Prophecy And The Church,* by Oswald T. Allis, The Presbyterian and Reformed Pub. Co. (deals with Dispensationalism)
2. *The Time Is At Hand,* by Jay Adams, The Presbyterian and Reformed Pub. Co. (a commentary on Revelation proposing "Realized Millennialism")
3. *Worthy Is The Lamb,* by Ray Summers, Broadman Pub. (a commentary on Revelation from amillennial viewpoint)
4. *The Meaning and Message of The Book of Revelation,* by E.A. McDowell, Broadman Pub. (a commentary on Revelation - amillennial)
5. *Jeremiah—Lamentations,* by James E. Smith, College Press, pub. (esp. Special Study entitled "Jehovah's Witnesses and the Seventy Years Prophecy.") (a commentary)
6. *Thinking Through Thessalonians,* by Wilbur Fields, College Press, pub. (see all the Special Studies in this book) (a commentary)
7. *God's Prophetic Word,* by Foy E. Wallace, Jr., Gospel Advocate, pub. Out of print. (a series of lectures on dispensationalism)
8. *Prophecy & Premillennialism,* by James D. Bales, Bales, pub. (studies on New Testament fulfillment of Old Testament prophecies)
9. *Millennial Studies,* by George L. Murray, pub. Baker (an excellent refutation of basic errors of premillennialism)
10. *Daniel,* by Paul T. Butler, College Press, pub. (a commentary)
11. *Minor Prophets,* by Paul T. Butler, College Press, pub. (a commentary - see esp. Introductory section)
12. *Isaiah, in 3 volumes,* by Paul T. Butler, College Press, pub. (a commentary - see esp. Introductory section)
13. *The End Time,* by Russell Boatman, pub. College Pres

Articles

1. *Is the Lord's Return Imminent?,* by Rodger N. Elliott, Christian Standard, 6-9-74
2. *Signs Of Confusion,* by Earl D. Radmacher, Moody Monthly, May 1974

MODERN PROPHECY EXAMINED

3. *Why Eternity Must Follow the Second Advent,* by Wick Broomall, Christian News, not dated
4. *The Coming Judge,* by Seth Wilson, Christian Standard, 4-12-58
5. *When Is Jesus Coming Again?,* by Seth Wilson, Lookout, 3-11-56
6. *Outlines of Matthew 24 and 25,* by Paul T. Butler, 3-8-81/3-15-81, Xerox
7. *A Secret Rapture Considered,* by Seth Wilson, OBC Compass, Oct. 1973

MODERN PROPHECY EXAMINED

Acts 20:28-32

by Paul T. Butler - OBC Convention 1978

Introduction

I. There are both true and false prophets in the first century church.

  A. The New Testament is replete with instructions and warnings about those who are to be listened to and not listened to.

  B. The most frightening aspect of New Testament teaching on prophecy is that the false prophets will arise from *within the brotherhood of believers!* (Acts 20:30)

II. There was a special charismatic gift of prophecy given to some in the first century church.

  A. That was given only by the laying on of the hands of the apostles (see lesson from OBC Convention 1978 on Paul's Power To Give Charismatic Power).

  B. This ceased (and was intended to cease) when the perfected church arrived (see lesson from OBC Convention 1977 on Gifts, Miracles, by Butler), or when the apostles died.

III. So, we will look at the phenomena of Modern Prophecy from those two conclusions.

  A. Even when there were true prophets, not all who claimed to be prophets were to be followed . . . and

  B. The New Testament indicates the miraculous gift of prophecy was to cease with the apostles deaths, (cf. Eph. 4:13; I Cor. 13:1-13).

Discussion

I. Who are the Modern prophets and what are they prophesying?

  A. Ever since the end of the apostolic age self-appointed prophets have been predicting and revealing messages from God (so they say).

1. No two of them seem to agree on interpreting events or times.
2. Hardly any of them agree doctrinally (except on charismatic gifts for today).
3. There are hundreds of them just in the Midwest—let alone the other hundreds all over the world.
4. I will deal with just a few because they are basically all alike—false!

B. Salem Kirban, author of *Guide to Survival,* and other books and films

    1. Rapture must occur 7 years before 2000 A.D., but there is a 4-year error in our calendar, therefore the Rapture is to be in 1989 and the Millennium begins in 1996 (after the "rapture" and 7 years tribulation).
    2. Then Mr. Kirban states, "However, nowhere in God's word does He tell us the exact date . . . for the Rapture."

C. David Webber, Pastor of Southwest Radio Church, Oklahoma City, Okla. and publisher of The Gospel Truth

    1. Refers to George Orwell's *1984* for the prediction that by that date a world dictator would control all nations; refers to Hal Lindsey's book and to movies with "apocalyptic warnings" like The Birds, Earthquake, The Omen which "testify to these things which are soon coming upon the earth."
    2. Mr. Webber says, "Scripture indicates ministers and pastors who refuse to investigate the signs of the time leading to Christ's return, and warn the unsaved to prepare, are ignorant, hypocrites, and false prophets (Mt. 16:3; II Pet. 3:3-5)."
    3. Mr. Webber's time table is: 1974-78 Jewish temple rebuilt; 1981-85 Beginning of the Tribulation; Beginning of the Kingdom age 1997-2001.

C. American Board of Missions to The Jews, Inc.

    1. How the Jews are related to the ending of the Tribulation Period. "Christ will not come back to the earth until the Jewish people ask Him to come back . . . (quoting Hos. 5:15) . . . Christ will not return to the earth until the Jewish people ask Him to come back. . . . This is the basis of the Second Coming of Christ."
    2. "Satan . . . knows that once Christ returns his career will be finished. He also understands that Christ will not come back until the Jews ask Him to come back. If Satan can succeed in destroying all the Jews before they have a chance to ask Christ to come back, Christ will not come back and Satan will be safe. That is why Satan is in an all-out campaign to destroy the Jews."

3. "The power of the Second Coming of Christ is very much in the hands of Israel." From *The Chosen People* magazine, May 1975.

D. Oswald J. Smith, Pastor of the Alliance Tabernacle, Toronto, Canada, wrote a book in the 1920's, *Is the Antichrist At Hand?*
   1. Jerusalem destroyed by Nebuchadnezzar in 587 B.C.;
   2. Times of the Gentiles 2520 years;
   3. Jerusalem and Palestine promised to Jews by Balfour, 1917;
   4. Great Tribulation, Revival of Roman Empire, Reign of Antichrist, Battle of Armageddon must take place before the year 1933!

E. Morris Cerullo, World Evangelism, San Diego, Calif. (produced the T. V. program "Masada")
   1. Ezekiel's prophecy of the "dry bones" predicted the Nazi slaughter of 6 million Jews, and the survival of modern Israel.
   2. This is the "beginning" "the *exact* summer season."
   3. The "generation" that sees the birth of the nation of Israel . . . is in the "summer season" (he cites Lk. 21:29-33).
   4. "I tell you, I would not trade places with Moses, with Elijah, with any of the apostles. I would rather be alive today. This is the greatest moment of history, when the trumpet of God will sound, and your Lord and mine will come. . . ."
   5. "When I was only 15 years old . . . God dealt with me in a vision in which I was caught up into the heavens and I stood as close to the glory of God as when Moses spoke face to face with Him. . . . the brightness of His glory moved from the place where He had stoood, there were two holes in the shape of footprints left in the heaven through which I could see countless thousands of people going to hell without Christ . . . In the vision I moved to stand in these open footprints . . . and my feet fit exactly where His had been . . . I knew that God had called me to go to the multitudes of this world with the message of salvation. . . ."

F. Dr. Charles Taylor, Redondo Beach, Calif., author of *Get All Excited, Jesus is Coming Soon.*
   1. First predicted the Rapture in 1975
   2. Then changed, saying, 1948 Israel established
   3. Makes "this generation" (Mt. 24:34) point of reference; a generation in the Bible is 35 years according to Job 42:16
   4. Thus the Rapture will be Sept. 25th, 1976 (Feast of Trumpets and a Sabbath day)
   5. Millennium is to begin in 1983

271

THIRTEEN LESSONS ON REVELATION

G. Joel Darby, Book Fellowship Tract, (Tract entitled, *Why All the Vultures;* sent out by A.B. MacReynolds) (alleged to fulfill Ezek. ch. 38-39)

1. A new breed of vultures has appeared in Israel, a breed never seen before.
2. They are multiplying at 3 times the normal rate in Israel.
3. This is a sign of the end time, writes a former Rabbi Michael Esses, in his new book, *Next Visitor to Planet Earth,* pub. Logos, Plainfield, N.J.
4. Whereas these "buzzards" normally lay one egg at a time, they are now laying FOUR!
5. According to Reuters News Agency, Russia has bought large quantities of powerful archery equipment from the British, also draught horses from all over the world.
6. At any rate the amazing multiplication of the buzzard population right now should warn any careless Christian to get busy and work. . . . God would not be off on His timing. . . . He would not provide for the vastly increased buzzard population NOW if the need for them was 10 or 20 years hence!

H. Hal Lindsey

1. In his booklet, *Homo Sapiens, Extinction of Evacuation,* pgs. 20 ". . . within 40 years or so of 1948, all these things could take place . . ." pg. 54 ". . . You are the generation seeing these things; you are the generation which is not going to see physical death." "I expect one day in my life to be physically called to see the Lord in the air, without seeing death."
2. Lindsey has predicted 1988 for the Rapture.
3. There are a number of historical and exegetical errors in Mr. Lindsey's book, *The Late Great Planet Earth.*

I. Christian church people

1. Christian Standard, March 15, 1969, art. entitled "Crisis In The Middle East."
   a. Applies Daniel's prophecies in ch. 11 to the Second Coming of Christ, suggesting that Armageddon may be within "the near future."
   b. Applies Ezekiel 38-39 to return of the Jews to Palestine now and the immediate future.
2. At a widely attended men's clinic in the late 1950's a college professor's prediction of Communist terror "Within 4 years we'll all be dead or wish to God we were!" was proclaimed.
3. *The Exhorter,* a publication of Churches of Christ, Hammond, La. "With the amazing acceleration of human history in the

last few years, we would expect to see the fulfillment of these prophecies (Zech. 14; as applied to Israel's return to Palestine, etc.) in a very short space of time." date of paper, January 1969

3. A Christian church paper, Dec. 11, 1972

". . . Russia with all of her current satellites and all she might acquire in the future, will not be able to successfully invade Israel. *ISRAEL IS INVINCIBLE UNLESS GOD IS VULNERABLE.*"

This is just a drop in the bucket: Billy Graham, David Wilkerson, Oral Roberts, Richard DeHahn, Pastor Pack, Bill Bright, Rev. Moon, Armstrongites, J.W.s, 7th Day Adventists, Mormons, on and on they go, disagreeing both in prophecies and doctrines. MILLIONS OF PEOPLE GIVE MILLIONS AND BILLIONS OF DOLLARS TO PROMOTE PEOPLE WHOSE MAIN EFFORTS ARE SPENT PREACHING SUCH USELESS VERBIAGE.

II. Why are they prophesying thus?

A. There are some who mistakenly think such a *literal* view of the Old Testament Prophets and Revelation is equal to fundamentalism.

1. "If we believe the Bible as the infallible and inspired Word of God, then we must also believe that God has set a day before the literal return of Christ to the earth in which everyone will have to worship the Antichrist as God in order to get their code and number." from *The Midnight Cry,* pub. by Dr. Wm. F. Beirnes, Shoals, Indiana

2. "Numerous passages in the Bible predict the return of Israel to the land. It is difficult to find any doctrines taught more clearly or emphatically in God's word. Yet, many people have failed to accept this truth. They have either ignored these passages, or said that they were fulfilled in the return of the Jewish captivity from Babylon, or that they were figuratively fulfilled in the church." from *The Exhorter,* already cited

3. "He (God) made a covenant with Abraham, promising a large portion of the Middle East . . . for him and his descendants. The covenant is unconditional . . . and we, knowing Him who made the promise, totally support the people and land of Israel in their God-given, God-promised, God-ordained right to exist. Any person or group of nations opposed to this right isn't just fighting Israel, but God and time itself." in the *New York Times,* over the name of the American Board of Missions to the Jews, supported by 48 named churches.

273

B. Fascination with and psychological need for knowing the unknown
1. This has been true of people ever since the garden of Eden.
2. It was a problem with the first century church (Thessalonians, Corinthians, etc.).
3. Martin Gardner, reviewer of *Close Encounters of the Third Kind,* says, "Long having lost faith in science and politics, millions of Americans are now longing for a mystical breakthrough from the skies which will usher in the Age of Aquairius."
4. Many people are looking for God to solve the problems of the Christian who has to face an ungodly world by supernatural intervention rather than through hard, faithful discipleship.
   a. Fascination with all these details of so-called Bible prophecies relieves people from the hard things in Christianity.
   b. If we can believe that the main thrust of God's redemptive program is going to deal with circumstances (land, armies, temples, etc.) we may hope in that as His ultimate program.
   c. BUT THE MAIN THRUST OF GOD'S REDEMPTIVE PROGRAM IS THE CHANGING OF THE NATURE OF THE INDIVIDUAL.
5. The essential elements of all the dispensational, pre-millennial systems may be found in the Jewish Apocryphal writings.
6. The New Testament plainly tells us we do not need to know times or seasons which God has set in His own authority (2nd Coming, etc.). We do not need to know what type of resurrection body we will have. There are many things we do not need to know. . . .
7. C.S. Lovett, *Personal Christianity,* Baldwin Park, Calif., "The Holy Spirit has given us a unique method for unlocking the *deeper truths. If,* for example, you were reading *Lovett's Lights On Thessalonians,* the books that offer Paul's comments on antichrist and the rapture of the church (which I strongly believe in), *you'd find your imagination set on fire. . . ."*

C. Instant Evangelism
1. "The signs of our time indicate the days of this age are winding down, and God does not want us to be ignorant when the day of Christ's return is at hand. . . . We must be about the Father's business, urging the lost to be saved . . . before that terrible day of darkness falls upon the earth." from the *Midnight Cry* already cited.
2. "Unlike other missions, Jewish missions is not merely evangelistic. The purpose of missions in general is to evangelize and disciple. But Jewish missions is more so. Not only does Jewish

missions seek to evangelize . . . it is also a prophetic ministry. . . ." *The Chosen People,* already cited.

3. Hal Lindsey's books appeal for urgent evangelism because "the time is short. . . ."

4. In some way or another, these prophets seem to think they can by-pass the plain urgings of Jesus to insist that people count the cost, that Christian discipleship should be based on conviction, not emotion.

They think that all these "count-downs" and "horror pictures" will persuade people to repent.

Revelation 9:20ff. plainly says that all the terrible things symbolized by the Trumpets (judgments upon the Roman empire) did not cause the rest of mankind to repent!

5. I was in a Christian Service Camp a few years ago (Guadalupe, N.M.) and a preacher was showing his slides of the Holy Land and preaching on the Rapture, etc., and five or six young people became so upset they started crying and making long distance phone calls to make sure their parents were home.

D. Zionism is politically chic!

1. Some people consider it a test of your relationship to Christ that you believe the Jews have a biblical right to Palestine.

2. We have already cited the quotation in II. A. 4.

3. *Time* magazine continually prints editorials and articles on the Jews returning to Palestine "Thus Judaism . . . and Israel have a commanding moral claim to Jerusalem. . . ." *Time* 12-27-71.

4. U.S. Presidents from Truman to Carter have been forced by powerful Jewish opinion to politically support something that although politically expedient, was actually unethical! Oswald T. Allis, "Israel's Transgression in Palestine," *Christianity Today,* Dec. 24, 1956

4. What really upsets me is the fact that most of our U.S. congressmen blasted their own countrymen for trying to protect the sovereign land of S. Vietnam against invasion by N. Vietnam (agreed to by treaty), and on the other hand acclaimed the U.N. partitioning of Palestine in 1948 to the Jews, forcing Palestinians out, as right.

E. Ego-trip, fame, gather a following (III John 9).

1. The scriptures indicate this as a motive for false teachers and false prophets.

". . . from among your own selves will arise men speaking perverse things, to draw away the disciples after them . . ." (Acts 20:30).

2. The indication in I Corinthians 12-14 is that people were even using *bona fide* gifts of tongues and prophecy for ego-trips.
3. There are thousands and thousands of "itching-eared" people who do not want to endure sound doctrine and accumulate to themselves teachers to suit their own likings, and turn away from listening to the truth and wander into myths; II Tim. 4:1-5. THERE ARE EGO-HUNGRY PREACHERS WILLING TO EXPLOIT THESE ITCHING EARED PEOPLED TO MAKE LUCRATIVE LIVINGS AT IT!
4. Even the *People Of God,* led by Moses David, use modern prophetism to recruit and obtain members and money, Bicentennial Issue of *Que Sera, Sera* (would you help us with a donation, please!).

F. Money

1. One example; many others might be cited
2. Rex Humbard's Archives of Faith for Sinners

In anticipation of the *soon* coming of Christ, the rapture and the seven years of Great tribulation (during which it will not be easy for those who are left).

After Humbard and all other saved Christians have been raptured only unrepentant sinners will remain on earth.

Mr. Humbard will be on video tapes to tell them how to reach salvation. Just push a button, and he'll be there.

The right to record a personal testimony to a maximum length of four handwritten pages is now being offered to anyone for a donation of $100. These microfilmed testimonies will represent a reservoir of faith for those left behind. At the archives there will be a film explaining what has happened with the rapture, etc. The first one to record a personal testimony will be Johnny Cash . . . he will not have to pay the $100 because he has contributed liberally in the past.

The date of the rapture, according to Humbard, is uncertain, but all those who have been born again know we are on the verge of the Lord's return. While it is true that no one knows the day or the hour, there is something on the inside of each believer that tells him the Lord is soon to return.

Mr. Humbard emphasized that the inclusion of names or testimonies in the archives was not a guarantee of salvation. . . . "We're just fixing to memorialize some people who help us do the job."
3. Of course, the recent expose of the Armstrong fortunes reminds us that they got it from majoring in this kind of modern-day prophetism.

MODERN PROPHECY EXAMINED

Granted, not all those who think they are prophets today are Christians or ego-maniacs. Some of them probably would not even claim to be prophets but merely interpreters of Bible prophecies. This may be another subject for study altogether—however, it is interesting that practically all those who have claimed to receive revelations and prophesy, and those who give literal dispensational-pre-millennial interpretations to Bible prophecies AGREE on current events of history!

"And God told me to tell my partners that the moment they hear me say $77 or $777 or multiples, of 7's, to act upon it quickly" Oral Roberts, Abundant Life, January 1978.

III. What God Says about Prophets

    A. Biblical tests of a True Prophet

        1. They speak ONLY in the name of God or Christ, Deut. 13:1-5; 18:20.

            a. False prophets may pretend to predict the future or work pseudo-signs (Deut. 13).

            b. Satan can do pseudo-signs (II Thess. 2:9; Rev. 13:13-15).

            c. God may allow a prophet to be self-deceived and to deceive sinful people as punishment (Ezek. 14:9-11).

            d. This is not the *only* test because a false prophet may pretend to speak in the name of the Lord (Jer. 29:8-9).

            e. *In the name of,* means, *by the authority of.*

            f. We have not only the right but the obligation to challenge every alleged prophecy or prophet with the proposition that the ONLY AUTHORITATIVE WORD FROM GOD FROM NOW UNTIL THE END OF TIME IS CONTAINED IN THE 66 BOOKS OF OUR BIBLE!

            g. Even authentic prophets can be deceived! (I Kings 13).

        2. They speak ONLY by revelation or inspiration.

            a. If a prophet of biblical times practiced augury, sorcery, divination, they were rejected as false (Deut. 18:9-14).

            b. Heathen magical practices were not practiced by true prophets of God.

            c. Deceivers who prophesy lie (Ezek. 12:24; 22:28; Jer. 14:14; Micah 3:7, 11); they speak their *own heart,* not God's revelation (Jer. 23:16, 26; Ezek. 13:2).

            d. True prophets receive *direct* revelations from Jehovah (Num. 12:6).

            e. False prophets may claim visions and dreams (Deut. 13:1-5; I Kings 22:13-28; Ezek. 14:9-11).

            f. Modern day prophets appeal to soothsayers like Jeanne Dixon; scientists; military prognosticators; even to *Reader's Digest* and current events to validate their prophecies.

THIRTEEN LESSONS ON REVELATION

Examples:

The Midnight Cry (already cited): "The November 1976 *Reader's Digest* carries an interesting story related to our subject entitled "Coming Soon Electronic Money."

"This (cashless society) is what both the Bible predicts and financial experts now affirm."

The Gospel Truth (already cited): "George Orwell in his book, *1984*, predicted that by this date a world dictator would control all nations. Mr. Orwell may be proven to be a prophet with honor in this respect. . . .

"Financial experts predict that by 1980 . . . etc.; "A news release this past month stated . . . etc.; "President Valery Giscard D'Estaing of France said . . . etc.; "Henry Kissinger said . . . etc.; ". . . it was the consensus of scientists who worked there (Kennedy Space Center) that if man did not destroy himself by the year 2000 . . . etc."

Personal Christianity, Vl. 17, No. 6, June 1977, C.S. Lovett: "Antichrist is in the world this moment! Who says so? Jeanne Dixon, the well known Catholic soothsayer. She claims he will surface in the early 1980s. But do we consider her a true oracle of God? No way! Not all of her predictions come true. Nevertheless she has quite a record of accurate predictions when it comes to world rulers, such as. . . . "

3. They were conscious of a definite call—they could not mistake it!

   a. Moses (Ex. 4:10-12; Jer. 1:4-10; Amos 7:4-15).
   b. Samuel (I Sam. 3:19-20).
   c. Mrs. Oral Roberts, explaining God's calling her to:
      ". . . Lord . . . I'd like to hear Your voice as Oral does. . . . So as I walked I prayed in the Spirit at length. I couldn't understand the prayer language coming over my tongue. It sounded Oriental to me . . . and the interpretation came back in my own language one line at a time. . . .

      'No, you will not hear My voice as others do. . . . I speak to him (Oral) in an audible voice but I will not speak to you audibly. . . . I will speak to you out of the everydayness of your life. . . ." (*Abundant Life,* Jan. 1978).

   d. Morris Cerullo: "Theresa (his wife) excused herself to tend to some sewing but was soon fast asleep on the couch. When I noticed that she had fallen asleep, I thought, Now that's strange! We just woke up from a good night's sleep!

      I soon realized that God had placed that sleep upon her, . . . so that He might prepare the way for the supernatural visitation of His presence right there in my kitchen. . . . Then God spoke to me. . . .

"... while I was in the back of a bus coming from a crusade ... God had spoken to my heart ... so forceful was God's visitation to me on that occasion, that I left the other members of the team and went to the very back of the bus and let God speak to my heart. . . ."

It is strange that all modern day prophets get their "calls" from God when no one else can verify it!

4. True prophets did not seek the office, they were chosen by God and spoke by divine compulsion.

   a. Many of them resisted (Jer. 1:4-19) (Ex. 3:10-12) Ezek. 3:12-15; Jonah 1:1-3

   b. Even when Paul told the Corinthians, "desire the spiritual gifts" he also told them that the Holy Spirit distributed His gifts (miraculous) according to His will . . . and not according to the wishes of men.

5. The commission of the true prophet was authenticated by signs or miracles.

   a. Ex. 4:1-21 . . . Moses

   b. Joshua 3:7-13 . . . Joshua

   c. I Sam. 12:16ff.

   d. Miracles of Elijah and Elisha

   e. Paul, Peter, and those upon whom they laid their hands

   f. Signs and miracles may be copied or faked by false prophets, Deut. 13:1-5; Ex. 7:8-13; 7:20-22; 8:7; Mt. 24:24; Mk. 13:22; II Thess. 2:9.

6. The message of the true prophet was always in harmony with the whole will of God which had been revealed up to that time.

   a. Deut. 13:1-3 - could not contradict previous truth

   b. I Kings 13 - true prophet would not have been deceived by old prophet if he had used this test.

   c. Jer. 26 - leaders were going to kill Jeremiah because he predicted destruction of Jerusalem. Some elders remembered Micah years before predicted the same and Jeremiah was spared.

   d. I John 4:1-6

   f. This harmony with revealed truth applies to all the doctrines of the Bible . . . not just predicted history.

   g. Modern day prophets for the most part do not teach the full apostolic doctrine.

Billy Graham, for example, who interprets biblical prophecy and declares he is God's spokesman, said, "I used to believe that pagans in far-off countries were lost—were going to hell—if they did not have the Gospel of Jesus Christ preached to them. I no longer believe that. . . . I believe that there are other ways of recognizing the existence of God—through nature, for instance—and plenty of other opportunities, therefore, of saying 'yes' to God."

"Graham once believed that Jews, too, were lost if they did not convert to Christianity. . . . Today Graham is willing to leave that up to God. . . ."

"I've found that my beliefs are essentially the same as those of orthodox Roman Catholics. . . . We differ on some matters of later church tradition." *McCalls* magazine, January 1978

7. The message of the true prophet and the prophet himself was authenticated by historical fulfillments of his prophecies.

   a. Deut. 18:21-22
   b. Jer. 28:17

8. The moral character of the prophet and his prophecies must agree with God's full revelation.

   a. False prophets tend to be ungodly and preach ungodly (both morally and theologically).
   b. Jer. 23:10-17
   c. Matt. 7:15-20; II Pet. 2:1-22; Jude 1-23

B. We do not need modern day prophecies and prophets!

1. There is enough prophecy in the Bible, fulfilled in minute detail (Daniel, Isaiah, Revelation) to show that God is in control of history!

2. We do not need, beyond what is revealed in the Bible, to know future circumstances—because knowing the future of earthly history has nothing to do with our covenant relationship to God (I Jn. 3:1-3).

   It is not circumstances that save or destroy, it is faith or lack of faith—regardless of circumstances.

3. The Bible is all sufficient

   a. "And now I commend you to God and to the word of his grace, which is able to build you and to give you the inheritance among all those who are sanctified" (Acts 20:32).
   b. "All scripture is inspired by God and profitable for teaching, for reproof, for correction, and for training in righteousness, that the man of God may be complete, equipped for every good work" (II Tim. 3:16-17).

C. Modern day prophets need to take warning from Jeremiah, ch. 23 and Ezekiel, ch. 13.

MODERN PROPHECY EXAMINED

Excerpt from a Workshop on the Second Coming of Christ for the NACC, July 14, 1978, Oklahoma City, Oklahoma.
ZIONISM (Restoration of a Jewish nation in the land of Palestine) Modern Zionism strictly political; never intended to exclude Palestinians (Enc. Brit. "Zionism").

A. Some little known historical facts about Zionism and modern Jews

1. Theordor Herzl, founder of political Zionism, was schizoid, given to frequent fits of melancholy and depression and threatened suicide several times. He spent vast sums of money bribing Turkish officials in order to gain the Sultan's approval of a Jewish settlement in Palestine.

    Pauline, his first child, became a drug addict, had several men who left her, wound up overdosing and dying of drugs, at 40.

    Hans, his son was manic depressive, treated by Freud who diagnosed an extreme Oedipus complex. Committed suicide on the day of Pauline's funeral.

    Trude, married and became a mental case, her marriage broke down and she died after being an inmate of a number of mental institutions. . . . *The Hebrew Christian*, Winter, 1977, Vol. L, No. 4.

2. What about the Falashas? 50,000 black, East Central Africans who have practiced Judaism since 600 B.C., and who claim to be descendants of King Solomon and the Queen of Sheba. They observe all Jewish rites, sacrifices, and festivals except Hanukkah. . . . *Christianity Today*, 12-7-73, "Black Jews: A House Divided," pg. 52.

3. Most East-European "Jews" (Poles, Hungarian, Czech, etc.) are not really descendants of Israelites, but descendants of the Khazars, Caucasians who became converts or proselytes to Judaism about 900-1000 A.D. The Khazars were "Gentiles" from south Russia! . . . *The Thirteenth Tribe,* by Arthur Koestler, Random House pub., (so well documented and important a book it was reviewed by *Wall Street Journal*)

4. No Jew today can trace his ancestry back beyond two or three hundred years. So how do we know for sure that they are really Jews (true Israelites according to the Old Testament and from the 12 tribes)? . . . *Christianity Today,* 3-13-70, Jacob Gartenhaus, "The Jewish Conception of the Messiah." (He was born in Austria and educated in rabbinical schools there.)

5. *CBS, "Sixty Minutes"* program, 4-10;77:

a. As many people are leaving Israel to come to the U.S. as are going into Israel to live each day.
b. There are over 2,000,000 Jews in New York City and many have come there recently from Israel.
c. Some Jews who have lived in Israel from its very beginning in 1948 have recently come to the U.S.
d. A taxi-driver in New York, who couldn't make a living in Israel, has made over $100,000 in three years since coming to New York.
e. Why are they leaving? 30 years of War; no exemptions from army service; not enough space; inflation rate over 35%; strikes; bureaucracy; takes five year wait to get a telephone; corruption in government; income tax takes 65% of wage earner's living.
f. 1 / 10 of all Israeli citizens live outside the country.

6. The present Israeli government has made it unlawful to do Christian evangelism in that land. How will the millennium ever come about?

B. Zionism and the Bible

1. Repentance and obedience to God's commandments and prophecies was the *condition* upon which God promised to give the land of Palestine to the Jews in the Old Testament.

    Significantly, God gave the Jews into the hands of their enemies a number of times when they disobeyed Him. They were taken *out* of Palestine and brought back a number of times.

2. The ultimate disobedience of the Jews was the rejection of God's Son, the Messiah (cf. Dan. 9:24 ". . . to finish transgression" and Mt. 23:29-39 ". . . may come all the righteous blood shed on earth . . . and your house is forsaken and desolate"; and Luke 19:41-44 ". . . because you did not know the time of your visitation."

3. Jesus predicted the dispossession of the Jews by God in His parables in Matt. 21 and 22.

    a. King's marriage feast for his son . . . the king sent his troops (Rome's army, Mt. 24:15, "desolating sacrilege") and destroyed those murderers.
    b. The householder's vineyard . . . "He will put those wretches to a miserable death, and let out the vineyard to other tenants who will give him the fruits in their seasons." This is the sentence the Jews pronounced upon themselves! Mt. 21:33-41.

282

Then Jesus reinforced it, "Therefore I tell you, the kingdom of God will be taken away from you and given to a nation producing the fruits thereof."

4. Jesus predicted the Jews would ". . . fall by the edge of the sword, and be led captive into all the nations, and Jerusalem shall be trodden down of the Gentiles until the times of the Gentiles be fulfilled" (Lk. 21:24). The Old Testament era was the times of the Jews. The New Testament era is the times of the Gentiles. Judaism is a thing of the past!

5. The apostle Paul, speaking of the Jews nationally, said that "God's wrath came (*ephtasen*, Gr. aor. past tense) upon them *to the end* (*eis telos*), or "*to completion.*" I Thess. 2:16. *Judaism cannot be revived*, although individual Jews may be saved if they accept the gospel (Rom. 1:16-17). Daniel 9:27 calls the destruction of Jerusalem—the "*decreed end.*"

6. Once the Messiah has come and completed His work, God has dispensed forever with a special *place* of worship (Jn. 4:21-24; Acts 17:24-25); any other *sacrifices* (Heb. 9:26; 10:12-14), etc.

7. To populate Palestine with a theocracy of Judaism, reinstitute the Temple and its sacrifices, reconstitute a Jewish priesthood, would violate and contradict the very plain teaching of the New Testament that the church of Jesus Christ (composed of both Jew and Gentile on the same basis) is the primary object of God's redemptive work . . . and not the Jewish nation!

8. The book of Galatians makes it plain that "in Christ" there are no more racial or social distinctions ever again (Gal. 3:26-29). If we are in Christ, we are Abraham's "offspring." Or, to put it another way, a true "Jew" is one who is inwardly, not genetically (Rom. 2:28-29). The true Israel of God is that which is a *new* creation (Gal. 6:15-16).

9. True Zion is the church. Heb. 12:18-24

10. Judaism is the kingdom that was "shaken" and "removed." Heb. 12:25-27

11. Christianity is the kingdom that "cannot be shaken." Heb. 12:28

12. Judaism is "no lasting city" Heb. 13:14 and to go to Christ it must be outside the camp (of Judaism) Heb. 13:13.

13. The twelve tribes of Israel in Rev. 7:1-8 cannot refer to a literal return of Old Testament Israel to Palestine because that list leaves out the tribes of Dan and Ephraim, and inserts two tribes not originally given an inheritance—Levi and Joseph.

14. It is very significant that no New Testament writer mentions a future return of the Jews to the land of Palestine. Very

obviously the return of the Jews to the land of which the Old Testament prophets spoke had already occurred in the restoration of the captivities, or, figuratively in the establishment of the church.

15. Daniel's prophecy (Dan. 9:24-27) plainly teaches that *God would finish His work* for the redemption of the world *through the Jews* 490 years after the "going forth of the word to rebuild" Jerusalem. From 457 B.C. (see Ezra 7) to 34 A.D. (allowing for the 4-year mistake in our calendar) is 490 years. 34 A.D. was after the stoning of Stephen and when the gospel was initially taken to the Gentiles (Samaritans and Ethiopian Eunuch of Acts 8; Paul's conversion and commission Acts 9; Cornelius Acts 10).

16. Isaiah predicts that God will establish a "new" nation before the "old" one passes away (Isa. 66:7ff.) and that the new will be established with one stroke (Heb. *pa'am*). A land and a nation was brought forth with one stroke before the old passed away on the Day of Pentecost, June, A.D. 30. What the Old Testament prophets predict about the future of the glorious land has to do with the church of Christ, for the most part.

This does not mean, of course, that some who call themselves Jews today, will never go back to Palestine. They may even build a new Temple there some day. But it does mean that as any of them go back they do so entirely on their own, apart from any convenanted purpose to that end and entirely outside of Scripture prophecy. No Scripture blessing is promised for a project of that kind.

It may be that in years to come the Jews will possess a larger part, or even all, of Palestine. We do not know. But if they do they will secure it as other nations secure poperty, through negotiation, or purchase, or conquest NOT BY VIRTUE OF ANY AS YET UNFULFILLED PROPHECIES OR BIBLICAL PROMISES. THERE ARE NO SUCH PROPHECIES OR PROMISES!

In the meantime, Zionism, premillennialism and dispensationalism must bear part of the responsibility for the evil and dangerous situation that has arisen in the Middle East, since it has encouraged Jews to believe they are rightful owners of that land and that it is divinely ordained that they are again to possess it.

The British had no ethical or political right to promise Palestine to the Jews at the end of WW I. The UN had no right to partition it. It should have legally been returned to the Palestinians. Ever since the partitioning, the Jews have extended their borders beyond those set by the UN.